BROWN IN BALTI

BROWN IN BALTIMORE

School Desegregation and
the Limits of Liberalism

Howell S. Baum

CORNELL UNIVERSITY PRESS, ITHACA AND LONDON

First published 2010 by Cornell University Press
First printing, Cornell Paperbacks, 2010
Printed in the United States of America

Library of Congress Cataloging-in-Publication Data

Baum, Howell S.
    Brown in Baltimore : school desegregation and the limits of liberalism /
Howell S. Baum.
        p. cm.
    Includes bibliographical references and index.
    ISBN 978-0-8014-4808-9 (cloth : alk. paper)
    ISBN 978-0-8014-7652-5 (pbk. : alk. paper)
    1. School integration—Maryland—Baltimore.   2. Segregation in
education—Maryland—Baltimore.   3. Race relations in school
management—Maryland—Baltimore.   4. School choice—Maryland—
Baltimore.   5. Baltimore (Md.)—Race relations.   6. Liberalism—
Maryland—Baltimore.   I. Title.
LC214.23.B35B38   2010
379.2'63097526—dc22   2009044416

Cornell University Press strives to use environmentally responsible suppliers
and materials to the fullest extent possible in the publishing of its books. Such
materials include vegetable-based, low-VOC inks and acid-free papers that are
recycled, totally chlorine-free, or partly composed of nonwood fibers. For further
information, visit our website at www.cornellpress.cornell.edu.

Cloth printing   10 9 8 7 6 5 4 3 2 1
Paperback printing   10 9 8 7 6 5 4 3 2 1

In memory of my parents, Ruth and Irving Baum, who had a passion for justice

In memory of Ralph Goodwin, who taught me an unforgettable lesson about race

and

In honor of the many principled and courageous persons who struggled to desegregate schools in Baltimore and elsewhere

Contents

School segregation is so much a fact of American life that few of us remark on it. After decades of struggle to desegregate, the language of "segregation" and "integration" seems anachronistic. Yet segregation continues to limit the academic development and social and economic opportunities of black children, particularly if they are poor, and it prevents all children from learning to work and live with others who differ by race, class, and culture.

School desegregation programs in the second half of the twentieth century took many forms. Sometimes they were voluntary; often they were forced on school boards and families. Some boards desegregated entire districts at once; others moved incrementally, often doing as little as necessary. Sometimes desegregation proceeded peacefully; sometimes it was punctuated by violence. Some boards maintained desegregation over decades; others let it lapse as soon as possible. Desegregation techniques varied widely, ranging from free choice to mandatory busing, with zoning, pairing, clustering, and magnet schools in between. Occasionally cities desegregated with suburbs.

Thus desegregation has been no single policy or experience, and it eludes easy assessment. However, the evidence shows that where school boards firmly implemented desegregation, and where it had time to become accepted reality, not only did white and black children attend school together, but both groups benefited. Black children gained academically, and they were more likely than peers in segregated schools to postpone childbearing, keep clear of the law, graduate from high school, attend college (including integrated colleges), enter occupations that traditionally had few blacks, work in integrated offices, have white friends, and live in racially mixed neighborhoods. Black and white children both learned to get along better with one another.[1]

The Supreme Court's 1974 *Milliken v. Bradley* decision was the first of a series of court rulings that eventually made deliberate desegregation nearly impossible, but there was a window of about thirty years after the 1954 *Brown* ruling when school boards might have desegregated, and some acted decisively. During that time, accumulating experience and social research showed that desegregation need not disrupt communities and could be a boon. Hence one should ask why school officials did not do more to desegregate. Much of the explanation is that boards followed public sentiment. While whites might be comfortable with impersonal relations with blacks in voting places, public accommodations, stores, workplaces, and medical institutions, many remained anxious about the greater intimacy of living next door, socializing, and sitting together in classrooms. Many white board members themselves were anxious about blacks. However, rather than resisting desegregation with expressions of animosity, white officials often avoided thinking about the realities of black children's lives by viewing them with a double consciousness that simultaneously recognized and denied their race. This peculiar frame of mind shaped what Gunnar Myrdal called an American Dilemma: whites espouse a creed that all are equal but treat blacks badly.

Race controls much of Americans' lives, and yet we understand race poorly. Most of us, at best, can talk superficially about race. We can use the words *white* and *black* or *African American,* we may count numbers of whites and blacks living or working or attending school together, but we have great trouble knowing just what we think about race that has led us to conduct lives largely governed by skin color. We may be aware of anxiety, guilt, shame, or anger encountering others defined as racially different, but we have hidden from ourselves the assumptions about morality, sexuality, and aggression that shaped and maintain racial identities. So long as these emotional premises remain unconscious and unavailable for discussion, some of us will continue to benefit at others' expense, and all will suffer.

Ignorance about race is both culturally normal and normative. It makes possible the familiar institutional and personal offenses against black Americans, but it also hinders well-meaning reformers from grasping racial discrimination firmly enough to attack it realistically. The latter problem is the concern of this book. The book examines the history of school desegregation in Baltimore as a way of understanding American difficulties dealing with race in public policy. Baltimore officials embraced the *Brown* decision as authorization to act on their conscience and end school segregation. However, they proceeded in two ways that limited what they could accomplish. First, though race was the reason for segregation, they avoided talking about race and officially ignored students' race in planning for desegregation. Second, they made desegregation voluntary, refusing to control enrollment, letting individual students decide where to attend school, and remaining officially indifferent to whatever racial makeup resulted. Black community leaders encouraged and supported this approach. In the end, unregulated family choice of schools, compounded by white withdrawal from city public schools, produced only modest, temporary desegregation, followed by resegregation and the steady growth of a black student majority. In fifty years the racial composition of schools changed from 60 percent white to 89 percent black.

Freedom of choice in Baltimore neither significantly desegregated schools nor evidently stemmed white flight. In other words, many whites left city public schools even though their children had little contact with black children. Paradoxically, a policy that did not force integration may have motivated whites to leave by creating uncertainty and anxiety about the racial makeup of schools. The book examines how school officials and city residents thought about desegregation so as to adopt and maintain this policy despite its increasingly apparent inefficacy in desegregating. Black community leaders, white liberals, and a predominantly white school board united behind the policy in 1954. As blacks gained power in the school system, they continued the policy, and two decades later blacks supported the policy more than whites. The book analyzes why and how Baltimoreans ignored race in making desegregation policy.

In this respect, the Baltimore story reveals something quintessentially American. The location of the city near the nation's North-South border exposed it to an intense confrontation of proslavery and abolition sentiments, segregationism and integrationism, and city leaders decided to stop talking about race in order to keep the peace. Baltimoreans carried out this strategy for avoiding racial conflict in a most American way—by thinking as liberals. Mid-twentieth-century Baltimore school officials espoused a liberalism that descended from John Locke to Thomas Jefferson to Walter Lippmann. They followed liberalism as simply common sense, in regarding children as independent individuals, relying on free individual choice as the means of determining where students would enroll, and limiting school board intervention. Liberalism made it seem only reasonable to think of children as raceless individuals—even when the issue was racial to the core—and school officials and most other city residents were relieved not to think about race. The book examines how liberalism, America's dominant public philosophy, addressed race, the nation's central problem, in the mid-twentieth century. The book is an historical study, but it puts liberalism in the present tense because the liberalism that influenced mid-twentieth-century school officials and civil rights activists continues to shape American thinking. Confusingly, some of the strongest twenty-first-century advocates of classical liberalism are those on the political right who use "liberal" as an epithet. The fact that they call themselves "conservatives" shows how deeply liberalism rests in the American grain.

A Note about Racial Labels

Racial labels have changed over time. In the first half of the twentieth century, whites and blacks referred to blacks as "colored." In the mid-twentieth century, "Negro" became a preferred label. In the 1960s, many black Americans started calling themselves "black," and some in the late twentieth century replaced that with "African American." The use of racial labels in the book follows three rules. All quotations contain the speakers' or writers' actual words. The word *colored* is used to refer to the designated "colored schools" of the Baltimore school system, but not the children attending these schools, even though they, their families, and school administrators frequently used that label. *Black* is used throughout to refer to people today called either "black" or "African American."

Organization of the Book

This book examines Baltimore school desegregation in terms of the American Dilemma. The study begins with an examination of race and liberalism—what race means and how liberal premises fail to comprehend it. The body of the book recounts Baltimore school desegregation efforts, with attention to how liberal thinking shaped a policy that avoided dealing with race. The Conclusion analyzes the history in the context of American school desegregation and in terms of American liberalism.

The Introduction presents the perspective on race and liberalism that informs the book. It examines what white Americans historically assumed about race, how these beliefs led to school segregation, and how liberalism made it possible to avoid thinking or knowing about race. Chapter 1 introduces Baltimore as an American city and examines how location on the nation's racial border shaped a parochial and moderate city character and a culture that avoided racial talk. This chapter also describes the development of separate, unequal schools for black children.

Chapter 2 begins the story of Baltimore school desegregation with black activists' campaign to improve their children's education. Starting in the mid-1930s, the account highlights community leaders' efforts to inform white policymakers of colored school conditions and persuade them, first, to equalize separate schools and, eventually, to end segregation altogether. Chapter 3 describes a 1952 Baltimore Urban League initiative to admit black boys to the select Baltimore Polytechnic Institute. The narrative reveals how civil rights activists persuaded school board members to integrate a school when the system offered no equivalent for blacks.

Chapter 4 presents the 1954 school board decision to desegregate all schools after *Brown*. The chapter examines school officials' assumptions about desegregation and their selection of freedom of choice and looks at black community leaders' reasons for supporting this approach. The analysis shows how liberal assumptions shaped policy. Chapter 5 describes public responses to the policy. The chapter looks at why few families, and virtually no whites, chose racially mixed schools.

Chapter 6 describes a 1963 protest by twenty-eight black and white parents against school system practices that maintained segregation despite its formal abolition. The discussion looks at how civil rights activists and school board members came to agreement on changes because all believed in free choice. Chapter 7 examines changes in the local and national civil rights climates in the 1960s, with growing sentiment for integrating Baltimore schools. The account shows how this movement was abruptly halted by Martin Luther King's murder, riots in the city, an attack by Governor Spiro Agnew on moderate black leaders, and white support for Agnew, with a resulting biracial retreat from integration.

Chapter 8 describes a 1974 U.S. Office for Civil Rights request that Baltimore develop a plan for citywide school integration and the school board response. The chapter examines how diminishing local support for racial mixing and school board resistance to deliberate integration limited city plans. Chapter 9 reviews city negotiations with the Office for Civil Rights. The chapter shows how school board actions to mollify parents by limiting integration led federal officials to give up on negotiations and move to cut off funding for city schools. Chapter 10 describes Baltimore court efforts to stop federal action against the city. The chapter recounts Baltimore's judicial victory and analyzes federal weaknesses influencing a school district. The story ends with the 1987 U.S. Department of Education certification that Baltimore had done everything possible to remove vestiges of legal segregation.

The Conclusion analyzes the Baltimore history in terms of race and liberalism. The chapter compares Baltimore events with desegregation in other school districts, and it interprets the course of Baltimore desegregation as a product of city culture and character. The chapter concludes by explaining how liberal thinking made it hard for school officials and city residents to grasp race, limited responses to segregation, and sustained the American Dilemma.

Many people provided invaluable help in this project. As someone who has lived in Baltimore only thirty-five years, I am indebted to people who generously offered deep knowledge of the city, schools, race, and the law and made it possible to understand not just events that preceded my time here, but also those that I witnessed but saw only dimly. Mike Bowler, who covered education for the *Baltimore Sun* for twenty-five years, introduced me to the history of the school system. He told many stories, provided *Sun* articles about school desegregation, and identified and helped locate dozens of participants. Matthew Crenson, who knows more about Baltimore politics and political history than anyone else, pressed on me his observation that Baltimoreans are singularly reluctant to talk about race. That insight led me to see how Baltimore developed desegregation policy that avoided dealing with race. He provided many useful comments as I proceeded with research and writing. Edward Berkowitz, an historian of twentieth-century America who has written about Baltimore schools, gave solid advice about how to think and write as an historian. Many conversations about the city, schools, and race helped me see a coherent story in disparate events. Antero Pietila, who also covered schools for the *Sun* for many years and has written a history of Baltimore housing discrimination, offered ideas about segregation, as well as many extraordinary nuggets of information. My brother, Lawrence Baum, who has studied courts for a lifetime, helped me understand the decisions and legal procedures related to Baltimore school desegregation. Michael McGandy at Cornell University Press has been all that I have wanted in an editor. Besides his continuing interest in the book, he has provided careful comments that immeasurably improved its contents.

Many people have offered thoughtful observations about race, schools, civil rights, liberalism, and Baltimore over the years. They include Fred Alford, Ira Berlin, Melinda Chateauvert, Jack Dougherty, Benjamin Feldman, Barbara Finkelstein, John Forester, Rodney Harrell, Charles Hoch, Steven Janes, Harold McDougall, James McPartland, Sherry Olson, Garrett Power, Connie Putzel, Beryl Radin, Leo Ribuffo, Jo Ann Robinson, John Rury, William Salganik, Clarence Stone, David Taft Terry, Mark Tushnet, Denton Watson, Jacqueline Watts, and Juan Williams.

The book depends on interviews graciously offered by people who made Baltimore desegregation policy, taught, attended school, parented a student, organized community involvement in desegregation, or participated in civil rights activity in the city, served in federal civil rights agencies, or were otherwise familiar with desegregation events and actors in Baltimore. These include Nelson Adlin, Cynthia Attwood, Bernard Berkowitz, George Brain, Billie Bramhall, Cynthia Brown, Eric Carriker, Joel Carrington, Nicholas Carroll, Fred Cioffi, Carl Clark, Carolyn Cole, George Collins, Milton Cornish, Robert Crain, John Crew,

James Crockett, Thomas D'Alesandro III, Betty Deacon, Stephen Derby, Robert Edwards, Beverly Ellinwood, Hayward "Woody" Farrar, Homer Favor, Edgar Feingold, David Feldman, Richard Foster, Edith Furstenberg, Martin Gerry, Larry Gibson, Herbert Goldman, Jack Greenberg, James Griffin, Lloyd Henderson, Kalman "Buzzy" Hettleman, Sidney Hollander Jr., Peter Holmes, Edward Holmgren, Freeman Hrabowski, Frank Krueger, Brian Landsberg, David Leeman, Marshall Levin, Robert Lloyd, Leigh Manasevit, Jeannie Marsh, Peter Marudas, Joseph McNeely, Barbara Mills, Keiffer Mitchell Sr., Arthur Murphy, William Murphy, Margaret Neustadt Randol, Sandra Pollard, Irona Pope, John Roemer, Alexander Ross, George L. Russell Jr., Sheila Sachs, Robert Schaefer, June Shagaloff Alexander, Larry Shugarman, Edgar Silver, John Sondheim, Walter Sondheim, Roma Stewart, Melvin Sykes, David Tatel, William Taylor, Robert Thieblot, James Wego, Gertrude Williams, Elizabeth Wolfson, and James Wood.

Librarians are by character exceptionally helpful, and I received extraordinary assistance from librarians and archivists, including Vanessa Williamson at the Robert S. Rankin Civil Rights Memorial Library of the U.S. Civil Rights Commission, Adrienne Cannon at the Library of Congress, Patrick Connelly at the Mid-Atlantic Region Archives Facility of the National Archives and Records Administration, Joellen ElBashir at the Moorland-Spingarn Research Center at Howard University, Rebecca Gunby and Tony Roberts at the Baltimore City Archives, Steven Kinsey and Mignon Conners at the Multimedia Department of the Morris A. Soper Library at Morgan State University, Thomas Hollowak at the Special Collections Department of the Langsdale Library at the University of Baltimore, and Erin Titter at the Jewish Museum of Maryland.

Two organizations gave crucial financial and associated moral support for the research. A 2003 Summer Research Award from the University of Maryland College Park General Research Board made it possible to formulate important research questions and identify relevant literatures. A John Simon Guggenheim Memorial Foundation Fellowship in 2004–5 provided extended time to read those literatures, conduct archival research, and interview people. This time, an extraordinary gift, permitted the immersion and reflection on which research depends.

The Urban Studies and Planning Program at the University of Maryland College Park supported the work in several ways. Students Ethan Bindernagel and Colleen Mitchell provided important research assistance, as well as ideas that were valuable in shaping the beginning of the project. Gregory Vernon created maps for the book. My colleagues James Cohen and Gerrit Knaap helped get needed technical assistance.

I appreciate the patient participation of my wife, Madelyn, and our daughters, Elena and Maya, in years of conversations about race and the schools. These challenging discussions enriched my thinking and improved the book.

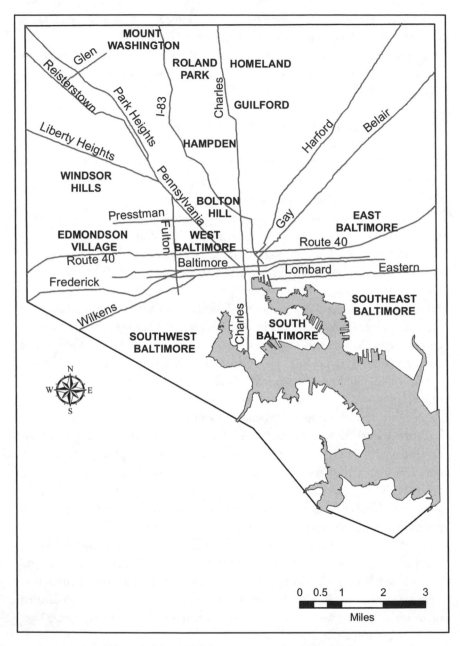

Figure 1. Selected Baltimore streets and neighborhoods

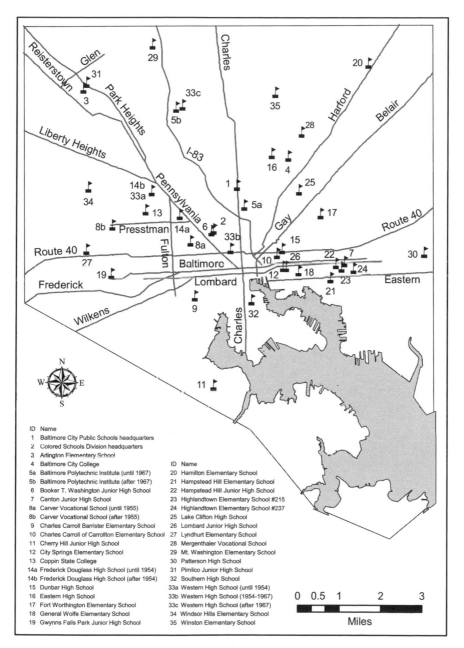

ID	Name	ID	Name
1	Baltimore City Public Schools headquarters	20	Hamilton Elementary School
2	Colored Schools Division headquarters	21	Hampstead Hill Elementary School
3	Arlington Elementary School	22	Hampstead Hill Junior High School
4	Baltimore City College	23	Highlandtown Elementary School #215
5a	Baltimore Polytechnic Institute (until 1967)	24	Highlandtown Elementary School #237
5b	Baltimore Polytechnic Institute (after 1967)	25	Lake Clifton High School
6	Booker T. Washington Junior High School	26	Lombard Junior High School
7	Canton Junior High School	27	Lyndhurt Elementary School
8a	Carver Vocational School (until 1955)	28	Mergenthaler Vocational School
8b	Carver Vocational School (after 1955)	29	Mt. Washington Elementary School
9	Charles Carroll Barrister Elementary School	30	Patterson High School
10	Charles Carroll of Carrollton Elementary School	31	Pimlico Junior High School
11	Cherry Hill Junior High School	32	Southern High School
12	City Springs Elementary School	33a	Western High School (until 1954)
13	Coppin State College	33b	Western High School (1954-1967)
14a	Frederick Douglass High School (until 1954)	33c	Western High School (after 1967)
14b	Frederick Douglass High School (after 1954)	34	Windsor Hills Elementary School
15	Dunbar High School	35	Winston Elementary School
16	Eastern High School		
17	Fort Worthington Elementary School		
18	General Wolfe Elementary School		
19	Gwynns Falls Park Junior High School		

Figure 2. Selected Baltimore schools, 1940s–1970s

BROWN IN BALTIMORE

INTRODUCTION

Liberalism, Race, and the American Dilemma

During World War II, black Americans worked in military plants and the armed forces to defeat the Nazis, and yet they still suffered discrimination in employment, the military, and much of the rest of life. Seeking victory against racism not only abroad but also at home, they inaugurated a "Double V" campaign. However, though the fight against Nazism would make it harder for white Americans to live with racial discrimination, Americans had other things on their minds after the war, and whites gave little attention to race.[1]

The postwar years were a time of belief and hope but also doubt and disillusionment. Postwar prosperity vindicated capitalism. After the Depression and wartime scarcities, the economy was delivering goods, and people had money to spend. Millions of third-generation Americans now established their bona fides as citizens by working hard, producing, and above all, consuming. With help from the GI Bill, families bought suburban homes. Parents looked to the schools to give their children what it took to make it in the middle class, or even higher. Markets were working, and government intervention no longer seemed necessary. General Motors president Charles Wilson, President Eisenhower's defense secretary designate, summarized the mood at his confirmation hearing: what was good for GM, he declared, was good for the nation, and vice versa. In contrast with fascism and, now, communism, America demonstrated the possibility and value of a free democratic society.

And yet, all that notwithstanding, Nazism had shocked the American moral system, baring the worst of human capabilities. The Soviet pact with Hitler and Stalin's prison camps disillusioned the American left. The bomb created the possibility of annihilating the species. The war thrust America into an international domain where it had to take a role but lacked control as it confronted a Soviet Union intent on world domination. Soon enough, the Russians got the bomb, China fell to the communists, and the United States got bogged down in Korea. Unaccustomed to defeat, Americans searched their midst for spies and traitors who must have aided the enemy. Thus Hitler and Stalin challenged Americans' faith in human goodness and a belief in state benevolence. After massive New Deal and wartime government initiatives, Americans gave up grand schemes for human improvement. In the tautness of the Cold War, they moderated their expectations and concentrated on getting along and getting ahead. Although some on the left criticized the middle class for conforming unthinkingly to materialist values and bureaucratic norms, most Americans were content, and the critics had no model for a better society.[2]

In these ways, midcentury America was a decidedly liberal society. Americans believed in themselves and in the market system. They were self-interested individual strivers in an economy they expected to reward their efforts. They were skeptical about big government, but they also believed, the GI Bill notwithstanding, that they didn't need it. If they thought about politics, they assumed it was shaped by pluralistic interest group competition, where sometimes one interest and sometimes another would get its modest way, but no one dominated it all. Few had faith in ultimate social values or held strong ideas about a good society other than what they had, but they had confidence in their own judgment of their interests. Given the freedom to choose what they wanted, they would do well. They associated free markets with the virtues of the free world.[3]

These Americans were liberals in seeing America as a society of individuals, valuing a right of individual economic and political choice, and preferring markets to government activity. They were also liberals in other, less explicit ways—with regard to what they didn't think about, what they ignored. They didn't think about the institutional structure of society. Even though they saw the manifestations of the market in their work organizations and in stores where they shopped, so long as prosperity continued, they didn't see a class structure or social groups fixed in place. Moreover, as dedicated workers and consumers, they concentrated their passion on economic competition. They tried to avoid recognizing or giving free rein to their emotions, because they understood feelings to be a diversion from economic success. Psychologically, as well as economically, they were rational actors.[4]

The poor were invisible in this view. Those who were prospering did not see those who were not. They could easily assume that all who, like themselves, applied their talents would make it. In addition, particularly in the North, whites did not pay much attention to blacks and did not say much about them. In that respect, they followed the lead of liberal writers, such as Walter Lippmann, who wrote eloquently about relations between individuals, society, and the state, but said virtually nothing about race relations or black Americans. Whites' public silence about race, however, concealed abundant, obsessional private thinking on the subject. Not talking about race was an effort to avoid contradictory, frightening ideas about the structure of society and personal passions.[5]

Whites' Thinking about Race

Gunnar Myrdal was the chronicler of midcentury white Americans' thinking about blacks. The Swedish economist came to the United States at the invitation of the Carnegie Corporation to analyze American race relations, and he published his findings in a massive 1944 report. White Americans, he found, were of two minds about race. On the one hand, they believed in equality. Christianity told them all men were equally God's creations, the Enlightenment gave them their own liberty on the ground that all were equally reasoning beings, and the American Revolution had taken over English liberalism in insisting on the rights of all men equally to be free. On the other hand, many whites believed blacks were inferior. Whether by nature or by conditioning, they seemed less reasonable, less human, more bestial. While some whites believed mistreatment had forced blacks to live poorly, others imagined their poverty and problems were the inevitable result of impaired moral character. In the latter perspective, discrimination and segregation were only reasonable.[6]

An American Creed of equality competed in white minds with doubt about the full humanity of blacks. Many whites who believed blacks were equal had trouble seeing them as equal. Some who believed in black civil rights hesitated to impose them on whites who feared black equality. The creed pushed midcentury liberals to end segregation; misgivings about blacks held the liberals back. The problem, Myrdal said, was not just that whites had not come to know blacks realistically, but that whites had emotional stakes in misunderstanding blacks in specific ways.

More than three centuries after the first slaves were brought to America, nearly two centuries after the American Revolution, whites spoke about white and black in modern language, but they continued to express old fundamental moral distinctions. When white Europeans first encountered black Africans, they made sense of the startling color difference in religious terms. The whites, regarding themselves as Christians, understood the blacks to be heathens and took skin hue as a moral marker. As white Americans incorporated black slavery into a nation where both Christianity and the Revolution pleaded for equality, they rationalized slavery in the original moral terms. They assumed "the Negro was a heathen and a barbarian, an outcast among the peoples of the earth, a descendant of Noah's son Ham, cursed by God himself and doomed to be a servant forever on account of an ancient sin." During the eighteenth century, whites acquired a language of race to differentiate white and black. Some held that apparent differences in group qualities reflected separate biological origins. Others attributed differences to deeply seated, essentially immutable cultural values. While the formal terms mid-twentieth-century whites used to talk about blacks differed from the earlier lexicon, the moral matrix remained largely the same.[7]

In the period when the National Association for the Advancement of Colored People (NAACP) was developing a legal campaign against school segregation, many whites, Myrdal noted, hardly thought rationally about blacks. He observed that they held onto a

> concept of the Negro "race" [with] an irrational element which cannot be grasped in terms of either biological or cultural differences. It is like the concept "unclean" in primitive religion....In this magical sphere of the white man's mind, the Negro is inferior, totally independent of rational proofs or disproofs....in a deep and mystical sense....There is fear of the unknown in this..."superstition."

While anthropologists of the time catalogued various numbers of races, whites experienced race dualistically. In their "primitive," "irrational" thinking,

> the Negro becomes a "contrast conception." He is "the opposite race"— an inner enemy, "antithesis of character and properties of the white man."...As the color white is associated with everything good, with Christ and the angels, with heaven, fairness, cleanliness, virtue, intelligence, courage, and progress, so black has, through the ages, carried associations with all that is bad and low: black stands for dirt, sin, and the devil....On a deeper magical plane of reasoning...the Negro is believed to be stupid, immoral, diseased, lazy, incompetent, and *dangerous*—dangerous to the white man's virtue and social order.

Historian Winthrop Jordan and psychologist Elizabeth Young-Bruehl later added more explicit psychological analysis. Whites, they suggested, driven by Christianity and conscience to see themselves as pure, unconsciously engaged in complex mental contortions. They split their unacceptable impulses (such as sexuality and aggression) from their virtuous qualities, denied their vices, and then attributed to blacks what they could not tolerate in themselves. Troubled by their lust, for example, whites disowned it and then saw it in blacks, magnified in proportion to their guilt about it. Thus whites used blacks to purify themselves.[8]

This way of thinking made whites ambivalent about blacks. While overtly whites were disgusted by what they imagined blacks to be, they were also attracted to them. The deadly sins, after all, if only they weren't deadly, were enjoyable, and blacks seemed to embody these pleasures; thus whites were drawn to blacks as to the sensual delights. At the same time, whites were pulled to blacks because they recognized in them the part of themselves they had cast off; only by being with blacks could they somehow be whole. "Like the devil [the Negro] is enticing at the same time that he is disgusting," Myrdal noted. "The old theologians of the South meant something specific when they equipped the Negro with a disproportionate amount of original sin, just as Christian theologians generally characterize the devil as a fallen angel." Thus whites had considerable moral and emotional investment in a particular concept of race. The two races were not simply groups that had come from places with different climates and cultures. Rather, one race was wholly good, the other wholly bad. Each existed only as a contrast to the other. What it meant to be white depended on what it meant to be black. Whites needed blacks to think of themselves as good. This notion of race called on whites to subordinate and even mistreat blacks. These were the motives that opposed the American Creed.[9]

One might think the sheer irrationality of these mental processes would doom them: it would be hard to maintain such magical beliefs in the face of reality. However, Myrdal observed, whites insulated themselves from reality by keeping ignorant about blacks:

> There is no doubt…that a great majority of white people in America would be prepared to give the Negro a substantially better deal if they knew the facts. But…we must never forget the opportunistic desire of the whites for ignorance. It is so much more comfortable to know as little as possible about Negroes, except that there are a lot of them in Harlem, the Black Belt, or whatever name is given to the segregated slum quarters where they live.

Further, "The ignorance about the Negro is not…just a random lack of interest and knowledge. It is a tense and highstrung reaction and distortion of knowledge.…The blind spots are clearly visible in stereotyped opinions. The 'function' of those stereotypes is, in fact, to serve as intellectual blinds." The North was no different from the South in this respect. Many educated Northerners, Myrdal found, were "well informed about foreign problems but almost absolutely ignorant about Negro conditions both in their own city and in the nation as a whole." Such ignorance about blacks was not innocent in either its intentions or results: "The important thing and the reason for suspecting this ignorance to be part of the escape apparatus is that knowledge is constantly twisted in one direction—toward classifying the Negro low and the white high." In short, whites avoided knowing about blacks and race in order to secure their feelings of superiority.[10]

School Segregation

The ways of thinking Myrdal found were culturally normal, albeit normally unconscious. They led whites to consider racial segregation necessary and to resist ending it.

Race, Sex, and Segregation

Segregation has been justified or explained in economic terms, as a way of restricting black competition with whites. It has served that purpose. However, most acts of segregation and discrimination were designed simply to assert white superiority by keeping blacks "in their place," away from whites. The extraordinary violence of lynchings, typically based on trumped-up charges of black sexual aggression, suggested in extremis the complicated emotional and moral struggles of many whites when thinking about blacks. Whites who unconsciously regarded blacks as their "bad" counterparts felt segregation was necessary to keep themselves from moral contamination and danger. Sexual anxiety was central to school segregation, and it was the engine that powered Southern (and Northern) "massive resistance" to implementing *Brown*.[11]

Lillian Smith, a white Southerner born at the turn of the twentieth century, who spent some time in Baltimore during her adolescence, recalled that race and sex were both forbidden topics: "Neither the Negro nor sex was often discussed at length in our home." She discovered that the two were related and that their link required segregating both:

> By the time we were five years old we had learned, without hearing the words, that masturbation is wrong and segregation is right, and each had become a dread taboo that must never be broken, for we believed God, whom we feared and tried desperately to love, had made the rules concerning not only Him and our parents, but our bodies and Negroes. Therefore when we as small children crept over the race line and ate and played with Negroes or broke other segregation customs known to us, we felt the same dread fear of consequences, the same overwhelming guilt we felt when we crept over the sex line and played with our body....parts of your body are segregated areas which you must stay

away from and keep others away from. These areas you touch only when necessary. In other words, you cannot associate freely with them any more than you can associate freely with colored children.

"The lesson on segregation," she concluded,

> was only a logical extension of the lessons on sex and white superiority and God. Not only Negroes but everything dark, dangerous, evil must be pushed to the rim of one's life. Signs put over doors in the world outside and over minds seemed natural enough to children like us, for signs had already been put over forbidden areas of our body.

In short, whites instituted segregation in an effort to avoid the sexual temptations they associated with blacks. The variety of African-Americans' skin colors showed that the attractions often overwhelmed taboos, only redoubling segregative impulses. Jim Crow institutionalized efforts to keep blacks down and away.[12]

A minority of Southern whites were uneasy about racial discrimination, either because these practices violated moral or political principles or because they harmed Southern society. Even so, some who asserted black equality also supported segregation. They saw no inconsistency because they distinguished civil, or political, equality and social equality. The former, which they endorsed, included the right to vote. The latter, which they opposed, included participation in social relations with whites. Though it might be hard to establish a firm conceptual boundary between the two, whites drew a practical line where intimate contact could occur. Thus in 1889 liberal George Washington Cable made clear that black civil rights did not include "social intermingling." In 1948 the liberal Southern Regional Council declared that civil rights had "nothing to do with swimming pools and dating places." Dating, with all it led to, was a danger to be prevented by keeping white and black children apart. Hence when Southern and border states provided public schooling for black children in the late nineteenth and early twentieth centuries, they established separate schools. Because Southern whites and blacks lived near one another, children often rode buses great distances to separate schools.[13]

School Segregation at the Time of *Brown*

In May 1954, when the Supreme Court ruled separate schools inherently unequal, thirteen Southern states (Alabama, Arkansas, Florida, Georgia, Kentucky, Louisiana, Mississippi, North Carolina, Oklahoma, South Carolina, Tennessee, Texas, and Virginia), four border states (Delaware, Maryland, Missouri, and West Virginia), and the District of Columbia legally segregated white and black students.

Public schools in the seventeen states and the District enrolled nearly 11 million students, one-fourth of them black. Only the District had a black student majority (56 percent). Mississippi and South Carolina had nearly as many black students as white, and at the other end of the continuum Oklahoma and Kentucky had just 8 and 6 percent black students, respectively. In the border states only 11 percent of students were black, ranging from 21 percent in Maryland to 6 percent in West Virginia. Nearly all states were gaining both white and black students, particularly in the growing metropolitan (city and suburban) districts, though many rural districts were losing students.[14]

Southern states spent much more on white students than on black, with the greatest disparities in rural districts. Whites had better facilities. The per-pupil property value of white schools ranged around one and a half times that of black schools in metropolitan districts and nearly twice that in rural districts. Most Southern states spent more on instruction and operations for white students, with per-pupil disparities ranging between 10 and 40 percent. At an extreme, Mississippi spent about two and one-half times as much for a white student as for a black. School library expenditures were more unequal, with black children commonly getting less than half what whites got. At the extreme, Georgia spent no money on rural black libraries, and rural Mississippi and South Carolina districts spent only pennies per black student.[15]

Spending disparities, combined with black migration to the cities, meant that black teachers had larger classes than whites in most states, particularly in metropolitan districts, with black teachers commonly responsible for 10 to 20 percent more students. Black teachers in a number of states had levels of training comparable to, sometimes better than, their white counterparts, though the quality of training in black normal schools varied considerably. Metropolitan teachers were more likely to be college graduates than rural teachers, and in metropolitan districts black teachers often had more years of training than whites. At the top, in Florida metropolitan districts 98 percent of white teachers and nearly 100 percent of black had college degrees; in Maryland the percentages were 83 and 91, respectively. Even though blacks often had similar training and taught larger classes, white teacher salaries were higher than black in most states, especially in rural districts, though in metropolitan districts in about half the states black teachers' salaries were a little higher than whites'.[16]

More than one-third of students rode buses in the seventeen states, but in all except Maryland more white children than black were bused. At an extreme, Mississippi bused 60 percent of white children but only 30 percent of blacks. Except for Maryland, Delaware, and Oklahoma, states spent more per pupil on transportation for whites than for blacks. Racial spending inequalities were greatest in rural districts, a result of both school locations and practices of buying new buses for white children and handing down old buses for black.[17]

American Liberalism

Those who opposed racial segregation in midcentury America drew on the public philosophy of liberalism. In their campaign, the ambiguities of liberalism would make it a sword that was not only double edged but also too broad and blunt for accomplishing the task. Myrdal had faith in the emancipatory potential of liberalism because of its emphasis on individual liberty and reason, but the roots of the American Dilemma lay in liberalism itself.[18]

Mid-twentieth-century American liberalism derived from the work of seventeenth-century English political philosophers who developed arguments for freeing men from feudal serfdom. John Locke asserted human intellectual equality as the premise for replacing the monarchy and church with institutions giving individuals autonomy. These thinkers fashioned accounts of men living in an insecure state of nature who contracted with one another to create a government that depended on their consent for authority. The main challenge in designing new political institutions, as Hobbes emphasized, was controlling human passions. Desires, anxieties, hopes, laziness, and interests in property seemed to keep men from thinking reasonably. The philosophers' psychological perspective would today be called a theory of narcissism. Individuals had grandiose views of themselves, their possibilities, and their deserts. At the same time, they worried about their worth—whether they were worth anything, whether they had what it took to get what they deserved, and whether they could hold their own against others similarly motivated. Continually anxious about their value, accomplishments, and status, individuals were tensed to strike.[19]

Thus, while seventeenth-century political theorists heralded an "age of reason," they had little confidence in the power of most men's reason to govern their passions. Individuals could not be trusted to think clearly about issues confronting society. At best, with guidance, they might reason about their immediate place and actions. Hence liberals formulated a model of governance that accommodated human weakness. They advanced the idea of economic interest: individuals should avoid philosophical pretensions and, instead, think of themselves as producers and consumers with the primary aim of maximizing their material welfare. Rather than considering grand political issues, they should focus their competitive passions on getting the best exchanges with neighbors. Because liberal theorists associated government with the despotism of monarchy, they postulated that individual pursuit of economic self-interest, advanced through ongoing bargaining, would create sufficient ties to regulate society, without external coercion. Thus liberals developed a theory of governance that at once freed individuals from feudal absolutism and minimized the likelihood that fallible men would thrust their passions into politics and create a totalitarianism justified by democratic claims.[20]

This theory, however, offered only hypotheses regarding whether a society of individuals pursuing self-interest could govern itself. For the eighteenth-century products of the new liberalism forming an American government, this was more than a speculative question. Republicans such as Benjamin Rush optimistically imagined citizens could be educated in civic virtues that would enable them to deliberate about the public good and govern towns, states, and the nation on the basis of their conclusions. Thomas Jefferson, a Lockean, believed that men should first tend to their own affairs, though he expected that the conduct of private matters would lead men to find common interests and develop ways to govern themselves. Federalists such as John Adams worried about human passions and wanted governance arrangements that would accommodate and contain human weaknesses. "If men were angels," James Madison explained, "no government would be necessary." The federalists drew on Locke's intricate ideas about governmental mechanics to design institutions that would check and balance divisive factional impulses and let an educated elite decide and act for the general good. The federalists' Constitution provided the structure for American government, and the individualism of Jefferson's Declaration of Independence became the nation's public philosophy. Americans would see their government as the product of a social contract into which individuals had entered and which they might renegotiate.[21]

Twentieth-century American liberals sought to redesign governmental institutions to fit a world far larger and more complex than the Founding Fathers imagined, but the modern liberals worried about the same dangers of passion that bothered their predecessors. Walter Lippmann, for example, affirmed that "man...is endowed with the faculty of reason" but noted, too, "the primitive lusts of mankind." Moreover, modern men, he observed, felt free to follow their passions, believing "that reason is not the representative of the universal order— and therefore the ruler of our appetites—but that reason is the instrument of our appetites." Lippmann saw around him the same deficient thinkers and narcissists that the early liberals lamented: "The citizen gives but a little of his time to public affairs, has but a casual interest in facts and but a poor appetite for theory." "This modern man...is a being whose desires are limited, not by his reason...but only by the difficulty of getting more and more satisfaction." Echoing Madison, Lippmann asserted, "There is in human nature a disposition to evil, [and] government is not government which cannot restrain it." The frightful situation, he said invoking Hobbes's words, is that "unless the people are successfully organized in a state, so that they can act through officials who represent them under laws to which they have consented, the people's power is mere ineffective, self-destroying violence. Without civil organization the people are…each man against all the others in a life that is 'solitary, poor, nasty, brutish, and short.'"[22]

Observing world wars and the Depression, Lippmann articulated the predicament of liberalism:

> It is perfectly true that that government is best which governs least. It is equally true that that government is best which provides most. The first truth belongs to the eighteenth century; the second to the twentieth. Neither of them can be neglected in our attitude toward the state. Without the Jeffersonian distrust of the police we might easily grow into an impertinent and tyrannous collectivism; without a vivid sense of the possibilities of the state we abandon the supreme instrument of civilization.

Lippmann's concerns might be framed in terms of two questions. First, could a society based on individualism identify and serve collective interests? Second, could a society based on individual interest serve justice, particularly if justice required that all individuals' interests be fairly satisfied? In the context of segregation, these questions came to a focus on a third: Could a society based on liberal individualism address racial problems?[23]

Lippmann had little to say about this question, because race was unimportant to him. Likewise, other liberal public intellectuals in the first half of the twentieth century rarely wrote about race or civil rights. Nor did many liberal political theorists writing at any time during the century even mention race. Tacitly, this broad silence about race supported Myrdal's observations that whites chose not to know about blacks. Hence it is necessary to consider how liberalism hindered thinking about race.[24]

Liberal Premises

The early liberal movement freed the individual of monarchical and ecclesiastical bonds by declaring him capable of reason. However, over time, John Dewey complained, this negative concept of individual freedom, originally a means to emancipation, became regarded as an end in itself. Individual liberty and rights were understood simply as freedom from constraint, and consideration of the aims and purposes of freedom were subordinated. Liberals chose to forget that individuals formed their ideas about themselves and their interests in the context of social relationships, and they ignored individuals' interests in social relations and the interests of society that made liberty possible, all to hold pure and high a negative concept of individual freedom. In short, liberalism emancipated the individual but left him on his own. This ambiguity about individualism was evident in the three main premises of mid-twentieth-century liberalism, and it contributed to liberals' inability to grasp race.[25]

Liberal sociology is atomistic. The liberal perspective reveals society as an aggregation of individuals who are independent in two related ways. Socially, they are unencumbered. Except during childhood dependency on parents and teachers, other persons and groups do not control or influence individuals' thinking about their identity and interests, and they are free to act on behalf of their interests. Because of liberals' mistrust of passion, these interests are defined materially. That is, liberals formulate interests in terms of things, rather than persons or social relations. Interests in other people are matters of feelings, about which liberals are wary. Hence the liberal individual is also emotionally independent of others, just a rational calculator of things that can be autonomously enjoyed.

In this view, individuals are born independent and may create or join groups, communities, or organizations, commonly called "associations." Persons do not grow up in groups or communities that make deep emotional claims on them or strongly mold their identity. Rather, once they identify their interests, they may join with others to serve shared interests. Thus a community is a rationally chosen interest group, rather than the foundation of personal meaning or relations. Ties among members are practical and strategic, not formative or emotional. A few theorists recognize that membership in certain associations is involuntary, that individuals are forced to belong and, presumably, are shaped by membership; typical examples are kin groups, religions, and nations. Even so, liberals regard these affiliations as extraordinary and limited. In the liberal world, individuals act on personal interests, rather than collective identity or social attachment.[26]

Liberal ethics is individualistic and procedural. Liberalism puts primacy on individual choice as the means for allocating valued things. This principle includes two assumptions. The first is that only individuals have interests that matter; there are no valid collective interests that do not rest on or support individual interests. The second is that the process of determining how things are distributed matters more than any specific allocation. This latter position is associated with the Kantian distinction between the right and the good. Individuals have myriad interests and notions of what is good, and consensus is rare. Accordingly, liberal ethics defines justice not in terms of any particular idea of a public good, social arrangement, or economic allocation, but in terms of individuals' right to identify and pursue their own positions. Liberal sociology makes this seem feasible in depicting individuals as free of external influence, so they can determine their interests. Crucially, liberals are indifferent to the aggregate outcomes of individual choices, about the goodness of which people disagree, so long as the results do not jeopardize individuals' right and freedom to choose.

The emphasis on procedure over outcome is familiar in the market, a prototypical liberal institution. In the ideal free market, individuals pursue their economic interests in exchanges with those who have what they want and those who want what they have. Participants learn to refine their views of their interests and their demands and expectations. Gradually, as many individuals adjust their positions in many interactions, they succeed in making deals that serve virtually everyone's interests. The outcome may be considered just insofar as it rests on free individual choices; satisfaction with the outcome legitimates the arrangement. Tacitly, these assumptions link the right and the good: the right of choice seems to produce good outcomes.[27]

Liberal political theory opposes strong government. A big, active government would distort individuals' perceptions of their interests and hinder efforts to satisfy them, in violation of the liberal ethical position. In any case, in the society seen by liberal sociology, where individuals are prime movers, no great inequities arise that might call for outside intervention to correct or compensate. Individuals competing and bargaining with one another will avoid extreme positions and come to agreements that satisfy nearly everyone. And, because procedure matters more than the outcomes of aggregate choices, there is no need for government to impose any particular social arrangement or economic allocation. Besides protecting citizens from harm, the prime responsibility of government is ensuring the right of choice.

The apparent exception of the welfare state helps clarify the meaning of liberalism. Those who have supported the expansion of government in the welfare state are egalitarian liberals, and those who urge limited government, give primacy to the market, label themselves "conservatives," and sometimes excoriate "liberals" are libertarian liberals. The two groups apparently disagree over the optimal size of government, but they share a belief that any government intervention should focus on insuring the right of choice, rather than controlling outcomes. Their central difference concerns who they believe deserves occasional government aid; the libertarians sympathize with business, while the egalitarians want to aid the economically disadvantaged. The welfare state is a liberal institution in that it represents public action intended to improve individuals' ability to participate in the market and other social choice situations. It aims not to alter outcomes but to secure the right of choice for those who lack resources (such as education, health, or income) needed for choosing knowledgeably and effectively. As economic institutions have grown, greater intervention seems necessary to establish individual freedom, but the state makes only temporary, ad hoc adjustments to conditions for choosing, giving individuals the minimum assets required for acting on their interests, and then leaves them alone.[28]

The Invisibility of Race

Myrdal hoped that the liberal belief in equality, bolstered by public education, would improve race relations and the conditions of blacks. However, the liberalism that nurtured his optimism also hindered understanding race and blocked progress. Race was largely invisible to liberals for three reasons.

Races are groups. The liberal prism that sees individuals barely recognizes groups. The main groups visible in the liberal perspective are interest groups. Thus liberals recognize that black persons form or join racially defined groups, such as churches or civil rights organizations, to further their interests. However, the liberal premise that individuals are born autonomous excludes the possibility that groups or communities form persons—that, for example, children born to black parents experience little choice about identifying with, feeling attached to, and thinking along the lines of a somehow-defined black racial group. Rather than allowing the possibility that being born black or white gives individuals significantly different experiences and identities (as well as some commonalities), liberal sociology considers all individuals idiosyncratic. In that view, a white person and a black person are as likely to see things similarly as differently.

Race is a relationship. The liberal prism recognizes autonomous individuals but misses most of their relationships. The main relationship visible in the liberal perspective is one based on common interests. Noninstrumental social relations are peripheral. Race is one of the latter. The races are not groups completely independent of one another, such as ballet dancers and philatelists. Rather, race is a strong, binary relationship extending across society. White people would not think of themselves as "white" if they did not think of others as "black" and persuade those others to think of themselves as black people. The existence of each group depends on a relationship with the other. Such relations are conceptually undetectable in liberal thinking.

Race is defined by emotions. Race is a social construction, something people believe in only because they want to believe in it. In American history, race was the product of an emotional and moral project, in which "whites" sought to avoid guilt about disapproved impulses by disavowing them and fantasizing, instead, that only "blacks" had such impulses. Race relations are built on powerful, deep, irrational passions. Liberalism urges individuals to deny the existence of their emotions, not, in any case, to act on them, and to ignore them in others as well. For these reasons, rational liberal actors are likely to be unaware of the passions in themselves or others that constitute racial relations. If they sense these feelings, they regard them as a poor guide to and constraint on materially self-interested action. The rational individual keeps his or her mind on the surface of things.

Thus, at best, individualistic liberal sociology recognizes racial groups only as interest groups. However, the other two liberal premises even limit the influence of racial interest groups with regard to civil rights. The procedural emphasis on individual choice, to begin with, does not recognize group rights claims. Only individuals have the right to choose. This position opposes a role for racial groups in influencing or exercising choice for members of their race; it rules out the possibility that, for reasons of equity or solidarity, members of a racial group might make collective choices in negotiations with others. More subtly and pervasively, the position denies the possibility that members of a minority racial group confront common historic obstacles to choosing or need common assistance to exercise a right to choose—in other words, that for certain purposes, they should be treated as a group rather than unrelated individuals. In addition, the procedural ethic is indifferent to outcomes. It downplays substantive equity concerns that matter to minority racial groups. Generally, the emphasis on individual choice, coupled with the assumption that individuals can make consequential choices, results in holding individuals responsible for their situation. It minimizes group and institutional discrimination that have constrained members of minority races, giving primary attention to how individual shortcomings may limit the ability to choose. Thus, in prescribing intervention to strengthen the ability to choose, this position focuses on changing minority individuals, rather than social institutions, public policies, or corporate or collective practices that limit members of minority groups.[29]

Liberal political norms resist racial groups' assertions that coercive government power is needed to remedy or compensate for certain racial disadvantages. A belief in limited government restrains public action and emphasizes that inequities, as any unsatisfying arrangements, should be corrected through voluntary negotiations and private contracts, rather than public policy. Moreover, the assumption that remedies for disadvantages in choice involve aiding individuals, rather than changing institutions, requires little government action.

The American Dilemma might be understood as a conflict between humans' better and worse natures, between their reason and their passion, a contest that Myrdal in his most optimistic liberal faith believed public education would mitigate. That formulation of the Dilemma is accurate but incomplete. It represents a conflict, as well, between an egalitarian norm and an ethic that gives primacy to individual choice. In fact, Myrdal noted not only that whites resisted knowing what education had to offer them, but also that they invoked a contract theory of the state when they wanted to avoid complying with laws that would impose conditions they considered illegitimate. The American Dilemma lay in liberalism.[30]

Liberalism and School Desegregation in Baltimore

Liberalism embodied a tension between egoistic individualism and obligations of a collective identity. Could a philosophy of individual rights provide the basis for a compelling national identity? Was it possible to assert a societal identity as anything other than the coercion of individuals? Could individuals see it in their interests to attach themselves to a broad and diverse community?[31]

Local school boards confronted these questions in contemplating desegregation. Desegregation would reorder race relations. By diminishing physical, social, and emotional distance between the races, it would alter white identity. Blacks would assert their individual rights to attend desegregated schools. Using the same language of rights, whites would assert their choice to attend segregated schools. These claims conflicted and, expressed in terms of rights, could not be reconciled. Confronted with this procedural impasse, school boards could acknowledge the conflicts between rights and seek Solomonic wisdom to divide them. Alternatively, they could try to articulate a collective school districtwide identity of which black and white both were part and on the basis of which they would have to find a place together. The emotional obstacle to both approaches, as boards knew, was whites' anxiety about blacks. The intellectual obstacle to the second approach, as boards might discover, was that liberalism gave them little to work with. It was hard to formulate a collective identity that did not seem to infringe on individual rights.

Mid-twentieth-century Baltimore school officials and civil rights leaders were not doctrinaire liberals, all holding precisely the beliefs described here. They recognized that individuals and firms participated unequally in markets and society. They preferred certain outcomes of market activity and public policy over others. A great majority supported the relatively new welfare state. Most favored government activism in some areas. They disagreed about explanations for inequalities and remedies. The clearest line was racial, though it corresponded roughly to a division between those who wanted to change school policy and those who were responsible for making and maintaining it. Civil rights activists, many though not all black, had no doubt that race affected the allocation of social, economic, political, and educational opportunities, that public and private institutions were complicit in these inequalities, and that government intervention was necessary to remedy injustices. School officials, almost all white, were more likely to talk about individual differences and interventions. Part of the explanation for this emphasis, whatever else was in their minds, is that the conventional vocabulary of schooling portrays and evaluates learning as an individual accomplishment.

Yet, despite their various nonliberal beliefs and different emphases, civil rights activists and school officials spoke a substantially similar, consistently liberal language. It provided the dominant legitimate perspective for interpreting social conditions and formulating public policy. Whether or not people called themselves "liberals," they found in liberalism a way of thinking that seemed essentially reasonable and fair. Its principles required no obvious justification. Individual rights were an unquestionably important American tenet, the raison d'etre for the Revolutionary War of the eighteenth century and the rallying cry of the Cold War of the twentieth century.

Most theorists acknowledge that the experienced world is not quite the world presented in formal philosophy, and they recognize the challenges in translating simple principles into complex institutional arrangements. School officials and civil rights leaders, in any case, were not philosophers, but practical men and women. Saddled with responsibility for fashioning policy, they took guidance from the American public philosophy. Particularly when they addressed controversial issues like racial segregation, they found it reassuring and persuasive to rely on time-honored principles. If the result for some was to act, or justify action, in ways that might have seemed not exactly right, still, liberalism made sense of their choices and the results.

AN AMERICAN BORDER CITY

Even in 1950, when Baltimore peaked at nearly a million residents and was America's sixth largest city, its inhabitants thought of themselves as living in a small town. More than that, Baltimore had long been a city of neighborhoods, and residents were as likely to identify with such ethnically, racially, religiously, and economically distinct enclaves as Highlandtown, West Baltimore, Roland Park, and Hampden as with the city as a whole. Baltimoreans were parochial. They were wary of outsiders, and they put a premium on self-reliance. They did their best to get along with one another by moderating extreme behavior and covering over conflicts with a veneer of civility.

The city's character was shaped by Baltimore's location on the nation's North-South border and the consequent impossibility of escaping America's racial conflicts. In the early nineteenth century, Baltimore struggled for autonomy against rural state legislators who punished the city because it had a large free black population and abolitionist sentiments. Within the city, growing battles over slavery led the local elites to agree not to talk about race or slavery in order to keep the peace. Baltimore tried to stay neutral when civil war approached, but when fighting broke out, federal troops occupied the city. The war dashed the city's ambitions of becoming the financial center of the South and delayed its entry into the Northern industrial economy until it was too late. Efforts to navigate a middle course between slavery and abolition left Baltimore a second-tier city. By the middle of the twentieth century, when racial segregation became an issue and the Supreme Court rendered *Brown*, the city's response would express

Baltimoreans' sense of being a community largely on its own in a nation moved by forces beyond its control.

The City's Origins

Baltimore had a history of dependence on outsiders, and started out slowly as a city able to chart its own course. Although Leonard Calvert settled at St. Mary's City as Maryland's first governor in 1634, the villagelike beginnings of Baltimore were not laid out until 1730. In 1752, Baltimore had just twenty-five houses, but by century's end the hamlet had grown into a small city, housing thirty thousand and becoming the most important city in the state. Yet what historian Sherry Olson called "the empty century" preceding this growth shaped the city's identity "as a people struggling" against outsiders, among them state politicians hostile to cities and British invaders. Baltimore developed a pattern of internalizing external conflicts, playing them out among local residents divided by race, class, or party. After the Revolutionary War and establishment of the new nation, Baltimore became a commercial center, linked to international shipping, finance, and communications. Population grew, with at least half the labor force involved in commerce, and the city developed a differentiated class structure. Construction of the Baltimore and Ohio (B&O) Railroad in the early nineteenth century linked the city to the western hinterlands.[1]

Within decades, however, Baltimore was surpassed by cities that diversified their economies and attracted larger numbers of workers. For one thing, the railroad industry failed to develop an integrated economy around the B&O, and equipment manufacturing and repair work located in or relocated elsewhere in the region. In addition, the city's capitalists were conservative. Bankers lent money mainly to other locals and invested relatively little in industry. Merchants thought of manufacturing primarily as a means of support for their commercial operations. On top of this, national settlement patterns constrained the possibilities of commercial expansion. The B&O contributed relatively little to the local economy, as population growth in the Midwest favored railroads in Cincinnati, St. Louis, Kansas City, and Pittsburgh.[2]

Economically, because of the limited potential of the B&O and the parochialism of city capitalists, Baltimoreans depended on initiatives by outsiders. Within the city, those not doing well took out their dissatisfaction on designated surrogates. In the 1840s Protestants organized a Native American Party, which started with attacks on Catholics and grew to take on Jews, other immigrants, and blacks. That nativist party was succeeded by the American (Know-Nothing)

Party, which enjoyed singular success in Baltimore and in Maryland as a whole. In the 1855 and 1857 elections, the party captured the Baltimore mayoralty, a majority in the city council, the governorship, and a majority of the state legislature. In 1856, Maryland was the only state to go for American Party presidential candidate Millard Fillmore.[3]

However, despite the city's momentary congruence of political orientation with other parts of the state, in important respects Baltimore was in thrall to the rest of Maryland. As the city grew during the early nineteenth century, the state legislature, dominated by agricultural and slave interests who feared Baltimore's growing free black population and opposed its abolitionist sentiments, limited the increase in city representation to less than the new size warranted. In addition, as another instance of the city's subordination, until a revision of the state constitution in 1851, the city was legally part of Baltimore County, subject to nonresidents' decisions on representation, taxation, and criminal justice. The separation made little difference, however, because the city and all twenty-three counties lacked home rule, and the state legislature repeatedly interfered in Baltimore matters. Even at the height of national progressive urban reform, rural legislators hostile to the city and its black population resisted home rule. At last, a 1915 state constitutional amendment let local voters choose a charter form of government with an elected executive and a council with legislative powers. Three years later, Baltimore adopted a charter increasing the city's authority. This marginal, slow growth of the political and economic authority of Baltimore highlighted the larger and more profound legacy of isolation and disenfranchisement of the city.[4]

Race in Antebellum Baltimore

A sizable black population played an important role in the development of Baltimore's economy and shaped its political culture. Maryland was a slave state, but it had the largest free black population of any state: seventy-five thousand in 1850, somewhat fewer than the ninety thousand slaves. The number of free blacks reflected three influences: Revolutionary rhetoric and religious scruples, particularly among Quakers and Methodists, which led owners to manumit slaves; the decline of tobacco, which required a full-time labor force, and the rise of wheat, which demanded less labor and, in any case, was often farmed by German immigrants opposed to slavery; and a racial tolerance nurtured by Baltimore's proximity to the North. Just before the Civil War, free blacks in Maryland nearly equaled the slave population: eighty-four thousand, compared with eighty-seven thousand. Free blacks constituted the fastest growing group in Baltimore, where in 1850 they numbered twenty-five thousand, more than in any other American city. Seventeen percent of the Baltimore population was black in 1850; the vast majority, 14 percent of residents, were free. Free black laborers were an integral part of the city's commercial economy—moving goods as stevedores, warehousemen, and haulers, working in the construction trades, and building ships, with a near-monopoly of ship caulking.[5]

Nevertheless, some whites opposed black freedom, and some shared white Southerners' amorphous fear of black rebellion—even though most Baltimore blacks were free and, therefore, had no reason for uprising. Supporters of slavery worried that the city's racial liberals encouraged black violence. Whites periodically attacked free blacks out of resentment of their autonomy and accomplishments. Proslavery interests threatened white abolitionists. In 1830, Baltimore officials jailed William Lloyd Garrison for "libelous" antislavery statements and subsequently forced him and abolitionist colleagues Daniel Raymond and Benjamin Lundy to leave Maryland. Recurrent violence and fear of violence led city leaders to develop distinctive norms for addressing racial issues in the early nineteenth century.[6]

As whites supporting and opposing slavery fought over Baltimore's policies and soul, both sides worried that their battles would tear the city apart, and they sought a modus vivendi. An 1840 British visitor, James Silk Buckingham, saw signs of the emerging detente in a peculiar public stance on racial matters. Baltimore, he said, stood out from New York and other American cities he had visited in the frequency with which citizens condemned slavery and supported abolition (though he might have noted that many advocated both emancipation and African colonization). Yet he was most surprised by another distinction: "In all our intercourse with the people of Baltimore, and we were continually out in society, we heard less about slaves and slavery than in any town we had visited." Expediently, Baltimore elites reached a tacit agreement to stop talking about racial controversies in public.[7]

More formal political developments similarly signified an interest in avoiding conflict over slavery. Baltimore's Know-Nothings reined in their attacks. Where they had once divided the city between native Protestants and foreign Catholics and other immigrants, in the late 1850s, rejecting the national party's position, they sought to include these groups in a coalition of moderate whites who would resist Northern and Southern extremists threatening the nation's survival. Anthony Kennedy, a Baltimorean representing the American Party in the U.S. Senate, feared racial violence if slaves were freed but worried still more about sectional violence if the nation broke up. He started advocating a new party that would emphasize the Constitution and Union—and avoid slavery as an issue. In a state divided between slavery and abolitionism, the new Union Party aimed to balance interests, subdue passions, and avoid conflict.[8]

The Civil War and Its Aftermath

Despite Baltimore's efforts to escape the conflict over slavery, the Civil War derailed local ambitions for national economic prominence. In the 1860 election, Maryland went for John Breckenridge, one of two Democratic candidates. Although Baltimore commercial institutions had ties to the Northern economy, the city's location in a slave state and its significant number of Confederate sympathizers drew federal attention. In February 1861, fear of violence led Abraham Lincoln to sneak through Baltimore on the train from Harrisburg to his inauguration in Washington. In April, after the attack on Fort Sumter, he ordered a Massachusetts regiment to Washington to defend the capital. However, when the soldiers arrived at Baltimore's President Street Station and disembarked to march a few blocks to Camden Station for the last leg of their journey, a mob stoned them, producing the war's first military and civilian casualties. Lincoln suspended habeas corpus in Maryland to secure the passage of troops through the state. In May, General Benjamin Butler of Massachusetts brought Union troops to Baltimore and encamped on Federal Hill, overlooking the city. Other regiments occupied Patterson Park in east Baltimore. Butler imprisoned citizens for treason without trials, and his men seized weapons and looted local establishments. When he left, other Union forces continued the occupation, and their commanders arrested many more Baltimoreans before federal troops withdrew at the end of the war. The indignities were quickly memorialized in 1862 by James Ryder Randall in a nine-stanza poem. The first line, declaring "The despot's heel is on thy shore," opened an account of the street battle with the Massachusetts troops and was followed by verses exalting Maryland valor in the face of Union cruelty. The last lines spurned "the Northern scum." (The poem became the official state song in 1939.)[9]

The eventual Union victory was a shameful defeat for Baltimoreans with Confederate sympathies and an upending for whites who depended on black enslavement for their identity and status. More than that, the war defeated aims of catching up with other cities in the growing national economy. City financial leaders had invested greatly in the Southern economy and striven to make Baltimore the financial center of the region's development. The wartime occupation, disruption of North-South links, and the diversion of Southern resources into the war dashed these hopes. Beyond immediate financial setbacks, city businesses lost their nerve. They became still more conservative in their politics and investments, less ready to take risks. As the postwar nation increased its investment in industry, Baltimore moved slowly from commerce toward manufacturing. Although the B&O gave the city vast westward connections, New York had advantages of rail and water links to the interior, greater proximity to Europe and regular transatlantic shipping service, and larger population and business resources. Philadelphia, for its part, moved more quickly to establish manufacturing. In contrast to cities where financial leaders developed collective strategies for building local economies, such as Pittsburgh, Baltimore was a city of cautious independent entrepreneurs. Except for a growing textile industry, small firms comprised much of the city's postwar industrial development.[10]

When Baltimore entered manufacturing in earnest, its late start limited the capital available to entrepreneurs and, consequently, the size and reach of their enterprises. Chicago and Pittsburgh, for example, became industrial centers, and New York an unrivaled central-office city. As industrial titans forged national corporations and trusts through mergers, buyouts, and hostile takeovers, Baltimore was a loser, its firms becoming merely regional offices. In about eighteen months in 1898 and 1899, outsiders bought up most of the city's industrial base. Ignominiously, the B&O, after overreaching in an attempt to regain dominance, went bankrupt in 1896 and entered receivership. It reemerged in the hands of meatpacker Phillip Armour, department store owner Marshall Field, and two other Chicagoans.[11]

The city's economic subordination was a piece of broader changes following the Civil War. More than anything else, Lincoln had sought to hold the nation together. Yet the fact of secession raised not just constitutional, but also social and cultural, questions about American identity. While Reconstruction may have failed to impose a federal order on Southern states, other, more powerful changes were transforming and unifying the country. The nationalization of the economy was one. As immigrants filled cities to work in new factories, self-appointed Progressive reformers created institutions to socialize them and manage the cities they populated. Centralized, common school systems and professional teacher and administrator training programs came early on. More broadly, national bureaucratic networks challenged small town localism and community folkways. Many Baltimoreans regarded the professional middle class as just a more civilized, and permanent, occupying force. However, the imposition of national standards was imperfect. Baltimore's failure to become a dominant part of the new economy left it lacking strong local institutions with the desire and power to impose a national order on inhabitants. Moreover, there were ways to opt out. Catholics, for example, rejected the Protestantism of the common schools and established parochial schools. Many Baltimore neighborhoods remained urban villages where ethnic cultures persisted and personal relations governed.[12]

The Black Community and Segregation

Whatever the economic setbacks and national constraints, white Baltimoreans did better than blacks. Even though most Baltimore blacks were free before the

Civil War, few had been able to acquire real estate or other forms of wealth. Of free black populations in fourteen major American cities in 1850, Baltimore's was least likely to own property. A half century later, when the Baltimore black community of eighty thousand was by far the largest in America, it ranked seventy-second among seventy-three Southern communities in homeownership, while the Baltimore white homeownership rate was highest. Unlike in some other border and Southern cities, Baltimore blacks did not develop their own bank during the nineteenth century.[13]

Difficulties acquiring wealth encouraged the development of a black middle class based on occupational status and education. As the class grew, it founded community institutions. Centrally, churches established the schools on which social and economic mobility depended and sponsored broad social, cultural, and political activity. Gradually, a black elite emerged, characterized by education, occupation, economic success, and light skin, and they built free neighborhood schools, a high school, an orphan asylum, an aged women's home, a seminary, and a teacher's college. By the end of the nineteenth century, Baltimore had a large, structured black community. At a time when Northern cities such as Detroit had few black residents, Baltimore had an educated black middle class prepared to promote racial causes with white city leaders.[14]

This institutional development reflected the success of a growing middle class, but it was also a product of necessity, as white Baltimoreans began imposing Jim Crow practices of discrimination and neglect in the late nineteenth century. The city's border position, mixing Northern tolerance with Southern customs, created greater ambiguity about race relations than found farther South and made whites (particularly the working class) anxiously uncertain about their status, with the result that whites imposed stricter segregation than in many other places. Close contact between white and black workers in the factories suggested that the races were equal and thus moved whites to limit interaction in other spheres. Paradoxically, Baltimore's industrial development, which might have given blacks entree into the larger society, induced more pressure for segregation than in less-industrialized Southern cities.

In this respect, Baltimore was a national innovator. In 1911, the City Council passed a racial zoning ordinance designating where blacks could live. In reaction, the next year twenty-five blacks and whites founded the nation's second branch of the NAACP. Meanwhile, other border and Southern cities copied Baltimore's law and enforced it until the Supreme Court declared Louisville's version unconstitutional in 1917. After this legal defeat, whites in Baltimore, as elsewhere, inserted racial covenants into housing deeds, a practice that remained legal until the Supreme Court rejected it in 1948. Socially and economically, the city was a web of segregative practices comparable to any in the Deep South. Public and private schools, colleges and universities, hospitals, hotels, restaurants, theaters, parks, golf courses, swimming pools, tennis courts, beaches, restrooms, water fountains, political organizations, professional associations, churches, taxis, and cemeteries were segregated, though, unlike the rest of the South, buses and trains were not, and blacks retained the vote. Department stores refused to let blacks try on clothes, because many whites would not buy items that had touched black skin or hair. The stores' Santa Clauses let only white children get on their laps and tell their Christmas wishes. Government and private employers discriminated against black workers in hiring, pay, and promotion. Police abused and killed blacks with impunity.[15]

In 1922 the Urban League found Baltimore a city of exceptional racial isolation: "The pronounced demand for separation has retarded contacts of acknowledged value to both races even further south.... The sentiments of the far south have been there, but without the sympathy frequently manifested by certain of the influential white leaders of that section."[16]

Schools for Black Children

Although Baltimore had the nation's largest antebellum free black population, the city government did not provide schools for black children. When the Progressives moved to raise and nationalize education standards, Baltimore had begun public schooling for blacks, but their schools were separate from and unequal to white schools.

Voluntary Black Schools

In 1826 the Maryland General Assembly created public primary schools for white children under ten. Three year, later, Baltimore opened its first three public schools. Before then, children attended private schools of varied curriculum and quality. The first of a number of church-sponsored Sabbath schools for black children, the African Academy, for children of free black parents, had been established by Quakers in 1794. Under the 1826 law, blacks paid school taxes, but the revenue supported only white schools. Accordingly, black leaders asked Baltimore government either to relieve them of the taxes or provide schools for their children. The mayor and city council rejected petitions in 1839 and 1844. In 1850, 90 blacks petitioned for public funding for schools for free black children, and 126 whites signed a supporting document. City officials rejected this request as well, leaving the black community to educate a growing number of children on its own. Black churches and white Methodist, Presbyterian, and Quaker congregations opened additional Sabbath schools. In 1854, twelve hundred children attended these schools, all staffed by white teachers.[17]

Even for white children public education was limited. Most children worked; less than one-third attended school. Few poor whites were students. Moreover, the slave interests that controlled the state legislature spent little on schooling. One-third of students went to private schools, because they offered better or culturally compatible education. The wealthy patronized private academies and high schools. German and Irish Catholics attended religious schools, and German Protestants went to their own private schools. The public schools were the domain of advancing middle-class white Protestants.[18]

In 1859, black leaders formed the Colored Sabbath School Union of Baltimore to improve black education and to fund poor children to attend the private schools. At that time the city had fifteen such schools. In 1864, thirty white businessmen, lawyers, and ministers, mostly Quakers, formed the Baltimore Association for the Moral and Educational Improvement of the Colored People to promote a system of black schools. Within a year, they had established seven schools in Baltimore, with an enrollment of three thousand. The association continually struggled to raise money, drawing heavily on Northern aid societies as well as local Quaker philanthropists and Jewish congregations. By its peak in 1867 it had set up more than a hundred schools, most in Baltimore and on Maryland's Eastern Shore. That year the organization established a normal school to train black teachers.[19]

Public Schools for Blacks

In 1867, as the association's fundraising ability flagged, a state constitutional convention called for public schools for blacks. The schools would be separate physically and fiscally. White school tax revenues would go to white schools; revenues from blacks, who had little wealth, would fund black schools. Local jurisdictions would build schools, choose textbooks, and hire teachers. The Baltimore City Council directed school commissioners to set up black schools. The Baltimore association turned its schools over to the government, which renovated and relocated some of the buildings and assumed responsibility for thirteen black schools. School commissioners, one from each ward, selected teachers, librarians, clerks, and janitors; they overlooked blacks because of their race and because they were Republicans. By the end of 1868, only whites taught in black schools.[20]

Although separate funding doomed black schools to inferior buildings and lower teacher salaries, the overall school system was hardly robust. Only 30 percent of children attended any school, and only 4 percent of those went to high school. Baltimore compared poorly with other cities in retaining, promoting, and graduating students. White and black enrollments increased during the late nineteenth century, but a meager local budget, poorly supplemented by state funds, could not keep up, and most black and white students attended crowded, unsafe, and unhealthy schools. Schools were a victim of politics, as bosses preferred spending money in ways that brought them greater returns. The 1873 school board president boasted that the city had spent less on buildings, teachers, and students than nearly any other large city. Baltimore superintendents were paid less than others elsewhere. Even so, the board spent in ways that differentiated races and classes. In 1878 the city ran seventy schools for thirty-six thousand pupils, with 14 percent in black public schools and 9 percent in public German-English schools. With a state subsidy that provided more per white pupil than black, the board constructed new schools for middle-class white students and put black and German children in old school buildings or rented space, such as church basements or old houses. As populations moved, schools built in the 1840s for white children became German schools in the 1870s and, by century's end, black schools. The board reserved its greatest investments for building high schools, attended by children from elite white families.[21]

A group of black leaders active in the large churches began lobbying city officials to improve their schools and increase black control over them. In 1873 and 1875, they unsuccessfully petitioned the mayor and city council to build a black high school. They began strategizing to get a black on the school board. In 1882 the city created a two-year Colored High School and housed it with the Colored Grammar School in the old city hall building. The next year, blacks petitioned the board to hire black teachers. In 1888, Colored High and Grammar schools acquired a new building. That year the mayor signed a law allowing black teachers, and the district hired its first in 1889. In 1896 the high school, enrolling about ninety students, moved into its own building.[22]

Despite the law authorizing black teachers, school commissioners still treated the jobs as patronage, and blacks continued to complain. In 1896 the black schools employed 175 white teachers and 35 black teachers, all of those at one school. Change came with an 1897 city charter, pushed through by a Republican mayor. The twenty-two-member, ward-based board was replaced by a citywide board of nine members appointed by the mayor for staggered six-year terms. The board chose the superintendent, who headed a department of education. The superintendent had responsibility for hiring and administration, while the board attended to policy. The Democrats soon returned but acquiesced in hiring black teachers, so long as they taught only black students. By 1906 all teachers in black schools were black. Still, they had no formal salary or promotion schedule, in contrast with white teachers, who were civil servants and whose salaries were raised to compete with other white women's occupations.[23]

The start of the twentieth century saw a growth in overall school attendance, an expansion of black schools, and solidifying inequality between white and black schools. By 1900, 40 percent of Baltimore children attended school. Since the first public black schools opened in 1867, black enrollment had grown from 901 to 9,383, including 93 high school students. Although black enrollment increased by half over the next two decades, the system built no black schools between 1898 and 1915. Periodically, when a building was judged no longer fit for white students, the board changed its number and name and made it a black school. However, these dilapidated facilities did not provide sufficient space for blacks, and crowding became chronic. After 1905, to deal with overcrowding in the black schools, most black children attended school half time, on shifts.[24]

Early-Twentieth-Century School Conditions

City school conditions were systematically assessed in a 1920 report to the school board by Columbia University Teachers College professor George Strayer, who found much to be concerned about in both white and black schools. His report described white elementary schools with toilets lacking proper drainage, unlighted classrooms and corridors, fire traps without fire escapes, defective stairways, and combustible material stored by a main stairway. Black elementary schools included these features plus others: dilapidated furniture, inadequate teachers' desks, lack of electric lighting, foul and inconvenient toilet arrangements, structural faults in buildings, unsafe and noxious coal stoves, an open sewer in front of a school, dark portable classrooms, and inadequate playground space. The average age of the 113 white elementary and junior high schools was thirty years, while the 25 black schools averaged forty-three years. The extra years represented differences in design and technology, as well as added wear and tear. While majorities of both white and black classrooms lacked what Strayer considered sufficient space for students, a much higher proportion of black classrooms were crowded. Overall, the report gave white elementary schools an average rating of 423 out of 1,000 and black elementary schools 284.[25]

Strayer noted that Baltimore spent less on nearly all government activities than fourteen other major American cities and that by several measures its spending on schools was worst. Los Angeles and Boston spent twice as much per capita on schools, and New York, Newark, and Pittsburgh spent nearly twice. Baltimore, he summarized, "has not been spending on the education of her school children what other cities have found it very necessary to expend in order to maintain high standards."[26]

Strayer recommended renovating, closing, and replacing schools. He urged immediately abandoning and replacing 34 percent of white schools (38) and 43 percent of black (12). He recommended abandoning and replacing less decrepit schools in specific time periods. Regarding teachers, Strayer observed that too few in Baltimore had adequate training. Fifty-eight percent of elementary teachers and 46 percent of high school teachers lacked a standard four years of high school and two of normal school. In comparison, the respective Massachusetts percentages were only 16 and 29. A primary explanation, Strayer held, was low salaries, which could not attract trained professionals and required many teachers to work second jobs.[27]

While discussing the superintendent's office, Strayer considered how to supervise black schools in order to improve them. He noted that blacks lived in separate communities and recommended appointing a black to a new position of colored school supervisor. Black leaders, including the PTA president, NAACP branch president, pastors, and *Afro-American* publisher Carl Murphy, lobbied for the position. In 1922, the school board hired Francis Russell, a Cincinnati high school principal. However, Baltimore's Colored High School principal opposed having his authority limited, and Russell became supervisor of only elementary schools and the teacher training school. Superintendent Henry West gave him no office, secretary, or stationery the first year, insisted he get permission before calling meetings, and commonly ignored or countermanded his actions. Russell quit in 1924 with complaints about salary and authority. He was succeeded a year later by Francis Wood, a Kentucky high school principal, who would hold the post for two decades.[28]

In 1933, Wood issued a progress report on colored schools during his tenure. Enrollment had nearly doubled from 14,448 in Strayer's time to 26,695, and the number of school buildings had increased from twenty-nine to thirty-nine. Of the twelve buildings Strayer had recommended immediately abandoning, the system had closed six, plus four others Strayer had urged eventually abandoning. Ten new schools had been built for black students. In addition, the system had given black students twelve buildings deemed no longer suitable for whites. Another hand-me-down building, adjacent to Booker T. Washington Junior High School, became Wood's office, a mile and a half from system headquarters. Along with some additions and renovations, Wood reported, these changes produced a "vast improvement…from makeshift classrooms, inadequate spacing, lack of playgrounds and unsanitary conditions." All black students now attended class full time. The system had recently opened Coppin Normal School to train black teachers, parallel to Towson Normal School for whites.[29]

Baltimore in the 1930s

In 1930, as Baltimore settled into the Depression, the city had 805,000 residents. Blacks comprised 18 percent, about the same as in 1850. Native-born whites were far more numerous, 73 percent, but blacks outnumbered the 9 percent who were foreign-born whites. Although immigrants and native-born whites shared racial identity, they lived nearly as separately as whites did from blacks. Only three of the city's twenty-six wards contained at least 15 percent each of native whites, foreign whites, and blacks. The greatest mixing was in the southeast: nearest the harbor were neighborhoods of first settlement for many Europeans, such as Oldtown and Canton, and farther north was home to the east-side black population. Though some foreign-born remained in the southeast, including Highlandtown, many had moved toward the city's periphery. Jews were in the northwest, along Liberty Road and Park Heights Avenue; Protestants had gone north, up Charles Street; and Catholics occupied the suburban edge of the east side, out Eastern Avenue and up to the northeast around Harford and Belair roads. Most blacks lived in a band that ran through the middle of the city from west to east, with the elite in Old West Baltimore. Native-born whites were concentrated in the city's outer neighborhoods—most of the Jews in the northwest, the Protestants in the north, including the elite Guilford, Homeland, and Roland Park neighborhoods; and the Catholics largely in the northeast, as well as west out Route 40 and southwest along Frederick and Wilkens Avenues. Baltimore neighborhoods were clearly demarcated by lines of race, ethnicity, religion, and class.[30]

Blacks and whites occupied largely separate parts of the labor market. Forty-three percent of working whites had manufacturing jobs, and 24 percent were in trade. In contrast, 42 percent of black workers were in domestic or personal service, and 26 percent were in manufacturing. The 8 percent of white workers in professions, along with entrepreneurs, were the strongest part of the middle and upper-middle class. The 4 percent of black workers in professions, as well as black businessmen, constituted the core of the middle class and elite.[31]

The white middle and upper classes included most of Baltimore's whites with progressive social and political views, the egalitarian liberals. Most prominent were descendants of the city's early Quaker residents and overlapping groups of German immigrants, refugees from repressive European regimes, and Jews. Business and professional contacts tied many to the North and the larger world; they were cosmopolitans in a parochial city. Their families' economic position bought access to higher education, which gave them broad knowledge and exposed them to liberal ways of thinking.

Working-class whites were more diverse. Native whites were socially and racially conservative. Their views, often reflecting their family origins, were closer to those of Southerners. They were the most vocal proponents of segregation. Part of their racial attitude derived from competition in a labor market where firms used blacks as strikebreakers and hired blacks at low pay to repel white wage demands. Part reflected efforts to assert their status as whites in a world where they had little as workers.

Baltimore's immigrant population was larger than in most Southern cities, though smaller than most in the North. Late- nineteenth- and early twentieth-century immigration tempered the city's white racial views. Although taking a white identity offered newcomers quick American status, these immigrants had no ties to American racial history. Some rejected discrimination outright. Those who encountered skilled black workers could not easily dismiss blacks as inferior. However, as recent arrivals to the city labor market, immigrants were vulnerable to black competition. Still, they did not see themselves as united with the white elite. Working-class families aspired to middle-class comforts, but many resented bosses' ethnic prejudices and economic power. And many, rather than revering professionals, disdained them as effete. In the end, however, working-class whites tamped down economic and racial animosities in keeping with the city's norm of moderation. Baltimore workers were less militant than their Northern counterparts and did not join unions in great numbers. An observer of Baltimore Catholics noted that "public opinion is of the quiescent sort...agitation is unknown, [and] popular feeling has never burst into tumult since the [Civil] war." Expediently, working-class whites took political direction from white machine bosses who traded patronage and protection for loyalty.[32]

The black middle class and elite resembled their white counterparts in several ways. Well educated and, in many cases, scions of long-standing, distinguished families, they identified with W. E. B. DuBois's "Talented Tenth," took pride in their community institutions, considered themselves better off than blacks in the Deep South, and regarded themselves as leaders of the city's black residents. Self interestedly and as a matter of conviction, they were liberals, espousing the principle of individual opportunity and illustrating it with their own success. Most were integrationists, and they regarded civil rights as a precondition for their personal advancement and that of their people. Geographically and politically, they were close to Washington and Northern progressive movements. Strategically, however, they were moderates who went along with Baltimore's modus vivendi. They preferred to work with powerful whites, rather than attack them. They bargained with political bosses and negotiated with elected officials. If necessary, they would go to court against white-dominated institutions. A 1933–34 "Buy Where You Can Work" boycott of discriminatory employers, part of a thirty-five-city national protest, was exceptional. Normally, Baltimore black leaders did not take to the streets but sought what they could get in back rooms, board rooms, and court rooms.[33]

The majority of blacks had little formal education and struggled economically. One-third of men worked in manufacturing, though typically in lower-skill and lower-status positions than whites and for less pay. Half the city's unskilled workers were black. Five in six black women worked in domestic or personal service, making up two-thirds of Baltimore service workers. Some blacks proudly claimed to be more assertive toward whites than deferential Southern blacks. However, a national NAACP official would characterize Baltimore blacks generally as "lethargic and…prone to accept the status quo." Many, particularly those recently from the South, were comfortable with separate black institutions. They relied on black leaders to secure improvements in their conditions.[34]

In the end, whatever blacks and whites thought of one another, segregation limited the extent and depth of their encounters. The most direct and equal interracial contacts involved a small group of black leaders and white public officials and political bosses, and both groups abided by Baltimore norms of tactfully expressing differences, carefully balancing opposing interests, and above all, preserving civility.[35]

A LONG BLACK CAMPAIGN FOR EQUALITY

In the mid-1930s, two black Baltimore community institutions launched a campaign to improve black children's education. The *Baltimore Afro-American* had protested black school conditions since the newspaper's founding in 1892. When Carl Murphy succeeded his father as editor and publisher in 1922, he kept up the crusade. The Baltimore branch of the NAACP, established in 1912, quiescent in the twenties, was revitalized by Lillie May Jackson in 1935. Together, the *Afro* and the NAACP, Murphy and Jackson and her daughter Juanita, focused efforts on equalizing black and white schools. They had close ties to Thurgood Marshall, who left Baltimore in 1936 for the NAACP's New York headquarters, where he and Charles Hamilton Houston mapped out a national campaign to end school segregation by forcing local school districts to equalize separate facilities and making it too expensive for them to do so.[1]

Desegregation Leadership

Carl Murphy's father, John, a former slave, had merged three church papers to create the *Afro-American* in 1892. Under the senior Murphy's guidance, the paper campaigned for employment and fair pay for black teachers, and advocated appointment of a black to the school board and a black administration for the colored schools. The *Afro-American* also pressed for black students to have a curriculum that better prepared some for college and others for vocational success, demanded better school facilities, and urged improvement of black colleges and desegregation of the University of Maryland. Carl, born in 1889, graduated from Howard University in 1911, got a graduate degree at Harvard, and studied at the University of Jena in Berlin. He began an academic career in 1913 as chair of Howard's German Department. In 1918, when his father's health declined, the family called him home to help with the paper. On his father's death in 1922, he took over. He expanded the *Afro* into thirteen editions, including local editions in Baltimore, Washington, Richmond, Philadelphia, and Newark. A national edition competed successfully with the *Chicago Defender,* the *Pittsburgh Courier,* and the *Amsterdam News,* and the *Afro* became the most widely circulated East Coast black paper. Murphy was a member of the NAACP, and publishing gave him financial security that permitted political independence.[2]

Lillie May Jackson, also born in 1889, claimed a distinguished lineage, including many educators. One paternal great-grandfather was Charles Carroll of Carrollton, a signer of the Declaration of Independence. A maternal great-grandfather was said to have been an African chief who was never enslaved; he married an English woman, and their free children included teachers and ministers. One of Jackson's mother's uncles owned land in Montgomery County in 1832, unusual for blacks at the time. Her father was born in 1836 on the Carrolls' Doughregan Manor Plantation in Howard County and was taught to read by women in the big house; he later became commissioner of county colored schools. Her mother was a teacher who stressed the value of owning property. Lillie May would buy houses and draw on rental income for financial independence that would give her political freedom. She was a community activist, a leader in civil rights programs, and an active member of the Sharp Street Memorial Methodist Episcopal Church.[3]

Her daughter Juanita went to the University of Pennsylvania and returned to Baltimore in 1932 to teach secondary school. After Philadelphia's racial freedom, she could not adjust to the segregation she reencountered in Baltimore. With her mother's encouragement, she organized the City-Wide Young People's Forum, which brought prominent national figures to speak to black youth about civil rights. In 1933, angered by employment discrimination in the depths of the Depression, she led the forum in organizing the local Buy Where You Can Work campaign.[4]

This grassroots activism was only loosely tied to the national NAACP civil rights campaign. The Baltimore branch had withered. Some whites contributed money, but few participated openly. The remaining black members were mostly an elite of doctors, teachers, lawyers, and ministers, and only a handful were active. The nationally publicized 1931 lynching of Matthew Williams on the Eastern Shore moved NAACP executive secretary Walter White to try to revitalize the branch, and he contacted Murphy, who was a member of the national board. In late April 1935, Murphy asked Lillie May Jackson to lead a reorganization effort, and she launched a membership drive. Earlier that month, Thurgood Marshall had sued the University of Maryland Law School on behalf of Donald Murray, a black Amherst graduate seeking admission. Juanita Jackson went to the 1935 national NAACP convention and boasted that Maryland was now "the laboratory of the NAACP" in inviting the organization to hold its 1936 convention in Baltimore. Lillie May Jackson secured the convention, pushed membership rolls past two thousand (toward four thousand by 1940), and raised thousands of dollars. With Murphy's endorsement she was unanimously elected branch president in late 1935. She quickly came to personify the Baltimore NAACP and civil rights activism and would remain branch president for thirty-five years.[5]

White urged the Baltimore branch to take the lead on Maryland civil rights. Thurgood Marshall was practicing law in Baltimore after training with Charles Hamilton Houston at Howard University. Hence, in 1935, when blacks in Baltimore County, surrounding the city on the west, north, and east, asked for help on a school issue, Murphy and Marshall responded. The county ran eleven white high schools and none for blacks. Black children who wanted to go to high school had to take an examination, and if they passed, the county paid for them to attend a city high school. About one-third of those taking the test passed; most ended formal education at the seventh grade. Marshall took the case, his first as lead attorney for the NAACP, suing the county to build a black high school. The NAACP lost, but the case established the interest of the branch in elementary and secondary education. While moving that case through the courts in 1936 and 1937, the NAACP, led by Murphy and Marshall, organized a statewide campaign to equalize black and white teacher salaries. After negotiating equal-pay agreements with seven counties, the NAACP sued recalcitrant Anne Arundel County. In November 1939, the U.S. District Court would rule for the teachers, and in April 1941, the legislature wrote equal salaries into law.[6]

Challenging Separate and Unequal Schools

With a revitalized NAACP branch and new education initiatives, Carl Murphy wrote Lillie May Jackson about Baltimore's colored schools on February 1, 1938:

> Report has reached us that the School Board proposed to inaugurate the staggered class system in [Booker T. Washington] Junior High School #130 under which classes will operate from 8 a.m., to 4:30 p.m. We desire to protest against any such system of overcrowding our children by putting 2,000 children in a building which can accommodate 1,400. We are

asking for a seat in the public schools for every child. Douglass High School is also over-crowded and under the circumstances we do not see why the School Board should accept pupils from Baltimore County.

City schools had enough room for all children, but separation into white and colored schools produced a scarcity of seats for the fourth of students who were black. The only remedy the school board considered was to operate Booker T. Washington on shifts, giving every student a seat while keeping black children away from white. The arrangement, besides shortening instruction, would force some children to start school early in the morning and others to stay late in the afternoon. Because the teaching staff would not be increased, black teachers would work longer days. Douglass High School suffered insult as well as injury. It was the only black high school until 1939 and thus became the destination for Baltimore County black students. County discrimination increased crowding at Douglass.[7]

Four days after Murphy wrote Jackson, the *Afro* reported that the NAACP would investigate. Murphy, a branch executive committee member, chaired the new investigative committee. The thirty members of the Citizens Committee on Current Educational Problems of Negroes in Baltimore included Lillie May Jackson, Baltimore Urban League executive secretary Edward Lewis, Morgan State College president Dwight Holmes, and representatives of major black social, professional, religious, civil rights, educational, and political organizations. A month later, as the study proceeded, the *Afro* angrily reported that Mayor Howard Jackson had filled the three openings on the nine-member school board by reappointing the white incumbents.[8]

While the committee worked, the *Afro* documented the inequalities of segregation. In March 1940, reporting that, once again, the mayor had reappointed three white board members, the paper complained about black school conditions. An elementary school had only old chemical toilets, and the board refused a health department request to replace them with modern sanitary facilities. A number of colored schools had been condemned for nearly fifteen years, but Superintendent David Weglein said no funds were available to replace them. Black children were attending school in a portable building missing 285 windows; it was winter, and the windows had been missing since September. Only a black board member, Murphy insisted editorially, would give black children what they needed.[9]

Portable buildings offered the most dramatic examples of the neglect of black children: many of these facilities did not have toilets with running water, were infested with rats, lacked adequate lighting, were filled with smoke from coal stoves, reeked with filth, or were just generally dilapidated. The board skimped on black children's education in many ways. Black classes were large, averaging thirty-eight students per teacher, compared to thirty-four white pupils per teacher. The system spent little on black school buildings, which averaged in value 34 percent of the average of white buildings (exclusive of land value). Put differently, the value of black school buildings per pupil averaged only 39 percent of the per-pupil value of white school buildings. The board spent less to operate black schools: per-pupil black elementary school operating budgets were 90 percent those for white elementary schools, and the secondary school ratio was 84 percent. Although black and white staff salaries were close, black principals and teachers were paid less per student, despite the fact that one-fourth more black teachers had college degrees.[10]

The Citizens Committee presented its findings to the school board on June 20, 1940. It made several requests, framed in terms of equalizing separate schools and intended to raise the costs of segregation. Some involved money—to construct a vocational school to prepare black students for contemporary occupations, build more elementary schools, hire teachers to equalize white and black workloads, and transport elementary children forced to travel more than eighteen blocks to school. A request for relief from overcrowding seemed to petition for new colored schools, though crowding could be remedied simply by removing the color barrier. The committee repeated its longstanding request that the colored school director be given the position of an assistant superintendent.[11]

In response, the school board did nothing; that would remain its most consistent response to black requests to improve school conditions. After three months, Murphy wrote board president Forrest Bramble to ask what the board had decided. Getting no answer, two weeks later, Murphy and Lillie May Jackson met with Mayor Jackson and Superintendent Weglein to ask how many of thirty schools to be built with a new school loan would be for black students. Despite prodding from the mayor, Weglein would not give a definite answer. Still lacking a response to most requests, the Citizens Committee addressed the board's Rules Committee on November 14. Murphy asked the mayor to get the board to move. Two weeks later, the board replied, rejecting virtually all requests. It said it could do nothing about high student-teacher ratios because it would not hire more black teachers and would not ask teachers to teach additional classes on shifts. It rejected a request for a new colored junior-senior high, and although it said a black vocational school had priority, it had not selected a site. It said its policy forbid transporting students to school. And it wouldn't make Francis Wood assistant superintendent. The only thing the board offered was "a considerable number of projects for colored schools" from the new school loan.[12]

In February 1941, NAACP branch attorney W. A. C. Hughes drafted litigation to press the board to make improvements, including building a new vocational school. Thurgood Marshall, now director-counsel of the NAACP Legal Defense Fund in New York, suggested to Hughes a different strategy for ending the vocational school problem:

> What about having qualified Negroes to apply to the white vocational schools for courses not offered in the Negro vocational schools and, upon refusal, have them apply directly to the City Superintendent of Schools? He, of course, will refuse to give them the training. After this is done, what about using Section 43 of Title 8 of the United States Code which provides [for civil action for deprivation of Constitutional rights]. It seems to me that an action for damages against the superintendent in the Federal courts will just about break up this whole thing.

During this time, A. Phillip Randolph, president of the Brotherhood of Sleeping Car Porters, was organizing a March on Washington to protest discrimination in war industries, and the committee held up litigation to see if the march might accomplish their purposes. President Roosevelt issued an executive order establishing the Fair Employment Practices Commission, and Randolph called off the march. The committee did not proceed with its suit, but a decade later the NAACP would follow through on Marshall's idea.[13]

In the face of school board obduracy, the Citizens Committee seized whatever openings it could find to press for improving black children's education. Shortly, the Department of Education released test scores showing Baltimore black junior high students about a year behind white students. The committee's response shows how the Baltimore branch was connected to a national network of civil rights activists and how it used social science to argue its case. Murphy asked education experts at Morgan State College and Howard University to interpret the test data. Believing that children's intellectual performance reflected home and school environments, not genetics, the committee prepared a report for the board noting "no significant difference" between white and black scores in Los Angeles, where schools were not segregated. Accordingly, the committee held the Baltimore system responsible for academic disparities and asked the board to equalize buildings, equipment, teacher quality, and teaching load so as to equalize student performance. The committee's February 1942 report also called attention to an issue near Murphy's heart, equalizing teacher quality. Black teachers attended the school system's Coppin Teachers College, which was unaccredited and unequal to white State Teachers College in Towson. The report summarized Coppin's deficiencies. Few of its teachers had graduate degrees, and they struggled against an excessive workload. The library had few books or periodicals. The committee asked the board to make Coppin as good as the Towson school or else transfer Coppin students to an accredited state college.[14]

The board offered no response, but a month later, Mayor Jackson declared once again that the time was not right to appoint a black to the school board.[15]

March on Annapolis

Racial tensions increased around the country in the early 1940s. The Depression was not over, and discrimination made it especially hard for blacks to find work. Many Southern blacks moved North in search of employment. As blacks looked for jobs and housing, the Double V campaign sensitized them to racial injustices. Competition for work and space in Northern cities, compounded by racial anxieties and resentments, provided the tinder for riots. In Detroit, a rapidly growing black population faced housing and employment discrimination, police brutality, and widespread segregation. In February 1942, when black families integrated a new public housing project, whites started a riot that ended in injuries and arrests. In June 1943, 100,000 whites and blacks gathered in a Detroit park to beat the summer heat, and some started fighting that sparked full-blown riots. After two days of destruction and death, federal troops authorized by President Roosevelt restored order. That August, racial tensions and black grievances in Harlem, ignited by rumors that a white policeman had killed a black soldier, gave rise to two days of rioting and shooting. Baltimore, in contrast, had no riots in the 1940s. In 1942, black Baltimoreans expressed their grievances about discrimination and police violence in a march to the governor's office in Annapolis. That event revealed much about their approach to addressing wrongs.[16]

By February 1942, the Citizens Committee had been waiting nearly two years for the school board to act on its requests. The last straw in the black community's relations with city government, however, came from another quarter. Robert Stanton had become police commissioner in 1939, and with his ascent abuse and brutality toward blacks had sharply increased. Under his watch alone, nine blacks had been killed, and not a single officer was punished. On February 1, 1942, Thomas Broadus, a black soldier, went with friends to see Louis Armstrong in the black Pennsylvania Avenue entertainment district. Just after midnight, Broadus's group hailed an unlicensed taxi. A white officer, Edward Bender, stopped them and insisted they take a licensed cab. Broadus said something to Bender, and Bender hit him with a nightstick and tried to arrest him. Broadus grabbed the club, hit Bender with it several times, and ran. Bender shot him. While Broadus lay in the street, his companions tried to take him to the hospital, but Bender prevented them. By the time a patrol car arrived and took him to the only hospital that treated blacks, he was dead. Broadus was the second black Bender had killed. On February 25, the grand jury charged him with murder, but a few days later the grand jury reconvened and dismissed the charges without explanation. Stanton took no action against Bender.

Carl Murphy moved the NAACP to protest the murder and insist on discussing the range of black grievances with Governor Herbert O'Conor, who agreed to meet in late April. Murphy helped assemble 150 organizations in a Baltimore Citizens Committee for Justice. He became its chair, and Juanita Jackson Mitchell served as director. (By this time, Jackson had become a lawyer and had married Clarence Mitchell Jr., who worked with the federal government on securing black employment in war industries and in 1950 would become director of the NAACP's Washington bureau.) Civil rights leaders recalled planning for the March on Washington, and the NAACP invited B. F. McLaurin, executive secretary of the porters' union and one of the 1941 March planners, to help organize a march on Annapolis.[17]

With planning for the march underway, fifty Citizens Committee members met on April 9 with Mayor Jackson, to ask him to appoint at least one black when he filled three school board openings. Murphy argued that black children, comprising a third of city students, needed someone to advocate for their needs, and he named five candidates. The mayor said he would give the request "very serious consideration."[18]

The night before the march, April 23, the Citizens Committee held a mass meeting, where Adam Clayton Powell, pastor at the Abyssinian Baptist Church in Harlem and a New York City councilman, addressed twelve hundred people. The next morning, two thousand protesters traveled by car, bus, and train to Annapolis. A small group, including Carl Murphy, Lillie May Jackson, Juanita Jackson Mitchell, Edward Lewis, and W. A. C. Hughes, met with Governor O'Conor for two hours. They asked the governor, who appointed the city police commissioner, to investigate police administration in black neighborhoods. They requested that he appoint black uniformed policemen (the city had three black policemen but did not put them in uniform so as not to intimidate whites), a black police magistrate, and an additional black policewoman. They asked him to appoint blacks to several state boards. The Citizens Committee presented petitions with four thousand signatures for the removal of Commissioner Stanton. Jackson noted that she represented six thousand NAACP members. The committee insisted gubernatorial action was urgent. Mitchell characterized the march as "born of desperation" over police brutality. Just weeks after the Detroit riot, Hughes called attention to the police killings and warned that "a serious racial conflict may result unless some remedial steps are taken."[19]

O'Conor was noncommittal. His main response, on May 18, was to appoint five blacks and thirteen whites to an Interracial Commission to Study Problems Affecting the Colored Population. Many public officials who feared racial violence were doing the same thing: during the 1940s, 1,350 localities set up intergroup relations committees. Murphy and Jackson doubted O'Conor's seriousness, and the Citizens Committee soon accused him of using the commission to "whitewash" issues.[20]

The march showed much about Baltimore black leaders. They included businessmen and professionals, people with education, money, familiarity with the white world, and the confidence to deal with that world. The two thousand who traveled to Annapolis could take a day off work. They did not have illusions about white officials or business leaders, but they believed in the propriety and strategic value of asserting their equality to their adversaries and reasoning with them rather than leaving grievances to street protest or riot. Mitchell explained, in reflecting on the march,

> the march on Annapolis in 1942 when 2,000 of us marched to Annapolis to protest the police brutality and the like, I am positive that kept us from having a riot in Baltimore. They had a riot in Detroit and a riot in Harlem....they didn't have a riot here because we channeled the frustration and resentment and bitterness into constructive protests, went to Annapolis to protest and got some results.

As an alternative to violence, black leaders offered community members ways to convey grievances to public officials. The governor and mayor, after all, talked with them. Even if the results disappointed, a two-hour meeting with the governor was a major accomplishment. Black leaders understood the importance of organization. While riots went on elsewhere, the Baltimore NAACP registered voters. Although city population was declining in relation to the rest of the state, in 1940 Baltimore still had 47 percent of Maryland residents, and in 1942 blacks constituted 17 percent of city voters. They warranted an audience.[21]

Moving from Equalization to Desegregation

A month after the Citizens Committee met with Mayor Jackson, he reappointed two white school commissioners and put another white in the third open position. On May 15, the committee wrote him, declaring black board membership a matter of "essential justice." The letter repeated requests from the unaddressed petition of two years prior. It protested whites-only vocational courses and held the mayor accountable for improving the colored junior high schools and Coppin. Jackson replied that many of the charges of school inequalities had no factual basis, and he explained how racial neutrality had led to appointing three whites to the board. Since he had planned to reappoint two of the three incumbents, he said, he had only one position to fill, and he followed the city charter in not distinguishing nominees by race. Because he had no formal responsibility for schools, he was forwarding the committee's letter to board president Bramble. Bramble referred it to Superintendent Weglein.[22]

At last, on June 25, 1942, the board replied to the June 20, 1940, requests of the Committee on Current Educational Problems and its subsequent critiques of school policies. The board held that the assessed values of white and colored facilities were close enough as not to warrant building new colored schools. It denied that poor facilities contributed to poor test scores by identifying substandard colored elementary schools where students did well. The board downplayed the importance of inequalities in elementary school student-teacher ratios. It justified meager vocational offerings by arguing that black students showed little interest in vocational training and noting that, in any case (in contrast with its accompanying statement about the adequacy of colored facilities), colored schools lacked the capacity to offer more courses. Concerning Coppin's teacher training program, the board minimized the importance of accreditation and observed that Coppin graduates, in fact, advanced in the city's colored system.

Carl Murphy, advised by Howard University education professor Martin Jenkins, presented the committee's rejoinder to the board on December 10. The committee's report characterized the board's response as "a series of evasions and rationalizations of present inequities that are unworthy of those who pretend to accept the concept of democratic education." The committee reiterated descriptions of inequalities and emphasized that good facilities, small classes, and qualified teachers were crucial at the elementary-school level for low-income children. What the committee said about vocational education stood ahead of the national NAACP legal position. The NAACP believed it could make a case for desegregating public graduate and professional schools because Southern states lacked separate black programs and providing equal programs would be prohibitively expensive. The likely result, as in the Supreme Court's 1938 *Gaines* decision, rejecting segregation at the University of Missouri Law School, was that the court would order blacks admitted to the white program. A case for desegregating undergraduate education and elementary and secondary education, where states provided separate facilities, was harder to make in court. The committee asserted, however, that *Gaines* set a precedent for secondary school vocational education. Black students, it insisted, had a legal right to the same offerings whites received, regardless of how many enrolled.[23]

The school board, on receiving the committee report, considered the matter closed. Three months later, the state Commission on Problems Affecting Colored People sent the governor its recommendations; regarding education, it urged making Coppin accreditable. Governor O'Conor took no action on Coppin. In

November 1943, Baltimore elected a new mayor who viewed black interests sym-
pathetically. Theodore Roosevelt McKeldin, a liberal Republican who had failed
to unseat O'Conor in the 1942 gubernatorial election, defeated Howard Jackson's
reelection bid and became mayor.[24]

While Baltimore black leaders pinned their hopes for a school commissioner
on McKeldin, they closely watched national NAACP legal action and considered
whether they should also turn to the courts. In March 1944, the *Afro* reported
that a black Washington, D.C., parent whose child was refused admission to the
school nearest home would contest the legality of segregation in court. (In fact,
it would be another six years before Spottswood Thomas Bolling Jr., became the
lead plaintiff in a suit to desegregate the capital's schools that would be one of
the school segregation cases decided by the Supreme Court in 1954.) Murphy
asked the NAACP legal department to study whether the Baltimore branch could
"compel the city with its jim-crow system to provide the equal accommodations
which the law guarantees."[25]

At last, in late March, McKeldin, after naming Roszel Thomsen to replace
Forrest Bramble as school board chair, designated George W. F. McMechen, a
black man, to fill one of three board openings. McMechen had graduated from
Morgan College and Yale Law School and had practiced law for forty years. He
was familiar with Baltimore segregation, since he had made history of a different
sort thirty-four years earlier. In the summer of 1910, as a rising young lawyer,
he got a new house in a fashionable neighborhood. The house was on the white
side of the city's informal color line. Whites threatened his home, and he had to
request police protection. In reaction, the City Council passed a racial zoning
ordinance.[26]

Stepping up the Attack on the Inequalities of Segregation

The *Afro* kept attention on ways colored schools were unequal to white. It decried
teachers' working conditions. Not only was the school system responsible for
educating black children, but 1,700 black adults earned livelihoods as teachers.
When schools opened that fall, the paper noted that 108 black teachers had left
since the previous year. Most, it said, had found better pay, facilities, and working conditions elsewhere. School officials, the *Afro* charged, had long known of
problems driving out veteran teachers but threatened retaliation against those
who complained and did nothing to improve the situation.[27]

When assistant superintendent William Flowers died in January 1945, the
Afro wanted the position filled with a black who oversaw colored schools. The
NAACP asked the board for autonomy for colored schools within the segregated
system. It asserted that only a black administrator would competently manage

black schools and proposed an arrangement like the one used in Washington: a black assistant superintendent to supervise staff responsible for colored schools. The NAACP said it was making the request in the context of segregation it did not accept. Juanita Jackson Mitchell noted that blacks were the only segregated racial minority; Chinese students, for example, attended the Baltimore Polytechnic Institute. She said the NAACP was determined to end segregation because it harmed black children: "It is generally known that the curriculum in Negro schools is a year behind."[28]

Board president Thomsen conceded that "no one would pretend that colored and white schools are on an equal level." He declared the board's intention to correct disparities but said doing so would take years. He said the system could not afford to equalize curriculum: because few black students would enroll in certain courses available to whites, providing the courses for blacks would be too costly. War conditions made it impossible to build schools to relieve crowding. A new colored vocational school remained on the agenda, but still no site had been chosen. He rejected the request for an autonomous black administration and noted that Elmer Henderson, who after Francis Wood's death had become colored school director, attended meetings of the superintendent and assistant superintendents. He doubted black supervision was inherently best for managing black schools and said current structures were adequate.[29]

Near the end of the school year, speaking to the black Frontiers' Club, Thomsen reported some developments. The board might name a black assistant superintendent. In the fall, the Carver Vocational School would add courses to become a black vocational high school, though the courses would have to be offered in the school's crowded old building for at least two years until a new facility was built. In addition, a $10 million postwar construction loan would pay for three black elementary schools to replace buildings condemned in the 1920s, and funds would be spent on improving other black facilities. Thomsen noted that the board was selecting a successor to Superintendent Weglein, who would retire in June.[30]

On November 1, the board elevated Elmer Henderson to the new position of assistant superintendent for colored schools. In making the announcement, Thomsen denied that the board had acted in response to the NAACP request. The *Afro,* reporting the victory, matter-of-factly called Henderson "superintendent." The *Afro* then put Henderson's feet to the fire, insisting he do something about overcrowding. Urging the board to find more space, the editorial echoed Murphy's letter to Lillie May Jackson seven years earlier:

> The fact remains that Booker Washington Junior High has crowded 2,500 pupils in a building meant to house only 1,200, and that Dunbar

Senior-Junior High has nearly that many. Both schools must resort to double shifts. In addition, at least eleven portable buildings are used to help relieve overcrowding in elementary schools. Not a single junior high school for white pupils has this kind of overcrowding.

Overcrowding was a direct result of segregation; seats lay vacant in white schools.[31]

In January, the NAACP pushed against segregation. As Thurgood Marshall and Carl Murphy had urged earlier, the branch sought to enroll black students in specialized white schools, arguing there were no comparable black facilities. The NAACP submitted three youths' names to the Mergenthaler High School of Printing, a white school offering unique printing courses. The NAACP announced it would present a student for admission to the Robert E. Lee School, where white students completed an accelerated junior high curriculum. School officials, however, held to their separate-but-equal policy. They rejected the Mergenthaler applications but promised to install linotype instruction machines at Douglass. Instead of admitting blacks to Lee, the board voted to open a similar school for blacks in the spring semester.[32]

Black leaders then focused on Booker T. Washington Junior High in their campaign against segregation conditions. A delegation representing a thousand members of the school PTA presented a report and petition to the board on January 17. They criticized overcrowding and part-time schooling and catalogued the school's problems. Books were in such short supply that students could not use them every day, and some pupils seldom saw books. Several classrooms lacked sufficient seats for students, and some children shared chairs. Windows were filthy, and the building hadn't been painted in years. Shops and athletic facilities had antiquated equipment and were nearly useless. Toilet facilities were filthy. The auditorium had broken seats and a torn stage curtain. The cafeteria was so small that students had to eat in shifts from 10:00 a.m. to 2:00 p.m., its walls were dirty, and rain came in through holes in the ceiling. The building was a firetrap. The PTA committee asked the board immediately to eliminate overcrowding and shifts; clean, overhaul, and modernize the building; renovate the facility and install needed equipment; and provide an adequate new junior high school building. Thomsen acknowledged that he had heard similar reports from other schools, and he conceded that Booker T. Washington was one of the worst. However, he blamed conditions on a meager maintenance budget and passed some blame onto the principal, saying that, if there were book shortages, he should have asked for books and would have gotten them. Thomsen asked a committee of board members and administrators to investigate.[33]

The first action, ironically, came in response to another NAACP request. The system would set up its colored alternative to Robert E. Lee at Booker T. Washington, adding to overcrowding. The *Afro* sustained a drumbeat of protest against conditions at the school. It noted that problems were old and reflected the indifference of officials who did not care about black students. In response, the board approved $12,500 for renovations there and at Carver. The NAACP got Theodore McKeldin to make a surprise visit to the school. The mayor, noting that his wife had gone to school in the building when it was the elite girls' Western High School, found conditions deplorable and promised to talk with Thomsen. McKeldin asked why colored school headquarters, on the school's back lot, were not torn down and the administration moved to the system's main office, "where it belongs."[34]

The *Afro* stepped up its campaign with a series of illustrated articles showing dismal conditions in black schools. Schools condemned by George Strayer in 1921 continued in use, including one built in 1886, designated unfit for whites in 1921 and turned over to blacks in 1944. These schools were still as Strayer had reported: variously, they lacked sewerage, accessible fire escapes, safe heating, modern toilet facilities, adequate light, running water, classroom space, recreational space, office space, and maintenance.[35]

While the series ran, William Lemmel came to Baltimore from Wilmington, Delaware, to take over as superintendent. He was a liberal on social and educational issues, and the black community welcomed him. However, his arrival did not instantly change entrenched practices. In January 1947, the board proceeded with plans to relieve overcrowding at Booker T. Washington by turning a white elementary school into a temporary black junior high. As was its practice when transferring schools from the white division to the colored division, the board changed the school's number, which had been 60, in the 1–99 white series, to 137, in the 101–199 colored series, and changed the name from the Druid School to the Harvey Johnson Junior High School. A month after the school reopened, the *Afro,* echoing Strayer's assessment of the building, pronounced it "unfit for junior high school use" and demanded a new building. Ironically, Harvey Johnson, a late-nineteenth century Baltimore Baptist pastor and civil rights activist, had lamented the condition of black schools and become a separatist after despairing of working with whites.[36]

Making the Case for Integration

During the fall of 1947, the *Afro* ran an eight-part series titled "Segregated Educational Facilities Are Legally Indefensible," by Harry O. Levin. Levin and his son Marshall were Carl Murphy's personal and corporate attorneys. He argued that Maryland law permitted, but did not require, segregation. The state code, he said, held that if districts provided racially separate schools, they had to be equal. If a district decided not to provide separate facilities, it was obligated to admit blacks to the facilities provided. Thus Baltimore had discretion to integrate.[37]

September test results showed Baltimore students of both races below national norms. On average, black students did worse than white, with disparities increasing with grade levels. Mary Adams, assistant superintendent for elementary schools, observed that many black children had come during the war from Southern communities with poor schools. Lemmel noted that racial differences in scores had nothing to do with inherent ability but, instead, reflected living conditions, and deputy superintendent John Fischer offered a similar view. Henderson, taking Booker T. Washington as evidence, added that crowding, prevalent in black schools, hindered student performance. Henderson's interpretation implied school reform, but Lemmel and Fisher's analyses left improvement to the larger society.[38]

The *Afro* presented a tacit brief for school integration in articles describing amicable residential integration in the city. A "scientifically conducted study" showed "both races can live together in harmony." In another instance of civil rights activists' employing social science to make their case, the Urban League had studied the experience of black families moving across the Fulton Street color line in West Baltimore, where the GI Bill had enabled returning black veterans to buy homes. After initial violent resistance, whites began to accept black neighbors. Thus "racially divergent groups can live in harmony if allowed to do so." A few months later, a front-page story proclaimed, "Residents of Mixed Areas Like Situation: Lessons in Democratic Living Being Learned." The article offered idyllic images of neighborliness in an area where the city's first blockbusters had panicked white homeowners into selling to blacks in 1945:

> The children play together, sharing the same toys, games and discussions about books, movies and the like. Young mothers are drawn into conversation by mutual problems concerning their offspring. Food prices and everyday happenings in the home are shared by the adult female homemakers through over-the-fence conversations as they hang out their weekly wash. A faulty sparkplug or flat tire on the family car is enough to draw the men together.... A bowl of home-made ice cream is handed over the back fence in time for Sunday supper.[39]

While the *Afro* presented the legal and social case for integration, activists began pushing the system to integrate if it could not equalize separate programs. In challenging segregation itself, they allied themselves with new thinking in the national NAACP, where Thurgood Marshall was organizing local branches to attack segregation directly. In April 1949, the Urban League reported to the board on how segregation limited blacks' educational opportunities. It noted that three exceptional schools admitted only whites: Mergenthaler, which taught printing (a subject dear to Murphy, who wanted to hire black pressmen); Baltimore Polytechnic Institute (Poly), where good grades in the "A" course let graduates enter college engineering programs as sophomores; and City College, which offered two years of junior college. The League wanted blacks admitted to these programs because no comparable alternatives existed. In response, the board neither opened admissions to the three schools nor established comparable black programs. When school started in the fall, Murphy noted the continuing juxtaposition of crowded black schools on shifts and white schools with empty seats, and he urged the NAACP to sue to open all white schools to black children.[40]

Years had gone by since the school board agreed to build a new Carver Vocational School. While students shuttled between the school's main building and three satellite facilities, the board could not find a site that satisfied both black civil rights advocates and whites. During the summer of 1949 the system had started buying property on West Baltimore's Presstman Street for a new Carver site, but white opponents sent the board a petition with fifteen hundred signatures in September. Some signers lived far from Presstman Street. The stated reason for opposing the location was that it was not central to the area where blacks lived. In fact, blacks were moving into West Baltimore, and the petition reflected worry about that change. This was one of the first incidents where anxiety about blockbusting and the breakdown of residential segregation found expression in the school arena. The controversy dragged on, with the board, superintendent, and mayor all hesitant to act. Thomsen told Presstman Street neighbors that, even if the board did not put Carver on the site, it would build another colored school there. The Urban League and NAACP supported putting Carver on Presstman. Finally, in April, Mayor Thomas J. D'Alesandro Jr., who succeeded McKeldin in 1947, asked all parties to make their case before the Board of Estimates, whose members—the mayor, comptroller, and city council president—decided on capital budget requests. The Board of Estimates approved the Presstman site.[41]

That September, just after schools reopened, the Baltimore Urban League introduced Furman Templeton as its new executive director. He had worked with the organization for a year in the early 1940s as industrial director. He left for civil defense work and returned to work for seven years as Carl Murphy's administrative assistant on the *Afro*. Templeton would take a significant role in desegregating schools.[42]

Setting Sights on Integration

In the winter of 1950, the school board sought a loan of $40 million for new construction and additions to accommodate an anticipated increase of thirty thousand students by 1958. In fact, enrollment would grow by forty-five thousand over the next eight years. Black students alone would increase by thirty-seven thousand. A district that was just over a third black would become nearly half black in 1958. Though the board could not know it, these would be the years when the city desegregated schools, and capital improvements would influence the outcome. One factor was whether schools would be in locations that suited black and white students and would have sufficient space to accommodate significant numbers of both. A second was whether dilapidated colored schools, many of which had already been cast off by whites, could be improved enough to persuade white parents to send children. Facility planning intended to provide space for racially separate populations did not necessarily lead in these directions.[43]

The board's plans included twenty-two new schools and additions to some existing buildings. One of three new senior highs would be a new Carver Vocational High School. One of four new junior highs would be Cherry Hill Junior High School, for south Baltimore black students, to complement Booker T. Washington on the west and Dunbar on the east. Five of fifteen new elementary schools would be for black students. Booker T. Washington would get an addition. The plans would not improve run-down colored schools, and they allocated hardly a third of new construction to black schools. With hindsight, one could expect that, if schools stayed segregated, black schools would become still more crowded, more likely to put children on shifts. Alternatively, desegregation would ease the challenge of allocating a rapidly growing student population.[44]

Carl Murphy had little faith that the school board would serve black children's interests, and he now favored litigation to desegregate. The *Afro* noted the suit initiated by Topeka parents against their school board, asking a federal court to rule against segregation itself. The particulars matched Baltimore, the newspaper said, and "a court suit in Baltimore may bring faster results than the promises of improvements made by city officials." In May, the *Afro* reported that NAACP lawyers had sued for Prince Edward County, Virginia, parents against their school board. The paper mentioned a similar South Carolina suit, which, with the Virginia action, would join Topeka, Wilmington, and Washington in the Supreme Court school segregation cases.[45]

When school opened in the fall of 1951, the *Afro* offered an assessment. On the plus side: seventy new classrooms, including two new elementary schools, two hand-me-down formerly white elementary schools, and new portable units at two schools. On the minus side: double shifts in at least five schools and continued use of many dilapidated buildings, including several condemned by Strayer in 1921.[46]

Shortly after schools closed in June 1952, a rapid series of events began to change the school system irreversibly.

OPENING THE RACIAL
DOOR SLIGHTLY

As black leaders concluded that only desegregation would improve black children's education, they found white allies—white liberals belonging to the NAACP branch, the Baltimore Urban League, and the local chapter of Americans for Democratic Action (ADA). On the school board, besides black member Bernard Harris, the eight whites included liberals who disliked segregation. However, unlike the activists, they believed that state and city law prevented them from acting on their principles. Whether they were aware of Harry Levin's *Afro* articles or not, they felt they had no choice but to live with policies they found personally distasteful. Then the Baltimore Urban League pushed them to admit black boys to Baltimore Polytechnic Institute. As that campaign progressed, local civil rights activists increasingly drew on people and ideas that were part of the national NAACP legal challenge to school segregation.

Integrating Poly

In May 1952, Furman Templeton, in his second year as Urban League executive director, addressed the ADA chapter. He argued for opening white schools to black students. His ideas excited ADA members, and they decided to work on integrating the schools. Board member Margaret Neustadt, chair of the Race Relations Committee, proposed starting with Poly, which offered a distinctive, nationally recognized advanced "A" course in engineering. Coincidentally, the

NAACP Annual Maryland Conference adopted a resolution urging greater efforts to integrate city schools.[1]

On June 16, Templeton convened a group, including representatives of the Urban League, ADA, NAACP, and Council for Human Rights, to form the Coordinated Committee on Poly Admissions (CCPA). In contrast to the NAACP branch, whose activists all were black, this coalition was biracial. The Urban League and ADA, unlike the NAACP, had racially mixed boards. They had previously worked together. Both groups' boards, particularly the ADA, had significant numbers of Jews, who were prominent among city liberals. A few people served on both boards in the early 1950s: Frank Furstenberg, his brother-in-law Sidney Hollander Sr., who was also on the national NAACP board, and Howard Murphy, an *Afro* staff member.[2]

Deciding to keep their efforts secret for the time being, they carried out a three-part strategy to get black students into Poly in the fall. First, they developed the legal argument for admitting black students to the Poly "A" Course, based on Harry Levin's articles. Templeton asked Marshall Levin, an Urban League member whom he knew from the Levins' legal work for the *Afro,* to prepare the presentation to the school board. Levin, who had a Harvard law degree and practiced with his father because the city's major firms did not hire Jews, was personally familiar with discrimination. Second, they contacted selected school officials and asked their support. Third, they began to recruit applicants whose qualifications for the "A" Course were unassailable and who had the strength to succeed under trying conditions.

To find the right students to apply to Poly, the Urban League asked black teachers and counselors to recommend candidates. League representatives then asked parents if they wanted their sons to apply to Poly and, if so, talked with the boys. Juanita Jackson Mitchell convened prospective students and parents at the NAACP office; Thurgood Marshall attended some of these meetings. The Urban League tested prospective applicants to make sure of their ability, and Templeton talked with families about what the boys could expect. Families whose sons eventually applied regarded Poly as a new educational opportunity, even though, because of segregation, few had even heard of the school. By the time the school board had held its last meeting of the year, on July 12, sixteen boys had applied to the "A" Course, and the system had judged ten fully qualified. The board declined to act on the applications but asked the city solicitor for a legal opinion and decided to consider that opinion in August. Meanwhile, the Urban League arranged tutoring for applicants who needed help to be ready for Poly in September.[3]

The board, to cover its obligations, instructed Superintendent Lemmel and J. Carey Taylor, assistant superintendent for secondary instruction, to design a program comparable to the Poly "A" Course in a colored high school. On July 25, Taylor wrote the sixteen applicants' parents to ask if their sons wanted to enroll in an advanced college preparatory program at Douglass. The Urban League urged parents to reject the offer on the ground that a program equal to Poly could not be set up in a month.

Templeton wrote Mayor D'Alesandro and now-Governor McKeldin to outline the Poly case and ask support. The mayor declined to take a position and deferred to the governor. McKeldin wrote Templeton a strong endorsement:

> The only question which remains is whether the School Board will act in accordance with the requirements of the law, and good standards of fairness and sound community relations, or will force court action to compel it to do what it should do voluntarily and graciously. From every point of view I am anxious that the former alternative may be adopted by the School Board, and that this just and progressive step may be taken without the heat and hostility that is liable to accompany litigation.

McKeldin sent a copy of his letter to the Maryland Commission on Interracial Problems and Relations, which cautiously urged the board to admit the applicants if equal separate facilities were unavailable.[4]

In late July, City Solicitor Thomas Biddison replied to the board. He focused on the 1936 Maryland Court of Appeals case *Pearson v. Murray*, which required the University of Maryland to admit black applicant Donald Murray to its law school. Biddison put weight on the court's ruling that the Fourth Amendment required "substantially equal treatment" in publicly funded facilities. He also noted *Briggs v. Elliott*, the NAACP's South Carolina school segregation case under review by the Supreme Court.[5]

At the end of August, the board announced it would consider the applications on September 2. The Urban League selected witnesses and worked out testimony. The CCPA discussed what to do should the board decide unfavorably, and they decided that the boys should accept the Douglass alternative, to maintain the case, while the CCPA sued the board. Still, one point of contention among the students' advocates centered on pride of ownership. Templeton considered the Urban League the prime mover, and Levin would address the board as a League member. However, after the NAACP resolution calling for city school integration, Carl Murphy invited Thurgood Marshall to address the board for that organization. The League resisted letting Marshall testify, but the board decided that anyone, certainly anyone of Marshall's stature, who wanted to speak should be able to, and they arranged for him to talk during public discussion after the Urban League presented its case.[6]

The Board Judges Whether Separate Is Equal

As events would turn out, the September 2, 1952, school board meeting was the only occasion when Baltimore school officials examined the meaning, merits, and limitations of the "separate but equal" policy. Debate was serious, dignified, and four hours long. Blacks and whites attended in unprecedented numbers. Normally, spectators at board meetings sat behind board members around a long table in the conference room, but the crowd of applicants, parents, school alumni, and interested citizens spilled onto chairs set up in adjoining rooms.[7]

President Roszel Thomsen opened the meeting with a statement about the gravity of the issue and asked all to join in silent prayer. A lawyer, he reviewed the city solicitor's opinion for legal guidance. It seemed to him,

> The only real question before the School Board is whether the proposed curriculum in one of the Negro schools which has been planned and set up by the Staff, will be substantially equal to the Polytechnic "A" Course. If it will be substantially equal, then under the City Code we must continue the policy of separate schools. If it will not be substantially equal to the Polytechnic "A" Course, then under the Constitution of the United States we must admit the boys to the Polytechnic "A" Course, or abolish the curriculum.

Thomsen summed up his assessment of Lemmel and Taylor's proposal for a preengineering "A" Course at Douglass. Noting that the school would have to offer only the first year of such a program for the first cohort of boys in September, he said he had no doubt that the system could offer a curriculum at Douglass identical to Poly's, with the same quality of instruction and "approximately equal" facilities, but the intangibles raised questions. Indeed, the superintendent's staff was divided on whether a graduate of a Douglass program offered for the first time in crowded facilities would receive the same sophomore engineering school standing as Poly graduates. It was even open to question whether a Douglass program graduate would get equal recognition and opportunity for local employment.[8]

Taylor presented the plan for a Douglass program. He reported on inquiries with admissions directors at Cornell, Lehigh, and Johns Hopkins regarding whether they would give graduates of a new Douglass program the sophomore standing they customarily gave Poly graduates. Although all seemed open to the possibility, they said they would want to see the Douglass graduates' college performance first. Houston Jackson, who had succeeded Elmer Henderson in 1951 as assistant superintendent for colored schools, emphasized that segregation harmed children and urged admitting the applicants to Poly as a matter of justice. Deputy Superintendent John Fischer, however, argued that if the tangible elements of a Douglass program were equal to Poly's, intangibles such as reputation and graduates' acceptance could be expected to be equal. Poly principal Wilmer DeHuff testified that a course like Poly's could be successfully introduced into any school that expected faculty and students to work hard.[9]

Furman Templeton introduced Marshall Levin to present the applicants' case. Levin agreed with Thomsen that the issue was whether Douglass could deliver a program substantially equal to Poly's. In reality, he said, one had to speculate, and the odds were poor. No Douglass program existed. No teachers had been identified. New teachers would lack the Poly faculty's experience. Douglass had no library or full-time librarian to care for "A" Course books. Overcrowding at Douglass would make it hard to find space for an "A" Course. Moreover, the school board could not guarantee the future funding needed to secure these things. In addition, he emphasized, the success of the Poly "A" Course rested on intangibles: nationally recognized teachers, national scholastic ranking, the position and influence of alumni, and tradition and prestige. Douglass could match none of these things. Colleges that accepted Poly "A" Course graduates offered no assurance they would accept Douglass graduates. It would be hard, Levin summarized, for Douglass ever to equal Poly's program. The crux of the school board's decision, he said, was a legal question. Supreme Court decisions on educational opportunity required integration where the state could not provide equal separate facilities. Unless the system could prove that Douglass met the test on both tangibles and intangibles, he concluded, black students must be admitted to Poly. When he was done, board members questioned him, and Thomsen tacitly supported his position by clarifying Supreme Court rulings on the necessity for separate black schools to be equal to white.[10]

At the end of the applicants' case, Thomsen recessed briefly before calling others who wished to speak. Alumni representatives from Baltimore City College and Poly argued for a segregated Douglass program. Finally, Thurgood Marshall took the podium. He directed the NAACP Legal Defense Fund, he had coordinated bringing the five school segregation cases to the Supreme Court, and in three months he would argue the South Carolina *Briggs* case before the nine justices. He began by reviewing High Court decisions pertinent to the Poly petition. Drawing from new arguments NAACP lawyers were making in the segregation cases, he invoked social psychological evidence that segregation harmed black children and hindered their learning. He emphasized the importance of the reputation of a program, in addition to tangible resources. While the NAACP was challenging segregation in court, separate-but-equal remained the governing legal principle, and Marshall assured the board they did not have to rule on segregation in the Poly case. The issue turned simply on whether a separate

Douglass program could be equal to Poly's. Douglass, he said, was "at best a gamble. A gamble is not what I consider equality." Then, warming to his task and gesturing toward board members, Marshall challenged them to find the courage to do what was right. He admonished them to admit the black youths to Poly at once, concluding with a threat to open all schools to blacks immediately if the board did not comply. Board member Walter Sondheim later recalled being offended by what he considered Marshall's condescension. From private discussions with other board members, Sondheim expected a majority to support the applicants. Marshall, he felt, antagonized the board, daring members to take positions that, in fact, they already held, and thus jeopardizing their support.[11]

Thomsen took the board into executive session to discuss the issues and procedure. They agreed to vote first on whether the Douglass program would equal Poly's and, if the majority voted no, to take the result as a vote to admit qualified black applicants to Poly. As members talked, it became pretty clear how each would vote. When the board returned to the public meeting room, Thomsen accepted a motion that Douglass be considered equal to Poly and called for a vote. "We knew from our *in camera* discussion how each member would probably vote," Thomsen recalled, "but the people who filled every available cubic inch in the hearing room did not know, and I have never seen a more tense and quiet group."[12]

John Sherwood, an oil company executive who came from an old wealthy Baltimore family, had no doubt about the inferiority of the proposed Douglass program and voted no. Dr. Bernard Harris, a surgeon who was the board's black member, concurred. J. Ben Robinson, dean of the University of Maryland Medical School, chose to give the Douglass proposal the benefit of the doubt, leaving the intangibles to speculation and arguing that any student who worked hard could succeed. He voted for the motion. Trueman Thompson, a Johns Hopkins civil engineering professor, made a lengthy, heartfelt personal statement. He noted that he was the only engineer on the board. He said that twice he had been a student in newly established courses, once in the city public schools and once in engineering at Johns Hopkins. He had found both experiences challenging and profitable. Moving to the question of whether a program equal to Poly's could be created at Douglass, focusing on the tangible requirements, he believed the answer was yes. He went on to say that he deeply opposed segregation, that he considered it unconscionable that, after black and white had risked their lives together in the recent war, they should be separated again in civilian society. However, he concluded, he did not believe he could properly let his personal position against segregation influence his public decision. Accordingly, he voted "aye." Tied at two.

John Curlett, an executive at McCormick Spice and a Poly alumnus, said he believed a Douglass program could be similar to Poly's. Next, Sondheim, executive at a major family-run department store, spoke. He regretted that the segregation issue had come up, since the board was not voting on that, only the equality of two programs. He said he had come to the meeting undecided on that question and was persuaded by discussion of the intangibles. He voted no. Tied again. Elizabeth Morrissy, in her fourth decade as professor of history and economics at the College of Notre Dame, stated succinctly that she did not believe the proposed Douglass course would be equal. Victoria Rysanek spoke next. A South Baltimore homemaker married to a physician, she was the "community" representative on the board. She often took her lead from Morrissy. She endorsed Sondheim's statement and voted no.

Thomsen announced that a 3–5 vote meant that the black boys would be admitted to Poly's "A" Course. For the record, he explained that the president voted only when there was a tie; had that been necessary, he would have voted against the motion. As Levin and Templeton thanked the board and everything seemed settled, DeHuff raised a question. Poly used "whites only" athletic fields; what if a black student made the football team? Thomsen assured him the board would work things out. Thomsen then asked Templeton and administration staff to get the qualified applicants started at the school.[13]

When classes opened, fifteen black students entered Poly. One of the applicants found the pressure too great and decided not to go. Twelve started the ninth grade. Three entered the tenth, confronting the added challenge of catching up on a first year of high school more rigorous than what they had gone through. Templeton met with the boys and told them to concentrate on academics and avoid extracurricular activities their first year. He would get them any needed assistance. The *Afro* praised the board.[14]

Fighting Segregation at Mergenthaler and Western

Carl Murphy, accepting congratulations on the victory from Edward Lewis, who was now New York Urban League director, confessed he had "never been more delightfully surprised...by the Board's decision." At the same time, he told Lewis, the Baltimore NAACP Legal Redress Committee had hired Howard University education professors Hurley Doddy and Ellis O. Knox to compare the city's white and colored schools. From their work, the committee "had sufficient information in hand to enable us to file a suit against the Board of School Commissioners and the city within ten days if the Board had given an adverse decision." "Our joy is tempered," he went on, "by the sad fact that we must take these institutions one by one.... We are continuing our survey and our first suit, I hope, will compel the

Board to utilize the vacant seats at Western High for the overcrowded conditions at Douglass. Our perennial problem is to open Mergenthaler School of Printing to all children."[15]

When the black boys entered Poly, members of the Park View Improvement Association went to female Western High School to try to enroll five black girls. Western, they explained, was the high school nearest their homes. The principal rejected them because of their race.[16]

In mid-January, Knox and Doddy reported their findings to the Citizens Committee. Colored schools were far more likely than white to be crowded and black students more likely to be on shifts. Black students lacked an accel-erated junior high school. Colored high schools lacked curricula comparable to those at male City College or Western. The city provided junior college only for whites. Although black teachers seemed comparable to white, overcrowded, inadequate facilities hindered black teachers' efforts. Knox and Doddy urged razing all buildings Strayer had tagged for abandonment and immediately pro-viding decent schools for black students. The report outlined an agenda for end-ing segregation.[17]

Petitioning for Entry to Mergenthaler

At the beginning of the spring semester, the NAACP requested admission of four black boys to the Mergenthaler Vocational High School of Printing. They were rejected because of their race. The NAACP requested a school board hearing.[18]

The February 5 board meeting opened with a resolution memorializing Su-perintendent Lemmel, who had died from a heart attack suffered while testi-fying before the state legislature. John Fischer was acting superintendent and would succeed Lemmel. Thomsen opened the Mergenthaler discussion by re-viewing the city's printing programs. The Mergenthaler printing school for white students would become part of a new Mergenthaler Vocational-Technical High School. For black students, Douglass and Dunbar offered some printing courses, which while not equivalent to Mergenthaler's, had "certain features in common" with them. When the new Carver was built, a program "identical" to Mergenthaler would be set up there. Before getting to the heart of the mat-ter, he noted that none of the four applicants had taken the required entrance examinations, and thus it was impossible to know whether they qualified for Mergenthaler. Thomsen then framed the legal question as with Poly: whether the board could "provide a vocational high school program in the printing trade in a colored school substantially equal to the program offered at Mergenthaler." He reported that he had asked staff to begin to create such a program in a black high school. He recommended that the students not be admitted to Mergenthaler but be enrolled in a course in Dunbar for the spring, when the board might evaluate things further.[19]

Speakers for the NAACP hinted that they would sue if the board did not admit the boys. Juanita Jackson Mitchell noted that the system offered little printing training for black students. Echoing Marshall at the Poly hearing, she observed that scant offerings for black children hurt them emotionally as well as educationally and asked the board to admit the students to Mergenthaler as a matter of constitutional right. Clarence Mitchell, now director of the NAACP Washington office, praised the board's Poly decision and criticized the Mergenthaler recommendation morally and legally. He added that duplicate programs wasted tax money. Donald Murray, the beneficiary of the 1936 suit against the University of Maryland Law School, argued that the Douglass and Dunbar courses were not really vocational training, and thus not equal to Mergenthaler, and he, too, requested immediate admission for black students to Mergenthaler.

Thomsen emphasized that, whatever board members believed about segregation, they had no authority to eliminate it; they might only judge whether separate facilities were equal. More important, the cases before the Supreme Court, on which it was expected to rule imminently, could produce a decision outlawing school segregation, thus obviating legal action against the board. When he called for a vote, Bernard Harris, who expected a majority to reject the application, asked for an executive session. Privately, he criticized segregation and urged postponing a vote so he could look into the situation. Back in public, the board put off a decision pending study of whether an equal separate program could be created. Carl Murphy, who employed printers, was named one of three study committee members.[20]

A week later, Park View Improvement Association president Martha Pulley requested a board hearing on the fall rejection of the Western applicants. While awaiting a response, she contacted Juanita Jackson Mitchell, who asked Murray to meet with the association to prepare a suit. Aware of pending Mergenthaler legal action, Pulley asked Murphy, as chair of the NAACP Legal Redress Committee, to initiate litigation on Western, linking the two suits. The next week, the Legal Redress Committee met with Jack Greenberg of the NAACP Legal Defense Fund. He emphasized the impossibility of duplicating Mergenthaler's program and recommended suing to admit black students. The committee voted to proceed with litigation and began recruiting qualified applicants. It also voted to sue separately on behalf of five Western applicants.[21]

Murphy invited Thomsen and Fischer to his office to discuss Mergenthaler. He acknowledged that three of the four applicants did not meet entrance requirements. The fourth, highly qualified, was a high school graduate interested in adult programs. Murphy asked that the board just turn down the applicants and let the NAACP take the case to court. Thomsen said the board would co-operate in responding quickly to expedite the filing of test cases, but he urged Murphy not to create unproductive controversy at Mergenthaler. Murphy replied that Mergenthaler was only one step in what would be a campaign against all school segregation.[22]

In early April, Murray, coordinating legal action, told the NAACP Education Committee that the Mergenthaler suit was ready for filing. He had two fully qualified applicants, and he was willing to add the four original applicants to the suit. He told the committee to begin recruiting qualified girls to apply to Western. He allowed that the case there was not identical to that at Poly, with its unique "A" Course, but he considered it "analogous." On April 22, Lillie May Jackson forwarded the names of Carl Smith and James Grove to Thomsen as additional applicants to Mergenthaler. She reminded him of his agreement to act quickly. The same day, Juanita Jackson Mitchell and Murray informed Thomsen they had been retained as counsel by the two boys' parents. They said they also represented the four previous applicants and wanted swift responses to all six applications.[23]

On May 14, Fischer sent Mitchell the board's response on Mergenthaler. Three of the four original applicants failed to meet admission requirements. The fourth, interested in an adult program, would be admitted to the Carver evening program in the fall. Smith and Grove were qualified, but the city code required them to attend segregated schools. They were being registered for a printing program to be added to Carver in the fall. Bernard Harris had already told his colleagues that program would not equal Mergenthaler's.[24]

Making the Case for Admitting Black Girls to Western High School

The NAACP was not the only group pushing to admit black student to Western. The Urban League was coordinating a Western committee like its earlier Poly committee. Competition between some of the member groups and the NAACP created uncertainty, diffusion of effort, and bad feeling. Templeton met with Murphy. After long discussion, Templeton agreed to ask his groups to pull back from an active role at Western and to support the NAACP as it moved toward the courts, doing what it did better than other organizations.[25]

The first week in June saw advances on two fronts. Mitchell and Murray sent Thomsen a letter making application to Western for twenty-four black girls. Some were applying to the Advanced College Preparatory Program, some to other programs. Most would enter the ninth or tenth grade, but six wanted to transfer into the twelfth grade. Many parents emphasized the advantages of single-sex education. At the June 4 board meeting, Thomsen referred the matter to the superintendent and asked him to report on June 23. He anticipated that the Supreme Court would rule on the school segregation cases before then and make the matter moot. Instead, the court announced that it had not reached a decision and asked parties to prepare for reargument.[26]

The day after the board meeting, the NAACP filed suit in City Court against the board, Fischer, the vocational education assistant superintendent, and the Mergenthaler principal. The NAACP Legal Defense and Educational Fund assigned Marshall and Greenberg to work with Mitchell and Murray. They petitioned for a writ of mandamus to compel the defendants to admit Smith and Grove in the fall. Attorneys argued that the Mergenthaler program was unique. They held also that the city code provision ordering school segregation violated the Fourteenth Amendment and asked the court to rule the section unconstitutional.[27]

On Sunday, June 21, the school system released Fischer's report and recommendations on Western. The press release succinctly presented his position:

> The report calls attention to the City ordinance, which requires separate schools for children of the white and Negro races. It points out also that there is no evidence that enrollment in a co-educational school constitutes denial of equal educational opportunity. For these reasons the Superintendent recommends that the requests of the girls be denied since to grant them would involve violation of existing laws.

The crucial sentence in this syllogism was the obscurely phrased second sentence. The superintendent reduced the girls' application to a bid simply to attend a single-sex school. Otherwise, he contended, there were no curricular differences between Western and Douglass, which would start an advanced college preparatory program in the fall. There was no objective evidence, he said, on the superiority of all-girls' schools over coeducation (an assertion that challenged the rationale for Western itself). Ergo, because the system was initiating a separate advanced program at Douglass that would be equal to Western's, the sexual makeup of classes being inconsequential, the law required the board to reject the applicants. Should the board not accept this position, Fischer said, it might create a new separate high school for a few black girls, it might direct the superintendent to admit the applicants to Western, or it could try some short-term expedient and put off a permanent decision.[28]

On June 23, the board heard the case for admitting black girls to Western. Board members, the superintendent, and his staff sat around the long table, and about fifty spectators spread along the conference room's north and west walls and out into the hallway. Although the meeting drew fewer people than the Poly hearing nine months earlier, participants regarded the stakes as equally high, and deliberations took nearly as long, three and a half hours. Thomsen began by calling attention to Fischer's report. He then invited Mitchell to present the applicants' case. She turned to Murphy as Legal Redress Committee chair, and he introduced a series of speakers. Jack Greenberg framed the legal issues. The question of segregation, he noted, was before the Supreme Court, and the school board need not take a position on that. Rather, their concern should be whether separate programs were equal—in facilities, teaching, and intangibles. Any significant inequality required the board to give up segregation. With regard to all-girls' schools, the board had obviously found value in them by establishing one [actually, two] for whites, but none for blacks. This inequality required admitting black girls to Western.[29]

Howard University consultant Knox, comparing Western and Douglass, reported that Western had a superior physical plant, better facilities, more room, a lower student-teacher ratio, and traditions associated with its accelerated program. Naomi Richardson, an ACLU member and former Goucher College admissions dean, said it would take years to establish a Douglass program with the quality and reputation of Western's, and she doubted colleges would give much weight to a new Douglass program. Morgan College president emeritus Dwight Holmes said that in his seventy-five years he had "never seen a separate institution in a dual system which is equal." "I ask you to give us a break. You know as well as I do that Douglass High School isn't equal. We can't afford, as far behind as we are, to miss a point." Marshall Levin, representing the Urban League and the ADA, emphasized Western's uniqueness as one of two all-girls' high schools and one of three high schools with "A" courses. Since the board valued a separate girls' high school with an accelerated program, he concluded, blacks had as much right to it as whites.[30]

The board moved into executive session, where members debated at length. Because John Curlett and Trueman Thompson were absent, Thomsen asked Mitchell and her colleagues if they wanted to wait until all could be present. Mitchell said that, because they wanted to take an unfavorable decision to court in time to secure fall admission, they wanted immediate action. Privately, the board voted first on whether all-girls' schooling was inherently superior to coeducation; only Harris held that all-girls' schooling had advantages. Then the board voted on whether a Douglass accelerated program would equal the Western "A" Course. Again Harris was the lone dissenter, with Sondheim abstaining. Thomsen reconvened the public session and announced that a "majority of the board" had voted in these ways, and, therefore, the applications were denied.[31]

One might ask why, after six board members supported admitting black boys to Poly, only the black member voted to admit black girls to Western. One explanation, emphasized later by Levin and Sondheim, turned on the difference between Poly's technical curriculum and Western's liberal arts education.

Perhaps board members found it easier to evaluate and compare programs in engineering than in the humanities. The Poly documents and testimony extensively analyzed Poly and Douglass curricula, but there was no discussion of academic programs in the Western case. Alternatively, white board members may not have been as concerned about women's work and careers as they were men's—though this would not obviously be so for Elizabeth Morrissy, who voted against the applicants. Whereas with Poly the board weighed evidence on employment advantages accruing to Poly "A" Course graduates, no one made any claims about employment prospects of girls graduating from the Western "A" Course. Significantly, at the time, only 32 percent of Baltimore white females fourteen and over were in the labor force, and only 17 percent of them were in proprietorial or white-collar occupations. In contrast, 43 percent of black females were in the labor force. The vast majority, however, engaged in manual labor, and an "A" Course offered the next generation a better opportunity. Perhaps, finally, white board members felt it would be politically difficult to give black petitioners everything they asked, so that, after admitting some to Poly, they blocked others. Margaret Neustadt, who was involved in both cases with the ADA, recalled that at the time Sondheim told her the board expected the Supreme Court to outlaw segregation soon and preferred to let the court solve the problem.[32]

Murphy and Mitchell attributed the difference to the change in superintendents between the Poly and Western hearings. Whereas Lemmel had expressed clear doubt about the equivalence of a Douglass program to Poly's, Fischer insisted a Douglass program could equal Western's. Whatever the explanation, however, what mattered to Murphy and Mitchell was getting black girls into Western. Right after the board decision, Mitchell announced that the NAACP was going to court.[33]

Litigation

On July 15, attorneys for twenty-three black girls filed suit in U.S. district court against the school board, Fischer, the secondary education assistant superintendent, and the Western principal. The suit was similar to the Mergenthaler suit but was filed in federal court to establish another venue for fighting segregation. Attorneys W. A. C. Hughes, Greenberg, Mitchell, and Murray presented the suit as a class action for all black girls denied educational facilities equal to those offered whites at Western. Western, they noted, was the only high school offering girls an advanced college preparatory course with graduates accepted as college sophomores. They requested injunctions restraining the system from denying qualified black girls admission to Western on the basis of their race. In addition, they asked the court to find that board action violated the Fourteenth Amendment, that

Douglass could not give black girls an education equal to that at Western, and centrally, that the section of the city code ordering school segregation violated the Fourteenth Amendment and hence was unconstitutional.[34]

Meanwhile, the school segregation cases were near rehearing in the Supreme Court. After some legal skirmishing, City Solicitor Biddison asked the plaintiffs' lawyers to hold up litigation until the court ruled. If it outlawed segregation, the suits would be unnecessary. If not, the parties could proceed. Plaintiffs' lawyers agreed to wait.[35]

In August, U.S. Attorney General Herbert Brownell Jr., asked the Supreme Court to postpone reargument of the cases from October to December, to let government lawyers finish preparing their case. On September 8, Chief Justice Fred Vinson died of a heart attack. He had been perhaps the biggest obstacle to a decision outlawing school segregation. Three weeks later, President Eisenhower asked California Governor Earl Warren to serve as Chief Justice, and Warren was sworn in on the first day of the new session, October 5. The court heard reargument of the segregation cases on December 7.

In Baltimore in mid-October, to little public notice, two black men started a night course at Mergenthaler School of Printing. In February 1954, President Eisenhower appointed Roszel Thomsen to the U.S. District Court of Maryland. Mayor D'Alesandro named six-year board member Walter Sondheim to succeed Thomsen.[36]

In March, colored school assistant superintendent Houston Jackson convened a meeting at Booker T. Washington to discuss integration in light of impending court action. Clarence Mitchell joined a panel discussing integration in other cities and the local situation. As elsewhere, blacks planned for school desegregation.[37]

DESEGREGATION BY FREE CHOICE

At 12:52 p.m. on May 17, 1954, without prior announcement, Chief Justice Earl Warren began reading the Supreme Court opinion on *Brown v. Board of Education of Topeka.* After failure to reach a decision a year earlier and reargument in the fall of 1953 under the new chief justice, the court had come to a judgment, unanimously. The justices declared that "in the field of public education the doctrine of 'separate but equal' has no place. Separate educational facilities are inherently unequal." The court endorsed NAACP lawyers' psychological arguments that deliberately separating black students from white, even if schools were tangibly equal, "generates a feeling of inferiority as to [black children's] status in the community that may affect their hearts and minds in a way unlikely ever to be undone" and "has a tendency to [retard] the educational and mental development of negro children." Although the court said nothing about how and when this judgment should be implemented (and would give only ambiguous direction a year later in *Brown II*), the justices made clear that school segregation was no longer constitutionally acceptable.[1]

The School Board Responds to *Brown*

First Reactions and Preparations

Later that day, the *Baltimore Evening Sun* announced, "High Tribunal Bans Race Segregation in Schools." An editorial called the decision a landmark in the country's social history and declared, "It writes finis to the chapter in the educational development in the South based on the doctrine of separate but equal facilities for the two races." It characterized Maryland facilities as having "long been equal," and though the state had resisted planning for integration, editorial writers believed that, with time and patience, Americans would help implement the court's reasonable decision. The next morning, the *Baltimore Sun* declared in the top of three banner headlines, "Supreme Court Bans Segregated Schools." The two other headlines kept readers apprised of Cold War developments: the Soviets had shipped arms to Guatemala, and the Army-McCarthy hearings were in recess. After reporting the court action in great detail, the paper editorialized optimistically that resourcefulness and compassion would enable Marylanders to do what the decision rightly called for. The editorial the next day put *Brown* in the context of the Cold War:

> The Communists…have played on the theme of racial discrimination in the United States as much as they have played on any one theme.…The only way to fight this kind of Communist propaganda is by the simplest and plainest of facts.…Now, in the highest court's decision that segregation shall not be practiced in the public schools, we have another such fact.[2]

The *Afro* proclaimed, "MIX SCHOOLS," "Unanimous Verdict Most Important In This Generation," and "THURGOOD WINS." Three pages reprinted the decision, chronicled the school segregation cases, and quoted civil rights attorneys, local officials, and ordinary citizens. Governor Theodore McKeldin, the paper reported, had said, "Maryland prides itself upon being a law-abiding state" and expressed confidence citizens would comply. He would talk with the state school superintendent about implementing the decision. However, City Council president Arthur Price, owner of the Gwynn Oak Amusement Park, which did not admit blacks and would become the target of 1960s civil rights protests, the acting mayor while Thomas D'Alesandro was in the hospital, responded charily: "As good citizens, the Baltimore city administration will certainly follow the edict of the Supreme Court. As good citizens what else could we do?" Civil rights leaders were ecstatic. Lillie May Jackson proclaimed, "This is the day for which our fathers prayed, and for which we, their children have suffered and toiled." Furman Templeton declared the decision "marvelous in its unanimity and significance. It is the most effective answer since the Emancipation Proclamation to those who would deny full American citizenship to minority group members." He offered school officials the League's aid in desegregating.

Superintendent John Fischer noted that some staff activities were already integrated and expressed confidence that the community would accept the decision. Houston Jackson and Bernard Harris offered similar reports of the superintendent's staff and the school board, respectively: both groups had expected the court decision and had been planning for desegregation. However, Sondheim, who would lead the board's response, cautiously noted that he had not yet been confirmed by the City Council and said he didn't really understand what the decision meant. He would talk with Fischer.[3]

John Fischer had grown up in Baltimore and the city school system. His career was a Horatio Alger story. He got a diploma at State Teachers College in Towson and started teaching in 1930 at a school where he had been a student. Soon marrying and having two children, he balanced new family responsibilities and teaching duties with evening classes aimed at a bachelor's degree. For five years he taught science and physical education in secondary schools and then moved up into the first of two secondary school principalships. After a decade of night school he earned a bachelor's degree from Johns Hopkins. In 1942 he advanced into the school system central office as director of attendance and child guidance. A year later, Superintendent Weglein appointed him assistant superintendent of general administration, and Superintendent Lemmel subsequently promoted him to deputy superintendent. Fischer continued studying while working and went on to earn a master's degree and doctorate in education from Columbia University.[4]

When Fischer assumed the superintendency after Lemmel's death, he pledged to continue his predecessor's work and boasted that he knew of "no better school system." In an *Evening Sun* interview he explained that his political views came from the Founding Fathers. Articulating a classical liberal position, he emphasized that "government should be as decentralized as possible with as high a degree of local autonomy as can be achieved." He believed, as the reporter summarized, that "the present tendency to do things collectively should be counteracted by providing more opportunities for individual initiative." Accordingly, public education should prepare children to be responsible citizens, as well as good parents and workers, by teaching them the Three R's. Fischer's own rise through individual effort seemed to validate this view. The *Afro*, skeptical about the social conservatism of native white Baltimoreans, hoped he would continue the progressivism of out-of-towner Lemmel.[5]

Walter Sondheim, at forty-six just four years older than Fischer and also a Baltimore native, had arrived at his liberal views by a different route. He had grown up in the Jewish community when anti-Semitism was prominent. He attended the Park School, a progressive private school established in 1912 because other private schools did not admit Jews. His father was active in Jewish organizations. In this environment, Sondheim became sensitive to discrimination and interested in civil rights. He went to Haverford College, which encouraged his liberal thinking. His family owned the Hochschild-Kohn department stores, and after college he started work in the firm, becoming vice president and secretary in the late 1940s. The business provided financial security but also troubled Sondheim. Like the city's other major department stores, Hochschild's did not let black patrons try on or return clothing, did not serve them in its restaurant, and employed blacks only in menial positions. The *Afro* gave "orchids" and "onions" to stores according to their treatment of blacks; Hochschild's was among those getting onions "for Anti-Colored Policies." Lillie May Jackson, pushing for better practices, often emphasized the Jewish ownership of department stores, even though Christians owned some. Sondheim was troubled by both the charges against Jews and his store's policies.[6]

Sondheim contributed to the Baltimore NAACP and came to know national NAACP secretary Walter White. He arranged for White to meet Baltimore department store executives to try to change policies. He served on the Baltimore Urban League board. He was trying to change his company's policy and improve race relations in the city when, in 1948, Mayor D'Alesandro asked him to take the "Jewish seat" on the school board. He would join the board's designated Catholic member, black member, University of Maryland member, Johns Hopkins University member, and "community" member (a resident of a nonelite neighborhood), among others. On the board, while he disapproved of segregation, he followed the law, and the law called for segregation. Though he voted to admit black boys to Poly, later he would say that in doing so he had mistakenly followed his heart, rather than his head. Now that the High Court had outlawed segregation, he could act on his principles.[7]

While the court was deliberating on the school segregation cases, Carl Murphy, Lillie May Jackson, Juanita Jackson Mitchell, NAACP lawyer W. A. C. Hughes, Morgan State College president Martin Jenkins, Morgan president emeritus Dwight Holmes, and Thurgood Marshall met to devise an integration strategy for the city. They wanted school officials to move quickly, but they wanted more than students mixed. They also wanted an end to the practice of assigning white teachers to white schools and black teachers to black schools. At last, the group invited Fischer to talk with them. Murphy's daughter Elizabeth Murphy Moss recalled the meeting:

> Dr. Fischer....I can remember him coming to the *Afro* office with all these papers and he was sitting down talking, "Well, you can do this." I can remember seeing Juanita saying, "You can do this." Working out plans so that when the ruling came....already everything was moving....Because there had been this foresight in planning and there had been established a rapport between the school officials who wanted to do the right thing, but needed the prodding of the NAACP and the black newspaper which had influence in the community. It didn't just happen.

She described the black leaders' strategic approach with school officials. They went

> with the papers and the supportive data, and then the plans whether you can do this this way under Plan A or you can do this under Plan B, providing the options, etc., so the people could act, so they didn't feel they were back in a corner. But they had options which they were provided.... The black people of this community were willing to work with people of stature who had no selfish interest.[8]

This planning, alluded to by Houston Jackson and Bernard Harris, set the stage for board action once the court ruled.

The Board Acts

Three days after *Brown,* Sondheim convened the school board. Fischer said he could not report in detail and would just address one question: the Division of Colored Schools would be eliminated, but Houston Jackson would remain assistant superintendent. Sondheim appointed a committee of three, headed by University of Maryland Law School dean Roger Howell, to work with staff on implementing the court decision. Then the board moved into private session to consider options. Howell opened by declaring that the court ruling gave the board clear, immediate direction. Succinctly, he noted, "If we're denying constitutional rights, we wouldn't want to be a part of that, would we?" "That was about it," Fischer later recalled, "This was an expert on constitutional law speaking."[9]

Fischer gave a report to the board. He said it would be necessary to consult the city solicitor on the implications of the ruling. In anticipating integration, he reviewed "several facts" indicating that white and black schools were already essentially equal. School authorities, he said, had never made "qualitative distinctions...in providing facilities for white and Negro pupils." If blacks had old or crowded schools, the reason was that they lived in old and crowded neighborhoods. He foresaw "no major problem of equalizing the quality of physical facilities on a racial basis"; rather, the main challenge was providing adequate space for growing numbers of students. He said that school officials had treated white and black schools the same in all budgetary matters and that the system had never treated black and white teachers differently in hiring or promotion. He observed that teachers' professional activities had been integrated for several years. Fischer noted that under current policies students could enroll in any school designated for their race, subject to administrative approval. His cabinet, he said, believed this procedure should continue, with the change that a student's race would no longer limit his or her choice. The board concluded by agreeing to consult with the Urban League, NAACP, and citywide council of PTAs.[10]

On May 24, Murphy and Mitchell, representing the NAACP Legal Redress Committee, went to Fischer. They reviewed their expectations. They reminded him of the suspended Mergenthaler and Western suits and wanted to know whether the city would integrate or whether they should proceed to court. Fischer promised to meet with the board and ask City Solicitor Biddison for an opinion on whether *Brown* effectively disposed of the suits.[11]

The next day, the board contacted Biddison, and on June 1 he answered succinctly: *Brown* had made the city code section requiring separate schools invalid. With the board free to act, Sondheim began calling members to see whether they would support integration. To his pleasant surprise, he found only agreement. Sondheim then realized that, while the board was going to desegregate, no one had talked with the mayor or city council. He hastily went to acting mayor Price to tell him of the board's plans. Sondheim recalled, "Price started wringing his hands. He saw blood in the streets and everything else. I told him that if people complain to you, just tell them that City Hall had nothing to do with it. That satisfied him."[12]

When Sondheim convened the board on June 3, he knew he had unanimous support for desegregation. After ten minutes of routine matters, he read Biddison's opinion, accepted a motion by John Sherwood that the "system should be conformed to a non-segregated basis…by the opening of schools in September," took a vote, asked Fischer when he could deliver a staff report on implementing the resolution, and on hearing Fischer's answer of June 10, moved up the board's next meeting by a week to allow prompt action, all within perhaps "a minute and a half," without public discussion. Sondheim then noted that plans for the new Carver Vocational Technical High School had been changed to eliminate printing instruction, since the Mergenthaler facilities would meet all needs. The meeting ended about thirty minutes after it began. Baltimore would join Washington, Wilmington, Kansas City, and St. Louis in starting desegregation right after *Brown*. After the vote, Sondheim visited Mayor D'Alesandro in the hospital to inform him. "I don't know whether what you did was right," he recalled the mayor saying, "but the priests tell me you were right," and that, according to Sondheim, "solved the local political problem."[13]

The following week, John Sherwood and Roger Howell's sons graduated from Gilman, a select private boys' school. Thus, while some board members' elite backgrounds inclined them to liberalism, their social position insulated them from the consequences of desegregation. The white 1954 board members lived in neighborhoods where slightly under half of children attended public schools. In the elite white neighborhoods of Guilford, Homeland, and Roland Park, about 40 percent of children went to public schools, and between 19 and 31 percent of adolescents attended public high schools. In comparison, the black girls who were plaintiffs in the Western High School case lived in neighborhoods where 95 percent of children went to public schools. In nearly all-white Southeast Baltimore, where parents would later resist integration, an average of about two-thirds attended public schools.[14]

Before the board met to consider Fischer's desegregation proposal, just to be safe, it petitioned the courts to change the names of the defendants in the NAACP suits; Thomsen and Thompson had left the board, replaced by attorney Samuel Jett and Johns Hopkins genetics professor Bentley Glass. The parties would eventually agree to drop both suits, Mergenthaler in 1956 and Western in 1958. For all practical purposes, May 1954, was the last time any desegregation suit against the board was even pending.[15]

The board met on June 10 to consider Fischer's recommendations. His report began,

> All of the standards and criteria which are now in force with respect to the admission of pupils to schools, grades, or curricula shall continue in force except that the race of the pupil shall not be a consideration....transfers because of changes of residence are routinely approved. Transfers for other reasons may be approved by the two principals involved or by the appropriate Assistant Superintendent.

Centrally, "As in the past, no child shall be required to attend any particular school." Baltimore had never had and would not adopt "a districting policy which requires such attendance." However, there would continue to be one exception: "Where a building is overcrowded, specific district lines may be established [such that no] pupil who lives beyond such a line may then enter the districted school." Finally, staff assignment, promotion, and transfer would be based on merit, not race. Sherwood moved to approve the report, albeit after being corrected by an audience member for referring anachronistically to "colored schools," and the board assented unanimously.[16]

Four days later, Fischer described the policy to the city's twenty-four hundred teachers in the only public presentation on desegregation. School officials believed that "the less said in advance about integration the better, since talking about it would focus attention on presumed problems and create the impression that difficulties were anticipated."[17]

What the School Board Did

The new policy ended legal differentiation of white and black schools and let students transfer to any school, subject to space availability and administrative approval. This was freedom of choice, or open enrollment. Officials used the terms *integration* and *desegregation* interchangeably. Within a decade experience would give the terms distinct meanings. Most commonly "desegregation" would come to mean the removal of barriers to blacks' mixing with whites. As civil rights advocates distinguished two types of segregation, "desegregation" would acquire two different meanings. The most obvious segregation was de jure, ordained by law. Hence de jure desegregation meant removing laws that separated the races.

Often, however, segregation prevailed without a specific basis in law or public policy. This condition was called de facto segregation, implying that it somehow just happened, a result of private preferences and actions. In reality, the line between de jure and de facto was rarely clear, in that public policies influenced and ratified many ostensibly private decisions. Residential segregation was aided by discriminatory federal mortgage insurance, housing, and transportation policies, local public housing policies and zoning regulation, and government enforcement of restrictive covenants. Further, school policies, such as decisions about school locations and zones, influenced residential choices and neighborhood racial makeup. Thus, not only was it difficult to distinguish public and private responsibility for segregation, but it was hard to draw a boundary around school system influence over it. Moreover, if separate schools were inherently unequal and unacceptable, it did not matter who was responsible. Hence de facto desegregation would refer not to the removal of legal barriers, but to the actuality of whites and blacks mixing. These dual referents meant that parties could disagree about whether schools were "desegregated," one emphasizing the absence of discriminatory policies, the other pointing to the lack of interracial student contact.

Sometimes the term "integration" referred to the more exacting view of "desegregation": schools were "integrated" when white and black students attended class together. In addition, "integration" had a still more robust meaning: students not only shared space in a building, but also interacted significantly, regarding one another as equals and possible friends. Thus one end of this lexical continuum was "desegregation" denoting the removal of legal barriers to blacks' attending school with whites, while the other was "integration" meaning the creation of interracial school societies.

In terms that would be clarified later, the 1954 Baltimore school board acted to desegregate schools by ending de jure segregation.

School Officials' Liberalism

As school officials noted, free choice simply continued the district's historic enrollment policy, with the removal of racial restrictions. The board's preference for free choice and for desegregation over integration expressed members'

liberalism. Many would have endorsed Fischer's invocation of the Republic's founding, echoing Thomas Jefferson, as a statement of their beliefs. They
thought of the city as constituted of individual families, whose involvement in
groups or communities was incidental to children's educational expectations or
needs. While the board deferred to professional educators in determining what
and how students should learn, it delegated authority to select children's schools
to families. Centrally, officials construed students' freedom of choice, or individual liberty, in negative terms. They had in mind freedom from external restraint, rather than freedom to get or achieve anything in particular. While board
members had personal preferences regarding how things came out, they believed
they should not use their authority to establish these conditions. Hence, though
some wanted integrated schools, they believed they had legitimacy only to free
students from segregation. Whether schools became integrated would depend
on families' decisions, not school board direction.[18]

Consistent with liberal principles, board policy defined choice as freedom
from coercion: "No child shall be required to attend any particular school."
Fischer recognized that individual freedom could conflict with a social goal such
as integration, that individual students could make choices that hindered integration. In that case, he believed personal liberty mattered more than racial
mixing, as he explained to teachers: "Will our school system be reorganized to
integrate all schools? The answer to that question is 'No.' ... no effort will be made
deliberately to transfer children of either race for the purpose of 'mixing' schools.
We have had the last of placing children anywhere for racial reasons." If white
children's freedom to choose schools without blacks limited black children's freedom to choose schools with whites, these constraints, in city officials' view, did
not result from government policy, but were private acts based on personal preferences, to which the state should defer. The *Sun* contrasted the "flexibility" of
Baltimore's free choice with Washington's "rigid district rule," assigning students
to schools in racially mixed zones.[19]

Five years later, reflecting on free choice, Fischer summarized his views, probably those of most board members:

> Negroes have been free to remain in their own schools or, if they chose,
> to transfer to a white school. The one thing we have resisted is to manip-
> ulate people. We are just opposed to pushing people around. The school
> system has never adopted any plan to achieve a good balance. We feel
> there is no merit in having a particular racial composition.

Free choice represented a procedural liberalism that was indifferent to the aggregate outcome of families' decisions, so long as every student had the right to
select a school. Crucially, board policy asserted that "the race of the pupil shall

not be a consideration" in where a child enrolled. The statement indicated that
the board did not want a child's race to limit where he or she went to school. In
particular, it meant that the board would be concerned about unfair limits on
individuals, but because race was now invisible with regard to public policy, the
board would not be interested in any ensuing inequalities between racial groups.
Indeed, the board would not care about any resulting inequalities, because, as
Fischer indicated, it was officially indifferent to the outcomes of its policy.[20]

In 1962, Fischer, then dean of Columbia University Teachers College, spoke
about desegregation to the U.S. Commission on Civil Rights. His statement en-
capsulated the dominant view of Baltimore school officials in 1954:

> If we are to keep the focus of our educational effort on the welfare of
> the individual child, we shall do well to avoid what is sometimes called
> social engineering. The very term is inconsistent with the purposes
> and values of democracy. Even the most desirable end does not jus-
> tify manipulating people to create a structure pleasing to some master
> planner....I am disturbed about the growing pressure to locate schools,
> draw district lines, and organize curricula in order to achieve a pre-
> determined racial pattern of enrollment. By no means am I opposing
> the desirability of having in the same school children of different racial
> backgrounds....But decisions about school organization based entirely
> or primarily on racial criteria seem to me to violate the principle of
> nondiscrimination. All school districting arrangements should provide
> a maximum of free choice for all children.

Fischer's peroration against social engineering located the 1954 board's thinking
in larger political and cultural contexts. "Free choice" resonated with the values
of the "free world" in the Cold War. Russia's despotic central authority represented the dangers of government intervention. Further, as Defense Secretary
Wilson's equation of GM and U.S. interests declared, Americanism in the expanding postwar economy meant producing and consuming. Thus "free choice"
evoked "free markets," where individual effort improved a family's lot.[21]

Free choice, with its liberal emphasis on individual freedom and limited government, followed Baltimore traditions. In education, Baltimore, unlike cities
that zoned schools, adopted open enrollment in the nineteenth century. In racial matters generally, the policy reflected the city's historic laissez-faire stance
of avoiding government involvement. For example, two weeks after the school
board voted to desegregate, the Baltimore Housing Authority, following a Supreme Court decision banning public housing segregation, also adopted free
choice—letting residents select the project they would live in, making desegregation voluntary. Crucially, the school board position that "race...shall not be a

consideration," while overtly banning discrimination, endorsed the Baltimore custom of avoiding potentially divisive talk about race. Color blindly regarding all students simply as equal individuals made it unnecessary to mention race when desegregating.[22]

When all was said and done, Fischer suggested in his address to teachers, the new policy might not change much. "Will there be a large number of pupil transfers? There might not be," he concluded, asserting that the equality of white and black schools gave little reason to move. A half century later, Walter Sondheim identified simpler reasons why few families might transfer children: preferences for neighborhood schools and attachments to current schools. In a city where housing was segregated, normal interests in nearby schools would discourage choices leading to racially mixed schools. At the same time, Sondheim acknowledged the political virtue of open enrollment: "I don't think there was any other choice....The idea of telling people in Bolton Hill [the elite white neighborhood where he grew up, which gentrified in the late 1960s after wartime decline] that they had to send their kids some place else, instead of the [neighborhood] school...was just unthinkable." While respecting individual rights, free choice removed the school board from intervening in race relations. It seemed the policy least likely to arouse conflict or provoke resistance.[23]

In the end, free choice was an experiment. No one had tried to desegregate schools before. There was no recipe book of interventions. Although open enrollment did not lead surely to racial integration, neither did it preclude it. Thus board members who wanted schools to become models of democracy and others who wanted to end segregation but worried about extensive racial mixing could both endorse a policy the outcome of which was a matter of philosophical indifference and undetermined. Anything, so it might seem, was possible.

Black Community Responses to the School Board Policy

Black leaders celebrated the board's vote to end segregation. "We are face to face with integration," the *Afro* proclaimed. Lillie May Jackson declared, "This puts Baltimore in the forefront of those cities which are on the road to true democracy. May God bless each and every member of the board for this wonderful step forward." The NAACP took credit for board action and the adoption of free choice: "The policy statements of the Board issued on June 3rd and June 10th embodied the requests made by the [Baltimore] Branch."[24]

Some blacks shared some whites' desires for integrated schools and society and saw free choice as a first step. Others, however, endorsed free choice and "integration" for different reasons. They wanted their children to attend schools with whites not so much because they believed racial mixing improved education or democracy as because predominantly white schools offered better resources and opportunities. However, after the NAACP's legal pleadings that segregation was inherently problematic, blacks could not say publicly that they cared more about school quality than racial makeup without seeming to concede that separate could be acceptable, after all, if it were equal. To white ears, these different interests in free choice sounded similar.

In addition, some blacks were satisfied with all-black schools. Some of these schools, despite rundown conditions, educated children well. Some had teachers with good training from elite colleges as a result of a state black scholarship program. Like a number of other border and Southern states, Maryland barred blacks from the state university but gave scholarships to those who could get admitted and go to colleges and universities in other states. With this support from the mid-1930s until 1957, Maryland blacks studied at institutions like Columbia, Oberlin, the University of Pennsylvania, and the University of Chicago. Some black parents liked all-black schools because they were community centers. Some black educators wanted to maintain these schools because they feared losing not just community relationships, but also the employment, or at least the status, that a separate system gave them. These families and teachers liked free choice because it removed the compulsion and stigma of forced segregation while letting them stay where they were.[25]

Thus many blacks endorsed open enrollment because it served their purposes. Some with strong interests in integration may have regarded it merely as the best they could get from the 1954 school board. Most black leaders involved in trying to influence desegregation probably recognized, with school officials, that the policy was an experiment with an uncertain result. At the same time, it appealed to them for many of the same reasons it appealed to school officials, among which was their own liberalism.

Middle-class Black Liberalism

For Baltimore's black middle class, individual striving was at once a means of economic and social advancement and a liberal principle. In the early twentieth century, Booker T. Washington and W. E. B. DuBois debated the direction and strategy for black development. Washington argued for black economic self-sufficiency, while DuBois advocated integration into the larger society. Washington urged manual trades training for the black masses as the means for economic independence, and as a graduate of the Hampton Institute, he founded the Tuskegee Institute to advance that cause. DuBois, who had a Harvard doctorate, emphasized higher education for the "Talented Tenth" who would lead other blacks, and he was one of the 1909 founders of the NAACP, which campaigned for black civil rights to participate fully in society and the polity.

Baltimore's black middle class were DuBoisians in regarding themselves as an educated elite who had the ability and responsibility to guide the black community. They believed they had the qualities necessary to succeed in the larger society, and they saw themselves as emissaries between blacks and white power brokers. The *Afro* was their voice in giving advice on everything from political issues to social behavior. In the end, they generally accepted Washington's view of the black masses: manual training was their best hope for economic security. Thus the middle class campaigned for integration of the top public schools for the ablest black youths and expansion of vocational programs for others.

The black middle class, as middle classes generally, regarded their own social and economic advancement as a reflection of their ability and striving. Their entrepreneurial and professional positions affirmed an individualistic view of society, where effort led to success. Where the black middle class differed from the white middle class was in the ability to spend its money, acquire wealth, and exercise prerogatives associated with income and education. Hence the black middle class wanted civil rights. They wanted the right to spend their money in stores, theaters, restaurants, and hotels; the right to buy homes in desirable neighborhoods; the right to enter and advance in occupations of their choice; the right to enjoy public parks and beaches—and the right to send their children to good schools. In their meritocratic view of social and economic advancement, education was the key.[26]

This position led middle-class blacks to support free choice as a means of unleashing individual ability, and the *Afro* promulgated the perspective in articles and commentaries on *Brown* and open enrollment. The main headline on an article presenting the new policy to readers proclaimed, "What the Baltimore Schools Offer Your Child: Integration means more opportunities." Smaller headlines catalogued the opportunities: "16 kindergartens, 5 nurseries, 5 schools with advanced courses," "10 vocational schools now," "Special art, music, printing and other technical courses available," and "2 all-girls schools, junior college." The article began by explaining that desegregation would free children to develop as individuals:

> Baltimore public school's [sic] lead in abandoning the dual system follows closely the policy of providing the best for each pupil under its jurisdiction. The school administration long ago dispensed with rigid curriculum and promotion rules in favor of more elastic education which prepares the individual child for good and profitable citizenship.

The next section elaborated, as it distinguished the more talented children from the masses:

> The Baltimore school system maintains schools and general classes to fit the needs of the average child, whether a formal or vocational career is planned; the same for children with superior ability and for those whose ability is limited. With all city schools now open to all pupils, it is the duty of the parent, as well as the school principal and counselor, to see that each child is placed in the school where his abilities can best be developed.

Thus the "opportunities" that desegregation offered were not for the race as a collectivity, but for individuals. Indeed, free choice would increase differences among blacks. Once black children were released from schools that limited them, they could develop to their fullest and distinguish themselves by their abilities. Those with superior talent would pursue professional careers, while others with limited talent would follow vocational careers.[27]

Carl Murphy's daughter, Betty Murphy Phillips, discussed how open enrollment would free individual striving and make the city better in an *Afro* commentary on "What Integration Means to You, Me." She began by belittling white fears that integration would lead to intermarriage. Students did not come to school primed to mate with the first person they saw of the opposite sex (or the opposite race). They came to work hard and do the best for themselves. Phillips emphasized the point in chastising "that colored reader who says she has always liked segregated schools because they gave her child a chance to excel. Where did she get the idea he couldn't excel in any school? If he has it, he'll stand out anywhere." Now there would be "an opportunity for all children in Baltimore to take the type of training they desire and for which they can qualify." Phillips conjured up examples of white and black children whose parents could choose new schools that fit their talents and needs. Because housing was segregated and because most families would choose schools near home, she assumed "there will be only a few colored pupils in many schools in our city. But that's not important—the important thing is that Susie Smith, colored, and James Jones, colored, will now have an opportunity to avail themselves of all the public school facilities this city offers." Still, Phillips did not discount the importance of new social relations: "[White children] Jane Kelinsky and Mary Feldman as well as Susie Smith and James Jones will all benefit because they will have an opportunity to know each other while they are still young. If they start while they are in school, Baltimore will be a better place for them all 20 years from now."[28]

In a column titled "This Won't Happen under Integration," Phillips described another type of individual freedom she hoped the new school policy would spawn. After hearing about a white boy's chagrin that his school would "turn colored," Phillips wrote,

> In the next 15 years when we get all our young people—white and colored—to stop thinking in terms of race, this youngster won't make such an observation. And, as children have an opportunity to go to school together, as they play together, we will get away from this thing of "colored school" and "white school." And, thank goodness, the Baltimore school board has taken the first step by abolishing all racial designation in assignment of pupils and in naming of schools.

Phillips expressed a common hope that integration would end racial identities. Just as there would no longer be white or colored schools, there would no longer be white or colored children. All would just be individuals, each like everyone else.[29]

In a way, the *Afro*'s words were unremarkable. Individual development is a normal educational concern, and the new policy would let black parents choose schools suited to their children's talents. At the same time, the *Afro* expressed a liberalism similar to that of white officials. The normative concept of society was one composed simply of individuals, where neither racial identity nor attachments to racial groups encumbered personal thinking or effort. The black middle class put primacy on individual liberty and shared school officials' negative concept of it: they wanted open enrollment simply to remove the constraints of segregation, to free individual students to go as far as they could on their own. To be sure, black leaders held a more demanding view of what removing the bonds of segregation required. They wanted board activism in improving and replacing buildings, providing adequate equipment and materials, and integrating staff. However, they assumed government would take a limited role beyond that. They did not want it to assign their children to specific schools. Nor did they suggest that the board should ensure any particular academic outcomes for black students. Perhaps they doubted the government would take such a role, but it was good liberalism to insist simply that government provide an equal starting point for a race that children ran on their own. Those who subordinated sexual desires to competitive academic work would advance, and their aggregate efforts, free of government regulation, would make society better.

Free Choice and Desegregation

As Baltimoreans looked ahead to desegregation, they could note three aspects of the new policy. First, school officials had repudiated a public interest in racial mixing. Second, by putting everything on individual choice, the board legitimated white opposition—a choice for segregation was as acceptable as a choice for integration. Third, in insisting that race "shall not be a consideration," the board foreclosed discussion of racial justice and, crucially, obviated talk of the racial issues and feelings that had created and sustained segregation to begin with. Residents, whites in particular, could take comfort that no one was going to force families to do anything they weren't comfortable with. Integrationists, on the other hand, could find no certainty that racial separation in the schools would end. How Baltimore interpreted and implemented the Supreme Court decision lay in the hands of Baltimore parents, just as school officials wanted.[30]

MODEST CHANGE

After the school board adopted free choice, the school facilities director reported that his staff had "long anticipated" and planned for the end of segregation. Desegregation would require only "minor adjustments." The main challenge, he said, was to provide up-to-date schools for an increasing number of students. His confident report, however, ignored two issues that would affect the course of desegregation. One was that public school enrollment was not just growing rapidly, but also changing racially. The other was that many historically black schools were dilapidated.[1]

Opening Schools under Free Choice

When the board voted to desegregate, 182,000 Baltimore children attended school. One-fourth went to private schools, 21 percent in Catholic schools and 3 percent in other religious or nonsectarian schools. One third of white students, but only 3 percent of black, attended private schools. The public schools had 138,000 students, 63 percent white. The system had 194 schools, 110 white, 84 colored. Enrollment was increasing, though white and overall enrollment had declined during the Depression and the war and began to grow again only after the war. Black enrollment increased steadily over this period as part of the Great Migration, nearly doubling from 1934 to 1953 and growing from 23 percent of enrollment in 1934 to 32 percent in 1945 before reaching 37 percent in 1953–54. Although three straight years of enrollment increases of six thousand to seven thousand students a year put pressure on school buildings, the expansion of black neighborhoods would present a greater challenge to desegregation by free choice. Because most parents wanted children to attend school near home, even with open enrollment the location of facilities would influence the racial makeup of schools. The facilities director said nothing about siting schools so as to encourage or ease desegregation.[2]

Not just the location of schools, but also their condition, would affect how free choice played out. One-third of all parents and one-half of black elementary school parents were dissatisfied with building conditions, according to a 1951 survey. Black parents wanted new schools, along with the addition of gyms, auditoriums, cafeterias, and recreation space. The facilities director did not speak of renovating, closing, or replacing outmoded, rundown, unsafe colored schools, which the board now offered to all students under free choice. White parents would not consider participating in desegregation by sending their children to these schools; indeed, no parents, whatever their race or racial views, would choose such facilities.[3]

Two other factors limited the likely impact of free choice. The University of Maryland refusal to admit black students had left most blacks who wanted to become teachers to attend Coppin, which suffered from chronic neglect by the school system. Because city teachers were segregated along with students, concentrations of poorly trained teachers in historically black schools would deter parents from choosing these schools. Finally, in a city where few whites and blacks had contact, anxiety blanketed the racial boundary and made it unlikely that many, whatever their racial views or educational preferences, would choose schools associated with the other race.

Thus historically black schools presented few choices, and few families felt emotionally and socially free to choose anything besides what they already had. Creating choices depended on closing, improving, or replacing historically black schools, integrating faculties, providing remedial teacher training, and disseminating information and engaging in human relations efforts to address fears. The school system did none of these things, as if these problems did not exist, as if the past did not constrain the present.[4]

Anticipations and the Start of School

School officials did little to publicize or encourage transfers. In contrast, black leaders and the *Afro* urged parents to take advantage of open enrollment. Clarence and Juanita Mitchell went to a PTA meeting at Booker T. Washington Junior High to recruit students for desegregated schools, though they were jeered by teachers who feared that falling enrollments in black schools would jeopardize their jobs. A counselor at the school identified girls he thought would do well at Western High School and encouraged parents to send their daughters. Teachers offered tutoring to help students succeed at Western. Over the summer, black parents weighed commitments to racial pathbreaking, assessments of educational opportunities, and calculations of children's safety, and hundreds made decisions that would integrate city schools.[5]

Many middle-class and elite black families sent children to the newly open white schools. The Mitchells enrolled their son Keiffer in Gwynns Falls Park Junior High School. It would let him develop his artistic interests, but they stressed to him that he had a responsibility to open a path for the race. Knowing the principal opposed integration, they expected difficulties. Blanche Dogan and W. A. C. Hughes decided to send their daughter Alfreda to Western, invoking a similar mission and urging her to recruit friends to go with her. They wanted young black women to attend the elite girls' high school, despite rumors that the principal had "declared that 'niggers' would come to her school over her dead body." Carolyn Holland's parents moved her to Arlington Elementary School, despite worries about her safety, because they believed it offered better opportunities than the small historically black neighborhood school.[6]

When classes opened in September, Baltimoreans waited to see whether schools would be racially mixed and whether changes took place peacefully. Daily, the newspapers tallied the rolls. The September 4 *Afro* announced, "Many Mixed Classes as Schools Open," while the September 8 *Sun* reported, "First Day Passes With Few Complaints, No Serious Clashes." The *Afro* quoted parents who had chosen white schools for the benefits of attending a school within walking distance of home. The *Sun* reassured readers that, "Although more than a score of schools enrolled mixed classes, the total number of Negroes listed as students in hitherto white schools was relatively small, officials said, and only two Negro teachers were directing the studies of white pupils." The September 11 *Afro* headlined "1,200 Classes in 47 Schools Mixed" but put the changes in perspective editorially:

> To be sure, total integration did not arrive in Baltimore's public schools on Tuesday. There are and will continue to be schools which will have either an all-white or all-colored enrollment. But the makeup of these schools will be caused not by designation by the School Board, but by the residential patterns of the city wherein some sections remain predominately white while others remain predominately colored.

Enrollment would fluctuate, and precise counts would be elusive, but the broad numbers showed big differences in black and white interest in mixed schooling. The October 31 count found 143,688 students, 60 percent white and 40 percent black. Among blacks, 1,379 elementary students, 3.5 percent of black public elementary students, entered 36 formerly white elementary schools among the city's 133 elementary schools. Another 196 black students, 1.4 percent of black public secondary students, entered 13 of the city's 32 junior or senior high schools. Six white elementary students entering three historically black schools represented 0.007 percent of white public elementary students. No white families sent children to once-black secondary schools.[7]

Signs of white resistance to integration appeared in mid-September. Charles Carroll Barrister Elementary School, Number 34, in working-class white southwest Baltimore, now had 11 black children among 561 students. White parents complained that neighbors had not been consulted before the school was opened to blacks and demanded that the superintendent meet with them. Fischer declined. On September 30, about thirty whites, mostly mothers, some with children, began picketing the school. One sign declared, "Segregation Is Our Heritage," and another demanded, "Let the Taxpayers Decide." Adults stopped neighborhood children on their way to school, warned them of harm from black students, told them school was cancelled, and urged them to stay home. Some parents walking children to school, seeing the pickets, who at one point grew to about seventy, took their children back home. By the end of the day, when picketers disbanded, attendance had been only 20 percent. That afternoon the school board held its scheduled meeting. Recognizing the seriousness of the protest, it unanimously adopted a statement that acknowledged anxiety about changes but asserted that schools would remain open and that police would ensure safety. The board invoked American traditions of individual freedom and the Cold War:

> One of the things that had made the United States the great bulwark against Communism and Fascist totalitarianism is the fact that, by common consent, we accept the principle of government by law and believe that adherence to law, especially when it concerns the rights of our fellow men, is a primary obligation of citizenship.

Undeterred, pickets at School 34 announced demonstrations at other desegregated schools the next morning.[8]

With picketing at several elementary schools in the background, Southern High School took center stage on Friday, October 1. Formerly the white high school for largely white working-class south and southwest Baltimore, it now had 39 blacks among 1,788 students. White students picketed and urged others to stay out of school. Phone callers, many anonymous, told parents of panic, violence, and pandemonium in and around the school and urged them to take children home. Principal John Schwatka encouraged compliance and attendance. Student government officers helped maintain order, and white football players included a black teammate in the afternoon's game. Meanwhile, some white Southern students traveled to City College and Patterson high schools to spread the strike.

During the summer, someone had burned a cross on Walter Sondheim's lawn, and several people had sent him anti-Semitic and racist messages and threats. No one knew how strong the emotions behind the picketing were, whether it might turn violent. Police patrolled at School 34 and Southern. Sondheim, armed with emergency phone numbers, kept watch at Southern with Police Commissioner Beverly Ober. When a rotten tomato sailed past their heads, Ober made an arrest. Yet uncertainty about whether picketing would spread, whether the two thousand absent students would increase, and whether isolated violence would become contagious led Fischer and Sondheim to confer with police officials, the city solicitor, the state attorney general, and civic leaders about what to do over the weekend to assure orderly school opening on Monday.[9]

Ironically, black leaders had been campaigning for Commissioner Ober's dismissal for years. They regarded him as incompetent, corrupt, and dangerous. In September 1951, the Grand Jury reported that Ober had not investigated charges that police took bribes and tipped off vice squad raid targets. Blacks felt he gave unwarranted protection to officer Jerome Glass, who had not only been accused of taking bribes but had shot six blacks, two fatally. The NAACP had demanded Glass's removal for trigger-happiness. When a delegation went to Ober after Glass's second killing in late 1950, Ober simply replied, "In both of the killings, [Glass] has been exonerated by the courts. After all, the only persons he has killed have been disreputable characters. Wait until he kills one of your good colored persons, then maybe I'll change my mind about him." The *Afro* repeatedly attacked Ober, declared him a "dictator," and insisted that Governor McKeldin replace him. Now blacks depended on Ober for their children's safety.[10]

After meeting with Fischer, Sondheim, and others, Ober issued a statement that the police would keep order. Fischer expressed confidence that integration would proceed without trouble. Mayor D'Alesandro called for calm. Nineteen civic, religious, educational, and labor groups formed the Coordinating Council for Civic Unity to plan a peaceful opening of schools on Monday. Pastors delivered weekend sermons supporting integration.

Serendipitously, a break came on Sunday afternoon. Leon Sachs, director of the Jewish Community Council and part of the Coordinating Council's steering committee, got a call from William Manchester. Manchester, who had written a biography of Baltimorean H. L. Mencken and a novel about race, crime, and politics in the city, who would later write books on President Kennedy's death, midcentury America, Douglas MacArthur, and Winston Churchill, was then a *Sun* reporter. By Sachs's account, Manchester, whom he had never met, was drunk and animated. He began by deriding Sachs's competence as a lawyer and then told him of sections 92 and 223c of Article 77 of the Laws of Maryland, which banned school building picketing intended to discourage student attendance. Monday morning, Sachs brought the other steering committee members to meet with Fischer and Sondheim. They agreed Sachs would inform Ober of the statutes and ask him to make a statement that the police would enforce the law by arresting violators. Meanwhile, a group of white students was marching to high schools in the central city, urging others to join them, at one point trying unsuccessfully to see the mayor and then moving to Southern, where the police sent them on. Sachs found Ober and talked with him for two hours. Ober checked with the attorney general's office and recorded a statement. Although the student march petered out by the end of the day and never threatened anyone's safety, twelve hundred of seventeen hundred Southern students stayed home. That evening, radio and television stations repeatedly broadcast the police commissioner's statement.

The next day, only a few adults picketed at scattered elementary schools and quickly dispersed when police arrived. Half the Southern students stayed out, but the superintendent announced that any student who failed to attend school without a legitimate excuse would be suspended or expelled, and most students returned on Wednesday.[11]

Varied Experiences of Desegregation

A study of the white protesters found something striking. Their schools and neighborhoods had few blacks—generally, 3 percent or fewer. Schools with high black enrollments in racially changing neighborhoods did not have protests. The protesters also contrasted with whites at other schools with few blacks who did not demonstrate. Those who resisted had especially low incomes, educational levels, and job skills. Many of their neighborhoods were deteriorating, and they lacked the resources to leave. Perhaps they were less tolerant than others, but they were also less able to move if changes upset them. Even a few blacks could seem threatening.[12]

In fact, students' and teachers' experiences varied. For example, Gertrude Williams, a black teacher starting her career at Charles Carroll of Carrollton Elementary School in east Baltimore, was unaffected by desegregation. No white families transferred children into her all-black school, and as far as she knew, no children left for historically white schools. Her students were the same before and after board action. Liz Wolfson, a white teacher starting her career at Lyndhurst Elementary School in west Baltimore, saw uneven evidence of desegregation across neighborhoods. It was significant in Edmondson Village, where she taught, but not in Mount Washington or Cross Country elementary schools. In general, black families were more likely to send children to schools in working-class white neighborhoods near a racial boundary than to more remote middle-class white neighborhoods. Williams's impression that none of her students' transferred out suggests that low-income black families rarely acted on the new policy. At the least, because the system did not provide transportation for transferring students, parents could not afford to get them to a distant school or to buy clothes that would make them presentable in middle-class schools. Finally, as Williams indicated, whites were unlikely to send their children to any black school.[13]

Sometimes black children's entry into formerly white schools presented great challenges, and sometimes it easily became normal. Neighborhood residents' attitudes mattered; so did teachers' and principals' inclinations. A troubled experience was that of Keiffer Mitchell, who transferred from Booker T. Washington Junior High to Gwynns Falls Park Junior High, at the eastern edge of Edmondson Village. Seven other blacks joined him among 2,109 students. The school board policy brought the first black youths into the neighborhood, and the principal shared many residents' opposition to integration. Clarence Mitchell, then NAACP Washington Bureau director, fearing what his son would encounter, accompanied him to school for the first six weeks.

At the end of September, when white parents were picketing Charles Carroll Barrister, some whites took up the cudgel at Gwynns Falls. Mitchell described what happened to his son on September 30 in a magazine article:

> During the lunch hour ... a colored student [Keiffer Mitchell] was struck in the face by two white men who came on the school property. The student reported that one of the men asked him what time it was. When the student replied that he did not have a watch, the man struck him in the face. Both men then ran from the school property. The Police Department staged a line-up which included the operator of a car that had driven away from the school at the time the incident occurred. The child, who was the victim of the assault, was unable to identify his assailant in the line-up. The driver of the car said that he had come to the school to pick up his sister because he had heard there would be a race riot at the school.

On Monday, October 4, white parents began picketing the school and urging students to go home. Mitchell concluded from observations and license plates that the demonstration was organized by outsiders. Though well known for his equanimity, he stormed to school headquarters and broke in on Fischer and Sondheim, who were trying to respond to multiple protests, insisted they do something at Gwynns Falls, and said he would counterpicket at the school.

Sondheim tried to dissuade him, but Mitchell marched. In response to signs including one urging "Niggers Go Back to Africa," his proclaimed, "I Am An American Too."[14]

Though the demonstrations quickly subsided as a result of Commissioner Ober's announcement, Keiffer Mitchell never gained a normal existence at the school. White students harassed or avoided him. A neighborhood gang of older youths once attacked him on the playground. In the winter, whites behind him on the bus put lighted cigarettes in the hood of his garment. Nevertheless, Gwynns Falls had advantages over Booker T. Washington, which was overcrowded, offered little food in the cafeteria, and had gangs demanding protection money. Mitchell's refuge and satisfaction at the school were art. He painted. He designed the cover for the Christmas edition of the school paper, taking advantage of materials unavailable at his former school. His art teachers gave him attention, though other teachers, perhaps fearing ostracism, kept a distance. Overt hostility subsided after a year, but white students continued to shun him. He stayed close to the classrooms and kept a careful routine. He interacted with other black students, but they did not form a close group, and he was often alone during his two years at the school. Painting became a source of pleasure that complemented his practice of medicine later in life, but his education in art came with the strains of white anxiety about desegregation.[15]

White residents of Edmondson Village saw integration of the school as the portent of neighborhood decline. Blockbusting realtors stimulated and exploited this fear, and whites started leaving. Black families began moving into the area around the junior high school. Although they were stable families with income comparable to those of the whites already there, their neighbors could not recognize these class similarities, but only saw the racial difference. The white exodus accelerated.[16]

Carolyn Cole, in contrast, had an easy time settling into Arlington Elementary School. Fifty years later, after becoming a school principal, she remained friends with several women she met as a student when she was Carolyn Holland. She grew up in the Pimlico neighborhood in northwest Baltimore, where three blocks of black families lived among mostly Jews. Under segregation, she went to first grade at School 157, an unnamed school handed down to black children when it proved unfit for whites. The school had two rooms, one teacher and three grades in each, without a kindergarten. It had no cafeteria or gym. Despite those drawbacks, School 157 was a community center, where the teachers were highly respected, PTA meetings were command social events, and parents assumed the school was good enough.

The predominantly white neighborhood where she lived differed from those where parents demonstrated against desegregation. Jews, who had faced discrimination, could understand blacks' victimization and their drive for equality. Many Jews were active liberals or sympathetic with liberal causes; they shared blacks' desire for integration and were personally comfortable with blacks. Moreover, a number of elite Jewish families lived in Pimlico and sent their children to public schools. Blacks and whites were more likely to have cordial relations around work or commerce there than in most other parts of the city.

Many people in the Holland family's lives were white. Perhaps the owner of the Pimlico Race Track, where her father was a jockey, was one who encouraged him to transfer his daughter to Arlington when the school board adopted its new policy. The school was just around the corner from home. It had a playground and gym, modern equipment, and new textbooks, and it offered courses unavailable in the two-room school: science, language, music, and art. Her father worried whether she would be safe at Arlington, but he decided the historically white school would be better for her.

On the first day of school, scared about what to expect, Holland dressed up in new clothes and walked to school with her mother. Her teacher greeted her at the classroom door and exclaimed, "Aren't you a pretty little girl!" A dozen black children had entered Arlington, a large school with 1,753 students, and the principal paired white students with new black classmates to help them settle in. The principal met Holland and told her she was happy to have her in the school. Quickly, Holland became comfortable. At the end of elementary school, she and some of the other black Arlington students went on to predominantly white Pimlico Junior High School, and she later went to predominantly white Forest Park High School. Looking back as an adult, she considered Arlington the best experience of her life. Reflecting on the ease with which she integrated the schools she attended, she observed, "I think I was so warmly embraced because 95 per cent of the kids I went through school with were Jewish, and Jews were a big help to getting Baltimore schools over the desegregation hurdle."[17]

Anxieties about Integration

In a city where few had contact with the other race, whites and blacks regarded one another with curiosity, often shading into apprehension. Innocently, a Jewish boy at Arlington went home after the first day of school and asked his family's maid whether black children would also be coming to his Hebrew school class. Some white girls at Western High School had more primitive questions, as a new black student discovered. After a physical education class, she and other black girls were in the shower with some white girls. The white girls kept staring at them, until she asked why. "They thought we had tails, that's why they were staring…they were looking for our tails."[18]

As that incident shows, much concern about integration had to do with physical intimacy. White parents at a southwest elementary school charged that black students lacked proper hygiene and threatened their children's health. At another elementary school, a white mother complained to the principal that her daughter had contracted a serious infection from a toilet seat because a black student used it. Rumors of toilet seat infections and trench mouth took wing in south Baltimore also, while public health officers worked with school officials to investigate complaints and issue reports declaring them groundless. At two high schools white parents protested racially mixed swimming classes. Western High School made showers optional.[19]

Concerns about physical contact reflected deeper anxieties. A letter to the *Evening Sun,* expressing "the thoughts of the average white person living in a community where we are surrounded on all sides by Negro people," described "the monstrous thing" unleashed on whites by desegregation. The writer ridiculed arguments for integration: "A Negro who wants to worship the Lord may do so very well without sitting next to a white person, just as a colored child may also learn in school without sitting next to a white child. The way the authorities go on you would think a colored person could hardly breathe unless they were in a group of white people." She proceeded to the crux of her concerns, "the social aspects":

> Will my child have to go to a school prom and dance with colored children? Where will these things lead? Suppose we do tell our children that everyone is alike, that these people who have only three hundred years of civilization behind them are the same, then a son or daughter brought home a Negro boy or girl friend. Would you be happy? Suppose they marry, would you be happy? Suppose they marry, would you be happy wondering whether your next grandchild would be black or white?

In short, black and white children sitting next to one another might come to know and like one another, date, marry, have children, and confound families' bloodlines.[20]

Such anxiety found expression in widespread concern about dancing and dating. At Oliver Cromwell Elementary School, where neighborhood racial change contributed to a black enrollment of 321 along with 382 whites, a white mother worried to the principal over who would dance the Virginia reel with her daughter. The principal explained that children were free to choose their partners. After the Southern High School demonstrations, New Rochelle High School, in New York, invited Southern students to visit and see how blacks and whites got along in a more extensively mixed school. Southern paid for two boys and two girls to spend five days in New Rochelle. When they returned, local papers, television

stations, and national wire services interviewed the boys, and they spoke at public meetings. A rural Baltimore County audience raised typical concerns:

> Most of the questions related to the social aspects of school integration:
> dances, dating and the like. The boys explained that this was something
> they themselves had been anxious to learn on their New Rochelle trip
> and that they had found out that while white and Negro students mixed
> freely in all school activities, they went their separate ways after school.
> They said they particularly pressed for answers about dating and were
> told on all sides that whites and Negroes did not date. The boys said that
> at New Rochelle dances both white and Negro couples attended but that
> the white students danced only with white students and the Negroes
> with Negroes—in short, no mixing.

Western High School, where the principal did not like integration, restricted social affairs in the building to those involving only girls. It left coeducational social
events to parental sponsorship elsewhere. The 1955 junior prom was held at a
hotel; black girls brought dates of their own race, and the hotel admitted them
because they were part of a larger, predominantly white group. Another school
sought to prevent interracial dancing by eliminating the stag line and adopting a
rule of one escort per girl. Another stopped selling dance tickets to the public.[21]

The First Years of Free Choice

While some whites worried that sharing classrooms led to dancing, dating, and
more, blacks were satisfied with new educational opportunities. At the end of the
first year, Lillie May Jackson thanked Superintendent Fischer for his efforts. The
NAACP, she wrote, was "very proud of the leadership you have given our community in this time of transition.... You richly deserve every award and com-
mendation. May God continue to bless your efforts." NAACP executive secretary
Roy Wilkins praised Baltimore's policy:

> We feel that the desegregation progress in Baltimore has been of very
> great significance, even though the numbers involved may be less than
> in some other communities. The principal factors are two. In Baltimore,
> students may transfer freely under its system—yet, despite the threats
> of adult agitators, no exodus of white students occurred when Negro
> students enrolled in the former all-white schools. Secondly, Baltimore
> has as deeply rooted traditions along the color line as many Deep South
> cities. Yet the transition proceeded smoother. We believe that Baltimore
> could be a model for the South.

Whether "the numbers" seemed large or small depended on what one expected or feared.[22]

Choices

Enrollment figures showed two trends: slowly growing but modest racial mixing and movement toward a majority black district. In the second year of free choice, 3,457 black children, 8 percent of black elementary students, attended 48 formerly white schools, and 916 black children, 2 percent of black secondary students, attended 17 once-white schools. Only 20 white children, 0.04 percent of white elementary students, went to seven previously black elementary schools, and no whites attended historically black secondary schools. Not until the fall of 1958 did any white students (5) enroll at formerly black secondary schools, making a total of 58 white pupils in 11 historically black schools with a total black enrollment of 13,686. By 1961, the number of black students choosing formerly white schools grew from 1,575 to 31,983, a third of black enrollment, while the number of whites choosing previously black schools rose from 6 to 86, 0.1 percent of white enrollment.

Not only did far fewer whites than blacks choose to desegregate, but the district, and thus available choices, was in flux. While overall enrollment increased for 15 years after Brown, the racial makeup was already changing in 1954. In the first year after desegregation, the system gained about 6,000 students, but blacks increased by 5,000 while whites grew by only 1,000. White enrollment began to drop in 1957, led by a decline of about 2,000 in the elementary schools. Only half of the white children born in Baltimore in 1951 were enrolled in city public schools in 1957. Baltimore became a majority black district in 1960, with 87,675 black students and 82,547 white students.

Open enrollment let blacks choose integrated schools, but many black parents who chose historically white schools preferred those nearby, close to the (moving) racial boundary in the residentially segregated city. Whites who became uncomfortable with racial changes could use open enrollment to avoid integration, and if they had the means, they could send their children to private schools or move to the suburbs. In the context of growing black enrollment, these decisions produced many single-race schools. Resegregation followed desegregation. By early 1959, when one-fourth of black students attended once-white schools, 15 formerly white elementary schools and two junior highs had become predominantly black, with 8 more than 90 percent black. In 1961, when a third of black students attended once-white schools, more than half the elementary schools were segregated: of 146 elementary schools, 30 were all white, and 44 were all black. Only 31 had at least 10 percent of students from each race. Secondary schools, because they drew from larger areas, were more likely to be mixed: 18 of 51 had at least 10 percent from each race.

Consequently, few students encountered many of the other race. In 1961, 65 percent of white students attended schools at least 90 percent white, and 80 percent of black students attended schools at least 90 percent black. In other words, only 35 percent of white students and 20 percent of black students attended schools with 10 percent from the other race. In addition, tracking into separate academic programs reduced interracial contacts in classes. One measure of the system's continuing segregation is the dissimilarity index, which indicates the proportion of white or black students who would have to transfer to give all schools the same racial composition as the district as a whole. The index was 0.94 in 1955 and dropped to 0.82 in 1961—four-fifths of all students would have to choose different schools to produce schools matching the district's overall composition, about 40 percent white.[23]

In short, a growing black majority made it harder for families to choose schools that were racially mixed. In addition, the fluidity of registration set in motion by free choice and compounded by white withdrawal made it difficult for parents to choose schools with any certainty about the race of their children's classmates.

School Policy and a Change in Administration

After the decision to open enrollment, school officials said little more about desegregation. In May 1959, John Fischer resigned to become dean of Columbia University Teachers College. The local Sidney Hollander Foundation had given him its 1955 award for his stewardship in integrating schools. The American Association of School Administrators' *School Executive* had recognized him, two other educators, and Adlai Stevenson for "outstanding statesmanship in education" in 1956. On his departure, the *Afro* lauded him as one of the city's "great school superintendents" and acclaimed the "success of school integration in Baltimore."[24]

In a farewell interview, Fischer expressed concern that Baltimore's leaders did not realize how much the city depended on good schools but said integration had been successful. He stated that, although the system had approved nearly every student transfer request, because black and white families alike preferred neighborhood schools, most changes in the racial makeup of schools had resulted from residential moves. For the first time, he acknowledged that "our colored schools were not as good as our white schools before 1954 and the differences have not been completely eradicated in five years."

Fischer affirmed the liberal perspective that led him to support open enrollment initially. Asked whether the city could have done more to prepare for desegregation, he rejected the idea that the school board might have sponsored workshops or discussions with parents. In his view of individual autonomy and limited government, the school system could not, or at least should not, influence parental choices. He framed integration as a dilemma that downplayed the influence of either race or schools on children's learning and put primary responsibility on individual families. Whenever possible, he said, a student

> should come to know persons of other races, other religions, other ethnic origins, other social and economic groups. An integrated school would normally give more opportunity for varied contacts than a school attended by children chosen from a narrow range. But when children from a broad cultural range are assembled in one classroom, teaching problems are increased, because the interests, ambitions and academic ability of children usually vary with the cultural level of their homes.

In 1959, "cultural level" was an increasingly common way of avoiding race. It reformulated racial differences as class differences, and it associated class with a "level" of "culture" roughly defined as adherence to the Protestant Ethic: those with a higher "cultural level" tried harder and accomplished more. This view of class differences emphasized the efficacy of individual striving and attributed much greater responsibility for success or failure to families than to social institutions. Apparently forced by the dilemma to choose, Fischer said he cared more about aiding students at the bottom, white or black, than about racial integration. While recognizing that a number of black students were performing well in integrated schools, he suggested that much of the credit lay with their parents' education, ambition, and encouragement, rather than integration per se.

Fischer confidently answered a question about dancing by reporting that no unwanted interracial intimacy occurred:

> Boys and girls date members of their own race for school dances as they do for private affairs. Most of them spend the evening with small groups of their own close friends and dance only with their own dates. I have heard of no mixed dancing at school affairs. In social activities our pupils tend to follow the prevailing patterns of the community.

Thus Fischer indicated that integration did not produce the physical contact that many feared. At the same time, he tacitly endorsed the liberal view that students succeeded by adhering to a "culture" that suppressed sexual impulses and channeled energy into academic work. And yet his preference for minimal government, which relied on "prevailing patterns of the community" to guide behavior, presented him with another dilemma. Whatever the realities of dancing and dating, fantasies about these things contributed to white parents' resistance to desegregation; a school administration that avoided discussions or workshops with parents about such matters threw away means by which it might have made desegregation more successful—in the extent of mixing or children's academic development. A liberal perspective that viewed all children as autonomous individuals could not address the ways race constrained many of them.[25]

On July 2, the school board announced the appointment of George Brain to succeed Fischer, effective January 1, 1960. He was superintendent in Bellevue, Washington, and his candidacy was suggested by the American Association of School Administrators and Teachers College, where he had taken his doctorate. When Baltimore hired him for twenty-five thousand dollars a year, the highest salary the city had ever paid a superintendent, *Time* magazine called him "the fastest-rising educator in the United States public school system." Coming from a nearly all-white rural and suburban school district with sixty thousand residents and twelve thousand students, Brain, just thirty-nine, was a subject of great curiosity. A *Sun* headline, "From Teacher to Superintendent In 14 Years," presented him as an educator on the move, and the article noted his "meteoric rise" and national reputation, but much of the story focused on his character, shaped by a Horatio Alger odyssey not unlike Fischer's. Growing up on a farm, he had "trudged" more than two miles to elementary and high school. He was active in 4-H and played high school basketball, baseball, and football. He had always wanted to be an educator. To pay for college, he worked nights for a towing company. One night on a call he gave a ride to a girl whom he began dating and married a year later. After Pearl Harbor, he joined the Navy, learned Japanese, and took part in invading Iwo Jima, where he was injured. When he finished his education after the war, he began teaching and became Bellevue's youngest superintendent in 1953.

Early articles gave hints about Brain's educational thinking. He was concerned about young persons' moral direction and recognized that the schools had assumed some responsibility for that as parents had lost their way, but he believed schools should concentrate on basic education. Families, churches, and other community institutions should resume their role in guiding youth. Although he had high hopes that social science could help by analyzing and solving community and urban problems, he did not seem to follow the progressive education philosophy that considered the community part of the curriculum.

As an incoming superintendent, Brain noted, he would be working with a staff that was already in place. He would be challenged to get to know a much larger district than he had worked with before. He confessed that the size of the system was "a little frightening." A *Sun* article concluded optimistically that Brain's practice of involving community members in schools would enable him to learn about Baltimore and guide him toward policies that fit the city's needs and culture. The *Afro* reported that the Seattle NAACP and Urban League had heard no complaints about Brain, and it quoted a favorable assessment of him by Bellevue's first black teacher: "He is really a brain. He is not the type person who is going to preach brotherhood but he's going to practice it." Brain seemed to hold the liberal views of individual responsibility and limited government that the city liked, and white and black alike looked forward to his arrival.[26]

PARENTS' PROTEST AGAINST CONTINUING SEGREGATION

A year after his arrival, in February 1961, George Brain spoke to a conference of the U.S. Commission on Civil Rights. His written statement reminded the commission that "the Baltimore public schools rejected the idea of deliberate mixing of the races" and summarized the results: "Changes in the composition of student bodies came as families changed their places of residence or as pupils applied for transfers for specific educational reasons.... There was no mass movement of children through transfer [in 1954] nor has there been any very great number of requests for transfer subsequently." Brain's testimony, however, was more specific. Some black parents, he explained, asked that their children be placed in schools in white neighborhoods because they were better than schools in black neighborhoods. And when the result was "a heavy Negro concentration," "parents of white children desire to have their children attend a school with more white classmates....white parents....will request a transfer to a new school plant more frequently than would the Negro family. The Negro family tends to remain in the neighborhood and the community." In other words, changes in school makeup did not necessarily reflect neighborhood changes, and while blacks chose schools because of their educational quality, many whites chose schools because of their racial composition.[1]

Criticism of Limited Desegregation

George Brain was managing a school system in a racially changing city. In 1950, the population had been the highest the census would record, 949,708.

Three-fourths of residents (723,655) were white, and one-fourth (225,053) were black. By 1960, the population was down slightly to 939,024, but blacks had increased by nearly half to 325,589. The city had lost more than 100,000 whites, who now numbered only 610,608. The demographic changes alone would expand black neighborhoods. In addition, blockbusting in the 1950s unsettled whites and panicked many in northeast and west Baltimore into leaving the city. Thus, as Brain conceded, whites used free choice to avoid desegregation at the same time that civil rights leaders and white liberals promoted open enrollment as a means to integration and new educational opportunities. These advocates were becoming disappointed with free choice.

A Black Administrator's Complaints

A few months after Brain spoke to the Civil Rights Commission, Houston Jackson, who had been assistant superintendent for a decade since succeeding Elmer Henderson, rendered a distinctly negative judgment on Baltimore desegregation in a *Southern School News* interview. He said the city had more segregated black schools than before *Brown,* because most historically black schools remained all black while many formerly white schools had become predominantly or entirely black and eleven new schools had been built in black neighborhoods. "That leaves more Negro children today in essentially segregated situations than we had when segregation was compulsory." Integration, he observed, had been "a one-way street" for students and teachers: blacks went to white schools, but whites did not move the other direction. Indeed, even among the fifty or so white pupils in once-black schools, most were children of shopkeepers who chose the schools simply because they were near the family store. Generally, as black enrollment at historically white schools grew, white students and teachers left: "When the Negroes in a school reach 50 percent, that's when the white teachers begin to ask for transfers. The white pupils have already begun to move out, and the teachers follow."

Black children, Jackson said, continued to suffer educationally. Many of them, particularly the poor, needed special academic attention. He mentioned "many pupils who are culturally deprived. On top of this, thousands of new children who are backward in education and culture because of limited schooling in the South are coming into the city to add to the school load. This applies to white Southern migrants as well as colored ones." Though Jackson spoke of "cultural deprivation," unlike Fischer, he saw black children's exceptional needs as an argument for integration. An important reason was that many of the city's historically black schools had been inferior to white schools and academically inadequate, and remained so. Douglass, Dunbar, and Carver high schools might be exceptions, he said, but black elementary schools were certainly problematic. Not only were facilities outmoded, rundown, and too small, but also many black teachers were not as good as many white teachers. In an assessment that provoked strong black reaction, he observed that Coppin was inferior to Towson and said that black teachers did not instruct students as well as white teachers. The better black college students, he said, were going to integrated institutions; those who became teachers would improve the schools. But, even though Coppin was getting better, it continued to turn out poor teachers. A third of its graduates failed the city teacher examination. For the time being, putting white teachers in black schools would raise standards.

Jackson believed that integration would help black students because they could learn from whites, but he saw that emotions engendered by segregation prevented many blacks from taking the benefits free choice offered. "When a pupil is set apart," he said, "he feels inferior. He is filled with race consciousness when he should be worried about his grades. That applies to Negro teachers as well." Hence more than two-thirds of black children stayed in historically black schools because segregation "has made them feel so inferior. They are afraid they can't meet the white standards, afraid they will lose their class positions and local prestige, afraid they will be left out." However, Jackson rejected directive alternatives to open enrollment, such as biracial zones. He thought that residential segregation limited possibilities of drawing biracial zones, and in any case, "forcing integration" would only push whites out. He believed that white resistance to integration was so strong that even improving the quality of schools would not attract or retain them and zoning could not hold enrollment stable in racially mixed schools. As a black educator, in contrast to the white superintendents he had served, he considered integration necessary for aiding black children academically, but he concluded that whites' and blacks' feelings about one another defeated realistic educational options.[2]

The *Afro* editorially agreed that many historically black schools were inferior to white and concurred that Coppin's program was inadequate. It insisted, however, that the purpose of desegregation was to create educational opportunities for black children, not to integrate schools. For this purpose, free choice remained the right policy, and Jackson should do whatever he could to aid black students wherever they went to school.[3]

Parents' Charges of Continuing Segregation

About this time, David and Billie Bramhall moved to Baltimore from Philadelphia. After getting a doctorate at the University of Pennsylvania, David was starting his academic career at Johns Hopkins University in fall 1961. They found a house in Kenilworth, in north central Baltimore, and they were happy to see a new school, Winston Elementary, across the street. Their street was all white, but over the summer they discovered black neighbors and were pleased to be living in an integrated neighborhood. They enrolled their two children at Winston. When Billie Bramhall took her children to school in September, she discovered that they were the only white students in their classes, even though the neighborhood was predominantly white. Her white neighbors had used free choice to enroll their children at all-white Northwood Elementary, two-thirds of a mile away, and the school system bused black children to Winston from overcrowded black schools. The Bramhalls were disappointed that their children would not be attending an integrated school. They kept the children at Winston and were pleased with the education, but they worried that school policies would lead white families to leave and destroy the neighborhood racial balance, and they wanted to prevent such a development.[4]

Billie Bramhall, who had been a community activist in Denver and had taken city planning courses at Penn, began investigating and seeking others who shared her concerns. She found Baltimore Neighborhoods, Inc. (BNI), an organization that promoted housing opportunity and integration, and met its new director, Ed Holmgren, who had recently arrived after a long career as a Chicago open housing activist. She joined a group trying to get the school system to change school boundaries and busing practices to make Winston racially similar to the neighborhood. In January 1962, she wrote Superintendent Brain that unless school officials worked with community organizations, integrated neighborhoods such as hers would lose white families, and schools could become increasingly black and segregated. She argued that the system's hands-off approach to desegregation let "ignorance, hysteria and fear" defeat student choice and the possibility of integration.[5]

Across town, another white mother was engaging in her own battle against the results of free choice. Dorothy Sykes had learned that, because Windsor Hills Elementary School was crowded, her daughter would have to attend part-time. She requested a transfer and was turned down by the principal. She protested to assistant superintendents and contacted the U.S. Civil Rights Commission and Office of Education. She, too, went to BNI, and Holmgren put her in touch with Bramhall. In August 1962, Sykes met with Brain and cited Windsor Hills and Winston as cases in a general complaint about shifts and the ways the administration of open enrollment, in fact, limited students' choices. Putting schools on shifts, she said, instead of dispersing students to other schools, generally limited instructional time and specifically contained black children in a few schools rather than sending them to predominantly white schools. She wanted to know why the city could not be zoned to reduce crowding. Brain denied that racial considerations had anything to do with putting schools on shifts and said that board policy did not allow zoning. She complained that system practices made it hard for parents to transfer children out of crowded schools. The administration published no list of schools with space, and when parents asked for transfers, principals often rejected requests that were not based on residence change. She noted that, when the system did bus students out of crowded schools, the choice of receiver schools produced "unnatural" majorities of black students in white neighborhoods such as Windsor Hills and Kenilworth "and hastened the exodus of white families."[6]

Sykes finally got her daughter into full-time schooling, but she helped Bramhall organize black and white parents against school system policies and practices that maintained segregation despite formally open enrollment. They called themselves the 28 Parents. Seeking legal help, they contacted Holmgren, who recommended Melvin Sykes (no relation to Dorothy), a BNI founder and board member. Pro bono, he agreed to help the group draft a report to the school board.[7]

Melvin Sykes had attended City College, the selective public liberal arts boys' high school, had graduated with honor from Johns Hopkins, and at Harvard Law had served on the Law Review before graduating magna cum laude in 1948. He clerked for Judge Morris A. Soper on the U.S. Fourth Circuit Court of Appeals and then went into practice with his father, who had been Chief Judge of Orphan's Court of Baltimore City. Rather than joining a large firm, he preferred developing a practice that suited his liberal convictions. From time to time, he served as reporter or consultant to state commissions. When Bramhall found him in 1962, he was a member of the Baltimore City Charter Review Commission. With regard to race and the schools, he disagreed with those who considered the schools segregated de facto. He had no doubt that segregation was de jure, a product of law and public policy.[8]

Indeed, in 1969, Melvin Sykes would draft the most ambitious suit ever formulated for integrating Baltimore schools. It would assert that most students were racially segregated and black schools were poorly funded because state and local policies had discriminated against blacks in education and housing and because officials had done little to eradicate past practices and their results. State and local governments had promoted metropolitan residential segregation by enacting planning and zoning practices that created suburban jurisdictions and allowed building by developers who discriminated, enforcing racially restrictive housing covenants until the 1948 Supreme Court ban, and licensing savings and loan institutions and realtors that discriminated. Then the state funded the predominantly black Baltimore schools that resulted from these practices at a lower level than other school districts, and the city administered "a dual school system based on race." These policies, the 1969 complaint would declare, violated the equal protection clause of the Fourteenth Amendment by giving black children inferior schools. The actions harmed black students by contributing to lower test scores, higher dropout rates, less job access, and higher unemployment than for whites. Further, white students were "deprive[d] of the equal protection of the laws by denying them the opportunity to receive a good education together with Negro children." White parents were "den[ied] the opportunity to send their children to quality integrated schools" and were "harm[ed] by…pressure…to move to certain areas of the Metropolitan area in order to obtain a quality public education for their children."[9]

The complaint would target all government agents responsible for school segregation, including not only the Baltimore school board, superintendent, mayor, city council, and fiscal officers and the Maryland board of education, school superintendent, and fiscal officers, but also the boards of education, superintendents, and treasurers of Baltimore and Anne Arundel counties, which took part in residential discrimination and operated largely white districts with students who were unavailable for integrating city schools. As relief, the suit would have asked the court to require jurisdictions to develop a metropolitan education plan to "remedy the inequalities and provide such administrative and other changes in the structure of the Metropolitan Area as are necessary to provide plaintiffs with equal protection and due process of the law." These views led Sykes to assist the 28 Parents in 1962.[10]

Parents Protest Continuing Segregation

George Brain endorsed the liberal open enrollment policy that emphasized a process of determining enrollments through individual choice and was indifferent to the resulting racial makeup of schools. The 28 Parents wanted desegregation policy to result in racially mixed schools, and they believed that school system policies and practices, in fact, maintained segregation by restricting students' choices. They advocated reforming the process of determining where students attended in order to change the outcome.

Seven Years of Desegregation in the Baltimore Public Schools

From late summer through the winter of 1962, Dorothy Sykes, Billie Bramhall, and Melvin Sykes prepared an analysis of the schools, titled *Seven Years of Desegregation in the Baltimore Public Schools: A Report*. In early March 1963, as they were finishing the document, school board vice president William McElroy, a Johns Hopkins biology professor, attended a meeting of the Council of Great City Schools in Chicago. Participants talked about desegregation in several cities, with particular attention to a recent suit against the San Francisco school board. McElroy, a liberal, returned home wondering whether Baltimore districting and transportation policies were promoting segregation and asked Brain to investigate. Brain agreed. Shortly after, on March 27, Melvin Sykes and Ed Holmgren, whose organization had endorsed the Parents' report, met with recently appointed school board president Eli Frank Jr., to present *Seven Years*.[11]

Frank had succeeded Sondheim in the board's Jewish seat in 1956 and was promoted to president in 1962. He was a fifth-generation Baltimorean, the son of Judge Eli Frank, who had served on Baltimore's Supreme Bench for twenty-two years. The senior Frank had been a Park School founder and the first chairman of its board. He also had served on the city school board. Eli Frank Jr., as Sondheim a few years after him, had grown up in Bolton Hill and attended Park. Following graduation, he preceded Melvin Sykes by a generation at Johns Hopkins and Harvard Law. From Harvard he returned to Baltimore and joined a prominent law firm of which his father was a founding partner. He followed his father on the Hopkins board. Politically, he was a liberal. He was sixty when he became school board president.[12]

The Parents' report described continuing school segregation. After seven years, the proportion of black students attending predominantly (at least 90 percent) black schools was down to 83 percent, but the number of blacks in these schools was up by one third. Only 31 of 146 elementary schools had "significant desegregation," at least 10 percent from each race. Secondary schools were somewhat better, but three-fourths of blacks still attended predominantly black schools, and their numbers had increased by one-fourth since 1954.[13]

Part of the explanation was the growing black student majority, but just as important, the Parents charged, were policies and practices that restricted student choices. The report attacked districting, restricting "overcrowded" schools to neighborhood children, as "inconsistent with the free choice policy." Moreover, as implemented, districting contained black students in a limited number of schools built for a smaller black population, while excluding them from historically white schools, even when they had room. Moreover, inconsistencies in districting suggested that these results were intentional. Not all schools that were so crowded as to require part-time instruction were districted, and not all districted schools were, or ever had been, on shifts, and the variations were associated with students' race. For example, of twenty elementary schools that continued on shifts without being districted, fifteen were predominantly black, and none were predominantly white. Of the nineteen predominantly black elementary schools that were districted, eighteen were on shifts, whereas of the thirteen predominantly white districted elementary schools, none was on shifts, and only one had ever been. While only 58 percent of elementary students were black, 90 percent of students on four-hour shifts instead of full five-hour days were black. Six of fourteen junior high schools were districted; all were in largely white neighborhoods and enrolled 55 percent of white city students. When the system bused students to relieve overcrowding, the Parents said, it moved students to schools with similar racial makeup. The cumulative effect of districting and transportation practices was to reinforce segregation and, because of the scarcity of space in predominantly black schools, keep black students on part-time schooling.[14]

In addition, the Parents reported, school officials built new schools in locations likely to draw students of a single race and thus maintain segregation. Enrollment grew by more than 40 percent during the 1950s, from 120,000 to 170,000. Decisions about new school locations, given parents' preferences for nearby schools, influenced the racial makeup of schools. Baltimore officials selected sites in racially homogenous areas. Of twenty-nine schools opened between 1955 and 1961, twelve were predominantly white, and twelve were predominantly black; only five could be considered integrated. The board thus limited opportunities for black and white children to attend school together.[15]

Finally, the Parents charged, administration of the transfer policy at the heart of free choice was biased to encourage white choices and limit black choices. Some principals recruited white parents or urged whites to transfer out if many blacks came in. Some principals discouraged black parents from requesting transfers to predominantly white schools or turned down black requests to transfer in. The principal of Roland Park Elementary, in an elite white neighborhood, put students requesting transfers on a waiting list, admitting them at her discretion. Sticking to the letter of policy, some principals insisted that black transfer requests involve no racial considerations and that they concern only "educational" issues. Some rejected requests to transfer to white schools on the ground that the travel distance would harm a child educationally.[16]

> Cumulatively, these practices had the effects of bottling up part-time [black] enrollments in overcrowded schools adjacent to districted [white] schools, of stabilizing racially changing enrollments (often with the result of hastening the segregation of another school), of creating all-white enrollments by the exclusion from school districts of blocks with Negro populations, and of establishing "exclusive" schools, particularly in schools with above average educational attainment.

Two years earlier, the U.S. Civil Rights Commission had observed, similarly, that Baltimore had "had a marked increase in the Negro population, but only a slight increase in the percentage of Negroes attending schools with whites."[17]

The Parents proposed ending districts and replacing free choice with school attendance zones that, as far as possible, included at least 10 percent of each race and would be redrawn as necessary to maintain racial balance. They wanted transportation provided to increase racial balance, part-time instruction eliminated, and school staffs balanced by race and experience, with special training and status for inner-city teachers. Frank said the board would study the report and asked McElroy to chair a committee.[18]

A New NAACP Initiative

Around the time the 28 Parents began drafting their report, in July 1962, the NAACP held its annual convention in Atlanta. Delegates passed resolutions urging stepped-up litigation and direct action to force school desegregation. Two weeks later, the Maryland State Conference of NAACP branches met in emergency session in Baltimore. Juanita Mitchell asked NAACP executive secretary Roy Wilkins to send June Shagaloff, the organization's chief education expert.[19]

Shagaloff had started out working with Thurgood Marshall in the NAACP legal department in 1950. Marshall believed the success of litigation depended on families' understanding court rulings, demanding integration, and sending their children to integrated schools, and he hired Shagaloff to do community organizing. Everywhere she talked with black parents, she found courageous people who struggled with segregation and wanted good education for their children. The white New Yorker got her baptism by fire in 1952, when Marshall sent her to Cairo, Illinois, to help the NAACP branch end school segregation. While she was there, an NAACP member's home was bombed, and she and several local NAACP officials were arrested for conspiring to "endanger the health and life of certain children." Marshall flew to Cairo and got her out of jail. Her organizing eventually helped desegregate schools in several southern Illinois towns.[20]

Meanwhile, the Supreme Court was considering the school segregation cases. In June 1953, a divided court, unable to reach a decision, asked the parties to address five questions in preparation for fall reargument. Some concerned how the legislators who drafted and ratified the Fourteenth Amendment thought about segregated schools. Some concerned whether a desegregation decision should require immediate or allow gradual compliance. Marshall recruited academics for his research. Shagaloff aided historian John Hope Franklin by reading the congressional hearings on the Fourteenth Amendment to discern intent regarding schools. She also collaborated with psychologist Kenneth Clark in examining experiences desegregating various institutions. They found no evidence that gradualism offered advantages over quick action, in terms of either the effectiveness of desegregation or the avoidance of resistance. If anything, extended time let the disgruntled organize. Crucially, they found, prejudiced whites would change their behavior to comply with desegregation if officials unequivocally asserted policies. They found evidence that larger-scale desegregation was more likely than smaller initiatives to get acceptance and avoid overt resistance. Clark concluded, *"There is evidence to suggest that there can be effective desegregation of elementary schools in the southern states."*[21]

When Shagaloff came to Maryland in 1963, she was in her second year as Wilkins's special assistant for education. Her charge was to implement a 1961 NAACP convention resolution demanding "the end of all segregated public education in fact or by law by all means available" in the North as well as the South. She traveled extensively to help Northern branches investigate conditions, negotiate with school boards, prepare integration plans, organize demonstrations, and if necessary, take legal action. On her arrival in Baltimore she pronounced Maryland segregation "appalling," and Mitchell announced an initiative to document and challenge county practices. Pointedly, the NAACP was looking at Baltimore schools, in light of "evidence suggesting that administrative policies in the city were serving in some instances to foster all-white or all-Negro schools." Bramhall learned of NAACP interest in city schools and contacted the branch for support.[22]

The Superintendent's Response

On May 22 Brain responded to McElroy's request to report on desegregation with a 157-page critique of the Parents' 44-page report. The superintendent began by affirming the liberal premises of the 1954 school board, giving priority to individual rights to choose a school over integration as an outcome. He defined segregation as legal restriction on children's enrollment because of their race, and he considered schools desegregated once this constraint was removed. Invoking John Fischer's language with the Civil Rights Commission, Brain rejected zoning to mix races as "repugnant...social engineering." He would not use school zoning as a palliative to housing segregation because he did not believe "two wrongs make a right." As for the Parents' request to manage enrollment in integrated neighborhoods to keep it consistent with residential composition and stabilize the neighborhoods, he argued that such actions "would violate the right of the individual."

Nevertheless, Brain defended an exception to his position that government should not restrict individual freedom: districting overcrowded schools. He cited board rules authorizing the superintendent to create districts when a school was even "likely to be crowded." He listed conditions under which schools were "usually threatened with overcrowding." The first was when "the neighborhood in which the school is located is in the process of changing from a white to a Negro residential area." Thus the superintendent might district schools to defend white children from a black influx.

However, Brain rejected government action to secure integration, not only because intervention was improper, but also because there was no standard for "appropriate racial balance for a given school," and hence "fixed racial quotas" were "impracticable." Courts had ruled, he contended, that "a free, private choice of segregation does not violate the Constitution." Under this view of segregation and the role of government, Brain concluded, "An undistricted school with a pupil enrollment of only one race must be considered a desegregated school, since any child wishing to attend may do so." "It does not necessarily follow that because there are schools which today enroll 100% Negroes, that there is 'continuing segregation' in the Baltimore City Public Schools." Because racially homogeneous schools resulted from individual preferences and choices, it would be wrong, and unnecessary, to zone schools or bus students to mix the races.[23]

Presentations to the School Board

After McElroy's committee received Brain's report, they prepared findings and recommendations. The board met on June 6 to receive the committee's report and, at the Parents' request, to hear their case. Television stations sent camera crews. Many of the hundred citizens present had to stand against conference room walls or outside in the hallway. Melvin Sykes spoke for the 28 Parents. The group had updated their report, now *Eight Years of Desegregation in the Baltimore Public Schools: Fact and Law,* with additional evidence of how system practices segregated students. Centrally, the report argued that school policies inherently influenced race relations and that, therefore, the board should act to integrate, rather than segregate.[24]

Sykes began by describing school segregation. Three-fourths of white elementary students and one-half of white secondary students were in predominantly white schools, and 45 percent of white elementary students were in all-white schools. More than three-fourths of all black students were in predominantly black schools, and 42 percent of black elementary students were in all-black schools. Sykes attacked Brain's indifference to the racial makeup of schools by reminding school officials that the Supreme Court had declared separate schools inherently unequal. Moreover, he emphasized, school policies had contributed to segregation and were thus "unconstitutionally depriving large segments of the student population of Baltimore of equal educational opportunity and the equal protection of the law." The school board, he stressed, had no choice about ending segregation. Sykes found "most disturbing" Brain's contention that the system lacked authority to end segregation because it could make no decisions based on race, when, in fact, its policies continued to discriminate among students on the basis of race.[25]

As remedy, Sykes presented new recommendations that were more sweeping but less specific than earlier. The Parents now asked the board to "recognize and rectify" discriminatory policies and practices and to declare "the educational undesirability" of racial homogeneity in schools, regardless of the cause. The Parents no longer advocated racial zoning, because some thought extensive residential segregation made mixed zones hard to draw and because some worried that zoning would drive whites out. Instead, the Parents simply asked the board to "encourage policies and programs" that would "achieve actual integration of pupils and staff in schools throughout the city."[26]

McElroy followed Sykes with his committee's report. He said the group had found no evidence that system practices had even unwittingly contributed to segregation. Insofar as schools were predominantly one race, housing patterns were to blame. Using some of Brain's text, the committee articulated the board's liberal premises. Emphasizing "free choice," it refused to consider racial mixing as a goal or take race into account in correcting for past discrimination. It rejected the Parents' earlier recommendation of biracial zones because they would "violate the rights of the individual." If schools with high proportions of low-income black students had academic problems, the proper remedy was not forcing integration on whites, but giving blacks compensatory programs. Finally, while reaffirming free choice, the committee urged action to free up choices. It recommended eliminating all districts as of October 31 and reducing overcrowding in other ways. It proposed removing authority over transfers from principals to an assistant superintendent and approving requests for reasons other than residential change on a first-come-first-served basis up to limits of normal class size and school capacity. The committee urged ethnic, cultural, religious, and educational (though it did not specify racial) diversity among school staffs. It recommended eliminating part-time schooling as soon as space could be provided through temporary facilities and other means. The board unanimously adopted the report and its recommendations.[27]

Next, Juanita Mitchell addressed the board for the NAACP, which had prepared testimony independently of the Parents. She endorsed the Parents' findings and then attacked the board for maintaining segregation, in violation of the Constitution and to the psychological detriment of blacks and whites. She demanded "immediate action" to eliminate racially homogeneous schools. She criticized the new board policies for lacking specifics and not addressing "the basic problem...what can be done to reduce racial segregation...to an absolute minimum." Hence the policies were "totally unacceptable."[28]

When she finished, Mitchell introduced Shagaloff, who attacked the board. "De-Segregation," she declared, "never took place to begin with" in Baltimore. Board policy was just "token de-segregation." She lamented "extensive" school segregation and compared Baltimore to Birmingham and Mississippi. She told the board not to use housing segregation as an excuse for school segregation. In agreement with the Parents, she wanted the board to act for "full integration." Unlike the Parents, she was making not recommendations, but "demands." Shagaloff wanted "a policy recognizing the educational undesirability of public school segregation in fact, and unequivocally committing the board to achieving maximum desegregation," an end to discriminatory practices, and "a long range city-wide plan" to integrate schools. The NAACP wanted higher educational standards in "deprived neighborhoods" and staff desegregation. If the board did not comply by September 1, Shagaloff warned, it could expect picketing, sit-ins, demonstrations, and a lawsuit.[29]

Frank thanked the speakers but was upset by charges that policies harmed black children. "We may have been fooling ourselves," he said. "We always thought all our policies were non-discriminatory." He said the board and staff would give the reports and presentations careful consideration, but he could not promise the board would comply with all requests or could respond fully by September 1. Shagaloff asked for a considerable start.[30]

Carl Murphy signed a front-page *Afro* editorial endorsing the criticism of school policies and continuing segregation. The *Sun* acknowledged disparities between predominantly white and black schools and supported ending any policies that kept black children from changing schools. At the same time, it blamed segregation on the housing market, for which, it said, the school system could not compensate. Within that constraint, the board should increase black children's opportunities but should not impose "compulsory integration."[31]

Ironically, in her testimony Shagaloff invoked former superintendent John Fischer against Brain and the board. Fischer, now Columbia University Teachers College president, after trying to help several New York communities integrate, had abandoned the views that shaped Baltimore policy. Reached by a reporter after the board meeting, he explained, "I once thought that simply letting things happen naturally was all that's necessary in this field.... But I now think it's necessary in some places to take special steps to achieve integration." Though once he had expressed indifference to school racial composition and excoriated "social engineering," now he believed "we have to use every opportunity we can to create schools that will contain within them a cross section of the entire school population." The methods would vary from place to place, and he was hesitant about busing, but if students were transported to relieve overcrowding, they should be relocated in ways that also integrated schools.[32]

Negotiations, Meetings, Protests, and New Policy

The Parents considered the board action just a "first step" and wanted more. Melvin Sykes, who had a relationship with Eli Frank from professional and community activities, would negotiate with the board president. Days after the board meeting, Brain announced he would convene a national conference of urban school officials and civil rights organizations to analyze integration issues and identify strategies to address them. He noted that a number of cities had been proceeding as if they were doing enough, only to run into activist criticism. On June 19, the board approved the purchase of a hundred portable classrooms and additional buses to reduce part-time schooling. After that vote, the two black board members complained about "tokenism" in desegregating schools and hiring black administrators. White and black members traded charges and shouted at one another. The superintendent missed the fracas because he was at President Kennedy's White House conference on school integration.[33]

Integration, Education, and Race

Board member William Stone, who also missed that meeting and could not attend the next, wrote Frank expressing consternation about so much talk of race. "I am concerned," the University of Maryland Medical School dean said,

> that the School Board has allowed its program to become almost exclusively involved with problems of race during the last three months....very little time has been available to consider the educational needs of the students....We have had endless discussions on mixing of students without considering the educational needs of the individual....I know of no evidence that would indicate the educational progress of the individual can be improved by mixing of students in classrooms without regard to their ability or rates of progress in education.

Stone's letter, in which he opposed "race" to "education," framed issues central to school boards. *Brown* was a civil rights suit, focused on equalizing blacks' access to public schooling. It was tied to education through the assumptions that many white schools closed to blacks were better than many black schools and that black students' opportunities to exchange views with whites were essential to their education. In addition, the court endorsed a psychological link pushed by NAACP lawyers, formulated by the Topeka case appellate court and quoted in *Brown,* that state-sanctioned segregation produced in blacks a "sense of inferiority [that] affects the motivation of a child to learn. Segregation with the sanction of law...has a tendency to [retard] the educational and mental development of negro children and to deprive them of some of the benefits they would receive in a racial[ly] integrated school system." For all these reasons, the court considered separate black schools educationally unequal to integrated schools.[34]

Stone's position could be understood in several ways. One was to reject the importance of civil rights, or at least assert their subordination to some kind of educational rights. In this formulation, all children had legitimate claims on the state for a good education, but the social conditions under which they attended school—for example, classroom racial composition—did not matter so long as they learned. This position, denying that segregation affected black children psychologically or educationally, could accept separate schools if they were somehow pedagogically equal. Alternatively, Stone might be willing to endorse integration if evidence showed that racial mixing contributed to learning. It would be another year before Johns Hopkins sociologist James Coleman would begin the Equality of Educational Opportunity Study called for in the 1964 Civil Rights Act, but he would amass evidence that black children's cognitive outcomes were strongly associated with classmates' socioeconomic status. Low-income black children in classes with middle-income white children did considerably better than poor black children segregated with others like themselves, while the white children suffered no educational harm. These findings would be published in 1966, though Billie Bramhall, whose husband taught with Coleman, and others locally would hear the results earlier. Finally, however, Stone's position could be understood more simply. He spoke in the tradition of Baltimoreans who wanted to keep the peace by avoiding talk of race. In opposing "race" to "the individual," he insisted on the liberal view that students were just unencumbered persons, whose preferences and abilities had nothing to do with racial conditions.[35]

In mid-July, while Sykes and Frank talked, Mitchell announced that the NAACP would look into the details of the district plan to bus 4,700 children to 134 vacant classrooms and 70 new portable classrooms. The branch would investigate complaints that plans to reduce part-time schooling would maintain segregation. Shagaloff would assist when she finished advising the Boston NAACP on strategies for desegregating that city's schools. Meanwhile, Brain announced that the Ford Foundation had funded an August 5–7 Conference on Practical Problems of Public School Desegregation. Participants would include eight big-city superintendents, three state superintendents, representatives from the NAACP, Urban League, and Congress of Racial Equality (CORE), and

federal staff from the Department of Health, Education, and Welfare; Justice Department Civil Rights Division; Housing and Home Finance Agency; and Civil
Rights Commission.[36]

The board met on July 31 to review plans for eliminating part-time schooling. Mitchell and Shagaloff had discussed busing proposals with the board the
day before. After three hours of often heated argument, they declared the plans
"unsatisfactory" because they would keep black children segregated. Now, while
the board met, Mitchell and Shagaloff joined forty picketers outside singing civil
rights songs. Shagaloff threatened picketing of board members' homes, sit-ins at
white schools with empty classrooms, and demands for removing administrators
implementing discriminatory practices. The *Afro* stated, "The demonstrations
marked the first time in history the local school board had been picketed for any
reason" and proudly published demonstrators' names and pictures.[37]

The Superintendents Conference on
Public School Desegregation

On the evening of August 4, Brain previewed the next day's conference for
the press. After his earlier emphasis on individual choice and denunciation of
"social engineering," he surprised reporters by declaring that de facto segregation
harmed students and that he would propose remedies. Essentially endorsing the
28 Parents' view while his board had not, he emphasized that his position was
"personal."[38]

About forty people gathered at the Sheraton-Baltimore Inn near the Johns
Hopkins Hospital in east Baltimore the next morning for three days of talk
that would be candid, sophisticated, and prescient. Participants recognized that
school segregation was linked to a web of national political, social, and economic
institutions, including housing policy and the housing market, employment
policy and the labor market, and race relations generally. They noted that the
residential segregation that complicated school desegregation resulted not just
from personal prejudices or private locational decisions, but also from public
housing, urban renewal, and racially discriminatory mortgage insurance policies that concentrated black families in city neighborhoods. The superintendents
recognized that the Supreme Court had not conclusively ruled on de facto segregation, but they agreed that "the school board that places geographic zoning
on top of racially restricted areas is, in a sense, compounding a wrong created by
another arm of the government."[39]

The educators asked civil rights organizations what they thought. The
Urban League, which focused on employment and job discrimination, and
CORE, which was engaged in wide-ranging direct action to desegregate public

accommodations, had the least involvement in education. Both urged integration but recognized that city school boards lacked control over suburban schools or students. CORE rejected "neighborhood schools" in residentially segregated cities as inevitably segregated and urged "qualitative integration"—not just mixing black and white students, but ensuring that they have first-rate educational programs. The Urban League seemed to concede that full integration was unlikely and urged "a massive Marshall Plan" to make "slum schools...just as good if not better than the suburban schools."[40]

June Shagaloff, speaking for the NAACP, reiterated the organization position that segregation, whatever its causes, harmed students and that school officials had to do whatever they could to end it. She acknowledged the difficulty of integrating large school systems but insisted on the "maximum desegregation" possible. She expressed NAACP opposition to giving black students in inner-city schools "compensatory" programs as a substitute for integration. Educators had to expect more of black children and do more to teach them while administrators did as much as they could to desegregate. Shagaloff turned to desegregation methods. In 1961, the NAACP had urged open enrollment on big cities, but Shagaloff now held it the least desirable desegregation strategy because the least likely to desegregate. The NAACP was most concerned about Southern districts that used open enrollment to sustain segregation but was also souring on the policy in places, such as Baltimore, that adopted it in good faith. The NAACP regarded it as only a last resort when extreme housing segregation made other methods ineffective. Shagaloff recommended that schools be zoned to include black and white students. As one way of doing this, the NAACP urged adopting the Princeton Plan. Named for the city where it was devised, it paired adjacent schools (one historically black and one historically white) into single attendance zones. Children might attend grades 1 through 3 in one building and 4 through 6 in the other. The NAACP was also interested in creating educational parks, where elementary and secondary schools would be located together on a site drawing white and black students from a large geographic area. Whatever strategies were adopted, the NAACP urged closing all-black schools, which, besides being segregated, were often run down. This action would make desegregation logistically easier and perhaps more acceptable to white families. Shagaloff said that the NAACP recognized that different methods worked in different places and that these changes would take time. It simply insisted that school officials commit themselves to the effort, and she offered assistance.[41]

The superintendents agreed that "schools should assume responsibility for combating de facto segregation and should proceed to bring about a racial balance in as many schools and classrooms as possible within the framework of local conditions." In this effort, they recognized a "need to examine the issues on a metropolitan basis rather than on a community or city basis." In moving forth, they would reassess the neighborhood school concept, think about biracial zoning, and consider merging districts for purposes of integration.[42]

At the end, Brain held another news conference, in which he repeated his new opposition to de facto segregation. He attributed much to housing patterns but said the school system should do what it could to end segregation. He characterized civil rights organizations' position as "realistic demands and requests." In discussing desegregation methods, he was particularly taken by the notion of constructing an educational park at the beltway between the city and suburbs. Though it would be legally and politically complicated, he thought desegregating city schools might require giving up neighborhood schools and taking a metropolitan approach. In closing, he espoused a broad view of schools that embraced the "social engineering" he had recently attacked. He urged superintendents to think of the school "first as an educational institution, and second, as an institution for ameliorating social conditions that have been created in part if not in whole by other institutions in society." Shagaloff issued a statement that the NAACP would continue its campaign to end de facto segregation wherever it existed, whatever its causes, and put the superintendents on notice: unless they made commitments and set timetables, the NAACP would go to court.[43]

Considering a New Board Policy

Following the Superintendents Conference, Brain considered possible new policies, and Sykes continued talking with Frank. Frank assessed what would be acceptable to conservative board members Stone and Maree Farring. Farring, on the board just a year, held its "community" seat. An activist in Brooklyn, at the southern tip of the city, she spoke for concerns of white working-class constituents. A grandmother, she said, "My family comes first, then my community, my state and my country, right or wrong." She was president of a garden club, a Sunday school teacher, and a former Girl Scout leader, and she managed her husband's insurance business.[44]

Shagaloff and Mitchell weighed the next NAACP moves, but most in the civil rights community were swept up in preparations for the March on Washington three weeks later. The August 28 march would take place around the time City Solicitor Joseph Allen was supposed to render an opinion on the school board's legal obligations regarding 28 Parents and NAACP demands and de facto segregation. The excitement of the Washington event encouraged local activists to see their school battle as part of a national civil rights struggle.

Allen delivered his opinion to Frank on August 29, with two messages. On the one hand, the legal minimum, underlined in his thirty-two-page letter, was simple: "Discrimination is forbidden, but integration is not compelled." The board's June 6 policy generally satisfied that principle, though Allen identified ways the policy might be implemented that could raise legal questions. However, he went on, "There is…a wide uncharted area between what is constitutionally mandated or prohibited and what is constitutionally permissible." A "broader view…a comparative newcomer to the mainstream of the law…imposes an affirmative obligation upon the school system to take active steps to mitigate the effects of adventitious segregation and the educational inadequacy deemed to accompany such a condition." Allen noted sociological arguments about the educational value of diversity and concluded, "There seems to be reason to believe…that affirmative policies encouraging integration will be held to be constitutional, even though failure to adopt such policies…will not be unconstitutional." In the end, he said, the board had to make its own judgment.[45]

The board met to respond to the 28 Parents and the NAACP on September 5. Schools had opened that morning with part-time enrollment down to about 7,500. Nearly 3,000 students, 90 per cent of them black, were bused among 43 schools to get full-day schooling. When 146 black children from Fort Worthington Elementary arrived at nearly all-white Montebello Elementary in northeast Baltimore, they delightedly learned that the school had a library from which they could take books home. In contrast, less than three miles north, when 96 from Fort Worthington arrived at Hamilton Elementary, which had 1,176 white students the previous year, 100 parents protested the blacks' presence and their assignment to classes with white children. A big, angry group of Hamilton parents and neighbors pushed their way into the school board's conference room for its meeting that afternoon. Frank, confronting a raucous crowd, decided to hold audience hearings before considering a new policy. For nearly an hour and a half he tried to maintain order with repeated use of his gavel, at one point threatening to adjourn. The speakers, sometimes interrupted by audience members for not protesting strongly enough, mostly argued against bringing black children to Hamilton. One parent complained about "forced integration." Some audience members privately shared racial epithets in expressing dislike for black children. Brain defended busing as necessary for reducing part-time schooling. Board member John Sweeney pointed out to a speaker that 87 percent of students who had been on shifts, 13,000 students, were black and challenged him to say that part-time schooling was as good as full-time.[46]

Eventually Frank ended the discussion and turned to the new draft policy. The 28 Parents had backed away from biracial school zones and asked the system simply to encourage policies extending integration. School officials, who supported free choice, embraced changes increasing choices along with a general commitment to ending educational inequalities. Under the new policy, all districts would end as of September 30, a month earlier than previously planned, though "the neighborhood school concept," left undefined, would be preserved. Transfer requests for reasons besides residence change, such as interest in desegregated schools, would be routinely approved in the order received until school capacities were reached. Families would continue to be responsible for transportation costs associated with transfers.

The policy statement introduced unprecedented language prescribing an active role for the school system in ending segregation—"not merely to eliminate the educational problems inherent in racial imbalances, but more significantly to counteract the discriminatory aspects of the practical problems that result from the countless practices of modern urban living." To begin, the board would "recognize and work toward the maximum resolution of...inequities that may result from racial imbalances in certain schools." It would adopt "intergroup understanding as an important school objective." Beyond that, in language adopted at McElroy's urging over Stone and Farring's objections, "Insofar as racially imbalanced schools may lead to educational, psychological, and sociological problems, the Board will do all it possibly can to remedy this situation." In the end, however, the board reaffirmed that "no child shall be required to attend any particular school." And, while the board asserted the desirability of racially and otherwise diverse staffs, it reaffirmed existing policy of assigning staff solely on merit. Two hours after convening, by a vote of 6 to 2, the board adopted a policy that contained new language but stuck with liberal principles and free choice.[47]

Theodore McKeldin, who had become mayor in 1963, expressed confidence that the "fine, religious" people in Hamilton would accept black children in their school, and he praised blacks and whites for cooperating in moving toward equal rights. He vowed to maintain order in the schools but said he doubted extraordinary police action would be necessary. The *Sun* editorialized in favor of transporting students, reminding readers that the aim was to reduce overcrowding and part-time schooling, not to mix the races. The board, it said with regard to the new policy, had no intention of "integrating merely for the sake of integration." The 28 Parents, with whom Frank had shared the draft policy earlier, approved it. They were uncertain whether it would desegregate schools, but they believed the new busing would significantly reduce part-time schooling. In any case, though *Eight Years* was written like a legal brief, the group lacked the resources to go to court, and it was unclear what more any court would require of the board. Mitchell cautiously endorsed the policy as a "first step" leaving "much yet to be done," but the national NAACP ebulliently announced, "The NAACP scored a major breakthrough this week in its far-flung campaign to end de facto segregation." Reading the policy differently than the *Sun* and the

Parents, they saw in it not just the ending of shifts, removal of discrimination in transfers, and elimination of districts, but also a commitment to integrate schools.[48]

The School System Evaluates Itself

In March 1964, Superintendent Brain gave the board a progress report on implementation of the new policy. In the interim, he had said nothing more about educational parks, the Princeton Plan, or any of the other desegregation approaches that excited him in August. Now he simply looked at the effects of abolishing districts, easing transfers, and transporting students, suggesting they would be the system's main actions for providing "equality of educational opportunity." He invoked "moral commitments and democratic beliefs" in identifying "racial imbalance" as a problem but then called attention to constraints on what the schools could do. He observed that poverty limited children's ability to learn and that housing segregation limited the ability of the system to balance students racially. He rejected busing as a remedy for residential segregation, contending it "would eventually result in educational chaos."[49]

Brain measured the policy against modest standards. In a district that was 58 percent black, he defined "integration" as the presence of at least 5 percent from each race. A 95 percent black school would be considered racially balanced. He announced that the proportion of students in integrated schools had risen under the policy from 34 to 41 percent. Still, only 25 percent of black students were in such schools. The 28 Parents and other civil rights groups used a 10 percent standard as the threshold for "integration." By that measure, only 17 percent of black elementary students and 33 percent of black secondary students were in integrated schools. However, by either standard, nearly half the schools were still predominantly (90 or 95 percent) black, and only about one-third were racially balanced. The dissimilarity index had declined insignificantly from 0.82 to 0.81.[50]

With regard to part-time schooling, Brain reported significant progress: from September to January, students on shifts went down from 7,731 (8 percent of students) to 4,466 (5 percent). Moreover, busing, while intended only to reduce overcrowding, contributed to racial balance, though the numbers were more ambiguous than Brain stated. While the number of black children transported from overcrowded schools increased from 2,464 to 3,325, the proportion taken to schools considered balanced by the 5 percent standard declined from 88 percent to 71 percent.[51]

To accommodate growing enrollments, the system had opened six new buildings since the preceding July, but the report said nothing about the racial makeup of the neighborhoods around the schools, the 28 Parents' concern. Brain said location did not matter under open enrollment. He summarized transfer requests, reporting that 421 of 714 requests for reasons other than residential change came from black students, many presumably choosing schools with white students. Seventy-eight percent of black requests and 65 percent of white requests were granted. The rest were turned down because of class size limitations; applicants would be notified when room was available. Brain acknowledged that transfers could produce single-race schools and pledged to monitor changes.[52]

A comparison of predominantly white and black elementary schools showed mixed differences. Predominantly black schools had a higher proportion of teachers considered qualified by virtue of having tenure—80 percent, compared to 63 percent. However, predominantly white schools were significantly more likely to have gyms, libraries, and cafeterias and somewhat more likely to have auditoriums. The schools had the same number of students per classroom teacher—35.5—but white schools had a higher proportion of other teachers. At the same time, the system offered many instructional, guidance, and community programs for assisting "culturally disadvantaged children" in "deprived communities," presumably mostly black.[53]

Brain reported limited progress in integrating teachers. Nine years after *Brown*, a majority of 194 schools still had single-race faculties: 33 percent all black, 19 percent all white, and 48 percent mixed. An unstated constraint on staff integration was the administration's unwillingness to oppose teacher organizations and assign teachers against their wishes. Although black teachers were willing to teach in predominantly white faculties, Brain reported, few white teachers wanted to teach in predominantly black faculties. An "appreciable" number of black teachers requested transfers from all-black to mixed faculties, while white teachers sought to leave schools when staff mix reached 50–50. Black faculty movement desegregated historically white schools, while white movement helped make those staffs predominantly black.[54]

The system was hiring more black educators, but whites still dominated administration. Over the past decade, 70 percent of educators hired were black, moving them from 33 percent of educational staff in 1953 to 45 percent in 1963. However, while 46 percent of teachers in schools were black, only 30 percent of central administrators were black. One reason was low administrative turnover in an historically segregated system. Another was that the system was more likely to hire blacks as teachers than as administrators. A further reason was the lower proportion of blacks promoted generally and in the central office in particular.[55]

Brain portrayed conditions as showing that the new policy was successful. However, some details were ambiguous, and the future was uncertain. Changes under the new policy had moved toward racial balance, but it was unclear how the policy would further affect the makeup of schools. It was unreasonable to expect the policy to effect profound changes in an historically segregated system in a few months, but it was uncertain how much the continuation of a laissez-faire policy could accomplish, when for a decade it had let white impulses toward segregation proceed without moral or political challenge. Despite the invocations of morality, democracy, and racial balance, Brain made clear that policymakers would only react to others' choices, not try to influence or constrain them.

A Decade after *Brown*

In spring 1954, except for a few black boys at Baltimore Polytechnic Institute, city schools were segregated. In spring 1964, 59 of 192 schools had at least 10 percent from each race. The change was significant, particularly when measured against massive Southern resistance to integration. Still, 89 schools were at least 90 percent black. The number of all- or nearly all-black schools had increased by 30 since 1954. Five in six black elementary students attended schools at least 90 percent black, as did two in three black secondary students. Secondary schools, because they drew students from larger areas, were more likely to be mixed, but enrollments closely followed residential patterns. Inside racially mixed schools, tracking shunted black and white students into separate programs. After a decade of legal desegregation, most children attended class with majorities of their own race.[56]

The pattern of moderate desegregation and growing resegregation had three general causes. Overall, the racial makeup of the city and the schools was changing, starting with wartime black migration to Baltimore for jobs and postwar white movement to the suburbs under the GI Bill and FHA mortgages. In addition, anxiety about black neighbors or classmates increased white movement out of city public schools and out of the city altogether. Finally, it was open enrollment itself that allowed white parents to take their children out of schools when black parents put their children in. Over the decade since *Brown,* "desegregation" in Baltimore had become associated with free choice and its consequences— black movement into historically white schools, white freedom to leave, and many segregated schools.

Free choice had produced paradoxical results. One of its virtues for the 1954 school board was that it seemed unlikely to scare whites out of city schools, and yet, even if open enrollment was only one reason, whites were leaving the schools. Civil rights activists increasingly were pointing to the failure of free choice to desegregate. And yet they might also have been puzzled that whites were leaving city schools despite the fact that most white children encountered few black classmates.

GROWING INTEGRATIONISM AND THE MURDER OF MARTIN LUTHER KING JR.

In the two months before the 28 Parents made their case to the school board, Martin Luther King Jr. was jailed in Birmingham, and Bull Connor turned hoses and dogs on young demonstrators. A week before the school board adopted a new policy in September, a quarter of a million black and white Americans joined in the March on Washington. Ten days after the board revised its policy, four black girls were killed in a Birmingham church bombing. Television recorded these events and brought civil rights to public consciousness. President Johnson built on national inspiration by civil rights activists, outrage over Southern violence, and mourning for President Kennedy to secure passage of the Civil Rights Act of 1964, which he signed three months after George Brain's progress report. Challenged and carried along by the civil rights movement, Baltimore school officials and parents alike increasingly viewed policies and programs in terms of their impact on the racial makeup of schools and the quality of black and white children's education. As more Baltimoreans questioned open enrollment, the school board considered new integrationist initiatives.

The Civil Rights Act of 1964

The 1964 Civil Rights Act created a federal interest in school desegregation as part of a broad initiative on voting, public accommodations, public facilities, employment, and education. Title VI authorized federal intervention into local schooling and other activities that received federal funds if they discriminated in using the money. Title IV, which covered education, defined school systems' obligations negatively. "Desegregation" meant only the removal of racial barriers, "the assignment of students to public schools and within such schools without regard to their race, color, religion, or national origin." It did not entail the affirmative action associated with "integration": "'desegregation' shall not mean the assignment of students to public schools in order to overcome racial imbalance." Title VI provided that a school district or other local entity suspected of discriminating would be notified of federal concerns and given the opportunity voluntarily to comply with nondiscrimination requirements. If voluntary compliance could not be negotiated, Title VI set out a process for terminating federal funds, including a hearing and possible judicial review. Any such termination would be limited to "the particular program, or part thereof, in which such noncompliance has been found."[1]

When passed, the act did not much disturb Southern school boards, because the federal government gave out little education money. Conditions changed the next year, when Congress passed the Elementary and Secondary Education Act, making Washington a considerable revenue source. The Office of Education (OE) in the U.S. Department of Health, Education, and Welfare (HEW) disbursed federal education money. When John Gardner became HEW Secretary in 1965, he created a central Office for Civil Rights (OCR) to enforce Title VI for all HEW programs. The structure incorporated three antagonisms into Title VI enforcement in education. First, the federal government would intervene in schooling, traditionally considered a local responsibility. Second, federal and local educators, who thought first about teaching and learning, would be challenged by civil rights advocates who focused on access to schools. Third, nearly everyone would be shunted aside by lawyers, who were responsible for interpreting the law. There was no clear role in all this for children, parents, or teachers. The devil of implementation would lie in the details of Title VI guidelines, development of a political constituency for OCR, and OCR's ability to negotiate with local school districts.[2]

Growing Baltimore Support for Integration

George Brain had submitted his resignation to the school board two weeks before giving his desegregation progress report. He would leave at the end of 1964 to become dean of the Washington State University College of Education in Pullman. He had received offers from other school districts and private industry, and he had just been elected president of the American Association of School Administrators.

In a national search, the board selected Laurence Paquin, the integrationist superintendent of progressive New Haven mayor Richard Lee's administration, who had attended Brain's desegregation conference. Though hired in August 1964, he would not start in Baltimore until the next July, and an interim super-intendent would fill in. As one of the first urban superintendents to take on de facto segregation, Paquin had introduced busing and pairing and faced a suit from white parents. He wanted to use his last New Haven contract year to solidify his initiatives. Fifty-two years old when he took the job in Baltimore, he had taught high school social studies in New Hampshire and New Jersey, earned a doctorate at New York University, and served as superintendent in Glastonbury, Connecticut, before starting in New Haven in 1962.

Paquin was a pragmatic integrationist. When he started in Baltimore, he told a reporter that busing for racial balance was not as harmful as many believed. Still, he recognized that residential segregation and parents' preferences for schools near home were likely to produce segregated schools, particularly when the board allowed busing only to reduce overcrowding. Where low-income black schools could not be desegregated, he proposed a program he had supported in New Haven: community schools, which would include health, social, and rec-reational programs and stay open for adults to join youth in educational and community activities. The *Afro* had checked him out and expected good things from him.[3]

New Civil Rights Activism and School Reform

In spring 1965, while Paquin was still in New Haven, Baltimore CORE launched sit-ins, a sleep-in, and other direct action to push the school board to replace the Dunbar High School building. The organization forwarded its concerns to Paquin, and he invited them to meet when he got to Baltimore. Baltimore CORE was much smaller than the NAACP. In 1961, it had twenty-five members, a ma-jority white, many of them Jews. In September 1963, Jim Griffin, a twenty-six-year old black man inspired by the March on Washington, went to the CORE office to get involved in civil rights. A month later, he was elected to succeed Walter Carter as chairman, a position Griffin would hold for five years. His quick rise reflected the organization's need for members. Over the next three years, he would expand the chapter, developing an executive committee of eighteen, an advisory board of sixty, and a predominantly black membership.[4]

Many new black and white members were attracted by CORE's direct action to open up housing and public accommodations. CORE did little on education, partly because the NAACP had taken that initiative, partly because educa-tion was harder to understand and organize around than housing and public accommodations. The Dunbar campaign involved neither curriculum nor de-segregation, and CORE got involved at students' request. East Baltimore blacks regarded Dunbar as their community school and just wanted facilities and pro-grams comparable to other high schools. (In 1968, the city would hold a com-munity charrette to design a new Dunbar.) CORE spoke of school desegregation at a school board meeting in December 1965, a half year after Paquin's arrival. Marcia Kallen, chair of CORE's Education Committee, charged the system with maintaining "planned segregation." Free choice, she said, was not producing in-tegration but was "another form of segregation." The board had revised its policy more than two years earlier, but school composition had not changed much. The board should actively integrate students and staff, she said. She wanted a detailed plan to implement the policy. Paquin said he would talk with CORE, but then other matters got everyone's attention.[5]

Paquin was developing a plan for reducing segregation and improving educa-tion. A centerpiece was "comprehensive" high schools, modeled after a proposal by James Conant. Conant had been president of Harvard from 1933 to 1953, and in 1957 the Carnegie Corporation gave him a grant to develop a new model for the American high school. The resulting "comprehensive" high school of-fered a wide range of courses to serve all students. Paquin proposed converting Baltimore's high schools into comprehensive schools to educate intellectually and racially diverse students together. As part of his initiative, he would elimi-nate tracking, which he thought lacked any educational rationale and separated students by race. He believed that under open enrollment these reforms would reduce segregation.[6]

City College, historically a selective liberal arts high school, became a focus of controversy over Paquin's plan less than a month after Kallen's presentation. Melvin Sykes found himself opposing former allies in arguing against unlimited open enrollment. Under free choice, many black students had transferred to City College and enrolled in business and vocational courses, with two conse-quences that concerned Sykes. First, unchecked enrollment put the school on shifts. Second, attention to the growing numbers of business and vocational students threatened the school's college preparatory program. Addressing the board as a City alumnus, Sykes presented a report titled "City Forever?" in favor of making the school a college preparatory boys' high school specializing in hu-manities. The report, listing locally and nationally renowned school alumni, was cosigned by twenty civic leaders. Addressing those who believed the proposal was antidemocratic and anti-integrationist, Sykes argued that such specialized schools were essential for black children's advancement and crucial for retaining white children needed for integration. He pointed out that one-third of City's college preparatory students were black. Some of the 28 Parents, Marcia Kallen,

Juanita Mitchell, and the Urban League's Lloyd Michener testified against the proposal. Among those supporting it were 150 of the school's black students, led by student body president Kurt Schmoke, who in 1987 would become the city's first elected black mayor.[7]

In February, Paquin gave the board his recommendations, as well as a response to "City Forever?" All high schools would become comprehensive except for the two vocational schools and four "specialized" schools: Western, Poly, Eastern, and City. City would have a college preparatory humanities program, but also business and "general academic" programs. Every high school would have an honors program. No school could have more than 75 percent of students in college preparatory programs. "The question," Paquin wrote in language unprecedented for a Baltimore superintendent, "is no longer whether there shall be integration in the Baltimore City Public Schools, but how integration can be worked out so that the educational needs of *all* children will be met and safeguarded." Still, he recognized that "unless the movement of the white population from the City is halted, the question of integration will no longer have meaning for the City school system." The NAACP, Urban League, ADA, 28 Parents, and *Afro* endorsed the plan. CORE criticized it as accommodating white resistance to desegregation. White opponents picketed Paquin's home and called him a "Communist" and "race-mixer." Paquin emphasized that he meant to maintain high academic standards, and he reiterated that integration depended on keeping whites in city schools. The board held two hearings on the plan in May. Civil rights activists, including June Shagaloff, generally supported it, while some whites argued that it would trade off academic quality for integration. Later that month, Paquin tried to persuade teachers voluntarily to integrate faculties. In June, the board adopted his plan.[8]

In August, Paquin observed that ending de facto segregation would require combining such approaches as the Princeton Plan, educational parks, busing, and zoning, though he noted that the city seemed committed to free choice. When schools opened in fall 1966, only one in four had at least 10 percent of students from both races, 20 percent were predominantly white, and 53 percent were predominantly black.[9]

CORE Comes to Baltimore

A month before the board hearings on Paquin's plan, Jim Griffin and Floyd McKissick, CORE's new national director, held a press conference at CORE's New York headquarters to announce that the organization was coming to Baltimore in the summer of 1966 to make it the first "Target City." CORE would show how a national civil rights organization could address a city's housing, employment, and education problems. A week later, CORE associate director Lincoln Lynch, again with Griffin at a press conference, declared that Baltimore "embodies all the evil attributes of the south and all of the more subtle and discriminatory patterns of the north."

McKissick had been elected to succeed James Farmer as CORE director in January. He represented younger blacks who were turning away from Farmer's integrationism and nonviolence and toward militance, separatism, and a focus on the black poor. In this context, coming to Baltimore was driven more by national organizational considerations than by local issues. In late 1964, CORE set up a Northeast Regional Office to expand its efforts from the South to the North. The national office had become uneasy about the Baltimore chapter, which it considered middle class in its focus on opening up housing for those who could afford it, rather than organizing the black poor. Herbert Callender, CORE's new organizing director, believed he could work with Baltimore blacks. In spring 1966, the national office decided to go to Baltimore and then informed the local chapter. When Griffin appeared at press conferences, his members were uneasy about the organization's intervention.[10]

Juanita Mitchell attacked McKissick as "dishonest" and "arrogant" for disparaging the city's civil rights record and ignoring NAACP actions and accomplishments. Reverend Marion Bascom and the Interdenominational Ministerial Alliance supported the Target City campaign but said they would participate only if activities fit their principles of interracial cooperation, integration, and nonviolence.[11]

Baltimore had not had any civil disorder like that which had erupted in Cambridge, Maryland, in July 1963, and Watts in August 1965, or would break out in Chicago in July 1966. A year later, in October, 1967, after unrest in dozens of American cities, Mayor McKeldin would tell the Kerner Commission how to avoid riots. Mayors and their staffs, he said, "must do their utmost to communicate to ghetto residents that they are willing to extend themselves to redress the more immediate grievances, to create job opportunities and to show that they are concerned and sympathetic with legitimate desires for a better life. This may mean that normal channels and reasonable bureaucratic procedures have to be by-passed for immediate action." He understood the impulses that led ghetto residents to rebel: "Civil disorders reflect the plea for justice and opportunity...the plea to America to live up to its ideal of justice being replaced by a demand for recognition and power. It is a threat by the dispossessed to inflict injury if the majority group does not cooperate with them in achieving some of their legitimate ends." Such views, as well as political acumen, led McKeldin to welcome CORE to Baltimore.[12]

To underline the importance of Target City, CORE moved its 1966 national convention to Baltimore, opening on July 1. Organizers invited widely ranging civil rights leaders to speak, including James Farmer, Georgia state legislator Julian Bond, Muslim minister Lonnie Shabazz, Mississippi activist Fannie Lou Hamer, and Martin Luther King Jr. (who, after some early speakers attacked him, cancelled and was replaced by Stokely Carmichael of the Student Nonviolent Coordinating Committee). McKeldin went to the convention on opening night to present a key to the city. Asked not to speak as scheduled, he returned the next night. Following a speech by Carmichael attacking white liberals and invoking the "black power" he had first spoken of two weeks earlier in Mississippi, McKeldin welcomed the group. He told the crowd, "With the help of CORE, we'll achieve some of the goals we've been working toward. We are ashamed of ourselves, we need you here to help us do what we have not been able to do. We've got to have open housing." Police Commissioner George Gelston, who had already frustrated local CORE demonstrators by avoiding confrontation, followed with an offer of a countryside picnic or a river cruise with refreshments.[13]

The Target City project petered out the following spring because of weak conceptualization, poor organization, internal conflicts, tensions with the local chapter, scarce funding, and an inability to connect with the city's black communities. Nevertheless, it affected Baltimore. Above all, it informed officials and residents that civil rights was a national movement, that Baltimore blacks thought about race and acted toward injustices in ways that reflected talk and strategies across the country. In reaction, whites, themselves following others elsewhere, asserted their own "ethnicity."[14]

Renewed Attack on Baltimore School Segregation

When Target City started, McKeldin created a Mayor's Task Force for Equal Rights. While Target City had little interest in education, the Task Force Education Committee became a center for criticism of school segregation. The committee started during the summer with cochairs Martin Jenkins, Morgan State College president, and Hans Froelicher Jr., a Park School founder, former school board member, and "City Forever?" signator. In September, the committee went before the school board to urge it to integrate teachers as well as students. Billie Bramhall, speaking for the committee, observed that a tepid response to the superintendent's plea for voluntary faculty integration had done little to alter the pattern of matching teachers and students. In 105 of 155 elementary schools, more than 90 percent of faculty were of one race. Nearly two-thirds of elementary teachers taught in such faculties. Half of 52 secondary schools had segregated faculties, with half of secondary teachers in such schools.

Accordingly, the Education Committee asked school officials to conduct a "campaign for maximum faculty integration." Bramhall cited new federal Title VI guidelines that said school systems had a "positive duty" to reassign teachers to end segregation and called for a teacher exchange between predominantly black and predominantly white schools. She requested an assistant superintendent to oversee desegregation by informing parents of free choice procedures, eliminating discrimination in counselors' practices and the issuance of transfers, handling discrimination complaints, and identifying programs that could increase student and faculty integration and improve inner-city school quality.[15]

Two weeks later, the 28 Parents complained to the U.S. Civil Rights Commission that the system continued practices separating children by race, and the commission said it would look at the charges as part of its study of racial isolation in urban schools.[16]

The Education Committee pushed to integrate faculties, and in May 1967 reported to the board that staffs were still highly segregated. It was "virtually impossible to attract white teachers to schools where populations are entirely Negro." The committee lamented that the Baltimore Teachers Union and the Public School Teachers Association both opposed reassignment. The committee supported a Principals Association plan to integrate faculties through various means including mandatory assignment. McKeldin endorsed the report, saying teacher integration was as important as student integration. Paquin responded that the situation was not as bad as Bramhall had indicated but was still unacceptable. However, while he acknowledged that he had the authority to reassign teachers, in view of teacher organizations' opposition to forced reassignment and staff integration, he simply attacked their intransigence.[17]

In June, the Task Force sent the board proposals for action. Its report put Baltimore in a national picture by citing the Civil Rights Commission's new *Racial Isolation in the Public Schools,* which included the story of Winston Elementary School and portrayed high segregation in the city. The report pointed out that 84 percent of black elementary students attended predominantly black schools; 67 percent of white elementary students attended predominantly white schools, and 85 percent of black teachers taught in predominantly black schools. Even so, the Task Force thought 150 schools were integrated and could continue so if school officials took actions that both increased incentives for mixing within free choice and moved beyond laissez-faire. The Task Force recommended continuing busing to relieve overcrowding with concomitant efforts to reinforce integration; adoption of Paquin's high school plan; creation of educational parks, model schools, and magnet programs; implementation of the Princeton Plan where feasible; merger of the historically black and white vocational-technical high schools; and establishment of middle schools. Where integration was difficult, the Task Force proposed "compensatory education in the Negro schools." McKeldin, meeting with the Task Force in July, called for busing children from inner-city to outer neighborhood schools for the combined purposes of integrating and reducing overcrowding.[18]

By the time the board heard the report in September, Bramhall had moved to Pittsburgh, and Thomas Goedeke was acting superintendent in place of Paquin, who had cancer and would die in a month. The Southern Education Reporting Service noted, "Ironically, Dr. Paquin made his least progress with pupil desegregation, previously his forte, and remarked on several occasions that he saw little future for school desegregation in Baltimore if the flight of white families to county suburbs continued."[19]

Waning Support for Free Choice

At the time of Paquin's death, some who worried that white flight constrained city school desegregation were looking into metropolitan remedies.

Baltimore Considers Metropolitan Desegregation

Paquin had asked Johns Hopkins researchers to assess desegregation progress, and they found that white movement to the suburbs was "the most important segregating influence in the metropolitan area," followed by white departure to private schools. Their report identified two solutions. One was eliminating the importance of the city-county boundary by opening up suburban housing to blacks or linking city and suburban school systems. To accomplish the latter, the report favored putting educational parks on the boundary and busing in city and county children. The second remedy was desegregating private schools. The researchers conceded that only pressure from civil rights organizations or the state and federal governments could bring about either remedy.[20]

The Education Committee promptly proposed busing "a moderate number of Negro elementary school children attending inner-city segregated schools to several suburban schools, particularly those in wealthy neighborhoods and within a one-hour ride, for at least one school year," along with voluntary exchanges of small groups of black and white city and suburban teachers. McKeldin "enthusiastically" endorsed the proposal.[21]

Public discussion of the Hopkins report was stimulated by a mayoral campaign. Republican Arthur Sherwood, a lawyer, believed that the city-county boundary, by causing school segregation, posed a legal problem and urged city officials to work out a merger with the county before someone took the issue to the courts. (Two months later, he recanted, opposing busing and emphasizing neighborhood schools.) Democrat Peter Angelos, a city councilman, declared that improving city schools would integrate them by retaining white families; he opposed busing, which he considered the prime cause of white flight. Democrat Thomas D'Alesandro III, city council president, defended busing to relieve over-crowding and to remove children from deficient schools and proposed replacing obsolete schools and building educational parks to draw students from across the region. Metropolitan desegregation, however, had little chance, in the face of quick opposition from the state school superintendent, the Baltimore County superintendent, school board president, PTA president, and Teachers Associa-tion, and the Anne Arundel County executive.[22]

Still, whatever people's positions, these discussions moved away from the prevailing laissez-faire policy. Not only had free choice desegregated little, but some believed it contributed to white flight by creating uncertainty about the racial makeup of schools. Two new ideas entered Baltimore thinking. The first, more explicit, was that, if schools were to be desegregated, something besides open enrollment was necessary. The second, largely tacit, was that free choice was "social engineering" like any other policy and that, if it was legitimate, then other interventions also were acceptable.

Growing National Pressure for Integration

Baltimore did not come by these ideas alone. In an early 1967 Civil Rights Com-mission report, Berkeley, California, school superintendent Neil Sullivan cited Baltimore as showing the "strengths and weaknesses of open enrollment" and recommended that Baltimore give up neighborhood schools for a metropolitan approach to desegregation. For a couple of years, civil rights advocates around the country had raised questions about free choice. From the start, the NAACP and the Civil Rights Commission (created in 1957) recognized that, while free choice could integrate, it also served as a subterfuge to maintain segregation. The Baltimore NAACP endorsed free choice in the city but challenged it in southern Maryland and on the Eastern Shore. Typically, civil rights advocates took aim at Southern districts, but in fall 1963, the Boston NAACP challenged that city's new open enrollment plan, proposing instead biracial zones, at the same time that the Baltimore branch pushed just for truly open enrollment.[23]

The 1965 Office of Education Title VI guidelines accepted free choice, even as staff came to recognize Southern duplicity in using it. NAACP executive secretary Roy Wilkins attacked the guidelines and charged that federal acceptance of open enrollment had limited desegregation. In February 1966, the Civil Rights Com-mission issued a *Survey of School Desegregation in the Southern and Border States* that focused on free choice plans. The report acknowledged that most federal appeals courts had upheld the plans but described how they retarded integration.

Although the intimidation and harassment of black parents described in Maryland counties did not occur in Baltimore, the city was like nearly all Southern districts in maintaining schools that still had separate racial identities. The commission quoted a Virginia federal district court decision to argue that, so long as teacher segregation and other historic practices continued to identify schools as "black" or "white," simply ordaining free choice would not lead families to select anything different. The commission recommended that OE revise its guidelines to approve only plans offering real choice, based on faculty desegregation and eradication of other racial identification. If such changes still failed to desegregate, the commission said, then OE should reject free choice altogether.[24]

The 1966 Title VI guidelines continued to accept free choice, because the courts did, but moved a little toward requiring results. New guidelines called for "significant progress" in the number of transfers in each district. Wilkins wrote Secretary Gardner that free choice plans were not desegregating, and he wanted OE to "reject any such plan that has not in the past year produced substantial desegregation." The Civil Rights Commission, also disappointed, urged HEW to switch from measuring percentages of black children transferring to measuring percentages of black students in schools with substantial numbers of white students—in other words, integration as an outcome. However, all this would be moot, the commission noted, unless Congress appropriated money for enough HEW staff to enforce Title VI.[25]

Meanwhile, the NAACP Legal Defense Fund went to court to enjoin a free choice plan in New Kent County, Virginia. The NAACP regarded the plan as a ploy to satisfy Title VI while avoiding integration. The federal district court and Fourth Circuit Court of Appeals both upheld the plan, and in the summer of 1967 the NAACP requested Supreme Court review.[26]

Split Views on Integration in Baltimore

At this time, Baltimore schools were 65 percent black, 54 percent of schools were at least 90 percent black, 19 percent were at least 90 percent white, and the dissimilarity index was 0.82. While the school board searched for a successor to Laurence Paquin, an incident focused white misgivings about desegregation.

Racial Tension

In October 1967, Gene Burns, a newcomer to Baltimore and host of radio station WCBM's first call-in show, began talking with listeners about rumors of sexual promiscuity, drug abuse, and violence at Pimlico Junior High School.

Some students and parents had been concerned about disorder at the school for a while. Pimlico was overcrowded, with twenty-nine hundred students in a building for twenty-two hundred. Moreover, the school, as the neighborhood, was changing racially. In 1960 99 percent of students were white, but now more than one-third were black. (In four years the school would be 91 percent black.) The school had a black principal.[27]

State Senator Paul Dorf brought constituents' complaints to the school board in early November: "There is also harassment on school grounds, and certain types of drugs and birth control pills can be obtained very easily in the girls' lavatories." He blamed "forced busing" for conditions, though a board member explained that all busing was voluntary and intended only to relieve overcrowding. The lavatory concerns, accompanied by rumors of forty pregnancies, resonated with long-standing white anxieties about desegregation. The *Afro* noted that it was biologically impossible for so many girls to get pregnant so fast and, while recognizing problems, suggested what really concerned whites: "Pimlico is the first city school to even approach the concept of complete integration—as to both faculty and student body."[28]

The school board had conducted hearings at Pimlico in October. Few people offered specific, substantiated testimony, but anxiety continued. The PTA focused on overcrowding and sought to calm parents. Eight white Pimlico fathers, including Johns Hopkins professors James Coleman and Peter Rossi, wrote the *Sun* in support of the school. On November 16, board member John Sweeney gave the findings of an investigation he and William McElroy had conducted. They reported complaints of unwanted physical contact, threats, shoving, assaults, extortion, and fighting. However, they had found no solid evidence of guns or drugs, though it was possible some students used drugs. They noted that several parents and students praised the school's reputation, academic program, and integration. They attributed problems to overcrowding, "change in pupil population" (they referred to "a greater variety of socio-economic backgrounds" without mentioning race), and lax faculty supervision. They proposed some logistical changes, police surveillance, putting the school on shifts in the spring, and redistributing students in the fall.[29]

The incident highlighted racial differences in views of desegregation and the intermingling of realities and fantasies about it. Blacks saw desegregation as an extension of civil rights and an expansion of educational opportunities. However, the mixing of middle-class white students with black students, many from lower-income families, presented whites with unsettling behavior and led to some violent encounters. At the same time, some whites' unease about intimacy between the races fueled anxiety about aggressive and sexual attractions and threats. Complaints about the lavatories echoed 1954 charges, and rumors of widespread pregnancies gave voice to the worst fears. The school board report noted that people had distorted views of the actual situation. In addition, however, it acknowledged that, as had been the city pattern, no one in authority had made an effort to manage the racial transition by fostering discussion and regulating students' behavior.

Integrationism in City and School Politics

A week before the school board heard the Pimlico report, voters elected Democrat Thomas D'Alesandro III, son of the mayor from 1947 to 1959, to succeed Theodore McKeldin. D'Alesandro's campaign had involved the first citywide Democratic effort to recruit black support. He prided himself on his racial liberalism and felt comfortable with blacks, and he was a practical politician who recognized that the city's population was nearly half black. He had introduced civil rights bills during his four years as city council president, though the council passed none. He worked with the NAACP and the Interdenominational Ministerial Alliance. "Young Tommy," thirty-seven, had great ambition for his administration. After the election, he took advisors to Pittsburgh, Chicago, and Boston to see how they addressed urban challenges. In Boston he met with Daniel Patrick Moynihan, director of the Harvard-MIT Joint Center for Urban Studies, and presidential scholar Richard Neustadt, a founder of Harvard's Kennedy School of Government.[30]

D'Alesandro's attention to blacks was smart strategy. Blacks had been gaining power in the city. When President Johnson signed the Economic Opportunity Act of 1964, Baltimore created a Community Action Agency, and Mayor McKeldin named Parren Mitchell to head it. Mitchell, whose brother Clarence headed the Washington, DC, office of the NAACP, had done graduate work in sociology at the University of Maryland after suing for admission. He used the poverty program to organize poor blacks and register them to vote. (He would run successfully for the House of Representatives in 1971, becoming the first black elected to Congress below the Mason-Dixon Line in the twentieth century.) Yet, in a city where the races had little contact, many blacks were wary of an East Baltimore white ethnic like D'Alesandro. Many Little Italy residents, in turn, did not understand D'Alesandro's overtures to blacks. However, he ultimately carried all city precincts and claimed 93 percent of the black vote. As mayor, he would appoint the first blacks to the Board of Estimates, the Board of Municipal and Zoning Appeals, and the Board of Fire Commissioners.[31]

At his December 1967 inauguration, D'Alesandro pronounced Baltimore "the city of our hope" against despair and white flight. He promised "to root out every cause or vestige of discrimination." He wanted racially mixed schools and would talk about creating magnet schools to attract white suburban students, but he made clear at his inauguration that his first task was just to construct adequate facilities. More than one-fourth of the city's students attended eighty-four schools built before 1916; 70 percent of the children in these buildings were black, and 40 percent of all-black schools were built before 1916. Thirty-four of the fifty-eight schools that Strayer had recommended for abandonment in 1921 were still in use; 90 percent of the students attending these schools were black, and twenty-seven of the schools were all black. Sixteen of twenty-six portable schools had all-black student bodies, and another seven had black majorities.[32]

D'Alesandro dubbed Baltimore "Education City USA" and made changes in the school board. Eli Frank resigned the presidency, and the mayor appointed Francis Murnaghan, partner in a leading law firm, to succeed him. He had attended City College (and was a signator of "City Forever?"), gone to Johns Hopkins, and worked on the Harvard Law Review. D'Alesandro introduced Murnaghan to the city on a tour of schools, where both declared that obsolete, dangerous facilities needed renovation or replacement. The *Sun* and *Afro* endorsed Murnaghan. D'Alesandro named Jim Griffin to replace retiring black board member Percy Bond. As CORE chapter president, Griffin had led sit-ins and a sleep-in against the school system and had disrupted a city council meeting. He worked as an equal opportunity assistant for the state personnel office. He and his wife, a teacher, were active in their daughter's elementary school PTA. D'Alesandro and Griffin had both grown up on the east side, and two members of Griffin's family had worked for D'Alesandro's family. The Black United Front had urged the mayor to appoint Griffin, and white city council members balked at approving his nomination. The mayor said he valued Griffin's independence and wanted to give him responsibility for making decisions. The council finally approved Griffin in March 1968, holding black board membership at two, with Elizabeth Murphy Moss.[33]

At the end of March, the school board chose Thomas Sheldon, from Hempstead, Long Island, to head the schools. Sheldon was a small-town superintendent. Hempstead had 41,000 residents and 5,200 students, in comparison with Baltimore's 900,000 residents and 193,000 students. However, Hempstead was 70 percent black. Sheldon had a reputation for integrating the schools in a district he called the "inner city" of a Long Island metropolitan area. He had implemented a secondary school desegregation plan that ended a de facto segregation suit filed against his predecessor. The Hempstead NAACP liked him.

Search committee chair William McElroy recommended the forty-seven-year old Sheldon as someone who would "shake up" the system. As a sign of its faith in Sheldon, the board voted him a fifty-thousand-dollar salary, the highest for any American superintendent. Sheldon accepted with the understanding that

Murnaghan wanted him to "move the schools into an integrated society." From Hempstead, he expressed views on integration that echoed Paquin's pragmatism: "First of all…busing for itself isn't all harmful. If you can say you are busing children to give them a better education, then it's worth it. But children in the local school can get a darn good education. And for the moment, you have to go to work on individual schools. You have to look at each community to see how it feels about its school." Sheldon had three degrees from Syracuse University and was a former science teacher and baseball, football, and basketball coach. His seven children ranged from thirteen to twenty-five; those of school age would attend Baltimore public schools. He would start on July 1.[34]

Eight days after the school board announced its new integrationist superintendent, the Supreme Court heard the NAACP case against free choice. The next day, Martin Luther King Jr. was killed.

King's Murder, the Riots, and the Aftermath

On Thursday evening, April 4, when Mayor D'Alesandro heard of King's death, he ordered city flags lowered. The next day, as riots broke out in Chicago and Washington, President Johnson called soldiers from Fort Myers to defend the capital, Congress met in emergency session, and Americans across the land worried what would come next, Baltimore civil rights leaders urged black workers and students to stay home on Monday to mourn. Walter Lively, head of the militant Union for Jobs or Income Now (U-JOIN), exhorted blacks to stay home as a "general strike." Danny Gant, director of what remained of CORE's Target City project, blamed King's death on "criminals" in the power structure, including the press, police, and slumlords. The mayor endorsed civil rights leaders' requests by proclaiming Monday a day of mourning, ordering all city offices and schools to be closed, and urging private businesses also to close. He convened his cabinet and pledged "to eliminate from every area of public life in Baltimore all forms of injustice, discrimination and inequality," including creating "better schools." Community Action Agency director Parren Mitchell and Community Relations Commission director David Glenn put most of their staff on the streets. A *Sun* headline reported, "Baltimore Sad But Peaceful As Negro and White Mourn."[35]

Rioting and Ranting

On Saturday D'Alesandro proclaimed Sunday a day of prayer for King. About five-thirty Saturday afternoon, rioting began on Gay Street, in east Baltimore.

City police could not handle matters, and at the mayor's request Governor Spiro Agnew called in the National Guard and imposed an overnight curfew. Quickly the east side and then downtown became the site of fires and looting.

On Palm Sunday morning, when D'Alesandro had hoped pastors would counsel calm and prevent disturbances, he toured the city in a National Guard convoy. Trouble had spread to Pennsylvania Avenue on the west side. Still, despite 250 fires, he hoped the city had passed through the worst. But, as he, and McKeldin, walked the streets, signs were ominous. He encountered anger and defiance. Black leaders had no more success. From moderates to militants, from the NAACP and the Interdenominational Ministerial Alliance to CORE and U-JOIN, advocates for calm and order had little sway. Later in the day, Agnew wired President Johnson that an "insurrection" had occurred, and Johnson sent nineteen hundred army troops. The *Sun*, which featured pictures of looters, fires, and damaged stores, referred to the troops in a headline as the "First Federal Soldiers Called into City since 19th Century." The article identified the last occasion as an 1870s railroad strike, but reference to an "army of occupation," bivouacked in two parks and near City College, could also evoke Civil War images of federal regiments.

On Monday things got worse, as fifty-five thousand troops struggled to restore order in cities around America. In Baltimore arson and looting increased, as did injuries, deaths, and arrests. White and black groups confronted one another. D'Alesandro viewed the spreading wreckage from a helicopter. The headlines said it all: "1,900 More GI's Join Riot Forces as Snipers Peril Police, Firemen; Arrests in 3 Days Rise To 3,450"; "Federal Force Rises to 4,900 As Violence Fans Out from Slums"; "Looter Is Disorder's 5th Victim; 510 Injured; 900 Fires; 1,660 Lootings Reported; Mob Wars Averted at 2 Places"; "Baltimore's Weary Firefighters Get Help From Two Counties; City's 2,100 Fought 900 Fires in 3 Days." Tuesday morning the *Sun* declared and prayed, "Today Must End It."

Over Tuesday rioting abated. Sightseers toured some ravaged areas, now quiet. Yet people stayed on edge. The mayor awaited nightfall hopefully. Only three lootings and two fires occurred between nine and eleven. At eleven D'Alesandro called a press conference and declared, "Life in our city is returning to normal." A sixth person had been killed, and injuries had reached 600, including 50 policemen, but the worst was over. By the end, on Friday, 5,512 people had been arrested, nearly all black, about one of every 75 black citizens. There had been 1,208 major fires, and 1,049 businesses were destroyed. Nearly 12,000 National Guard and Army troops had occupied the city—one soldier for every 75 Baltimore residents.

Governor Agnew invited a hundred Baltimore black leaders to meet with him in Annapolis on Thursday. They included NAACP officials Lillie May Jackson,

Juanita Mitchell, and Clarence Mitchell Jr.; Interdenominational Ministerial Alliance president Frank Williams, Marion Bascom, and other pastors; state legislators Clarence Mitchell III, Verda Welcome, and Troy Brailey; former Community Relations Commission director Samuel Daniels and current director David Glenn; former assistant state's attorney Joseph Howard; Baltimore Teachers Union president Dennis Crosby; Parren Mitchell; Jim Griffin; parent activist and Morgan professor Homer Favor; and Baltimore Colts Lenny Moore and John Mackey (who both declined to attend).

The assembled, many exhausted from walking the streets trying to restore order, expected the governor's appreciation. Instead, he began reading a statement attacking them for encouraging and supporting the rioters. He identified them as "moderate" black leaders, the only ones he accepted, in contrast with the "circuit-riding, Hanoi-visiting type of leader," the "caterwauling, riot-inciting, burn-America-down type of leader." Yet some of them, he charged, had met secretly with the "reckless" "demagogue" who headed the local Student Nonviolent Coordinating Committee chapter, and all had declined to repudiate militants and advocates of violence, such as Stokely Carmichael, who "not...by chance" met with "local black power advocates and known criminals" just three days before the Baltimore riots began. "You were beguiled," he told them, "by the rationalization of unity; you...were stung by insinuations that you were Mr. Charlie's boy, by epithets like 'Uncle Tom.'" Hence they bore responsibility for the rioting. D'Alesandro had seen an advance copy of Agnew's statement and urged him to say something less "inflammatory," but Agnew followed his own muse.

As Agnew continued reading, black leaders stood up and walked out, until only about twenty remained. The *Sun* noted, "The startling aspect of the walkout was that it was staged by persons generally recognized as forming the 'moderate' segment of the Negro leadership." Those who left drafted an angry rebuttal. "Agnew's actions," they said, "are more in keeping with the slave system of a bygone era." He had decided who were legitimate black leaders, separating the "moderates" from the "militants," even going so far as physically barring some of the latter who tried to attend. In this way, they said, Agnew sought to divide the black community. Yet, if he insisted on tying the moderates to the militants, holding them responsible for the violence despite their efforts to prevent and stifle it, his words, a minister remarked, would have a paradoxical result: "He's forcing us all to become militants." These blacks felt especially hurt and betrayed because they had campaigned for Agnew in 1966, when he ran as an integrationist against Democrat George Mahoney, whose slogan "Your Home Is Your Castle—Protect It" unabashedly encouraged whites to keep blacks out of their neighborhoods.[36]

Reactions

Black and white Baltimoreans alike had taken pride in their city's placidity during the riot-torn summers of previous years. Important contributing factors were the civility and pragmatism of black leaders who preferred negotiation to confrontation with white officials. White political leaders responded favorably, even if blacks chafed at white misunderstanding, insensitivity, indifference, paternalism, and control. Mayor Howard Jackson and Governor Herbert O'Conor, neither a liberal, agreed to meet with protesting black leaders in 1942. After the war, westside Democratic boss Jack Pollack rewarded the growing number of blacks with patronage and a few electoral positions, until blacks gained the numbers and organization in the late 1950s to operate independently.[37]

The 1943 election brought in the first of a series of liberal public executives: Mayor McKeldin from 1943 to 1947, Mayor D'Alesandro Jr., from 1947 to 1959, Governor McKeldin from 1953 to 1957 and then Mayor McKeldin again from 1963 to 1967, followed by Mayor D'Alesandro III, in 1967. Faith in this tradition led the younger D'Alesandro to assume that Baltimore would have no riots after King's murder. Yet, after he had joined forces with black leaders, that alliance had not held the black community with him.[38]

Many whites found the riots confirming their worst fears about blacks. While some had sympathized with civil rights activists and could appreciate black anger at King's murder, few could understand looters and arsonists, who became blacks' public image. The unrest seemed to rationalize anxiety about black violence. What many had not said or had kept below the surface, they now thought and voiced openly. After Agnew's speech, a hundred telegrams an hour poured into his office, most from white Baltimoreans, most favorable. One praised his "act of courage" for "saying what every American hasn't had the courage to say." Another congratulated him "for standing up for the average middle-class American citizen when no one else did." Another said, simply, "Thankful to hear that the white people still have a strong voice in government." Several urged Agnew to run for president.[39]

Many white liberals were troubled or disillusioned by the riots. Some shared D'Alesandro's feeling that, after they had been earnest civil rights allies who took pride in the city's race relations, the riots had violated their trust. It was possible to distinguish the rioters from the black leaders and organizations with whom white liberals had worked, but the riots bludgeoned the senses. The liberals included many Jews, both activists and others who provided financial or moral support for civil rights causes and supported school integration. The vast majority of the 1,049 burnt-out and looted businesses were owned by whites. Many of these belonged to Jews, particularly in the Gay and Lombard street areas of east Baltimore and around Pennsylvania Avenue on the west. A Baltimore *Jewish Times* editorial observed, "Jews, owners for the most part of small business which seemed special targets for the looters and fire-bombers, were particularly hard-hit because their businesses were in the areas of the ghetto and the ghetto fringes closest to those who wreaked havoc." The editorial warned against a backlash against all blacks, but many Jews began emotionally and physically withdrawing from the central city into more securely Jewish territory. The riots marked a watershed in their history with the city.[40]

The riots shocked middle-class blacks in two ways. First, they discovered young blacks who were out of their control, who did not regard the middle class as models or leaders—who rejected middle-class civility and discipline because they doubted they could attain middle-class success. Not only would the NAACP have difficulty speaking for all blacks, but it was harder to see all blacks as part of one community. A breach between the middle class and the poor had opened. Largely as a result of the city's loss of manufacturing, the black male labor force participation rate would fall to 73 percent in 1970, on a slide from 81 percent in 1940 to 65 percent in 1980. In 1970, one in six black males between sixteen and twenty-one was a high school dropout who was either unemployed or not in the labor force at all.[41]

Middle-class blacks' second shock came from Agnew's peroration and whites' enthusiastic response. The governor had assaulted the black community, and whites had cheered him on. Leaders who for years had painstakingly maintained moderation, tempering their words so as not to upset white officials who did not understand or care about them, found that their education and civility counted for nothing; they were just black. Although D'Alesandro and members of the clergy had condemned Agnew's speech, few other whites had joined them. The circle of white allies was contracting, and moderation brought no returns.[42]

Free Choice Forever?

Seven weeks after the riots ended, on May 27, the Supreme Court ruled on free choice in *Green v. County School Board of New Kent County.* The justices considered whether the school board had satisfied the *Brown II* requirement to end segregation "with all deliberate speed." The court found that "the school system remains a dual system," and it ruled that "delays are no longer tolerable....The burden on a school board today is to come forward with a plan that...promises realistically to work *now.*" *Green* made two key rulings. The first was that free choice, as any desegregation policy, had to be judged by its results. The second was that school boards had "the affirmative duty to take whatever steps might be necessary to convert to a unitary system in which racial discrimination would be eliminated root and branch." In defining a "unitary" system, the court went beyond student composition to specify that "every facet of school operations" had to be indistinguishable: "faculty, staff, transportation, extracurricular activities and facilities." While not ruling free choice inherently unconstitutional, the court insisted that school boards adopt alternative policies, such as zoning, if they could more quickly and effectively create "a system without a 'white' school and a 'Negro' school, but just schools." Practically, because open enrollment rarely passed this test, the decision ended the constitutional acceptability of free choice.[43]

A Baltimore Opinion on the Supreme Court Decision

A few days after the Supreme Court decision, Baltimore Community Relations Commission director David Glenn asked City Solicitor George L. Russell Jr., for a legal opinion on *Green*'s implications for Baltimore. Glenn had grown up in the Cincinnati black community, where he worked with the NAACP and CORE. He came to Baltimore in 1952 to assist Furman Templeton in the Urban League. Mayor McKeldin appointed him Community Relations Commission director in 1967. Glenn vigorously opposed segregation, and the Community Relations Commission had a long-standing interest in schools. In September 1967, he sent school board president Frank a report focusing on deteriorating historically black facilities, advocating the Princeton Plan, and backing Paquin's staff integration efforts.[44]

Russell's family went back several generations in Baltimore. He grew up on the west side, attended segregated schools, and earned a law degree at the University of Maryland the year the Supreme Court banned school segregation. In 1966, Governor Millard Tawes appointed him to the Circuit Court, where he served as Maryland's first black state judge. He resigned from the bench in 1968 when Mayor D'Alesandro selected him as the first black city solicitor and member of the Board of Estimates. Personally, Russell was skeptical about integration. Although he had nothing good to say about the physical condition of schools he had attended, he liked the teachers and cherished the schools' familial climate and ties. To his mind, integration would break up important community institutions. In practice, he saw few positive results. When blacks tried to integrate schools or neighborhoods, whites moved out. When the school system integrated faculties, administrators mollified whites by transferring good black teachers into historically white schools and moving weak white teachers into once-black schools. Russell preferred to see improvement of predominantly black schools. He replied to Glenn at the end of November.

Russell began his nine-page opinion by summarizing *Green,* then turned to city schools. He noted that 34 percent of black children still attended all-black schools and that they were "still being deprived of their constitutional right of attending integrated schools." He recognized that the Baltimore board had adopted open enrollment in good faith. However,

> Baltimore would appear to have gone as far as it can to bring about integration under a "freedom of choice" plan.…while the "freedom of choice" method used in Baltimore has assisted in moving toward a "unitary non-racial system" of schools, the vestiges of the dual system in effect prior to *Brown* still remain.…sufficient time has elapsed to bring about a truly unified system: a new plan is required for students and especially for faculty, until every Negro school child has an opportunity to enjoy his full constitutional rights.

"In spite of [teacher organization] opposition," he continued, "the law requires the School Board to proceed immediately with a workable faculty integration plan." The conclusion was clear: "Unless the Board continues to pursue the objective of a fully integrated system and achieve that objective, we do not believe that there is or will be a valid ground for determining that the Board is fulfilling its constitutional responsibilities." The legal opinion suggested no new policies. It noted that residential segregation hampered integrative school zoning. Russell, speaking at a press conference, observed that zones and busing (which he opposed) might integrate schools and satisfy Baltimore's constitutional requirements.[45]

The city's top legal officer had just declared that, unless the school board did more to integrate, its policy was unconstitutional. Mayor D'Alesandro, who appointed board members and had directed Russell to respond to Glenn, ignored the opinion. School board president Murnaghan refused to say what he thought about Russell's opinion. Instead, he highlighted obstacles to integrating schools. One was housing segregation. Another was the complexity of student social relations. "Indiscriminate integration," he said, "can do more harm than good." For example, "If you put two kids together in the sixth grade—one from an advantaged environment, the other from a disadvantaged environment—this is more likely to confirm in the minds of both the myth of white superiority." Murnaghan added that integration would cost money. He reaffirmed free choice. He deferred to Superintendent Sheldon on responding to Russell's opinion. Two weeks after Russell delivered his report, Sheldon, who had been on the job only five months and was struggling to develop relations with his staff and the unions, said he had not yet received the document and would review it with administrators when he did. He never commented publicly. The most candid response came from

William Donald Schaefer, who had succeeded D'Alesandro as city council president and would follow him as mayor. He refused to revisit desegregation policy, he said, because "immediately the question of race comes in."[46]

Postriot Baltimore

Baltimore officials' inaction in 1968 contrasted with the 1954 school board's response to *Brown*, when members said they were glad the court had freed them to act on their principles. *Green* required the city to supplement open enrollment, and no one moved. Officials expressed practical objections. However, none of their concerns constituted a legal argument against the court ruling. D'Alesandro, Murnaghan, and Schaefer, all lawyers, ignored the law. In 1952 and 1963, the school board had responded to community pressure. Now, sixteen years after the Poly campaign, no biracial coalition pushed for expanding black educational opportunities. No civil rights group sued the system to comply with *Green*. Schaefer, whose four terms as mayor would show that he understood city residents, said clearly that after the riots Baltimoreans did not want to talk about anything tied to race.

Around this time, Melvin Sykes looked for funding for his metropolitan desegregation suit against the school board and city, state, and suburban officials. He needed an estimated twenty thousand dollars for expenses. The local NAACP did not readily collaborate with others and, in any case, had little money. Sykes approached the NAACP Legal Defense Fund but was turned down. He never found funding.[47]

Growing Racial Tension

During his superintendency, Thomas Sheldon oversaw $133 million in school construction, replacing many dilapidated historically black facilities. He used Elementary and Secondary Education Act funds to hire three thousand teacher aides, many black. He reorganized the superintendent's office and appointed three black associate superintendents and ten other blacks at cabinet level. After a year, the *Afro* approved his performance and exhorted him to be "more aggressive" on integration. However, following the riots, the school board became racially polarized, and a black-dominated bloc challenged Sheldon for control.[48]

After January 1969, four blacks and a white ally controlled the board. That month D'Alesandro added two black board members. Larry Gibson, a twenty-six-year-old attorney, had recently joined Murnaghan's law firm and was recommended by him. He had enrolled at City College two years after *Brown*. As a student he worked to desegregate restaurants. He had Howard University and Columbia University Law School degrees. During the summer of 1966, while interning at a Baltimore law firm, Gibson enlisted lawyers in helping U-JOIN conduct rent strikes. Samuel Daniels was a generation older and more experienced in civic life. After graduating from Coppin in 1948, he became a teacher. In 1955 Governor McKeldin named him director of the new Maryland Commission on Interracial Problems and Relations, and in 1960 he was appointed Baltimore Community Relations Commission director. When D'Alesandro tapped him, he directed the Council of Equal Business Opportunity, and he was Grand Master of the seven-thousand-member Prince Hall Lodge of the Masons. Daniels believed the black middle class should join with poor blacks in pushing for integration. Gibson, Daniels, Jim Griffin, and Elizabeth Murphy Moss made four black members. They joined forces with Philip Macht, a 1968 appointee with wealth from suburban development, as a five-member liberal bloc that began to assert black influence over school policy.[49]

A January 1970 incident shifted the balance of power. Growing tensions between a predominantly black student body and predominantly white faculty at girls' Eastern High School reached a crisis when a white teacher reportedly used a racial slur with a black student. Students protested, and someone called the police, who roughly treated students and eventually arrested eight. School was dismissed early, and many girls went to adjacent City College, where boys joined the protest, and City College was closed. At the next board meeting, Sheldon announced he would investigate. At once, Gibson introduced a resolution that the investigation be conducted jointly by a board committee and the superintendent. Murnaghan stated that the issue was administrative, the superintendent's responsibility. If the board approved the resolution, he would resign. Sheldon expressed dissatisfaction with growing board meddling in administration. Gibson, Griffin, Moss, Daniels, and Macht voted for the motion, and Murnaghan resigned. The *Afro,* praising Murnaghan, regretted he had not found a way to stay.[50]

D'Alesandro tried to persuade black businessman Henry Parks to take the presidency. The owner of Parks Sausages, at one time the nation's largest black manufacturing company, Parks had been on the city council from 1963 to 1967. He told the mayor his business required his time. D'Alesandro then picked lawyer Robert Karwacki. He had been an assistant state attorney general, and in 1964 had exonerated city police on charges of beating an arrested black man. Juanita Mitchell, who had represented the plaintiff, attacked D'Alesandro's choice. Parren Mitchell, who at the time had headed the Maryland Commission on Interracial Problems and Relations, believed Karwacki had protected the police; he wanted a black appointee. Daniels was "disappointed and disgusted" with the choice. Griffin would accept Karwacki if he were willing to join the movement to "stamp out institutional racism." Karwacki quickly found the "atmosphere so tense you could cut it with a knife. It wasn't only acrimony; it was hatred."[51]

The five-member majority's relations with other board members and the superintendent deteriorated over the year. In October, the group pushed to hire Samuel Banks to rewrite the social studies curriculum to emphasize black content, over Sheldon's protest that such changes would harm what should be a general curriculum for all students. Sheldon tried to decentralize system administration, but black members defeated the plan because they considered his districts racially imbalanced and because the proposal did not give community members control of schools.[52]

Increasingly, board members, the superintendent, and the press characterized the board as a "circus." After the December 4, 1970, board meeting, the *Afro* observed, "The conflict between the five-man liberal majority and the 'conservative' elements of the board has killed any pretense of reconciliation and harmony among the members.... There is open laughter and cheers and cries of derision as time and again the liberal majority defeats the conservatives, usually by a 5–2 vote." A "very unhappy" Sheldon, feeling "vilified" by the board, had reached the end of his patience when the board rejected 11 nominations for principalships, and on January 6 announced his resignation. When he was hired, the president of the Hempstead NAACP had praised him, saying, "His predecessor was an out-and-out cracker. It took Dr. Sheldon three years to straighten things out." Now, after three years in Baltimore, a black board member dismissed him, saying, "I think he...lacks sensitivity to civil liberties and human rights."[53]

On January 13, D'Alesandro, trying to bring peace to the board, appointed staff assistant Kalman "Buzzy" Hettleman to replace Macht, whose term was up. Hettleman was a thirty-five-year old lawyer, a former social worker, D'Alesandro's education advisor, an activist in Jewish and other community and civic groups, and a member of the NAACP and the Urban League. He was liberal, a white who knew and could talk with blacks, and conciliatory by nature. The mayor had resisted ninety black leaders' request to replace Macht with a black candidate they recommended, but he did reappoint Daniels. Two days later the mayor had a "heart-to-heart talk" with board members and the superintendent and said he "would not hesitate to remove the entire board or any individual member of the board" if public sessions continued to be discourteous and disorderly. "The screaming at the school board's public sessions must stop," he insisted. He chastised the board for attacking Sheldon and said he wanted Sheldon to stay.[54]

At the January 25 board meeting, after heated discussion, members voted 7–1 to release the superintendent from his contract. Then Daniels, complaining that he was scapegoated for the board stalemate by both conservative board members and black community members, announced he did not want reappointment. Moderate Sweeney announced his resignation, charging, as a newspaper put it, "that reasonable debate in board deliberations has given way to placards, singing and clapping." White city councilmen told the mayor they would approve Hettleman only if D'Alesandro removed Griffin; Hettleman was eventually approved while Griffin stayed. In early February, the board appointed Sterling Keyes, a black deputy superintendent brought by Sheldon from Hempstead, interim superintendent. A week later, the city council approved D'Alesandro's nomination of conservative lawyer Robert Thieblot despite negative votes from the four black city councilmen, who questioned his racial views. Meanwhile, a search committee interviewed candidates for superintendent.[55]

On July 16 the board hired forty-two-year old Roland Patterson as the first permanent black superintendent. A Washington, DC, native, he had graduate degrees from Columbia University Teachers College and had taught and been principal in New York, New Jersey, and Seattle. He was then a Seattle assistant superintendent, in charge of the city's Central Region, which resembled Baltimore in being 62 percent black. Patterson had devised the city's federally ordered desegregation plan, including grade reconfiguration and crosstown busing, against system and community opposition. He had a reputation for strongly asserting black educational rights and a concern for building interracial relations. At a Baltimore interview in June, he had startled some by observing that many blacks were in jail "because they are black" or "because they are political prisoners." Nevertheless, with only Maree Farring dissenting, the board voted 8–1 to hire him. Members spoke favorably of his intelligence, knowledge of urban education, and aggressiveness. He would start October 1, 1971.

Desegregation within Free Choice and More Racial Conflict

In April, a unanimous Supreme Court had delivered a landmark ruling on school desegregation in *Swann v. Charlotte-Mecklenburg Board of Education.* The Charlotte-Mecklenburg school district, including the city of Charlotte and suburban Mecklenburg County, was 71 percent white, but fifteen years after *Brown* two-thirds of Charlotte's twenty-one thousand black students attended schools at least 99 percent black. The court considered what remedies satisfied *Green*'s requirement to create "unitary" systems "*now.*" It would be unrealistic, the court said, to eliminate every single-race school, but the continued existence of predominantly single-race schools in a district where segregation had been law placed the burden on the district to prove school assignments were "genuinely

nondiscriminatory." Under such conditions, the court stated, color-blind policies
were inadequate:

> All things being equal, with no history of discrimination, it might well
> be desirable to assign pupils to schools nearest their homes. But all
> things are not equal in a system that has been deliberately constructed
> and maintained to enforce racial segregation....."Racially neutral"
> assignment plans...may fail to counteract the continuing effects of
> past school segregation....an assignment plan is not acceptable simply
> because it appears to be neutral.

The court accepted transfer policies letting students move from schools where
they were in the majority to others where they were in the minority but required
districts to provide free transportation and make space available. Beyond that,
Swann allowed the "gerrymandering of school districts and attendance zones,"
even if zones were "neither compact nor contiguous." In addition, pairing and
clustering of schools with mandatory assignments were acceptable. Finally,
noting that "bus transportation [is] a normal and accepted tool of educational
policy," the court allowed busing to desegregate schools.[56]

Baltimore had more than twice the students of Charlotte-Mecklenburg, was
a demographic mirror image of the North Carolina district, and contained no
suburbs. These differences, however, only affected what Baltimore desegregation
policies might accomplish. They had no legal bearing on the repertoire of acceptable means—now including gerrymandering and busing, as well as pairing.
Moreover, racially neutral policies were indefensible if they did not desegregate.
Baltimore headlines highlighted the approval of busing. However, unlike three
years earlier, after *Swann* no one asked the city solicitor for an opinion on the
implications for Baltimore schools. When the board met two days after *Swann*,
no one mentioned it. The main item was creating magnet high schools to reduce
overcrowding within open enrollment.

In discussing Larry Gibson's magnet school proposal, board members wres-
tled with the contradictions of open enrollment. The virtue of the policy in giving families freedom to select schools had two undesirable consequences. One,
the focus of discussion, was overcrowding at preferred schools. The other was
segregation, particularly at schools less desired by whites. Hettleman regarded
free choice as "a means to an end: the goal of integrated, quality education for all
children." However, in speaking for Gibson's proposal, he articulated the liberal's
dilemma while raising broader questions about what a school board could control: "He stated his belief that [open enrollment] has caused segregation rather
than integration by accelerating to some extent the exodus of middle income
families from the city leaving only the lower income families in the inner city.

On the other hand, Mr. Hettleman agreed that any form of districting is undesirable since it will preclude some children from attending the schools of their choice." For his part, Gibson regarded open enrollment and magnets not as integration strategy, but as simply the best means for students to get into good programs. Griffin observed, however, that realistic appraisal of open enrollment and long-range planning were "likely to lose out to the hysteria of recent events." He referred to attacks on white teachers at predominantly black Lombard Junior High, but that incident and reactions to it were just one manifestation of diffuse racial tension.[57]

On May 13, the board unanimously approved a magnet plan that gave priority to currently underutilized high schools and three new schools. The *Afro* reported the action in an article that reaffirmed free choice: "To end open enrollment, which now ensures students freedom of choice, would only damage student morale and initiative and serve to further polarize the community. [Proposals to restrict choice within districts for the purpose of integrating schools] address themselves only to symptoms and do nothing to improve the quality of education in the schools."[58]

When Roland Patterson arrived in the fall, attacks on him began almost at once. He was a black outsider in a city still narrowly majority white. The board was split along racial lines. Karwacki resigned in November. D'Alesandro, in his last appearance as mayor, urged support for the superintendent. When criticized, Patterson increasingly defined issues racially and identified with black interests. His supporters would hold that he became a lightning rod for racial animosities when he spoke uncomfortable truths about race. His adversaries would argue that he inappropriately racialized issues and invoked race defensively. An important factor would be William Donald Schaefer, who, after defeating black candidates George Russell and Clarence Mitchell III, was elected mayor a month after Patterson started. Schaefer believed in mayoral control, had little sympathy with racial pleadings, and as time went on, just did not like Patterson.[59]

School board meetings became televised public spectacles, attended by animated standing-room crowds. In October 1973, Buzzy Hettleman, D'Alesandro's intended peacemaker, resigned, unable to navigate the mines. His resignation followed those of Stephen McNierney and Robert Thieblot. Meanwhile, Elizabeth Murphy Moss and Jim Griffin, whose terms had expired at the end of 1972, stayed on without formal reappointment or replacement by Schaefer. John Walton, a white sixty-two-year old Johns Hopkins education professor whom Schaefer had named board president, had trouble managing the board. The mayor seemed to have washed his hands of the school system; at the least, he had little to do with board members.[60]

Virtues and Weaknesses of Free Choice in Racial Transition

Between 1963 and 1973 Baltimore public school enrollment held steady at around 185,000. White registration dropped 25,000 while black registration rose 23,000, increasing the black majority from 57 to 70 percent. Predominantly black schools increased from 89 to 118, 57 percent of schools in 1973. Of these, 57 were all-black, and 31 had five or fewer whites. Over the decade, the numbers of predominantly white and balanced schools both declined, and only 54 schools in 1973 had at least 10 percent from each race.[61]

One could read these numbers as a measure of the inevitable result of the city's changing demography. However, they also record the effects of a laissez-faire policy whereby the school board declined to do anything to influence school racial composition. The relationship between policy and enrollment seems obvious: absent system intervention, family choices directly influenced school makeup. Yet the policy also had a less apparent effect. Paradoxically, free choice, valued for disturbing school composition minimally and thus not scaring off white families, by removing any central control and creating uncertainty about school makeup, added to anxiety, frightened away white families, and affected school composition significantly. Thus open enrollment, by not managing school racial makeup, contributed to changes in city demography.

By the end of this period, not only were schools blacker and more segregated, but the system culture had changed. The board that encountered 28 Parents and NAACP demands in 1963 responded civilly, treating their petitioners and one another respectfully. In 1973, board members often acted individually and adversarially, apparently more interested in pursuing separate, frequently racially defined aims than in finding ground for agreement on policy that might have wider legitimacy. Part of the cause, but also a symptom of broader shifts in the city, was a change in mayors. McKeldin and D'Alesandro were egalitarian liberals who espoused civil rights and embraced the schools, but Schaefer had no particular affection for civil rights, openly disliked Patterson, and distanced himself from school policy. The earlier mayors sought inclusive consensus; Schaefer encouraged competitive interest-group politics. Another part of the explanation was black ascendance. Blacks comprised nearly half the population. Whites still ran much of the city, but blacks were gaining. The 1963 school board had seven white members; the 1973 board had four blacks. With Macht as partner, and, later, with a black superintendent, blacks dominated policy.

Part of the explanation for the cultural change was the trauma of Martin Luther King Jr.'s assassination and the riots. For many blacks, King's murder, the riots, and Agnew's lecture aroused anger at white society and raised questions about the efficacy of nonviolence, moderation, and interracial coalitions. For many whites, the riots evoked a fear of blacks and retreat from the city. However, the riots did not cause these changes so much as catalyze and punctuate shifts already taking place. Here it is helpful to recall a well-known optical illusion— a drawing that in one moment looks like two faces and becomes a vase in the next. The Gestalt shifts. The faces and vase are both present, but what was background becomes foreground. The riots shifted Baltimore's racial Gestalts. Ambivalences rebalanced.

Desegregation involved two ambivalences. Whites experienced what Gunnar Myrdal called the "American Dilemma." They simultaneously espoused the equality of individuals and thought about blacks in ways that could justify discrimination. They might believe in civil rights but also hold a low view of or fear blacks and try to keep them down or away. Black ambivalence was expressed in the debate between W. E. B. DuBois and Booker T. Washington. Blacks both believed in integrating into a color-blind society and wanted to maintain a separate society with their own institutions. They might want integration but regard whites apprehensively, doubting whites would accept them and worrying that integration would cost them cultural and political power.[62]

These ambivalences were individual, in that many people held both beliefs in some mental and emotional balance. At the same time, they were collective, in that more or less discrete groups within the races held one position more prominently than the other. Thus convention contrasted tolerant whites with prejudiced whites and integrationist blacks with separatist blacks. While these distinctions referred to real variations, people could exaggerate differences. For example, whites who wanted to see themselves as tolerant liberals could downplay any personal prejudices or fears and attribute racial anxieties to other whites, such as working-class ethnics. Blacks who wanted to find places in a color-blind society could suppress suspicions or fears of whites and attribute separatist impulses to other blacks, such as the less-educated masses.

As a result of the shift, whites and blacks emerged from the riots with little faith in racial cooperation and renewed conviction that even talking about anything associated with race was dangerous. After growing interest in school integration and more directive policy to that end, both races pulled back, determined to go it alone, or at least reconciled to doing so. Though desegregation remained policy, board members talked more about school quality. Black members focused on controlling a system where majorities of students and teachers were black.

The change in the political culture, the racial parting of the ways, and black efforts to assert power contributed to school board chaos, but that can also be linked to a constant over the decade: open enrollment. If anything, blacks supported it more than whites. Moreover, free choice was not just a default policy that lingered in place. Gibson actively asserted it, as did Hettleman. However, the difference in their rationales was telling. Hettleman justified open enrollment as a means to integrating schools. Gibson supported it as a way of opening educational opportunities. He emphasized black children's freedom to enter whatever school they wanted. In this respect, he was the truer descendant of the 1954 board, with his liberal emphasis on individual rights and process, whereas Hettleman wanted the process to produce a specific outcome.

Open enrollment persisted from a white-dominated board to a black-dominated one because of its multiple meanings and uses. Whereas some of the former thought of it as a path to integration, most of the latter considered it a strategy simply for desegregation. Throughout, the policy served boards similarly in letting them avoid intervening in race relations, or even talking about race. This need grew urgent after the riots. However, while offering board members these benefits, free choice contributed to the adversarial climate by emphasizing individualism. As enrollment policy, it authorized individual choice: everyone should decide what was best for him or her. By extension, what was right for students was right for board members. If something like the economists' hidden hand produced salutary results from aggregate school choices, then presumably, board members' self-direction would also lead to benign ends. The companion to the individualism in the policy was the renunciation of any responsibility for producing agreement.

More broadly, free choice gave up any concept of justice: all outcomes, school officials had said, were equally acceptable. Thus the board's liberalism disarmed it in two ways at a time of growing racial conflict. Politically, school officials had no way to assert a public interest binding everyone. Practically, open enrollment had never required the board to manage race relations, and now school officials lacked both the experience and authority to build interracial alliances. Free choice did not lead inexorably to anarchy, but it held seeds of the destruction of board and community cooperation. The policy made it seem natural, just as the riots made it seem necessary, to retreat from attempts at civic life into private worlds.

FEDERAL INTERVENTION

During the time black school board members were battling Superintendent Sheldon over his decentralization plan, in October 1970, NAACP Legal Defense Fund lawyers filed a suit against the Department of Health, Education, and Welfare in the U.S. District Court for the District of Columbia. Plaintiffs charged that HEW had ceased enforcing Title VI of the 1964 Civil Rights Act against segregated school districts (and states with segregated colleges and universities). President Nixon's OCR director, Stanley Pottinger, had not taken administrative or legal action against more than one hundred districts he knew to be out of compliance.

On February 16, 1973, Judge John Pratt decided *Adams v. Richardson* for the plaintiffs. "HEW has attempted to excuse its administrative inaction," he said, "on the grounds that it is still seeking voluntary compliance through negotiation and conciliation." However, eighty-five districts had one or more schools with a racial composition at least 20 percent divergent from the district makeup, and HEW had not even notified these districts that their practices apparently violated *Swann* and asked for explanation. The court gave HEW sixty days to write the districts asking them "to rebut or explain the substantial racial disproportion in one or more of the district's schools." The districts included entire Southern states, small rural counties, and seven large cities: Kansas City, Richmond, San Antonio, Jacksonville, Louisville, St. Louis, and Baltimore. Baltimore school officials had received national plaudits for their 1954 desegregation policy. Now, in a changed legal climate, federal agents would press the city to expand greatly the modest results.[1]

The Federal Government Confronts Baltimore

Peter Holmes, the new OCR director, would be responsible for enforcing the ruling, which could deprive Baltimore of federal funds. Holmes, thirty-four, had grown up in a small Ohio town and reached the top HEW civil rights enforcement position by advancing through Republican party politics. As a young man he was puzzled about why the local swimming pool was reserved for whites, but he was not active in civil rights. In his freshman year at Northwestern University, he pledged a fraternity that, against national organizational policies, decided to accept a Jew. "I guess that was the closest I came to a so-called civil rights issue," he reflected later. After graduating from Northwestern in 1961, he went to American University to prepare for the foreign service but left to intern for conservative Democratic Ohio Senator Frank Lausche. Afterward, he began writing for the *Congressional Quarterly*. In 1966 he joined Michigan Republican Robert Griffin's senatorial campaign and became Griffin's legislative director when he won. Griffin supported civil rights legislation until busing became an issue in Detroit.[2]

When Richard Nixon became president in 1969, he picked Leon Panetta, an aide to liberal California Republican senator Thomas Kuchel, for OCR director. Panetta wanted to withhold funds from segregated school districts but ran up against Nixon's Southern strategy and opposition to busing. To strengthen his staff, Panetta invited Holmes, whom he knew from the Hill, to be special assistant for congressional relations. Once on board, Holmes told another staff member, "I think we have just enough civil rights laws right now; we don't need any more. They should be enforced, but I'm no civil rights fanatic." Over time, Panetta ignored warnings from Nixon lieutenants John Ehrlichman, John Mitchell, and Robert Mardian not to push civil rights in the South, and Nixon fired him in early 1970 and put in Pottinger. Holmes stayed on as assistant director for public affairs and special assistant for policy coordination. In April 1973, Nixon named Pottinger assistant attorney general for civil rights, and HEW Secretary Caspar Weinberger made Holmes OCR director. Although Title VI enforcement turned on fine legal points, Holmes, unlike his predecessors, was not a lawyer.[3]

Days after Holmes's appointment, presidential aides Ehrlichman and H. R. Haldeman and Attorney General Richard Kleindienst resigned, and White House counsel John Dean was fired. A month after Holmes wrote the superintendents, Senators Sam Ervin and Howard Baker opened the Watergate hearings, and Elliott Richardson, Holmes's initial HEW boss and the *Adams* defendant, now Attorney General-designate, appointed former Solicitor General Archibald Cox Justice Department special Watergate prosecutor. The administration was coming apart around Holmes.[4]

Federal Engagement with Baltimore

While HEW geared up to enforce Title VI, Baltimore was already attracting federal scrutiny. The city had submitted a proposal for a language arts program under the federal Emergency School Aid Act, intended to help districts desegregate. Harold Davis, an equal opportunity specialist in the OCR Philadelphia regional office, found the request puzzling: Baltimore had neither the federally approved desegregation plan nor the desegregation court order that normally qualified districts for aid. He made a site visit.[5]

Davis grew up in Mississippi, where he became a school teacher. He was diligent and hardworking, arming a passion for integration with a detective's attention to facts. He would become the OCR expert on Baltimore, coming to know city schools by name, location, boundaries, and public transit access. His findings and analysis would be the basis for communications issued in Holmes's name. On his first Baltimore visit, he learned that the city had operated under free choice since 1954, and that policy made the district eligible for federal assistance. Nevertheless, when he analyzed Baltimore data, he found that the district was

> not in compliance with certain other assurances, one relating to faculty assignments.... There were a great number of schools that were outside [acceptable faculty racial ratios], and, in fact, there were a number of schools that had all white faculty, all white student bodies, all black faculty and all black student bodies.... to bring the schools within acceptable parameters... would have required approximately sixteen hundred transfers of faculty members. The second problem... was racial isolation. Approximately one third of the students were attending desegregated schools but within those desegregated schools there was further racial isolation.[6]

On April 17, while HEW appealed *Adams,* Holmes sent Superintendent Roland Patterson the same letter he sent eighty-four other districts, noting that *Adams* required HEW to ask Baltimore to account for conditions where a "20% disproportion exists between the percentage of local minority pupils in [one or more of] the schools and the percentage in the entire school district." In a district that was now 70 percent black, all schools had to be between 50 and 90 percent black. Holmes gave Baltimore until May 21 to submit data, including a map, concerning each school involved, and to explain how any disproportion complied with the law or delineate plans for relieving it. On June 4, the city wrote HEW describing school composition, the open enrollment policy, and desegregation efforts since 1954. Attributing persistent school segregation to "housing patterns and population shifts," Patterson argued that "the history of desegregation in the

Baltimore City Public Schools illustrates the system's sincere efforts to become a unitary non-racial system of schools." Eight days later, the United States Court of Appeals for the District of Columbia Circuit upheld *Adams*.[7]

Holmes replied on August 17 with his first specific comments on Baltimore. He asked for a map and data showing how Patterson's plans to create nine subdistricts would affect enrollment, along with faculty data, within 15 days. Patterson provided the information, and then OCR was silent for five months. Meanwhile John Walton struggled to manage the board.

On February 5, 1974, Holmes sent Patterson his judgment: "On the basis of the data available…I have concluded that further desegregation of Baltimore City Schools is necessary and feasible." Holmes emphasized three findings:

1. Most of the schools that were segregated prior to the 1954 *Brown* decision remain racially identifiable. All 30 of the formerly black schools that are still open continue to be all-black. Fifty-five of the formerly white schools still open remain identifiable as white; 14 of them are all white. Thus, they are clearly vestiges of the dual school system. Further desegregation is easily achievable; a substantial proportion of the identifiable black schools are in close proximity to identifiable white schools.

2. Open enrollment has not been effective in establishing a unitary, nonracial school system; therefore, it is legally insufficient to remedy the continuing effects of past state-mandated segregation....

3. The projected staff data you provided in your September 1, 1973 letter show that staff assignments to some of your schools are not in accord with the decision in *Singleton v. Jackson* [requiring every school to have the same staff racial makeup as the district]. In fact, there will be ten elementary schools with one-race staffs—nine black, one white.

Holmes gave Baltimore thirty days to submit a plan for further student and faculty desegregation that would be implemented by the start of the fall semester.[8]

This letter came at a terrible time for Patterson. The day before, the Public School Teachers Association, bargaining agent for eighty-four hundred teachers dissatisfied with new contract terms, called a strike. The city got an injunction, but most teachers walked out, and students followed. On February 5, only 20 percent of teachers showed up, and fewer than 30 percent of students attended; these numbers would drop. The strike would last a month, to be settled only when the mayor took $6 million from the treasury for a new contract.[9]

In the third week of the strike, sixteen days into the thirty Holmes gave the city to develop a plan, Patterson told the school board about Holmes's order. He said he believed Baltimore had "maximized the integration of its schools to the fullest extent possible." To do more would drive away white middle-class families and hurt the tax base. Invoking the busing bugaboo, he declared it "unconsciona-ble to think of moving the white children" to predominantly black schools across the city. He added that the gasoline crisis and the system's distressed fisc made it impossible to buy or run buses for further integration. In any case, he reported, he had written HEW about the strike and asked for an extension. Meanwhile, he would do nothing. Larry Gibson, noting the consequences of failing to provide a plan, reminding those present that integration was the law of the land, and allud-ing to the horrors of what courts did when they stepped in and wrote integration plans, moved that the superintendent prepare a plan in compliance with HEW directions with the participation of a community task force. The board approved the motion. Soon after, OCR extended Baltimore's deadline to April 30.[10]

At the next board meeting, Walton, who liked free choice, expressed doubt that doing what HEW asked would desegregate schools:

> In order to improve racial integration in the schools of Baltimore, it is necessary to increase the white school population. And to accom-plish this, we must provide the kinds of schools to the city that will be attractive to both middle class whites as well as middle class blacks.... I suggest, therefore, that we start with the schools rather than with inte-gration.... It seems impractical to me as well as trivial to attempt to distribute the 30% white students we have proportionately among all the schools in the City.

He urged that the city go to court if HEW tried to impose unacceptable con-ditions. Patterson then announced that a task force would meet on March 18. At a press conference the next day, Patterson asserted that free choice, properly modified, could satisfy the federal government. It was now clear that $23 million were at stake.[11]

Baltimore Responds to Federal Demands

Patterson appointed thirty-nine persons to a Desegregation Task Force, includ-ing parents, activists, the Community Relations Commission director, an Urban League administrator, a Chamber of Commerce officer, educator group represen-tatives, two elected officials, a board member, and four system administrators.

The Desegregation Task Force Gets Started

Four of the thirty-nine had asked to be on the Task Force. One was attor-ney Herbert Goldman, a parent at Mt. Washington Elementary School, in an upper-middle-class white neighborhood. Community members urged him to request a spot. He got involved because he was afraid of busing. His neighbors feared busing other children in and having their children bused out. That, as they saw it, was the federal government solution for segregation. Making the school 70 percent black to comply with the federal edict, he figured, could be accomplished only by sending the majority of neighborhood children, including his daughter, elsewhere. Elsewhere would probably be Pimlico Elementary, a place, he believed, that black parents did not like either. Mt. Washington residents could afford private schools but Goldman wanted to keep the elementary school for neighborhood children.[12]

Betty Deacon, on the other hand, was a reluctant Task Force member. An activist in white working-class southeast Baltimore, she was surprised to get a call from a friend one Saturday morning. He said the newspaper story about the superintendent's press conference listed her as a Task Force member. She ran out to buy a paper; when she got back, her phone was ringing with calls from neighborhood parents glad she would represent them. As in Mt. Washington, they were concerned about busing. Deacon was angry, however, about being named without being consulted. She said she would take part only if neighborhoods such as hers had fair representation and community members were involved in making decisions.[13]

At the first Task Force meeting, Goldman was elected chairman. Later in the week, Dewey Dodds, OCR Philadelphia regional director, met with the group. He noted that 180 of 210 schools had enrollments outside the 50–90 percent black range and said open enrollment had not worked. He urged the Task Force to consider alternatives, including busing, but assured them that HEW was "not expecting any kind of massive busing." Sheila Sachs, the school board representative and a Mt. Washington parent, told him that most Task Force members had ruled out busing anyway. A lawyer and civic activist, she staunchly defended neighborhood schools. Dodds reminded the group that the courts also required desegregating faculties. While he discussed desegregation approaches with the group, President Nixon spoke on radio urging the House of Representatives to pass antibusing amendments to the education appropriations bill. Deacon raised her concerns about community involvement, and the group agreed to increase membership to fifty and scheduled hearings around the city. The Task Force established work groups and planned to meet three times weekly in order to give the board proposals by April 19 so it could meet the HEW April 30 deadline.[14]

Soon after, Baltimore planning director Larry Reich wrote Mayor Schaefer recommending litigation to merge the city and surrounding county school districts to desegregate schools. The memo discussed a pending Supreme Court case involving such a suit in Detroit. Noting that Mt. Washington parents were talking about leaving city schools in response to the HEW order, Reich suggested that legal action would hold off HEW intervention.[15]

On April 4, Samuel Banks, the school system's social studies coordinator and the Task Force vice chairman, gave Task Force members his desegregation plan, pairing 47 predominantly white and 47 predominantly black elementary schools.[16]

Southeast Baltimore Concerns

Southeast Baltimore, where working-class white ethnic families kept mostly to themselves, had a history of organizing when threatened. The South East Community Organization (SECO) was formed in 1971 after a fight to stop demolition of homes for a highway. When HEW contacted Patterson, SECO already had an Education Committee, chaired by Deacon. After Patterson named her to the Task Force, she decided to do whatever she could to defend white and black eastside communities.[17]

By chance, the Task Force had scheduled a hearing in southeast Baltimore the night before Banks was going to present his plan to the Task Force, and Deacon organized against it. SECO circulated fliers about "forced busing" and urged residents to attend the hearing. Twelve hundred showed up. The mayor was on record opposing busing. City Councilwoman Barbara Mikulski (a future U.S. senator) rejected busing and endorsed a metropolitan desegregation suit. An aide to Representative Paul Sarbanes (also a future U.S. senator) reported that he had voted for the antibusing amendment to the education appropriations bill. City Councilman John Schaefer (not related to the mayor) railed against Washington for once again meddling in Baltimore affairs. Busing, he declared, was "another effort by big brother to control our daily lives.... If we have to bus our children in order to obtain justified federal funds for education in Baltimore then I say, let them keep their federal funds.... it will be difficult but we will not falter under the crush of liberal power mongers who want to run our lives from Washington." The crowd put the school board on notice: as it tried to satisfy federal officials, it would have to mollify southeast Baltimore. The next evening, a hundred angry southeast residents attended the Task Force meeting. The following day, four hundred south Baltimore parents protested Banks's proposal.[18]

Deacon would later describe her Task Force experience as a sociology lesson. In a segregated city, she had pioneered in building a biracial coalition to oppose housing demolition for highway construction in the late 1960s. The Task Force brought her first contact with some of the city's elite, white and black. When it started, she "very idealistically" would have supported busing, but she found little idealism among other Task Force members. Some just wanted to cut deals to protect their neighborhood children and schools. Some blacks wanted integration and supported busing, but others, while talking of desegregation, seemed mainly interested in controlling increasingly black schools. Still others shared interests in preserving neighborhood schools, regardless of racial makeup.

What upset Deacon, besides some members' disingenuousness, was a tendency to scapegoat working-class whites. Blacks and middle-class whites agreed that the white working class were the city's racists, the obstacle to satisfying the federal government. In addition to racial prejudice, Deacon now saw class prejudice, where the better-off denied their own biases and put them on the less powerful. "It became clear to me that it was going to be okay to desegregate schools with poor blacks and working-class white people. But it wasn't going to be okay to have upper-middle-class and high-class people in those schools." She drew what seemed an obvious conclusion: "I said, why not do metropolitan desegregation, go across city lines? I'd love to have my son bused out to Roland Park, Dulaney Valley [well-to-do city and county areas]. Mix rich and poor and working class. I said that to the Task Force and the press. Some said, this is probably a great idea, but it will not happen." And so, if that were the case, southeast residents would look out for their own interests.[19]

The Desegregation Task Force Proposes, and Residents React

Now aiming to finish by April 16, the Task Force reviewed eleven plans before an often unruly audience of two hundred at a two and one-half hour meeting on April 11. With a day to go, work groups prepared five separate reports for final consideration. When the Task Force met on April 16, after six wearying hours, members could not agree on an overall plan and voted 25 to 20 to send the board five plans. One would halt further desegregation until housing segregation lessened. Banks's plan recommended pairing grades four through six at ninety-two schools, with extensive busing of white and black students. A third plan would establish elementary school attendance zones with racial balance and encourage clustering elementary schools into racially balanced middle schools. A fourth proposed making high schools evenly balanced between white and black, with free choice within that constraint. A final plan included methods for desegregating faculty. Though the plans did not add up to a comprehensive strategy, most assumed open enrollment would have to give.[20]

The *Sun* was sympathetic with difficulties settling on a plan and saw even in the disagreement a consensus on "doing something." Carefully, the paper supported HEW's request:

> While Baltimore acted promptly to desegregate the schools in 1954 following the landmark Supreme Court decision, it has done little or nothing to halt the resegregation that occurred as many formerly all-white

schools gradually became all-black. The assumption has been that there was little that could be done, given the population shift within city limits, and the emphasis however imperfectly has been on trying to improve the educational quality of the black schools. But now the HEW is saying that Baltimore cannot simply throw up its hands on desegregation, that it must try to bring black and white children together to the extent feasible. We agree that the HEW is probably right about this. The difficulty is determining what is feasible without major dislocation, increased white departures from the city and extensive busing, which supposedly the HEW is not urging.[21]

Meanwhile, Deacon organized. Convinced that most blacks and whites preferred good neighborhood schools to integration by busing, she thought the races should join forces and formed the Southeast Desegregation Coalition. Again, she was struck by the interplay of class and race. Dunbar was the eastside high school for blacks under segregation. Despite the federal mandate, East Baltimore black leaders wanted to develop the school as a black institution preparing students for health careers. Patterson High School, the historically white southeast high school, was part of the desegregation plan. Deacon went to Dunbar to talk with two black politicians about how to incorporate Dunbar into a desegregation scheme. They told her they did not want white students at the school and added that, if she wanted black children to integrate white schools, she should visit the poor families in public housing projects. She did, and gained black allies offended by the politicians.[22]

On April 17, eight hundred people attended a SECO Education Issues Hearing. They assembled under the banner "We're Staying in Our Schools—No Busing" and voted unanimously against each Task Force plan involving busing. Parents talked about registering their children at the schools they wanted, regardless of what desegregation plans said. Mikulski supported them with a letter to the *East Baltimore Guide,* in which she declared, "I AM TOTALLY OPPOSED TO FORCED CROSS-TOWN BUSING." She had met with Mayor Schaefer and urged him to fight HEW in court.[23]

The *Afro* defended busing. The uproar, it editorialized, didn't alter two basic facts: "Baltimore is in defiance of the law.... Additional busing, already agreed upon by the highest court as a tool to be used in ending illegal school segregation, will be necessary to desegregate on an acceptable level." The paper asked rhetorically, "Are the white students, 30 per cent, so much more important than the blacks 70 per cent?"[24]

The school board held public discussion of the plans on April 25. Some in the audience carried antibusing signs. Deacon brought petitions with 4,625 signatures asking that southeast do its own plan. Some white and black parents complained that desegregation would destroy neighborhood schools. Walton expressed a wish for metropolitan desegregation and noted that the Supreme Court would shortly rule on Detroit's urban-suburban arrangement. The board, unprepared to assemble a plan, awaited OCR's response to another extension request. A week later, Holmes gave Baltimore until June 20 to come up with a plan of which "a substantial portion" could be implemented in the fall.[25]

On May 4, 800 delegates representing 170 community organizations attended SECO's annual Community Congress and voted to "resist in any way necessary the forced bussing of children out of S. E. Baltimore to integrate other schools." They asked every southeast school to hold a preregistration day so that parents could enroll children where they chose. If the system did not do this, SECO would "register" children at each school itself.[26]

Others publicly defended integration. Marion Banfield, a black social worker who was one of the 28 Parents, later cochair of the Mayor's Task Force for Equal Rights in Education, and now a member of the Desegregation Task Force, wrote the *Evening Sun* lamenting the baleful effects of racial anxiety and urging renewed integration efforts:

> Because we have not openly and frankly talked about our racial feelings in schools, we have quietly drifted in or remained with racial isolation....Segregation festers hatred. Hatred obstructs rational thinking....Politicians...take advantage of racial hostility to induce a hysteria which blinds normally intelligent people to rational problems and decisions....We as blacks and whites in America can find no hiding place from each other....Together is the only method for black and white citizens to survive.

The *Jewish Times* published a story on a neighborhood where blacks and Orthodox Jews lived together. It highlighted efforts to make integration work despite tensions. "The Glen Avenue story is important," the paper said,

> because the races must learn to live together or the city will continue its downward economic spiral....The people of Glen Avenue are showing that white and black Americans can live together....that housing patterns in urban America can be stabilized at a respectable black-white ratio. If this continues to prove true, then the public school systems of urban America could service all segments of the population in an integrated school situation without the upheaval of busing.

Black integrationists and Jewish liberals, however, were in the minority.[27]

The School System Assembles a Plan

On May 9, the school board gave the staff guidelines for developing a plan. Patterson asked deputy superintendent John Crew to direct efforts. The board's central directive, passed with five whites in favor and four blacks opposed, was to forbid busing for elementary school integration, though allowing busing for secondary schools. The board directed staff to get "the maximum amount" of elementary school integration without busing. (State law required transportation for elementary students attending school more than a mile from home.) Junior high and middle schools should be at least 40 percent black. With high schools the board approved "voluntary and involuntary techniques" to produce "maximum integration." The board said school staffs should resemble the district: in fall, 1974, between 35 and 85 percent black, the following fall between 50 and 75 percent black.[28]

On *Brown*'s twentieth anniversary, the *Sun* trumpeted the accomplishments of the ruling and urged continuing efforts to desegregate schools and society. Walter Sondheim reminisced about how simple the 1954 board's decision had seemed and how successful the results had looked when he left the board in 1957. "We'd like to think," he reflected, "that we had played a major part in the solution of racial inequality...but when you look back at our share, it seems much smaller than we had thought." John Walton lamented how complicated issues and options had become. In any case, he declared, *Swann* did not apply to Baltimore. Citing these two board presidents, the *Afro* contrasted the actions of city officials in 1974 with those in 1954:

> In 1954, the school board, under the leadership of Walter Sondheim, Jr., and others, obeyed the law and got on with the job promptly so that Baltimore complied with a minimum of problems. But here we are two decades later with a school board led by conservative Dr. John Walton, and Mayor Schaefer's administration...who are doing everything in their power to cause dissension. In 1954, Mayor Thomas J. D'Alesandro Jr.'s administration emphasized being law-abiding and supported the school desegregation program of Superintendent John Fischer. Today, we have city leaders encouraging those who yell, "If we have to bus, we will not obey the law."

The *Afro* told public officials to get on with integration, without getting distracted by metropolitanism or agonizing over busing. At the same time, the *Afro* drew another contrast with 1954 and bemoaned the absence of support for integration from business, education, and church leaders, including black pastors. It urged the NAACP to sue and get court approval for a desegregation plan.[29]

Six hundred citizens crowded into the May 28 board meeting to hear Crew present the plan. For elementary students, free choice was over. Students entering the system would attend the school nearest home; transfers would be limited to majority-minority moves, hardships, and other specified conditions. Twenty-seven schools, enrolling 18 percent of elementary students, would be paired. Crew outlined two possible junior high school plans. One ended open enrollment and created feeder links between elementary and junior high schools. It would be implemented in one grade each year, affecting only one-fourth of junior high students in the first year. The other clustered schools to produce a combined racially balanced enrollment, with different grades in different schools. Students would choose clusters, rather than schools. The high school plan mixed ingredients. Seven schools would have specialized magnet programs, seven would remain comprehensive neighborhood schools, four would stay citywide schools, and Mergenthaler and Carver would merge. High school students would have free choice within building capacities. The staffing plan proposed moving 865 of the system's 8,300 teachers by September, mainly through voluntary transfers and reassignment of faculty returning from leave.[30]

Public Reaction

Baltimore NAACP branch president Enolia McMillan, who had succeeded Lillie May Jackson when she retired in 1969, wanted to see the details but doubted desegregation could be accomplished without elementary school busing. McMillan, whose father had been a slave, had attended Douglass High School, earned education degrees from Howard and Columbia universities, and become a teacher in 1927. She had led the Maryland State Colored Teachers' Association and was one of a few black teachers in Baltimore to move to an historically white school in 1954. She threatened legal action if the city failed to satisfy federal guidelines.[31]

Mayor Schaefer, recognizing that the matter could end up in court, announced the retainer of attorneys William Marbury and Stephen Derby to represent city interests. They were advising Montgomery County on school desegregation at the time. Marbury, principal in one of the city's elite law firms, was a preeminent Baltimore legal figure. A Harvard Law graduate, he had served on the Harvard governing body for twenty-two years. Although his father had advised the sponsors of the 1911 racial zoning ordinance and argued for black disfranchisement in the Supreme Court, he was a liberal. He had represented his friend Alger Hiss in a libel suit against Whittaker Chambers, and he was an original member of the Lawyers Committee for Civil Rights Under Law. Derby was returning to Piper and Marbury after two years as a Maryland assistant attorney general. He had been a Baltimorean since 1954, when he graduated from Harvard Law. Marbury was in his seventies, and Derby, thirty-six, would become the lead attorney in this matter.[32]

Newspapers characterized the desegregation plan as "minimal" and "moderate," while "imaginative" and "practical." The *Sun* explained that the "relatively mild proposal" would "affect at least initially, only next year's new high school students and black and white families living in or near integrated neighborhoods." Noting that only elementary schools near one another were paired, it observed, "The plan thus avoids large-scale desegregation of pupils in the age range where integration is considered most meaningful, and it concentrates on schools whose pupils are most likely now to play and attend school with children of the opposite race." The analysis singled out the high school plan for its feebleness and possible unconstitutionality: "This plan is built on the city's long-established 'open enrollment' policy...banned by the courts where it has not enhanced integration....the magnet scheme has been in effect in the city for three years. Dr. Crew conceded that it has done nothing to enhance desegregation and that the basing of the new plan on a magnet approach 'is sketchy at best.'"[33]

In southeast Baltimore, parents objected to everything. White parents at General Wolfe Elementary did not want their children going to City Springs, the paired school, which drew black students from public housing. Further, these parents, as well as those at Hampstead Hill, Highlandtown #215, and Highlandtown #237, did not want their children "fed" into nearly all-black Lombard Junior High. The school's poor education, student insubordination, and physical danger, they said, made it a place neither black nor white parents desired. In addition, southeast residents resented the designation of Patterson High as a construction trades magnet. Venerated Patterson had proud alumni. Making it a magnet would dissolve community boundaries and force many southeast youths to leave while admitting many black students from outside. But the nature of the magnet—construction trades—was the rankest of class insults. Apparently the elite believed that working-class children had the ability only for manual labor, that they lacked the intelligence and motivation for mental work and college. (Making the school a construction magnet would also remove most girls.)

Southeasterners pushed ahead with "preregistration" plans and drafted a proposal to keep Patterson a zoned neighborhood comprehensive high school. The day after Crew presented his plan for Patterson to the board, 95 percent of twelve hundred students in the second shift at the school walked out, and five hundred paraded to City Hall, chanting, "Hell no, we won't go!" The next day Patterson students again cut class to demonstrate. They were joined by students from six other schools, about three thousand in all, in protests at City Hall and school headquarters. Hampstead Hill and Canton junior high students objected to clustering with a predominantly black school. Students at mostly white Mergenthaler protested merging with nearly all-black Carver. A southeast mother railed against integration as akin to communism: "This isn't Russia," she declared, "and nobody's going to tell my kid where to go to school." City Hall protests grew. On Saturday, two thousand people demonstrated. Sunday evening, southeast residents massed for a rally in Patterson Park. Monday morning, two thousand high school students blocked traffic outside City Hall for an hour. Blacks who spoke up argued for integration. The mayor expressed satisfaction with the proposals while the board contemplated the protests and considered making revisions.[34]

On Tuesday, June 4, Walton opened the board meeting by announcing that the plan had been modified. Elementary pairings had been reduced to seven, involving only 14 schools and 9 percent of elementary students. The board approved the revisions 7–2, with Gibson and Griffin opposed. For junior highs, the board chose the feeder plan, which would be implemented in only the seventh grade the first year. Gibson, Griffin, and new black member Beryl Williams, a Morgan State College dean, were on the losing end of a 5–3 vote. In a new high school plan, Patterson and four other schools remained comprehensive, and Mergenthaler and Carver remained separate. Gibson objected that the plan did little to integrate. Seven of the eight remaining magnet schools, he noted, were predominantly black and would likely stay that way as long as they were magnets. Williams observed that zoning schools at the city periphery would keep them nearly all-white or all-black. Gibson, Williams, and Griffin again lost 5–3. The board amended the faculty plan to limit transfers to ten teachers per school at a time. Only the five whites supported those changes.

Though whites generally favored the amendments, the audience raucously challenged the board. Students stormed the stage, demanding to speak. Parents complained about federal intrusion into community affairs. Mikulski alleged that the HEW desegregation order was just "a Washington scenario to take our attention away from the impeachment of the President." She argued for open enrollment. Gibson charged her with inconsistency, pointing out that she and her constituents supported the no-choice junior high feeder plan, apparently because it kept students in neighborhood schools.[35]

As Patterson prepared to take the plan to Holmes, litigation threats and legal action swirled around it. Schaefer threatened to sue HEW if it did not accept the plan. McMillan threatened to sue HEW if it did accept the plan. She criticized the mayor and the board's "conservative majority" for encouraging self-interested individualism that stood in the way of integration. She had more faith in children than in adults: if the schools were integrated, she believed, young children would "get along beautifully." The *Afro*, declaring that the plan "perpetuates segregation," urged the NAACP to go to court. Meanwhile, the NAACP Legal Defense Fund filed a motion with Judge Pratt in the *Adams* case to order Justice Department legal action or HEW administrative enforcement hearings to cut off funds to districts including Baltimore.[36]

Edgar Jones, an *Evening Sun* reporter who had been watching desegregation since 1954, saw an altered city:

> The disordered state of race relations in Baltimore was revealed with almost frightening clarity in the past several weeks, as large numbers of white high school students roamed the streets with impunity shouting "Hell no, we won't go." At public hearings before the School Board they were rude, crude and unattractive, not only booing and shouting derisively at board members but also showing total disrespect for School Superintendent Roland N. Patterson....
>
> Twenty years ago when a few hundred white students at Southern High School demonstrated...nearly every community leader worthy of the name denounced their disregard of law and order....In those days there was a fairly large reservoir of white goodwill toward Negroes. Many Baltimoreans knew that segregation was wrong and were willing to stand up for the School Board's efforts to eliminate it. In those days, too, the School Board acted unanimously and decisively and without looking to the Mayor for direction.

Now whites had given up on efforts to make a way with blacks:

> The past few weeks have shown precious little evidence of white goodwill toward either blacks or the School Board (or school administrators). Except for a few neighborhoods trying to preserve some integration, Baltimore's white residents by and large are buttoned up in their own diminishing sectors....The white kids who hooked school to shout their protests probably quite accurately reflected white parental attitudes, including the disrespect for authority.

And blacks had retreated from integration and the public schools:

> Also in slim evidence was support for the School Board from the black middle class and black politicians...The private and parochial schools have a goodly number of middle-class black children, including the offspring of black public school teachers, principals and supervisors. When there was a need for the white and black leadership to pull together to help bring about a rational school policy, the whites with a few exceptions let their rowdier elements do the yelling, and the blacks with equally few exceptions looked the other way.

Martin Luther King's assassination, the riots, and the aftermath had changed Baltimore.[37]

FEDERAL OFFICIALS, THE SCHOOL BOARD, AND PARENTS NEGOTIATE

A month after Roland Patterson submitted the Baltimore plan to OCR, on July 23, 1974, Peter Holmes, Lloyd Henderson, chief of the OCR Education Branch, and Harold Davis gave city representatives the verdict. The plan, which did little in elementary schools and left grades eight through twelve untouched the first year, would not "substantially desegregate" in September. Holmes accepted the proposed elementary school pairings as an interim plan but asked the district to add pairings, for which he offered staff aid. He found elementary school attendance boundaries ambiguous and asked the city to draw defined zones. He accepted the seventh grade feeder plan as an interim measure pending plans for grades eight and nine. He found the senior high plan confusing and wanted something clear and effective. With minor changes, he accepted the faculty plan. He asked the city to submit a revised plan for September by August 14 and a final plan by November 1. Otherwise, OCR would start administrative hearings to cut off funds.[1]

Two days later, the Supreme Court ruled against metropolitan remedies for segregation. In *Milliken v. Bradley*, a 5–4 majority held that interjurisdictional schemes were unconstitutional unless plaintiffs could prove the legal culpability of suburbs or the state in segregating city schools. The *Sun* editorialized that the court had removed the only realistic means of desegregating Baltimore schools and predicted that compliance with OCR demands would drive out whites and further segregate schools.[2]

Chaos in Baltimore

While school officials and OCR negotiated, much around them was in free fall. On July 30, the House Judiciary Committee voted out an article of impeachment against President Nixon, and on August 8 Nixon resigned. The evening Nixon announced his resignation, the white members of the Baltimore school board tried to fire Superintendent Patterson.

Conflict had been growing around Patterson for a long time. Critics charged he lacked the ability to manage the system, was insensitive to teachers' concerns in the strike, and had made bad appointments. Board member Robert Schaefer (unrelated to the mayor), chief financial officer at a local bank and chair of the school board Finance Committee, was disturbed that Patterson had ignored his request to interview comptroller candidates and was upset that Patterson wanted to lower admission standards for the Poly "A" Course. Some noted his hesitation responding to the federal request for a desegregation plan. Staff were leaving the system, and he had not filled positions as the start of school approached. Mayor Schaefer was concerned that Patterson showed no signs of planning for opening desegregated schools in September. Beyond specific charges, Patterson was a lightning rod for polarized racial feelings. As the first permanent black superintendent, he represented black interests in controlling the majority-black system. At the same time, he framed a wide range of issues racially and often labeled criticism racism. When the city was forced to desegregate, he became a symbol of whatever people liked or disliked about integration. To many blacks he could do no wrong, whereas for a growing number of whites whatever he did was wrong.

During the first week of August, the five white board members strategized to remove Patterson a year before his contract ended. Schaefer would introduce a motion, and Walton would call a vote, with five votes certain for removal. Black board members learned of the plan when white members contacted the two who were most critical of Patterson to ask their support. The two informed black residents, and hundreds came to the August 8 board meeting. After discussion of routine items, Schaefer introduced his motion, it was seconded, and then Patterson supporters shouted down the board. Walton pounded his gavel and called for a vote, but Griffin grabbed the gavel and said there would be no vote. A crowd rushed the stage, tearing out microphone cords and strewing documents. Griffin invited the audience to testify for Patterson. Parren Mitchell, now a member of the House of Representatives, condemned the five white members, called for order, and presided over four hours of mostly black testimony supporting Patterson. At the end, it was unclear whether the board had fired the superintendent. Patterson returned to work the next day. The mayor asked City Solicitor

Benjamin Brown to review meeting tapes to determine whether a vote had occurred. Brown concluded that there was no formal, binding vote.[3]

Five days later, awkwardly shifting gears, the board convened in emergency session to adopt a new modified desegregation plan. At least a dozen plainclothes police were on hand to ensure order. Crew introduced proposals for minor changes. On July 31, Harold Davis had shown city officials pairings of thirty-one elementary schools that OCR thought feasible. Crew's proposal added ten of these, from which the board, after community protest, removed one. Gibson argued that the busing ban limited pairings to densely populated areas that had several schools within walking distance—in short, only working-class neighborhoods. The plan passed 4–2 with one abstention, the latter three votes from Gibson, Griffin, and Williams, who criticized the plan for doing little. A slightly modified junior high plan passed 4–1, two abstaining, with Gibson, Griffin, and Williams again not in support. Walton announced that a high school plan would be ready by November 1.[4]

The board submitted the revisions to OCR and awaited a response while moving to open schools in two weeks. Deacon continued organizing parents and children to sit-in at schools of their choice. She arranged nonviolence training and sold raffle tickets to raise a legal defense fund. Meanwhile, middle-class white families exercised exit options. According to the *Sun,* parents in Bolton Hill, the seat of early gentrification mentioned by Sondheim as a neighborhood that families would leave if integration were forced, were putting children in private schools instead of a nearby junior high the quality and safety of which they doubted. The *Sun* reported that working-class whites were turning to Catholic schools to avoid desegregation. In fact, enrollment in the Baltimore Archdiocese, which included the city, suburbs, and rural counties, rose by less than 2 percent in the fall before resuming a long-term decline from a 1964 peak. Lower-income families had no choice; hence their vehemence about public school policy.[5]

Meanwhile, the school system announced that parents would not know where children were assigned until at least August 28, just a week before the September 5 opening. Teachers, 1,302 of whom would move, 964 involuntarily, would not know where to report until September 1. The Mass Transit Administration, which would transport secondary school students, waited in the dark, ready to do its best to add buses and adjust schedules or routes.[6]

In the middle of all this, on August 23, Holmes rejected the city's plan and declared "no alternative" to starting administrative enforcement proceedings. He offered to hold off, however, if the system complied with his earlier conditions for reassigning teachers, desegregating the seventh grade, and submitting a plan for grades 8–12 by November 1. In addition, he wanted the new pairings implemented, and he requested by November 1 "pupil locator maps and a map of zones indicating where students would be assigned if they attended elementary schools nearest their homes.…for considering the feasibility of further remedies to maximize desegregation." He reiterated that he regarded the city's latest plans as interim measures, pending analysis of the maps to determine what more could be done.[7]

City officials were defiant. A week before schools opened, Mayor Schaefer said he would personally alter the plan. City Council president Walter Orlinsky, citing a new federal law barring HEW from requiring busing beyond a child's second-nearest school, threatened to sue HEW. Superintendent Patterson stood nearly alone with the plan, and his support was tepid. Nearly the only prominent citizen advocating for the plan was the new archbishop, William Borders, who believed that the plan, even with its imperfections, would begin racial healing. On Labor Day, Schaefer and Orlinsky met with City Solicitor Brown, who told them that Schaefer could not change the plan and Orlinsky could not sue, and Schaefer then urged peaceful compliance. The Baltimore Urban Coalition, a biracial group of business and civic leaders, made a one-hour television appeal for all with influence to support an orderly school opening. The mayor approved a massive police deployment.[8]

Parents Modify the Plan

Desegregation affected only 20,000 of 180,000 students, but many parents, mainly white, demonstrated against the plan and informally amended it by keeping their children from assigned schools and, in many cases, taking them to preferred schools. Parents picketed or sat in at a dozen schools, most in white working-class south, southwest, and southeast neighborhoods and Hampden, but also in black east Baltimore. Junior highs were the crucial test, because they involved the most students and because students' ages aroused the greatest anxiety about sex and violence.

On opening day, school officials put a good face on things, asserting that 77 percent of junior high students were in school, not much less than 83 percent a year earlier. However, this figure included not only the seventh grade, which was subject to desegregation, but also the eight and ninth, which were not. The actual turnout by the end of the week was probably closer to 70 percent. Moreover, white attendance was only 50 percent, considerably lower than blacks' 78 percent. At the ten junior high schools that had been nearly all black, white attendance was only 20 percent. For example, 114 whites were assigned to Cherry Hill Junior High, but none showed up. One of 71 came to Booker T. Washington, and 3 of 87 turned out at Houston-Woods. Some schools had low white and black attendance. For example, at Lombard, the focus of southeast boycotts, where blacks comprised 87 percent, attendance was only 72 percent. At Clifton Park, 90 percent black, attendance was just 50 percent. At the paired elementary schools, attendance was a little better, about 74 percent. However, even there, white attendance lagged behind black attendance, 62 percent to 78 percent.[9]

The *Afro* recognized that attendance was low and reported incidents where white students harassed blacks or black intimidated whites. Nevertheless, emphasizing the overall calm, it proclaimed "Integration…a success." At Clifton Park Junior High, for example, it declared that integration was "working well," despite white attendance of only 43 percent, because attendance was rising and white and black students were getting along.[10]

In southeast Baltimore, more than a hundred white parents had "preregistered" children at junior high schools they preferred to the assigned Lombard. On opening day, about 80 parents took children to Canton, and about 50 went to Hampstead Hill, where parents and children took available seats. Administrators let the children stay. The mayor went to Canton and met with protesting parents, who cheered him. He praised their calmness and lambasted the "insensitive people at HEW…who don't care about people, only care about one thing, statistics." In Canton and Hampstead Hill classrooms, some teachers readily accepted the new students, while others refused to recognize them or take their homework. Gradually, most teachers included them in classes. The mayor returned to the southeast a week later to attend a boycott rally and argue for modifying the plan. Deacon would keep appearing at school board meetings to request changes in the feeder plan.[11]

On the first day of school, attorney Stephen Derby phoned Holmes. He described problems implementing the plan, most prominently seventh grade absenteeism. He asked Holmes what to do about white parents' refusal to send their children to Cherry Hill Junior High, and he suggested altering the plan.[12]

HEW Blows the Whistle

Four days later, while several thousand mostly white students stayed home from assigned schools, HEW notified Baltimore of a hearing that could be the first step in withholding funds. The city had twenty days to respond. The notice charged that Baltimore had never taken feasible steps to desegregate historically white and black schools, so that the city continued to "operate a substantial number of schools which are either one race or substantially disproportionate in student racial composition [outside the 50–90 percent black range]." In the 1973–74 school year, HEW reported, 123 of 212 schools were more than 90 percent minority, and 63 were majority white. Further, the district continued to assign teachers, principals, and other staff in ways that reinforced schools' racial identities. Holmes's August 23 letter had given notice that HEW "had exhausted attempts to secure…voluntary compliance with Title VI of the Civil Rights Act of 1964." In light of Baltimore's refusal to consider policies that would more quickly and effectively create a unitary system of racially indistinguishable schools, HEW requested an order terminating aid.[13]

The School Board Desegregates Less

John Walton opened discussion at the September 19 board meeting with remarks meant to reassure at least white parents. He mentioned the recent federal education amendments that forbid HEW from busing children beyond the school second nearest home. Under the law, he said, Baltimore might be able to reduce desegregation. Gibson followed by criticizing the junior high feeder plan for producing little integration. He called attention to the federal hearing notice and expressed chagrin that the city had not responded. Griffin added his concern that the board had done nothing to prepare a high school plan, due in six weeks. Then Schaefer moved that students at six junior high schools subject to white boycotts be allowed to transfer to their closest or second closest junior high school. He, Oscar Helm, a retired principal, and black member Eugene Scott, a Johns Hopkins physicist, voted for the motion. Gibson, Griffin, and Williams abstained. Walton broke the tie by supporting the change. The board thus ratified parents' noncompliance by revoking feeder patterns they objected to.[14]

After the school board vote, southeast parents ended their sit-in. Within a week, 900 students, including 138 at Lombard, applied for transfers. The vast majority were white, though a few black parents, concerned about travel distance or school safety, also wanted to move children. White south Baltimore parents keeping children out of Cherry Hill, however, got no relief because there was no nearby alternative and the board did not exempt it from the feeder plan.[15]

The *Sun* decried "desegregation without direction":

> If Baltimore could be said to have had a school desegregation plan for seventh graders, that plan has been disemboweled by the School Board's decision to return to a form of freedom of choice at the six junior high schools where desegregation protests have been heard most strongly.…But…it should be acknowledged that the feeder system had few supporters. Put together hurriedly at the goading of federal civil-rights officials, who are under a court order to eliminate the vestiges of pre-1954 dual school systems, the feeder system ran contrary to the continuing black interest in preserving a choice of schools and

the deep-seated white resentment of having relatively small numbers of white children assigned to overwhelmingly black schools....

Perhaps the most worrisome aspect is the lack of leadership inside or outside the school system on this crucial issue. The School Board is badly divided and at loose ends....School Superintendent Patterson has disowned the desegregation plans, saying they are the board's responsibility, yet the board members can only go as far as professional staff work makes possible. Mayor Schaefer dips in and out, not so much showing leadership as reflecting community indecision.

As a steady stream of parents requested transfers, the *Sun* said, a situation demanding thoughtful educational leadership was falling into the hands of political actors who neither knew nor cared much about education. Absent such leadership, it observed, many blacks treated the school system as a power base rather than an educational institution, and white parents yelled "no" at any racial mixing. The *Afro* lost all patience and urged the NAACP to sue the board for perpetuating segregation.[16]

The Office for Civil Rights rejected the plan revisions, and John Crew, City Solicitor Brown, and Stephen Derby met with Peter Holmes on October 15 to take stock. Holmes offered assistance drawing up plans. The next day, Harold Davis came from Philadelphia for the first of three October visits to observe grades one through seven and press for an elementary school pupil locator map and staff information. Boston schools had just blown up over integration, and the *Sun*'s front page showed a black student on a stretcher above a headline reporting "U.S. Troops Asked in Boston." In a kind of balance, the front page of the local news section showed an injured white Baltimore student below a headline reporting "Beaten Junior High Student Refused to Go Back to Desegregated School." The previous day the *Sun* had run a Boston op-ed that must have resonated locally: "Working Class Boston Wants Upper Class Whites Bused, Too."[17]

With a week to go before HEW's November 1 deadline for a high school plan, the board unanimously adopted a "concept" that would make eleven high schools comprehensive zoned schools and leave six others citywide magnets. Students who did not go to a magnet would attend their nearest or next-nearest high school. Students could transfer from schools where their race was the majority to any where they were the minority. The board revised the junior high plan to let south Baltimore whites transfer children from Cherry Hill to Diggs-Johnson. In other business, Joseph Kelly, Fraternal Order of Police president, reported on the shooting of a Douglass High security officer and suggested arming school police.[18]

The NAACP reacted angrily to the continuing retrenchment. "The board's lack of commitment to meaningful desegregation," Enolia McMillan complained, "resulted in a watered-down plan which made very few changes." "The board's willingness to yield repeatedly to the pressure of segments of population opposed to any change affecting its group has made ineffective much of the already weak plan." Therefore, she said, "the NAACP will again be forced to use the courts to secure the implementation of the laws of the land."[19]

Over the week, Derby and Holmes conferred. Regarding elementary schools, Holmes wrote that proposed boundaries should, within capacity limits, result in students' attending schools nearest their homes. For high schools the city got an extension until February 3, 1975. On the last day of October, the district sent OCR a map showing each elementary student's residence and his or her nearest school. Federal staff were not satisfied because some schools were located on zone boundaries and, in any case, the map did not include school capacities.[20]

Four board members' terms expired at the end of 1974, and Mayor Schaefer replaced two whites (Walton and Farring) and two blacks (Gibson and Griffin) with three black members (Howard Marshall, Grover McCrea, and David Sloan) and a white president, Norman Ramsey. The board now had a black majority. Marshall, an executive with McCormick Spice, had worked with the Baltimore Urban League. McCrea, a corporate recruiter, had taught at the Community College of Baltimore and Coppin, helped create a middle school, and was an officer in his children's elementary school PTA. Sloan, a lawyer, had been senior editor of the *Afro* and now wrote weekly *Sun* columns. Ramsey, fifty-two, was a partner in a prominent law firm. He had handled highly publicized cases involving federal tax evasion and political corruption charges. He had served on the American Bar Association committee that reviewed President Nixon's Supreme Court nominees Clement Haynsworth and Harrold Carswell. He lived in the elite Guilford neighborhood and sent his daughter to private school. A former Marine, he had a reputation for toughness and was rumored to be Schaefer's man to remove Roland Patterson. The *Sun* characterized the new board as "predominantly middle-class and middle-of-the-road."[21]

The Office for Civil Rights Sets Conditions

On January 8, Holmes wrote Patterson: the board's alterations to the interim plan, which was inadequate to begin with, had only increased segregation. The new junior high transfers had reduced desegregation. Moreover, a number of students had transferred to overcrowded schools on shifts. At least thirteen of the twenty-six junior highs were on shifts; the board seemed to prefer crowding to integration. Modifications to elementary school pairings had reduced desegregation. Faculty composition at thirty-one schools did not meet the goal of 50–75 percent black. Holmes told Baltimore to fix the seventh grade, elementary school, and faculty plans, provide a pupil locator map including school capacity, and submit a plan for grades eight through twelve—all by February 3. Otherwise, OCR would proceed to administrative enforcement hearings.[22]

The *Sun* tried to frame the HEW position reasonably. It assumed federal officials were acting in good faith to enforce the law. However, "the fact that it is often hard to know exactly what they want or which plans will meet with their approval or disapproval can be taken as an indication that they too are feeling their way in a very difficult and sensitive matter of human relations." Nevertheless, "while school desegregation by now has assumed the aspects of a numbers game with children assigned...to satisfy a racial percentage objective, at heart the legal compulsion to eliminate segregation has one purpose: to enhance the educational opportunities of black children." In a school district as predominantly black as Baltimore, the *Sun* observed, "desegregation would not appear to have any substantive meaning any more," but demography didn't change legal requirements. Accordingly, "the foremost obligation of Superintendent Patterson and the School Board...is...to make the desegregation moves which demonstrably further equal educational opportunities."[23]

Patterson staked out his position in a reply to Holmes's January 9 letter, on January 20. "Many of the assertions in your letter," he began, "are contrary to our understanding of the actual facts." While Holmes had criticized district actions and demanded remedies,

> you have not identified the asserted deficiencies with sufficient detail to permit the Board and the public school administration to consider means for correcting whatever deficiencies may exist. In view of your offer of assistance, we hope that you will be willing to describe in detail each deficiency which you believe exists, to explain what you believe must be accomplished to correct each deficiency, and to suggest measures which you believe would work to overcome the asserted deficiencies. Only then will the Board be in a position to respond to your request for "specific measures."

Holmes, Patterson said, had not identified the thirty-one schools that did not have satisfactory faculty composition, and he misunderstood the results of recent student transfers. With so much ambiguity, Patterson ended, the city would have difficulty submitting remedies by February 3.[24]

The City Responds Again

On January 30, a unanimous board approved a "working draft" of a high school plan. In a departure from open enrollment, twelve of seventeen high schools would be zoned comprehensive high schools. Five—Poly, Western, Mergenthaler,

Carver, and Dunbar—would stay citywide schools. Magnet schools, many of which were weak and few of which attracted white students to predominantly black schools, would close. Transfers between zoned schools would be allowed for residence change, selection of specialized programs, or majority-minority moves. A third of high school students would have to change schools in the fall. With a high school population 70 percent black, five schools would remain all black, with a sixth 96 percent black, down from nine all-black schools currently. Seven schools would meet federal guidelines, up from three. Eleven percent of black students would attend majority-white schools, 44 percent would attend schools at least 96 percent black, and 45 percent would be in "balanced" schools. Forty-nine percent of white students would attend majority-white schools, 49 percent would attend "balanced" schools, and two percent would be in schools at least 96 percent black. Patterson would be the largest and whitest high school, with 70 percent of its thirty-four hundred students white. To accommodate so many students, it would be the only high school on shifts.[25]

Deacon was prominent among whites endorsing the plan. Black leaders, contending that zoning would confine black students in poor schools, decried the elimination of open enrollment and magnets. State Senator Robert Douglass was among blacks disillusioned with integration. His constituents, he said, opposed the high school plan "because we no longer think that integration is the panacea." He complained that Baltimore integration mainly involved moving black children around, leaving most white children alone. While blacks had complied with desegregation plans "like good soldiers," Douglass said, the school board rewarded whites who defied the policy.[26]

Later in the month, Holmes responded to Patterson's complaints about inaccuracies and ambiguities. Harold Davis and Eric Carriker, of the HEW Office of General Counsel, had visited Baltimore schools in January, and Holmes believed they had accurately described deficiencies. He gave the district a week to tell him when it would remedy the problems and said he would get back to the superintendent on the high school plan when he had reviewed it.[27]

Meanwhile, the board geared up for a new junior high plan. As with the high schools, it turned to zoning. Because most larger schools and white students were at the city's edge and black students were concentrated in the center, some zones were long and narrow, radiating out like hands of a Dali watch. The plan would move 50–60 percent of current seventh and eighth graders. Twelve of twenty-three junior high and two middle schools would meet federal guidelines, up from seven under the feeder plan. However, ten would remain more than 90 percent black, and four would be majority white, with Canton whitest. Six percent of black students would attend majority-white schools, 47 percent would attend schools at least 98 percent black, and 47 percent would go to "balanced" schools. Thirty-one percent of white students would attend majority white schools,

67 percent would go to "balanced" schools, and 2 percent would attend schools at least 98 percent black.

After the Douglass High shooting, board member Eugene Scott decided to look at school violence, and his hearings, accompanied by frequent news stories on school incidents, had increased whites' wariness about predominantly black schools. Several white parent groups protested the junior high proposals and boycotted schools. The Southeast Desegregation Coalition, set on keeping children out of Lombard, proposed an alternative. After hearings and protests, on March 13, the board again amended its plan, shifting white students from predominantly black into predominantly white schools. New southeast zones would make Canton 74 percent white and Hampstead Hill 49 percent white, both on shifts, and Lombard 99 percent black. At the same time, the board reaffirmed the goal of matching the faculty makeup of schools to that of the system.[28]

By unfortunate coincidence, the same day Baltimore sent HEW its junior high and faculty plans, Judge Pratt issued a supplemental order against HEW in *Adams*. Citing a Civil Rights Commission report, he observed, "There appears to be an over-reliance by HEW on the use of voluntary negotiations over protracted time periods and a 'reluctance…to use the administrative sanction process where school districts are known to be in non-compliance.'" Of the eighty-five "*Swann*" districts, thirty-nine, including Baltimore, "remain unsolved more than 25 months after the issuance of this Court's Order, but HEW has not initiated enforcement proceedings against any of them. The time for securing compliance by merely voluntary means…has passed." Pratt gave HEW sixty days to start enforcement action against the districts. No matter that ten of those twenty-five months lapsed between Holmes's initial letter to Patterson requesting information and his next letter calling for a plan in thirty days. No matter that Holmes seemed willing to play things out a little longer with Baltimore. The court left little maneuvering room. The sixty days would run out on Tuesday, May 13. That would be four days short of *Brown*'s twenty-first anniversary, a generation.[29]

While the city awaited the federal response to its plans, the new board president, Norman Ramsey, began taking steps to remove Superintendent Patterson, whose contract would run out in October. Ramsey wrote Patterson that the board would evaluate his performance. Patterson allies and opponents girded for battle. Patterson engaged Larry Gibson as his attorney.[30]

The day after Patterson hired Gibson to save his job, Holmes sent Patterson his judgment on the latest plans. The May 2 letter, beginning with reference to Pratt's order, concluded by stating that OCR would initiate administrative hearings against the city. Legal action would be suspended if Baltimore submitted an acceptable plan and certain requested data. Seven pages specified objections to the plans. Many secondary schools still failed to satisfy the 50–90 percent standard, and southeast schools stood out as the worst violations. Thirteen junior highs did not meet desegregation standards. Significantly, three majority-white schools were adjacent to schools with 98 or 99 percent black enrollments, and all three would be enrolled beyond capacity, while the nearly all-black schools would have space. Holmes wrote that "the fact that the relationship between capacity and enrollment varies directly with the racial composition of the junior high schools in question" suggested that Baltimore was deliberately resisting desegregation.

Similarly, seven senior highs would fall outside desegregation parameters. Significantly, two majority-white schools—Patterson and Northern—would enroll 53 percent of all white students. Moreover, Patterson would have more than 1,000 above its capacity. Adjacent to each was a school at least 96 percent black. Holmes wrote that the existence of shifts as a result of over-enrollment suggested that the city was resisting high school desegregation. In addition, Holmes was skeptical that Dunbar truly prepared students for health careers and asked why the school, which would be 99 percent black, should not be zoned and desegregated by exchanging students with nearby Patterson. With regard to faculty, Holmes objected that the district would allow too much variation among schools, leaving many staffs racially identifiable. As for elementary schools, the district had failed to submit maps showing school capacities. Without this information, OCR could not determine how much desegregation was reasonable.[31]

Baltimore Tries to Cope

Baltimoreans increasingly couched resistance to federal demands as a defense of community norms and cohesion. The *Sun,* which earlier had reminded readers that the focal issue was improving black children's education, now complained that narrow-minded federal officials fixated on racial statistics and misunderstood local customs. Ramsey replied to Holmes in a thirteen-page letter. He regretted Holmes's not discussing his concerns before going to administrative enforcement, and he argued that many criticisms were based on inaccurate assumptions, misunderstandings, or "a failure to comprehend fully the negative consequences which are likely to flow from some of the alternative zoning suggestions to which you have alluded." After responding to Holmes point-by-point, Ramsey invited him to meet with Baltimore school officials.[32]

In mid-May the board met with Holmes, HEW regional director Gorham Black, Davis, and other HEW staff and lawyers from Washington and Philadelphia. The federal officials delineated deficiencies in the city's plans. The board presented a map with proposed elementary school attendance areas. A week later, Davis met with school officials and showed them zoning alternatives that would increase desegregation. Holmes followed up by asking for more information. On

June 20, Ramsey sent Holmes a revised school pupil locator map that showed attendance areas and included school capacities.[33]

Some board members talked about suing HEW, but the board was going to end up in court first as the object of a suit by its superintendent. While Ramsey was trying to work things out with Holmes, the board met for days on end with Patterson and Gibson. On June 9, it voted 7–2 to fire Patterson. He got a temporary injunction against dismissal from Supreme Bench Judge Joseph Howard. The city appealed and got a favorable decision from the Maryland Court of Appeals. Patterson asked the U.S. Supreme Court to intervene. Justice Thurgood Marshall signed a twenty-four-hour stay of board proceedings but two and a half hours later, after reading the briefs, denied High Court review. At last, on July 17, the board fired Patterson. It named John Crew interim superintendent, an appointment that would become permanent. Under these conditions, the city was fortunate that administrative hearings had been postponed from June 30 to August 4.[34]

John Crew, who had managed desegregation planning as deputy superintendent, was from South Carolina, where he had attended segregated schools. He came to Baltimore to study at Morgan, later getting an NYU master's and a University of Maryland doctorate in educational measurement. He started work with Baltimore schools in 1955 as an educational psychologist, later went to the state to supervise testing, and returned to Baltimore in 1969 as director of special education. Paterson appointed him deputy superintendent for planning, research, and evaluation in 1972. He had a reputation for forthrightness, an ability to work with diverse groups, including parents, and good relations with Mayor Schaefer.[35]

At the end of July, Baltimore awaited the opening of school and the hearings. As backdrop, a headline that "Boston Girds for School Violence" was the start of a steady drumbeat of stories about busing, protests, and violence in desegregating cities around the country.[36]

The Lawyers Take Over

With the commencement of administrative enforcement proceedings, informal, more or less voluntary negotiations between school officials and federal civil rights officers gave way to formal legal action, with both sides represented by attorneys.

Administrative Enforcement Prehearing Conference

On August 4, 1975, administrative law judge Irvin Hackerman convened a prehearing conference at Social Security Headquarters in Baltimore. Present were

Interim Superintendent John Crew, Deputy Superintendent Robert Armacost, Assistant City Solicitor Blanche Wahl, and counsel Stephen Derby from Baltimore and attorneys Eric Carriker and Christopher Hagen and investigator Harold Davis from the U.S. Department of Health, Education, and Welfare. The purpose of the conference was to hear a Baltimore motion to dismiss the proceedings. Hackerman, a New Jersey judge, had presided over several dozen similar cases and was a confident master of procedure.

Derby began by arguing that stability in Baltimore as an integrated city depended on a temperate school policy that did not drive out middle-class people (he did not mention race). He invoked the Boston tempest as a sign of how volatile schools were and how sensitively the federal government should consider what was feasible. Baltimore's commitment to desegregation, he said, could be seen in the presence of black school administrators, a black superintendent, and a black board majority. Then he got to the heart of the city's case: the federal government had failed "to identify with specificity exactly what programs [it] seeks to terminate, and exactly how discrimination has been practiced in the administration of these programs," as, he said, federal regulations required. Thus the district did not know either with what it was charged or what it must do to comply with the Civil Rights Act. Moreover, the city was still negotiating with HEW, and it would be premature, and contrary to law, to suspend these efforts to comply voluntarily and proceed to enforcement hearings. Derby dismissed Holmes's current request for elementary school maps by noting that he had not responded to the maps submitted on June 20.[37]

Carriker spoke for OCR. He had gone to Harvard and Boston University Law School and, at thirty, was a few years younger than Derby. He had started at OCR just out of law school the previous summer. His supervisor, David Leeman, was also assigned to the Baltimore case, but a small OCR legal staff stretched to handle a huge elementary and secondary education caseload, and Carriker was lead attorney. When Holmes first threatened Baltimore with administrative hearings in late summer, 1974, Carriker began preparing a legal case. Interpreting the mayor's stance as refusing to desegregate unless sued, he saw the hearings as crucial to changing the schools. He worked with Davis, who showed him Baltimore schools. They saw rats and broken windows in predominantly black schools, while predominantly white schools were noticeably better. Carriker was devoted to civil rights law and wanted to see *Adams* implemented in Baltimore, though he recognized that certain social and educational issues lay outside his legal expertise. It was for others to say, for example, how classroom racial composition affected learning.[38]

Carriker called Judge Hackerman's attention to what *Adams* required. Derby had talked about procedure—how the federal government worked with the city in identifying and responding to problems—but Carriker was concerned about substance: whether schools were segregated. The core of the federal case was that the "Baltimore City School District…was operating in a former de jure system, until 1953–54. For the last 20 years, they have operated a school system with rampant segregation of the schools." He agreed that the parties should consider what was feasible but argued that the school board, far from doing everything possible, had been "recalcitrant in attempting to…remediate that segregation." In response to Derby's complaint that the federal government had been vague, Carriker took up the example of elementary schools and characterized the city's attitude as willful obfuscation. Impatience for a response to the June 20 maps was misplaced, he said, because negotiations over elementary school desegregation had gone off the tracks a year earlier, in August 1974, when OCR staff concluded that Baltimore was misleading them. The district had given HEW the impression that pairings were built from schools with definite boundaries. In reality,

> Elementary students had been assigned wherever they wanted to go. There was a very amorphous standard whereby they attended the school nearest their home, whatever that meant, but they could transfer out. When we asked for a delineation of what it meant by nearest their home, it was found that…the boundaries within which most students attended a particular school were highly overlapping. There were no boundaries. There were no zones.

As soon as HEW staff realized this, they asked for specific maps of students and schools, which Baltimore took a long time to provide.[39]

Turning to the procedural issues underlying the motion to dismiss the hearings, Carriker cited a federal appellate court ruling that racial discrimination in parts of a school system "infected" the entire system. He argued that discrimination in some Baltimore programs had produced "massive systemic discrimination of the elementary and secondary system," and, therefore, the federal government did not need to "allege with great specificity what those programs are." "In fact," however, "we had submitted to the respondent, several months ago, a request…about information dealing with what those programs happen to be. Until this morning we had nothing forthcoming as to what they are. The respondent, indeed, was in a much better position than we were to determine what those programs were, and which programs were supportive of the elementary and secondary system." In this way, he conceded HEW's general weakness in enforcing the Civil Rights Act: local officials knew far more about what went on in schools than federal agents ever could. Even so, he concluded that it was "gossamer to contend that there is denial of procedural due process."[40]

Judge Hackerman, who said he had heard more than forty cases like this one, said he would make rulings without long explanations. And, without any explanation, he denied the motion to dismiss the hearing. Recognizing that Baltimore was trying to put desegregation plans in place in the final summer weeks, he postponed the hearing for forty-five days.[41]

Opening Desegregated Schools

The school system scheduled late-August open houses for new junior and senior high students and parents. Crew organized human relations training for several hundred persons who would serve on intervention teams. Civic groups, business leaders, and newspapers urged cooperation and peace. The school system set up rumor control lines. The chief of school security reassured parents and students that he did not expect trouble and, in any case, would have 126 officers on duty, nearly four times as many as the previous fall.[42]

The *Sun* and *Afro* put the same word in headlines to register their satisfaction, and relief, with school opening: "peaceful." Baltimore, many reassured themselves, was not Boston. Three-fourths of secondary school students turned out. Significant numbers of whites showed up at predominantly black schools, though sometimes it was hard to be sure how many were on the rolls. At Lake Clifton High School, for example, the desegregation plan projected 1,000 white students, but in August official white enrollment was 800, and when school opened, it was down to 583, out of 2,372 students. Moreover, many students stayed away. Only 409 whites showed up at Lake Clifton. Absenteeism generally varied by race, with attendance at a school higher for the majority. For example, at Robert Poor Junior High 80 percent of whites and 70 percent of blacks were present, while at Harlem Park Junior High 69 percent of blacks and 47 percent of whites showed up.[43]

When all was said and done, schools remained largely segregated. In a system where enrollment was 73 percent black, one-fourth of schools still had white majorities, and half were more than 90 percent black. Two-fifths of schools were 99 or 100 percent black. Only one in four satisfied federal guidelines. Because of residential segregation, elementary schools were most segregated, with two-thirds enrolling at least 90 percent from one race. Three-fourths of black elementary students attended schools at least 90 percent black, and 60 percent were in virtually all-black schools. Four-fifths of white elementary students were in majority white schools, and half were in schools at least 90 percent white. As a result of feeder links, junior high schools were somewhat more mixed than mostly neighborhood-based senior high schools, but only about 40 percent of both met federal guidelines. Nearly half of black junior and senior high students were in schools at least 90 percent black, and a third of each were in nearly all-black schools. One-third of white junior high students attended schools where whites were a majority, as did three-fifths of white high school students.[44]

In any case, the numbers were fluid. During the first two months of the school year, the Office of Student Placement received four thousand requests for transfers to citywide high schools, along with five thousand other transfer requests. An estimated eight thousand students got FAST transfers, where principals directly admitted students they believed lived in their zone. Some parents asked for transfers out of concern for children's safety getting to school. Others said that baby-sitting arrangements for their children would fall through if they went to a paired elementary school. Parents asked for schools closer to home or with better teachers. Some openly said they wanted their child with students of the same race, though most with racial concerns couched their wishes in other terms. Student Placement staff tried to interpret requests, encouraged parents to stick things out when anxiety seemed the issue, and approved transfers when reasons were legitimate, not obviously related to avoiding desegregation, and when moves would not jeopardize desegregation. Even so, Lake Clifton principal Boyse Mosley reported that 49 students had gotten FAST transfers out of his school in the first two months and that daily white attendance was averaging three hundred.[45]

As many Baltimoreans struggled against personal misgivings to comply with the federal mandate, national resistance to directed integration gained liberal allies. James Coleman, who at Johns Hopkins in 1966 had authored the report that found academic benefits for lower-income black students attending school with middle-income white students, now argued against busing on the ground that it would provoke white flight and thus thwart integration. The *Sun* reported Coleman's testimony but balanced it with an op-ed piece by Christine Rossell, a Boston University professor who had studied at Hopkins. She challenged Coleman's findings, observing that whites had left both school districts that desegregated and others that did not. Centrally, Rossell challenged Coleman's belief that voluntary desegregation arrangements would be more likely to reassure and retain whites:

> Under the present laissez-faire system there is absolutely no incentive for a white family to move into a neighborhood with a substantial number of black neighbors because, based on past experience, the neighborhood school will in all probability become predominantly black.... without a desegregation plan, the white family often does not perceive a choice between an integrated and an all-white school, but only between an all-white school and one that is almost certain to become virtually all black. The only way to break this cycle is to assure families that the

school will be integrated wherever they move within the city and will not become overwhelmingly black anywhere. This assurance, which can only be supported by a city-wide desegregation plan, could stem the flight of whites to the suburbs seeking schools that will not become all black in the near future.

In short, voluntary desegregation policies like the one Baltimore officials favored contributed to white flight by keeping school makeup uncertain.[46]

Black families were also leaving city schools, a *Sun* headline announced. From 1973 to 1975, the schools had lost about sixteen thousand students, and sixty-three hundred were black. Black parents' explanations were indistinguishable from what whites said when removing their children. Some complained about desegregation problems, but a mother who moved to the county focused on other concerns: her son "just wasn't getting an education. The schools were too crowded. There were shifts. He's not a big boy and he was getting beat up on all the time." A father acknowledged his disappointment that many county teachers seemed as undedicated to students as those in his son's city school but felt the move benefited the boy by removing him from urban problems. A ninth-grader who switched to a private school in the county noted that the city school to which he had been assigned was going on shifts. His mother said she sent her other children to private schools because she did not want them attending their neighborhood junior high, Pimlico, which had "gone down." A mother who had moved her tenth-grader into a private school summed up conditions and options: "The public schools are as good as they can be but they just have too many children. They have lots of problems that are part of the times, like crime and dope, so if you can get out you get out."[47]

The Federal Judgment

On November 5, Holmes sent Ramsey the final federal judgment on the city plan. The letter, he said, was a response to Ramsey's of June 20 and Armacost's of September 9; he apologized for the delay. Holmes chronicled a history in which he had tried to persuade Baltimore to create neighborhood school zones as a desegregation strategy and the city had resisted. "Because of the impasse in negotiations and the impending new school year," he had expediently accepted the flawed August 19 plan as an interim step but had requested the locator map to assess what the final plan should do. The Office for Civil Rights had rejected the June proposal because the map lacked solid and reasonable zone boundaries:

Rather than drawing all the zone lines so that children would be assigned to their nearest schools, taking capacity into account, your revised map includes some bizarre shaped zones that would assign many children to other than their nearest schools....The distorted zone lines often trace the boundaries between predominantly black and predominantly white residential communities. It is clear from your revised map that if all the zone lines had been drawn on a nearest school basis, they would have resulted in substantially more elementary desegregation.

When submitting the maps in June, Ramsey had said drawing zones was hard, but Holmes noted, he had offered aid, which Baltimore did not take up. In May, OCR had suggested zoning alternatives, but the city never responded.

Holmes again asked for previously requested data and some updated information. He concluded with a judgment about where things stood:

I believe that this office has continuously attempted to be fair and reasonable in our requests. Examples of this co-operativeness are the numerous extensions of time granted for the submission of compliance data as well as the numerous trips made by members of my staff to Baltimore to work with your staff....It is our desire that a resolution might still be achieved....Your posture appears to be one of convincing us why our desegregation requirements are wrong rather than demonstrating your willingness to work for the common goal of desegregation.

Hence the only way to resolve the impasse was to proceed with the scheduled administrative hearing. Again he offered to suspend legal action if the district submitted an acceptable plan.[48]

What Holmes did not know when he wrote Ramsey was that the latter had quietly left the board presidency in late September, after just nine months on the job. Reportedly, this was at least the second time he had asked the mayor to accept his resignation. Apparently a first attempt, shortly after Patterson's firing, was rejected because Schaefer thought it would give the unseemly impression that Ramsey had been appointed just to oust Patterson. Ramsey stayed nominally in place until the mayor named a successor.[49]

On November 17, the city and OCR returned to Judge Hackerman for another prehearing conference. Derby argued that Baltimore needed to interview Holmes to make its case, a matter of urgency in light of Holmes's departure on December 1. President Ford had appointed David Mathews HEW secretary, Mathews wanted his own OCR director, and Holmes was returning to Senator Griffin's staff. Hackerman denied the request, explaining that directors rarely thought for themselves, but just acted on what staff told them. After objecting, Derby insisted that Carriker put in writing the issues that would be the focus of the proceedings, and Hackerman asked the two to work things out for a February 3 hearing.[50]

Two weeks later, Schaefer, who had been resoundingly reelected on November 4, named Mark Joseph the third school board president in a year. Joseph, thirty-seven, had grown up in Reading, Pennsylvania, and graduated from Harvard Law School. In the 1960s he worked for Philadelphia Legal Services aiding welfare rights and tenant organizations and had fond memories of the War on Poverty. Among his accomplishments was filing a suit that blocked the Philadelphia urban renewal plan because it failed to provide low- and moderate-income housing. In Baltimore he had served the Schaefer administration as deputy housing commissioner in charge of public housing and as development coordinator before becoming a partner in a leading law firm. His five-year-old daughter attended kindergarten at Mt. Washington Elementary, but he disavowed any expertise on the schools. He did not consider his inexperience in education a handicap: "I don't think the process of making decisions in education is really different from making decisions in housing." He would proceed by "rational discussion."[51]

Meanwhile, Derby filed a document with Judge Hackerman to push OCR to clarify what it had asked of Baltimore and to seek its acknowledgment that, in fact, the city had complied. He noted that "Baltimore City was the first major city to integrate its school system following the Supreme Court's decision in *Brown v. Board of Education*." Carriker replied sharply, "Baltimore City schools have never desegregated. In a June 10, 1954 policy directive, the Board of School Commissioners ordered that the only change in student assignment policies would be that explicit racial criteria would no longer be used. Policies and practices of the Board have reinforced racial segregation of teachers and pupils since *Brown*." The legal battle was on.[52]

Liberalism versus Integration

The disjointed sequence of interim plans, plans, and revised plans for different grade levels could easily draw attention to details separated from any big picture, and the back-and-forth of these proposals and federal critiques could numb the mind, but the path that led Baltimore to enforcement hearings was straightforward. A wide range of black and white Baltimoreans were classical liberals, who believed that school enrollment should be a matter of individual choice, free of coercion by local or national government. Many blacks who remembered legal segregation did not want anyone of any race ever again telling them where to go to school. Many whites who were anxious about blacks wanted desegregation left voluntary in the hope that they could avoid mixing. School officials of both races, convinced that racial conflicts were unresolvable or at least certain that they lacked the knowledge and political capital to deal with them, embraced a laissez-faire position that removed the school system from responsibility for race relations. Some came to their position from explicit liberal principles. Some followed the tacit liberalism in American culture. All found that liberalism, besides making sense of troubling issues, conveniently served their interests.

Civil rights law also rested on liberalism, with an emphasis on individual equality. As all American law, civil rights law was clearer about individual rights and harms than about group claims or damages. However, the 1968 *Green* decision, with a demand for "unitary" school systems, shifted federal civil rights emphasis from a process of free individual choice to an outcome of racially mixed schools. Explicitly, this turn of attention from desegregation as a procedure to integration as a result broke with one liberal principle. Tacitly, it parted ways with another. Desegregation referred to an individual situation, whereas integration was a collective condition. Desegregation was indicated by whether individual students were free to attend school regardless of their race, while integration was measured by the extent to which a community or city had racially mixed schools. Liberal civil rights advocates might have difficulty justifying these new positions philosophically, but experience with the failures of laissez-faire desegregation pushed them to rethink what they wanted.

Thus Baltimoreans' traditional liberalism encountered a new federal integrationism. Postriot fears of racial contact viscerally reinforced philosophical resistance to federal demands. Because civil rights officials insisted that city policies result in mixed schools, many Baltimoreans thought of integration only as "forced integration." They objected to "statistics" not simply because the numbers abstracted from individual particulars, but because they measured and gave primacy to collective conditions. Baltimore resentment of federal intervention went back to the Civil War, as contemporary rants against "Washington" suggested. Now many residents resisted federal demands because they did not want integration. But many also resisted because they believed Washington had violated an American agreement to abide by liberal rules. The city lawyer addressing the administrative law judge concentrated on the fairness of federal negotiation procedures not just because doing so offered the best legal case, but also because Baltimoreans cared about process. In contrast, the federal attorney focused on outcomes: city schools had to be integrated. Liberal Baltimoreans collided with federal enforcers not simply because many residents didn't want integration, but also because they couldn't understand federal reasoning and thought that federal officials just approached matters wrong.

THE CITY'S COURT VICTORY

Legal confrontation over civil rights neither required nor allowed discussion of local culture, customs, and race relations. For better or for worse, civil rights law focused on the statistical bottom line and means of improving it. In many places, school officials invoked community norms to justify segregation and obstruct change, and yet black and white families lived and found meaning and security in community attachments and beliefs. As OCR tightened its grip on Baltimore, local residents took stock.

Baltimore Takes Account

The NAACP branch continued advocating for integration, as did the *Afro,* which urged busing where necessary. However, the five black board members were more conservative. Either they did not wholeheartedly believe in integration, or they doubted it was possible at this point. They endorsed plans that, even within the city's demographic limits, did little to mix white and black children. Many black parents complained that "desegregation" simply moved their children around, sometimes from one predominantly black school to another, without obvious educational gain. "And many blacks," a *Sun* reporter concluded, "resent the de-segregation plan because its zoning concept adopts the form, though not the philosophy, of the system of de jure segregation that restricted blacks to certain schools." Alongside the integrationists, Baltimore blacks had always included many who just wanted school choice. As blacks farther South, they did not want whites (or other blacks) telling them where to go to school. Unlike blacks farther South, they believed the local elite would give them more or less free choice. Federal pressure to replace open enrollment with zoning went against the preferences of black parents who wanted to make their own decisions for their children.[1]

In contrast with 1954, there were few white liberals urging integration. Those left recognized that schools were highly segregated, and many of them, at least retrospectively, were not sure that earlier school boards had done all they could to desegregate. They shared the *Sun*'s view that black children's education was the central issue. However, after 1968 they had lost much of their authority and many of their white and black allies. White participation in desegregation had fallen largely to the working class, partly because they comprised the majority of whites left in the public schools and partly because they had less power than the middle class. Now free choice was nearly gone, racial mixing was inescapable, and a sea change in city demography meant that white students would encounter numerous black students. Many working-class whites made clear that they did not want their children in school with blacks. Some were prejudiced, and many were afraid, as newspapers and rumor mills reported real and imagined dangers. More vulnerable than in 1954, they organized.

A number of whites urged metropolitan desegregation. For some, this talk was a way to get off the hook. Blacks should go to school with whites in the suburbs, where there were so many more advantages than in city neighborhoods. Yet, however self-serving such sentiments were, they had merit. Whites with resources had fled the city and blacks, leaving many others with less of nearly everything to solve the resulting problems. White ethnics were being portrayed as bigots, when their main lapse was being poor. Public officials spoke for many Baltimoreans when they complained that the federal government was picking on the city, blaming it for a problem others had made and insisting that it solve the problem alone while letting the culprits off scot free. The *Sun*, a constant advocate for metropolitan desegregation, noted that OCR had signed off on Baltimore County schools, despite a history of federal and local government activities that segregated county housing and schools, actions that incontestably contributed to city segregation. Still hopeful after Holmes's final letter, the *Sun* noted that the Supreme Court had approved metropolitan desegregation in Wilmington and Louisville.[2]

White and black Baltimoreans lived in the city through communities. Working-class white neighborhoods drew coherence from residents' shared ethnic origins and associated later-generation remnants, geographic interests, and mistrust of the larger world. Middle-income and elite white neighborhoods formed identities mostly on the basis of class-linked sensibilities, in addition to territorial interests. Blacks distinguished higher-status westside neighborhoods from what at least those on the west regarded as lower-status eastside neighborhoods, with different social histories shaping particular black community identities. At the same time, the *Afro,* speaking always in the first-person plural, nurtured an encompassing black community identity. Some whites invoked "community identity" to exclude blacks, but for them, as for most residents, "community" was not just rhetoric. Across racial lines, Baltimoreans regarded schools as institutions that strengthened and continued their communities by imparting culture to children. They experienced school policies as community interventions.

Mayor Schaefer encouraged this neighborhood consciousness. Renowned for revitalizing the city's inner harbor and making Baltimore a tourist destination, he loved the city and identified with it. He got massive federal funding for renewal and did anything he could to get the city publicity. He had his critics, more likely black than white, more likely poor than better off, who charged that he invested in public venues while doing little for less visible impoverished residential areas. Periodically, political candidates, outside observers, or grassroots leaders worried that Baltimore was congealing into two cities, one making it and one economically imperiled. Schaefer had little patience with such doubts, and he lashed into critics who questioned him. He touted Baltimore as a city of vital neighborhoods. Some were white, and some were black, but they were also Polish, Italian, Greek, Irish, German, and Russian, and they were Catholic, Protestant, and Jewish. This ethnic prism diverted attention from race, but it reflected the city's past. Schaefer might acknowledge racial issues, but he insisted there was much good in the city, and, in any case, racial problems would not be fixed in a day. Moreover, he believed, the schools did not cause them, and it was wrong to make children tools of social engineering. Moving students around would disrupt their lives and break up communities.[3]

Open enrollment had nothing explicit to do with either race or community: the policy offered choices to individuals. For a long time whites generally embraced its emphasis on personal freedom, because the policy let their children attend predominantly white neighborhood schools. As the proportion of black students grew, whites began to object to free choice on the ground that it let outside students bring alien values and loyalties into community schools. The Office for Civil Rights was centrally concerned about race, but the federal agency, too, concentrated on individuals: mixing those of different races. In its view, students might come from communities, but students did not represent or belong to communities. Community wishes and interests, particularly but not only those of whites who wanted to avoid blacks, had no standing. Nor were civil rights officials interested in community development, even for blacks. Individual rights trumped any and all community claims. The language of community got no purchase with civil rights officials.[4]

For these reasons, Baltimoreans felt unheard, misunderstood, and increasingly, harmed. City officials had been losing patience with Peter Holmes and OCR for a long time, and they handicapped their odds with the Nixon and Ford administrations. Though some held onto hopes of reaching an agreement, a growing number had been expecting a letter like that of November 5. Holmes recognized that the high proportion of black students presented challenges, and he gave signs of being flexible. However, he was responsible for hundreds of school districts, as well as other federal health, education, and welfare civil rights efforts, and gender discrimination, covered by Title IX of the Civil Rights Act, took a growing amount of his time. These obligations contributed to long lapses between communications with Baltimore. Perhaps the other demands made it hard for him to identify specific school infractions. Because Holmes was not a civil rights careerist, his persistence surprised those who expected a Republican Civil Rights Office to relent. Perhaps the young director was under the sway of the lawyers or staff like Davis. Perhaps *Adams* left him little leeway.[5]

Baltimoreans began talking about going to court to stop OCR. Herbert Goldman, the Desegregation Task Force chair, recalled a moment in the spring of 1974 when he watched federal officials with a map moving around pins representing children. It seemed cold, abstract, and dangerous. He sought out his neighbor and friend Mark Joseph, then in the mayor's office, and asked him to set up a meeting with Schaefer, whom Goldman urged to sue HEW. In May, the mayor retained lawyers William Marbury and Stephen Derby. After the school board submitted its plan in June, Schaefer threatened to sue if HEW rejected it. Later that summer, City Council president Walter Orlinsky talked about suing if HEW imposed busing. Derby became a regular participant in meetings with federal officials. When battles with and about Superintendent Patterson disabled the school board, Schaefer increasingly called the shots in the desegregation fight. Board president Joseph would report that the last straw was the December 23 response of HEW to a request for clarification of facts germane to the administrative enforcement hearing. The federal lawyers wrote that Holmes's May 2 letter rejecting the junior and senior high school plans and moving to enforcement merely "enumerated examples of inadequacies…and was not intended as an enumeration of all possible inadequacies of those plans."[6]

Baltimore Goes to Court

On January 8, 1976, at the mayor's direction, Baltimore attorneys filed suit in federal district court against HEW Secretary David Mathews; Acting OCR

Director Martin Gerry; the Department of Health, Education, and Welfare; and Administrative Law Judge Irvin Hackerman.

The City Sues

Baltimore requested a temporary restraining order and preliminary injunction to stop OCR from conducting administrative enforcement hearings and from deferring approval of federal funding. The city asked the court to enjoin OCR permanently from proceeding with enforcement unless it specified problematic programs and recommended specific remedies in writing, and negotiated reasonably on these matters. In addition to these procedural remedies, the city asked for a substantive declaration that Baltimore desegregation plans complied with the 1964 Civil Rights Act and the 1974 Equal Educational Opportunity Act. The latter favored neighborhood schools, minimized the importance of racial balance, and limited busing. Such a substantive finding would make procedural issues moot.[7]

The procedural complaint, elaborated in a January 27 memorandum, was that OCR had failed to negotiate according to its Policies on Elementary and Secondary School Compliance with Title VI of the Civil Rights Act of 1964:

> The first formal step of such negotiation is a letter from the Office for Civil Rights to the school system identifying the particular areas of non-compliance...and offering the school system assistance and guidance on the best manner to achieve compliance. If a school system submits a plan which is unsatisfactory in any respect, the Office for Civil Rights will inform the school system in detail and in writing of the areas in which the plan is not satisfactory. If local officials so request, the Office for Civil Rights will at any stage of negotiation recommend in writing specific steps the school system may take to achieve compliance.

In pressing for specificity and seeking to limit any sanctions, the city emphasized the Title VI reference to "programs": "the termination of or refusal to grant or to continue assistance to [a program found to discriminate] shall be limited in its effect to the particular program, or part thereof, in which such noncompliance has been found." Baltimore charged that OCR had never identified in writing all specific programs or parts it believed violated the Civil Rights Act. Nor, when asked what the city should do to comply, had OCR identified acceptable remedies in writing. Thus federal agents had not exhausted efforts to get voluntary compliance and lacked a basis for concluding such efforts had failed.[8]

On the one hand, Baltimore complained, federal enforcers were trying to impose statistical standards for racial balance that disregarded what was good for children's education and safety. At the same time, OCR had not told the city what exactly its shortcomings were, so that it could not properly defend itself at the administrative hearing. As a result, city lawyers were certain to make a weak case that might not hold up in later stages of the enforcement process and could lead to losing all federal funds. Anticipating such irreparable harm from going ahead, the city asked the court to take the extraordinary step of halting the hearing before a judgment was rendered.[9]

The Civil Rights Division (CRD) of the Department of Justice represented the defendants and responded to charges. Frank Krueger, of the HEW Office of General Counsel (OGC), prepared the document. He had come to OGC just a year before and was writing regulations in a different substantive area when Eric Carriker told David Leeman he was too busy to take on the district court part of the case. Krueger came in and joined CRD staff in defending HEW. As chance would have it, he had grown up in Baltimore, in the predominantly white northeast, and had attended Johns Hopkins. He thought middle-class whites in the city were fairly progressive but enjoyed the status quo. He did not believe the mayor was willing to make any hard decisions to desegregate. He drew on his knowledge of the city in responding to the Baltimore complaint.[10]

The response argued that OCR had followed prescribed procedures in going to a hearing. The law did not require OCR to provide the specificity the city asked. The Title VI reference to "programs" did not mean that OCR had to identify all programmatic violations prior to hearings; rather, it provided that an administrative law judge finding discrimination could impose penalties only on specific offending programs. In any case, simply listing individual programs would not take into account the ways discriminatory programs infected the whole system. Further, contrary to the complaint, in many letters, phone calls, and meetings over months of negotiations, OCR staff had given the city specific critiques of plans, beginning with the notice that free choice was unacceptable, as well as guidance for complying. The OCR policies required staff to provide specific written recommendations when a district requested them, but Baltimore, OCR held, never asked for suggestions in writing.[11]

Regarding judicial intervention to halt an agency hearing, federal lawyers argued that the case met none of the few established conditions justifying such action. Baltimore would not be irreparably harmed, since the process had checks and appeals. To the contrary, judicial intervention would harm the federal government and the public interest by hindering OCR ability to enforce Title VI against segregated school systems.[12]

Adams had directed OCR to move against not only school districts, but also states with racially segregated higher education systems. Maryland was such a state. In 1975, OCR had started enforcement hearings against Maryland, and in December the state had asked the federal district court to enjoin OCR from proceeding. Baltimore lawyers asked the court to join the two cases.[13]

Judge Northrop Hears the Case

Judge Edward Northrop was sixty-five when the Baltimore and Maryland cases came before him in January 1976. A Democrat, he had set out on a political career, in 1954 getting elected to the state senate from Montgomery County, a well-off Washington suburb. In 1959 he became senate majority leader. He planned a run for the U.S. Senate in 1962, but his path changed when a friend wrote Attorney General Robert Kennedy in 1961 to recommend him for a federal judgeship. President Kennedy named him to the U.S. District Court for Maryland in September 1961, making him the first Democrat and first lawyer from outside Baltimore to serve in a Maryland federal court since before the Civil War. He became chief judge of the court in 1970.

Northrop was regarded as more a pragmatic jurist than a legal scholar. He sympathized with states against federal intervention. He interjected his views in court hearings, and he could be irascible when annoyed. In the early 1970s he was known as the judge in the 1968 trial of the "Baltimore Four," including priest Philip Berrigan, who protested the Vietnam War by pouring blood on Selective Service files at the Baltimore Customs House. Sentencing Berrigan to prison, Northrop declared, "You have transcended the tolerable limits of civil disobedience....You deliberately set out to use violent means to destroy the very fabric of society."[14]

In the Baltimore school case, one of Northrop's first acts, before the court hearing, was to order Peter Holmes to submit to deposition on January 20. Stephen Derby, who had negotiated with Holmes, now had the opportunity to push him to clarify what he had said to city officials and to identify ways he had been vague, inconsistent, or arbitrary. Under questioning, Holmes was uncertain whether he had said OCR might direct the city to zone elementary schools. Derby and Holmes agreed that Holmes did not want the city to bus elementary school students, but Holmes, contrary to Derby's recollection, said he wanted the city to consider pairing schools in noncontiguous zones. Holmes recalled saying something to the effect that in a system 70 percent black some all-black schools were inevitable. After much prodding, he admitted that he had not conducted a school-by-school analysis prior to sending any of the letters about enforcement hearings. Derby tried to get him to endorse certain letters as his final judgment about what was acceptable, but Holmes resisted. As for giving the city guidance, he did not recall putting in writing any specific remedies for the elementary schools but said "it was very clear to the school system the steps that they could take to increase desegregation." Zoning and pairing, he repeated, were possible.[15]

The Pretrial Hearing

Judge Northrop convened the hearing on the motion for a temporary restraining order, preliminary injunction, and permanent injunction in the old U.S. Courthouse and Post Office on Calvert Street at 10:00 a.m. on January 30. He heard the Baltimore case before the Maryland case. Stephen Derby reviewed city contentions and then called witnesses. Sheila Sachs had led plan preparation, and Derby asked her about elementary school zones. Baltimore had never had zones, she said, and she did not recall that HEW had ever told the city to zone elementary schools. However, the system identified attendance service areas, representing where the students at each school generally lived. Federal officials had asked to see these on a map but found overlap and wanted the city to delineate clear boundaries. She said that city staff did so, but federal officials rejected the new maps without clear explanation. She suggested that the board would have negotiated with HEW to develop satisfactory service areas if given the chance. The main problem, she said, was that HEW never told the board which specific programs or parts did not comply with the Civil Rights Act. This vagueness created uncertainty that made it hard for the board to plan, drove out families who could exit, and left "the people who have no choice" in a system that could not serve their children.[16]

Alexander Ross, representing OCR, moved quickly to erase this picture in cross-examination. Derby's contemporary at thirty-nine, Ross was a career civil rights lawyer who had joined CRD after finishing the University of Miami Law School in 1962. He had started working on voting cases in Louisiana. Then the 1964 Civil Rights Act added public accommodations and employment, and the 1965 Voting Rights Act added more on voting. When CRD was reorganized around areas of litigation in 1969, he went to the Housing Section, formed after the 1968 Housing Act. In 1974 he became chief of the CRD Education Section. Ross was proud of the division. He had taken great satisfaction working under the legendary John Doar, who had accompanied James Meredith to the University of Mississippi; led the prosecution for the murders of civil rights workers Schwerner, Chaney, and Goodman; and written significant parts of the 1964 Civil Rights Act. Ross saw the civil rights lawyers he worked with as the active part of the Justice Department. Stanley Pottinger had become assistant attorney general over CRD in 1973, and Ross appreciated Pottinger's aggressive civil rights stance at a time when OCR staff felt increasingly constrained by the Nixon and Ford administrations.[17]

With Sachs, Ross wanted to clarify whether Baltimore now regulated where elementary students went to school, in an effort to integrate, or whether families still had choice, and could select racially homogeneous schools. He asked Sachs about the difference between attendance service areas and school zones. "A zone line is a rigid geographic line that has been drawn around a school.... An attendance service area meant that there was a basic area that this school was supposed to serve." Service area maps could be misleading, Ross noted, because open enrollment let students who lived far from a school transfer in, and they would not be reflected in a service area. Sachs agreed but said new transfer limitations would reduce that problem. When Ross finished, Derby returned to get Sachs to explain that attendance service areas were just "tentative or interim registration areas" for the fall, subject to negotiation with OCR. Later testimony would clarify, further, that these areas applied only to entering students, mostly kindergartners, and would take seven years to affect all elementary grades. In short, if service areas governed enrollment, many families would have choices for a long time.[18]

After a brief recess, Derby called Mayor William Donald Schaefer. Schaefer presented a picture of a mayor and citizenry more than willing to desegregate but pestered by federal officials making vague, continually new demands and threats. Ross was one of a number of federal staff who felt that Schaefer had little commitment to desegregation. For this reason, as well as because Ross thought that Holmes had given Baltimore vague direction, he wanted to tie Schaefer down to specifics. Under questioning, the mayor admitted that he did not know the details of the dispute and had only general impressions. One was that city representatives repeatedly met with federal officials and reached agreements, only to get letters saying the contrary. Pressed to give an example, Schaefer said he could not. Ross asked about the junior high school plan, and Schaefer did not know which plan was implemented. The mayor railed against HEW unreasonableness about where school boundaries could be drawn but, when asked, could not cite an example. Ross asked Schaefer about his complaint that HEW had not specified programs out of compliance. Schaefer was concerned about losing $20 million. The actual amount was $23 million, but Ross did not correct him. The more important point, which Ross found that Schaefer did not understand, was that funds could be withdrawn only from specific programs; the likelihood of losing the whole amount was small. Ross failed to get the mayor to understand that the commencement of hearings did not stop negotiations.[19]

With Schaefer still on the stand, Northrop began interrogating Ross about Title VI. The judge saw no legal basis for summoning a school district to a hearing without specifying programs not in compliance with the law. In any case, he rejected the notion that one discriminatory program could infect a system; each program should be assessed in isolation. Underlining the reference in the law to "voluntary" compliance, he chastised OCR for taking an adversarial position that hindered negotiation and voluntary agreement. With regard to specifying programs, Ross explained that HEW understood the law to designate hearings as the appropriate place for a judge to identify discriminatory and infected programs and noted that a judge's ruling could be appealed in court. As Schaefer stepped down, Northrop continued attacking HEW and zeroed in on fund cutoff: "They are not federal funds. They belong to the tax payers of—me, you, and everybody in this room. That's the funds you're dealing with and not something that the Federal Government has. The Federal Government gets it from the people."[20]

Now that the city had finished with its witnesses, the judge invited Ross to make opening remarks he had deferred until the end of Derby's presentation. Ross began by addressing what he considered a misunderstanding in something Northrop had said, and the judge interrupted to denounce the unfairness of withholding funds pending a lengthy appeal process. For better or for worse, Ross explained, that was congressional intent. Northrop said that he favored negotiations over adversarial proceedings and asked Ross if Congress had specified what would indicate that efforts to get voluntary compliance had failed. Ross said it had not, and, hence, that was a question for this court to rule on. What the HEW position amounted to, Northrop said bluntly, was "negotiating under the gun."[21]

After concluding his opening statement, Ross called his witness, Harold Davis. Davis reviewed OCR requests to Baltimore and city responses. He reported on his school visits. He indicated that student and faculty plans both failed to comply with Title VI, and he recalled a 1974 meeting with Baltimore officials when he identified thirty-one additional schools that might be further desegregated. In cross-examination, Derby led Davis back into the history of the maps. Derby insisted that Baltimore had acceded to every OCR request, and Davis noted the shortcomings of each map submitted. Moreover, the last map was so big and unwieldy, it had to be pasted up a wall and partly across the ceiling in the basement of an HEW office building, and people had to stand on a ladder to read it. After Derby took Davis through the rest of the OCR dealings with the city, the court recessed at 3:10 p.m.[22]

The parties agreed to put off the administrative hearing until March 9, to let the court first hold a trial and rule.[23]

The Trial

Judge Northrop convened court for the trial on the city and state cases at 10:00 a.m. on February 20. Attorney Edward Norton led off for Baltimore. He asserted that HEW had not followed regulations in dealing with the city—it had not identified programs alleged to violate Title VI, it had not specified remedies, and it had done little to reach voluntary compliance. Hence, to avoid irreparable harm to students and schools, court action to stop the administrative hearing was necessary. Northrop interrupted to reinforce Norton's argument. A key precedent, the judge said, was *Taylor County v. Finch*, in which the Fifth Circuit ruled that HEW was required to specify noncompliant programs in an order to terminate funds. Northrop said that *Taylor* required OCR to identify programs prior to the hearing, so the district could prepare an adequate defense. He encouraged Norton to describe the legal and practical problems created by the HEW stance and endorsed Norton's concerns. The judge then discussed with Norton what the court should rule. Norton summarized the city's request: "Hold in this case that HEW was required to go through the voluntary compliance stage as the statute requires…by identifying the particular programs." Although Norton noted that *Taylor* did not halt administrative hearings but only appealed the ruling afterward, Northrop offered his own argument for applying *Taylor*.[24]

When Norton finished, Derby took up the argument on voluntary compliance. Baltimore had negotiated in good faith, he said, but federal officials were vague, inconsistent, arbitrary, and adversarial. The city had gone to court reluctantly, just to get free of federal coercion so that local officials, who knew the schools best, could apply their judgment to educating children. Derby mentioned the 1974 federal education amendments. Northrop was pleased: "That's what I'm glad you're coming to." Derby explained that the new law forbade OCR from requiring busing students beyond the school nearest home. "Well," the judge chimed in, "not only students but teachers." Derby clarified that teacher provisions were different.[25]

After Derby concluded, Frank Krueger presented the federal position that, whatever the quality of negotiations between HEW and the city, the court lacked jurisdiction to halt administrative hearings: "It's a basic rule of law that Courts will not accept jurisdiction where administrative proceedings are in process and administrative remedies exist and…the parties seeking the relief have not exhausted those administrative remedies." Northrop asked Krueger about *Leedom v. Kyne*, in which the Supreme Court affirmed lower court rulings setting aside a National Labor Relations Board order and which Baltimore said authorized this court to halt the administrative hearings. Krueger noted that later decisions limited judicial intervention to instances when an agency blatantly violated the law. Judge Hackerman's hearing was the proper domain for resolving questions of fact and law. Krueger went on to emphasize the federal interpretation of "programs." Simply, "in the case of Baltimore City it's their [overall] elementary and secondary programs." Thus OCR staff just had to identify problems in the system as a whole, rather than anything smaller, such as individual schools, activities such as vocational education, or specific grants. In any case, he said, federal officials had many times provided details of Baltimore programs out of compliance with Title VI.[26]

In fact, while HEW lawyers had no doubt their case was stronger than that of the city, some felt the issue of programmatic specificity was the weakest in their argument. They were confident that HEW had established clear desegregation standards and that federal officials had done their best to negotiate with a recalcitrant school district, but the issue of whether OCR had to identify noncompliant programs prior to administrative hearings had not been litigated much.[27]

When Krueger finished, Derby challenged his view of "program." Rather than the entire elementary and secondary program, he said, the statute referred "to each specific project and grant...administered at a local level which is funded by federal programs." Northrop said he would take the case under advisement. At the 1:45 p.m. adjournment, Baltimore lawyers had addressed the court for more than two and a half hours, and federal attorneys had spoken for less than an hour.[28]

Judge Northrop's Decision

On March 8, one day before the enforcement hearing would resume, Judge Northrop rendered his decision. He said he would not comment on whether schools were desegregated or what further action might be taken, but would rule only on whether HEW had followed Title VI procedures in addressing these questions. He invoked *Leedom* in assuming jurisdiction over the administrative proceedings. The issue before the court, he summarized, "narrows to whether HEW sought to achieve, in good faith, compliance by voluntary means."[29]

In the Baltimore case, Northrop declared, "There is much authority for the proposition that Title VI requires HEW to employ a program-by-program analysis when reviewing federally funded institutions." And plaintiffs had demonstrated "the inherent futility of attempting to secure voluntary compliance of Title VI in a major system where the offending program is unknown." For its part, HEW had confronted Baltimore with a "lack of definitive standards." Northrop saw a "cavalier and arbitrary posture by HEW toward plaintiffs' requests for specificity." The court found HEW guilty of "a consistent pattern of...duplicitous and uncooperative behavior. Defendants have overwhelmingly refused to negotiate in good faith....Rather, defendants have sought to bludgeon compliance through initiation of unwarranted and premature enforcement procedures...in brazen defiance and in direct contravention of Title VI and...defendants' own policy statement." Thus HEW staff "have arbitrarily and whimsically failed to attempt to work toward compliance by voluntary means and have vindictively refused to assume a programmatic approach." Hence a preliminary injunction against HEW was appropriate.[30]

Northrop ordered HEW to discontinue enforcement proceedings and deferral of fund approval. He directed HEW not to reinstate proceedings before exhausting efforts to secure voluntary compliance, by informing Baltimore in writing of any unsatisfactory parts of current desegregation plans, recommending specific remedial steps in writing, specifying programs or parts not in compliance with Title VI, and allowing sufficient time and opportunity to come to voluntary agreement.[31]

The Federal Government Appeals the Court Decision

Federal officials had started enforcement proceedings after concluding that Baltimore would not voluntarily comply with Title VI. Accordingly, Justice Department lawyers appealed Northrop's ruling to the Fourth Circuit Court of Appeals, in Richmond. In briefs filed on June 30, they argued that the district court lacked jurisdiction to review an administrative hearing in progress. The appellate court would consolidate the appeals of the Baltimore and Maryland cases, both of which Northrop had decided against HEW.[32]

The NAACP Legal Defense and Educational Fund, which had initiated the *Adams* suit, submitted an *amicus curiae* brief supporting HEW. The fund considered the argument that the lack of a program-by-program analysis left the city without direction disingenuous. Supreme Court desegregation decisions were clear, and Baltimore had not followed them. Administrative proceedings were appropriate; *Adams* required them. The fund said that Northrop had misunderstood Title VI, case law, and common sense. All that said, however, the fund did not want procedural disputes to distract from the substantive issue: Baltimore had discriminated against black children in using federal education money.[33]

When OCR went to appeals, the CRD Appellate Section represented it in court. Brian Landsberg had directed the section since 1974. After graduating from the University of California Boalt Law School, he began a federal civil rights career at CRD in 1964. Like Alexander Ross, he started out on voting cases in Alabama. In 1965 he worked on public accommodations and school cases. In 1969 he became head of a new CRD Education Section, and he became part of an effort spearheaded by Attorney General Ramsey Clark and Education Commissioner Harold Howe to use *Green* and *Alexander* to desegregate big city and Northern schools. Landsberg took pride in the aggressive intelligence and public interest orientation of CRD. By the time he assumed responsibility for the Baltimore appeal, he had a great deal of experience with education and OCR.[34]

The Fourth Circuit had a distinctive practice in school segregation cases, hearing them en banc, with all judges sitting, to give the full weight of the court to decisions. The seven judges heard arguments on February 14, 1977. The court examined the two issues at the core of the dispute: whether HEW had appropriately specified programs not compliant with Title VI and whether HEW had allowed time and conditions for negotiations to proceed to voluntary compliance. Both sides agreed that the interpretation of "programs" was central.[35]

The court delivered its decision on August 19, 1977. Judge Harrison L. Winter wrote the opinion for a 4–3 majority. He grew up in Baltimore, went to Johns Hopkins, and got a law degree from the University of Maryland, where 1954 school board member Roger Howell shaped his legal thinking. He practiced law in Baltimore for fifteen years before becoming assistant and deputy Maryland attorney general and then serving as city solicitor from 1959 to 1961. President Kennedy appointed him to the federal district court for Maryland in 1962, and President Johnson named him to the Fourth Circuit in 1966. He was a liberal with a concern for procedural fairness, and he was inclined to uphold government agency decisions. Fellow Fourth Circuit judge John Butzner described Winter as one "of those indomitable federal judges in the South who, following Brown v. Board of Education, wrought a peaceful revolution by giving full effect to ... the Civil Rights Acts." Though he moved in this larger world, the *Sun* would characterize him as "a Baltimore boy totally," a citizen who lived in the elite Guilford neighborhood, patronized the arts, and served on the boards of major city institutions. His law clerks respected his intelligence, character, and understanding of ordinary people. One of these clerks had been Stephen Derby.[36]

Judge Winter wrote that Judge Northrop, in issuing an injunction, had ignored a "long settled" rule that courts should not intervene in administrative proceedings. The majority opinion found that HEW guidelines and directives, along with *Brown* and succeeding cases, made quite clear what Baltimore had to do to desegregate. Moreover, federal officials had given the city ample opportunity to comply voluntarily:

> The record reveals that there were extensive negotiations extending over a two year period.... if any party was responsible for the various delays and the ultimate breakdown of communication, it was more likely the City. Nonetheless, we note that nothing in the language of Title VI or HEW's own regulations specifies the quantity or quality of attempts to negotiate voluntary compliance.

Finally, Judge Winter considered

> the contention that HEW violated Title VI ... by failing to negotiate with the City on a school-by-school or program-by-program basis.... We do

not view § 602 as requiring negotiations on a programmatic basis. Its language is directed solely to the issue of remedy, once negotiations have failed and a finding of noncompliance has been made (after administrative proceedings with full opportunity to be heard).

In reversing the district court decision, the Fourth Circuit freed OCR to push Baltimore to desegregate.[37]

The *Sun* put the best face on this development. Federal officials, it assumed, would do more to specify their judgments and expectations. Even so, it counseled moderation, hoping HEW would "be enlightened enough to recognize that little can be gained, educationally or socially, from further shifts of children from one school to another to change racial percentages, unless specific instances can be found of intentional segregation."[38]

However, there was an unusual detail in the court's decision, an asterisk next to Judge J. Braxton Craven's name among the four-member majority. The accompanying note read, "Judge Craven died before the filing of the opinions which follow. Before his death, however, he concurred in the judgment and approved the language of Parts I and II of the majority opinion." In other words, before Judge Craven suffered a heart attack on May 3, he had reviewed the majority opinion but had not seen the dissents.[39]

Seeing the asterisk, Stephen Derby and his colleagues scrambled and found precedents on the basis of which they asked the court to discard Craven's vote and affirm the lower court decision on the basis of a 3–3 tie, or else rehear the case. They cited 1960 decisions in *United States v. American-Foreign Steamship Corp.*, which required that "en banc proceedings shall be 'heard and determined' by a court consisting of all the 'active circuit judges'" and that "a case or controversy is 'determined' when it is decided." Thus Judge Craven did not fully take part in deciding the case, and his vote should not be counted.[40]

The court took five months to announce a new decision, on February 16, 1978, more than two years after Baltimore first went to court, four years after Peter Holmes asked the city to prepare a desegregation plan, five years after Judge Pratt first ruled in *Adams,* and twenty-four years after *Brown.* Persuaded by *American-Foreign Steamship Corp.,* the court ruled that, because Craven died before the dissents were written and before the court decision was announced, his approval of Winter's draft of the majority opinion should not count. This change left the court evenly split and affirmed the district court preliminary injunction. The case returned to Judge Northrop for trial to determine whether the preliminary injunction should be made permanent.[41]

The Baltimore school board declared victory. President Mark Joseph proclaimed, "It means that there is no real threat of a loss of funding for the foreseeable future." He quickly added that winning or losing was not the issue, that the school system remained "committed to a desegregation effort." "The board," he said, "is very much in favor of integrating. We think we've been doing a good job. The attendance zones have accomplished a substantial integrative effect and we have reassigned 25 per cent of the faculty over a three-year period."[42]

The Department of Health, Education, and Welfare wanted to get Supreme Court review, but Justice Department lawyers decided not to appeal. Although Northrop's decision contravened other federal court rulings, it affected only Maryland, Northrop's rulings typically carried little weight elsewhere, and the Justice Department did not want to risk having the High Court affirm his decision.[43]

Not a Bang, but a Whimper

Nearly three years of legal wrangling set OCR back in the position of trying to negotiate voluntary compliance with Baltimore. During that time conditions for an agreement that would significantly change the racial makeup of schools had deteriorated. In fall 1978, city schools were 77 percent black, and the Eagleton-Biden Amendment to the 1978–79 HEW appropriation banned using federal funds to require busing to a school beyond the one nearest home to comply with Title VI.[44]

The Office for Civil Rights Regroups

As an alternative to resuming negotiations under the new restraints, OCR could have asked CRD to sue the city for violating Title VI. However, after the district court decision, the case would have been hard to win, and in any case, the ruling did not affect schools outside Maryland. The Justice Department was working on more urgent districts, where local officials overtly and systematically segregated students, and CRD was involved with demanding Northern cases, where segregation was informal and federal staff had to build up evidence that officials practiced segregation.[45]

With no easy course, OCR took stock of Baltimore. David Tatel had succeeded Martin Gerry as director in 1977. He was a University of Chicago Law School graduate in his early thirties. After teaching law at the University of Michigan for a year, he had joined Sidley and Austin, an old Chicago law firm with a strong tradition of pro bono work. Tatel alternated between private practice and civil rights activity. He served as director of the Chicago and National Lawyers' Committees for Civil Rights Under Law and general counsel for the newly created Legal Services

Corporation. He came to the OCR directorship with considerable civil rights interest and experience. Staff at OCR and CRD valued his aggressive support.[46]

In November, Tatel asked Lloyd Henderson, director of the HEW Office of Compliance and Enforcement, for a briefing memorandum on Baltimore. Henderson was an OCR veteran with a doctorate in history from the University of California at Berkeley and had taught at Pacific University in Portland. He came to Washington to work with Lyndon Johnson's 1964 campaign. In 1966 he joined the Office of Education as a civil rights investigator, working mostly in Mississippi. After OCR was formed, he became Education Branch chief. In that position he met nearly every superintendent concerned about desegregation requirements. Now he was in charge of enforcement across the country.[47]

In response to Tatel's request, Henderson forwarded a report from Dewey Dodds, the OCR Philadelphia director. In 1976–77, the last year for which OCR had Baltimore data, faculty composition was considerably out of compliance with the federal standard that school teacher makeup fall within 5 percent of the district composition for the grade level. However, these data highlighted a general OCR difficulty: as time went on, the office had less and less current information. The last on-site review had been Harold Davis's 1974 visit. While Baltimore engaged OCR in the courts, little new information passed from the city to the federal government. Thus OCR was trying to assess 1978 schools mostly with 1975 student data. Dodds's report said that in 1976 80 percent of Baltimore elementary students attended schools considered segregated by the 50–90 percent standard, most of these probably more than 90 percent black. Not only did Eagleton-Biden limit options, but a paucity of data made it uncertain what might be done. The document offered few possibilities.[48]

Occasionally Judge Northrop asked the parties for status reports, and Baltimore and OCR talked informally from time to time. Baltimore did not move to make the temporary injunction permanent, because it wanted to avoid an HEW appeal to the Fourth Circuit, where another liberal had replaced Judge Craven. Things drifted.[49]

Tatel left OCR in summer of 1979, and the new HEW secretary, Patricia Roberts Harris, asked Roma Stewart to succeed him. Stewart, a Fisk graduate with a Georgetown law degree, was a civil rights lawyer specializing in employment. In her early forties, she was teaching at Howard Law School and working on the eighth appeal of the Little Rock school desegregation case in the Eighth Circuit when Harris contacted her. Her tenure was likely to be brief, since President Carter's reelection prospects were slim and, in any case, a new Department of Education was being carved out of HEW. On school segregation, Stewart considered fund cutoff reasonable for noncompliant districts, but Harris resisted it as draconian.[50]

Stewart asked Eric Carriker and two other OCR staff members to lay out HEW options on Baltimore. In January 1980, she sent Harris a memorandum proposing alternatives. The report began by noting that enrollment in 1978–79 was 77 percent black. Accompanying maps and charts put that fact in two contexts. The first, quite familiar, was an historic expansion of census tracts with high proportions of black students, moving from the city core toward the periphery. The second, not noted in the report, was two occasions when the percentages of schools with more than 90 percent of students from one race dropped sharply— after 1954, when the board instituted free choice, and after 1974, when, under OCR pressure, the board took additional desegregation steps. Whereas 81 percent of schools were so segregated in 1973, only 59 percent were in 1978. The OCR allowance of a 20 percent variation would now consider schools 57 to 97 percent black in compliance with Title VI, and it was unclear how many schools fell outside this range, but the data showed that efforts to mix students had results.

The most effective method for desegregating schools within Eagleton-Biden constraints, the report said, was pairing and clustering. In mid-November, Davis had driven around Baltimore for four days, measuring distance and travel time between schools. He formulated two elaborate alternatives, one restructuring grades, the other reassigning students. Pairings and clusterings, many originally proposed in Samuel Banks's 1974 plan, would mix students while keeping travel time low. Moving either one-fourth or one-half of students, the alternatives would bring 117 of 201 schools into compliance with the 50–90 percent standard and leave only 45 schools over 90 percent black. Davis had figured out two ways that the city, even with many black students, could more broadly mix black and white students within federal busing limits.

Still, the hard question was what OCR could do in the face of the injunction and Baltimore officials' lack of interest in desegregating. The report contemplated metropolitan desegregation and considered research to see if Baltimore County activities met *Milliken* standards of responsibility for city school segregation but acknowledged that OCR lacked the staff for such a study. In the end, the report recommended reopening negotiations and pursuing a strategy to return the case to court and give the city an incentive to develop an integration plan. However, despite the conceptual and political ingenuity of the memorandum, it did not persuade Secretary Harris to move against Baltimore.[51]

Coming to an Agreement

While Stewart was trying to proceed with Baltimore, Shirley Hufstedler, Carter's designee to head the new Department of Education, was hurrying to get the agency running by a June 1980 deadline. The education part of OCR would move to Education and report to an assistant secretary for civil rights. When the department started up on May 4, Cynthia Brown became assistant secretary. When Ronald Reagan came in the next January, Frederick Cioffi took the post on an acting basis until Clarence Thomas's appointment later that year, and Harry Singleton took over when Thomas went to the Equal Employment Opportunity Commission in 1982. Singleton graduated from Johns Hopkins and was Thomas's classmate at Yale Law School. He had practiced law, worked with the American Enterprise Institute, and served as legal counsel and staff director to the Republicans on the House District of Columbia Committee. He was thirty-three when he came to Education. Soon after, the Baltimore case came to a head.

Four years had passed since the Fourth Circuit had sent the case back to district court, where a temporary injunction was now six years old. The case was one of the oldest on Judge Northrop's docket. As OCR tried to move against Baltimore, the federal court administration pressed Northrop to close the case. Baltimore took the judge's new interest in action as an opportunity to settle things permanently in favor of the city. In September 1982, Stephen Derby wrote Assistant Attorney General William Bradford Reynolds, who supervised CRD, proposing an agreement to make permanent all provisions of the preliminary injunction not by then moot. Singleton, who considered the injunction unjustified to begin with, persuaded Reynolds to oppose making it permanent. Northrop, spurred on by court administrators, abruptly set a status conference with the parties on October 22. After some back-and-forth, over Singleton's objection, the sides agreed to terminate litigation and continue with voluntary negotiations. Education would abide by the terms of the temporary injunction, now effectively permanent, and Baltimore would provide requested information so far as it could. On January 21, 1983, Northrop issued an order ratifying an agreement between Baltimore and the Justice Department, ending a seven-year legal battle.[52]

Baltimore Schools Move On

School Board president Mark Joseph had periodically updated the board on the litigation but did nothing further to desegregate after the Fourth Circuit victory. When his term expired in 1980, he summarized his accomplishments at a board meeting. "After almost a decade of steady decline," he observed, "while the system was embroiled in conflict over race, a teachers' strike, and the firing of Dr. Patterson, our students have now demonstrated a dramatic three-year gain on the national norms." He admonished board members and residents that "extraneous controversy must be avoided." Even though Derby had argued that the purpose of the injunction was to give city educators and officials breathing room to desegregate in ways that fit local conditions, Joseph did not mention desegregation as an accomplishment, and his only reference to race implied that the city should avoid discussing it.[53]

Superintendent John Crew retired in 1982 and addressed the board on that occasion. He did not mention desegregation among his accomplishments either. Board president David Daneker lauded Crew for bringing about "an air of harmony, a unity of purpose, and a measure of success which is uncommon to urban school systems." Black board member Howard Marshall underlined a main theme: "He brought a good deal of harmony out of a lot of disorder." After years of racial conflict, the board valued peace above much else, including desegregation.[54]

Alice Pinderhughes, a Baltimorean who had made her career in elementary education, succeeded Crew as the city's third permanent black superintendent in September 1982. The next month, the board asked her to review the status of the city faculty desegregation plan and directed her "to take any reasonable actions necessary to bring the school system as close to compliance as possible by February 1, 1983," a federal deadline. At the January 20 board meeting, Pinderhughes announced that twenty-nine secondary teachers would be moved among seventeen of the twenty-eight schools still in violation. She aimed at full compliance by September 1983, twenty-nine years after *Brown*.

Pinderhughes's announcement was followed by the most extensive public discussion of desegregation in a long time. Notably, speakers repeatedly referred to "HEW," in apparent ignorance of, or indifference to, the fact that the Education Department had held jurisdiction over desegregation for nearly three years. The announcement of twenty-nine teacher transfers found five parents and a city councilman protesting a midyear move and urging the board to wait until September. As a sign of how black thinking had changed, two parents and three elected officials urged unpairing City Springs and General Wolfe. Instead of having children shifted between schools from year to year, these advocates wanted City Springs to become a "complete" school again. Loretta Brown, president of the City Springs PTA, felt that white General Wolfe families had not participated in the pairing as much as black City Springs families. The result was to reduce City Springs enrollment. More importantly, she argued, moving students back and forth caused low test scores, poor behavior, and problems keeping up. She wanted children to go to a neighborhood school and was unconcerned about classmates' race: "Before the 1974 Desegregation Law went into effect, [City Springs] did not have a problem with desegregation. The school was already integrated. Furthermore, every time the matter of race is brought up, it is not the parents but staff or other persons who bring it up. To us, it is just not a problem."

In fact, in 1974 City Springs had 11 white students in an enrollment of 642, and this imbalance was why the schools had been paired, but Brown's comment made clear that this did not matter. She just wanted a school to educate her children.[55]

The *Afro*, reporting on the board meeting, singled out Baltimore Teacher Union opposition to midyear transfers as the obstacle to desegregating staffs. With understatement, the front page headline reported, "City School Desegregation Pace Still Slow."[56]

The End of the End

Harry Singleton represented OCR activists in trying to restart negotiations over student desegregation with Baltimore, but three new conditions worked against that effort. First, the city had few white students. Second, victory in court gave Baltimore little incentive to negotiate or make concessions. Third, the Reagan administration had no interest in desegregation. Quixotically, Singleton organized his troops for a last assault on the city. He asked Antonio Califa, director for litigation, enforcement, and policy service, who should serve on a new Baltimore team. Califa recommended several people, including Harold Davis, but Califa did not expect new negotiations to produce any agreement the earlier ones had not and wanted to turn the case over to the Justice Department for litigation.

After consulting with Davis, Califa gave Singleton a summary of 1983 Baltimore conditions. The district was now 80 percent black, and many schools were disproportionately black. The proximity of a number of disproportionately black schools and disproportionately white schools suggested something might still be done. However, on-site investigation was necessary, because information supplied by Baltimore was "incomplete" and "misleading and unreliable." Available data suggested that the district was intentionally segregating students and that some white city students were attending Baltimore County schools. Davis conducted a study while OCR waited for the district to provide bits of requested information. In September, Singleton wrote Mayor Schaefer, then in his thirteenth year in office, requesting a meeting to resolve problems getting data, but Schaefer did not reply. After more than a year, in June 1984, Califa got Singleton's permission to contact Baltimore staff, but his August progress report revealed the Achilles heel in federal dealings with local districts. The consent decree required OCR to specify programs and schools that did not comply with Title VI, but OCR did not know how federal money was spent in individual schools. Its staff could determine whether Baltimore was in compliance only if the city gave them that information, and Baltimore was not doing so.[57]

The Office for Civil Rights and the Baltimore City Public Schools (BCPS) traded correspondence for two more years, as the city submitted additional data,

OCR raised questions about possible discrimination, school staff interpreted the data benignly, OCR asked further questions, and so forth. The Education Department found it harder and harder to show that predominantly single-race schools resulted from school system actions and more and more impractical to devise policies that would improve the racial mix. At last, in March 1987, Philip Kiko, acting director of the department Policy and Enforcement Service (PES), conveyed his conclusion to Alicia Coro, acting assistant secretary for civil rights: "PES believes there is insufficient reason to warrant OCR inquiry. Although PES is not convinced that fostering or maintaining a balance of white and nonwhite elementary students was given a high priority by the Board of Education, the BCPS...was not unreasonable."[58]

On May 12, 1987, five days short of the thirty-third anniversary of *Brown,* Coro sent Superintendent Pinderhughes a short letter. "OCR has concluded," it said, "that there are no remaining vestiges of BCPS's prior de jure school segregation in its student and faculty assignment policies and practices." The correspondence was not reported at a school board meeting or noted in the press. The battle had been over for nearly a decade.[59]

CONCLUSION

Baltimore School Desegregation, Liberalism, and Race

Chance played a role in how Baltimore desegregation ended. If the city suit had gone to a different federal district court judge, the court might have directed that administrative enforcement hearings proceed, and Judge Hackerman might have imposed integration requirements on Baltimore. Alternatively, if Judge Craven had not died, the Fourth Circuit would have ruled in favor of enforcement hearings. Besides chance, local circumstances influenced the course of events. Baltimore had a race-aversive political culture that encouraged school officials to adopt a laissez-faire desegregation policy. The city's black leadership negotiated grievances with white officials, rather than battling in the open, and in any case, most middle-class blacks wanted free choice desegregation, so that no civil rights group had reason to sue the school system to do more. And the 1968 riots and aftermath broke up biracial support for integration and contributed to racial polarization that incapacitated the school board and gave control over desegregation to a mayor with little civil rights interest and hostility toward federal intervention.

Despite these idiosyncrasies, the course of Baltimore desegregation reflected the national conflict over race that Gunnar Myrdal characterized as an American Dilemma. School officials who espoused racial equality adopted and sustained a desegregation policy that eliminated some racial restrictions but tacitly maintained others. Crucially, school officials tried to desegregate schools without dealing with race. An important part of the explanation is that liberalism, the culturally normal American way of thinking about society and politics, presented an individualistic prism that made it hard to see and know about race.

Yet another part of the explanation is that all who had political or psychological motives not to talk or think about race could avoid the subject simply by following liberal common sense. Silence about the deepest meanings of race helped preserve domestic tranquility, but that came at the cost of the moral invisibility of black children's educational needs.

Black Children's Invisibility

By the time the U.S. Department of Education exonerated the Baltimore school system, a half century had passed since local black activists started campaigning for better education for their children. If they had been alive in 1987, they would have been pleased to see a succession of black superintendents and blacks' ascendance to power in the school system. On the other hand, schools were not integrated, and black students were not doing well academically in nearly all-black schools. Most black children suffered from a reconfigured segregation—attendance in city schools that were separate from and largely unequal to predominantly white suburban schools. Enrollment was 80 percent black, a mirror image of the district that was 75 percent white in 1937. In 2004, the fiftieth anniversary of *Brown*, city schools would be 89 percent black, and black children in Baltimore would have less chance of encountering white classmates than black students in any other large American school district. Although a 1987 observer would see a preponderance of black faces, what stands out in the decades of desegregation effort is black children's invisibility in school policy.[1]

In *Brown*, the Supreme Court held that deliberately separating black students from white, even if schools were tangibly equal, made black children feel inferior and hindered their intellectual development. The Baltimore school board never considered this possibility as an urgent reason for mixing white and black students. Even if board members doubted such psychological arguments, they could see the tangible inequalities in schools and recognize their educational consequences for black children. But the board did little to equalize facilities under legal segregation and did not rush to improve historically black schools after *Brown*. Although school segregation was enmeshed in extensive social segregation, the school board adopted a voluntary individualistic remedy for this institutional problem.

It would be unreasonable to expect 1954 school officials to anticipate all the results of their actions, especially since they were moving in uncharted territory. It is impossible to know what the board could have accomplished if they had tried to root out the institutional underpinnings of segregation in the school system and devised more directive desegregation strategies. However, the board never publicly considered such action, even though within five years members could see the limitations of open enrollment as desegregation strategy. Two superintendents excused the board from further action by disavowing an interest in whether many black and white children attended school together. Although individual board members rued black students' conditions, a series of boards collectively accepted them. In practice, "compensatory education" for the "culturally disadvantaged" became the main fix for the shortcomings of open enrollment as a strategy for improving black children's education.

How Free Choice Failed to Engage Segregation

Because the school board's free choice policy avoided direct explicit intervention in school racial makeup, the policy not only had limited efficacy in desegregating, but also hampered desegregation by contributing to white flight. These shortcomings can be understood by examining how the board, following liberal principles, created a market in school enrollments, in which individual preferences were regulated by voluntary mutual accommodation rather than government coercion. Market principles contained two flaws that limited desegregation. First, markets poorly fit the conditions through which education is "produced" and "consumed," and centrally, markets cannot force individuals to make choices they strongly dislike.[2]

Free Choice as a Misconceived Enrollment Market

The school board created a market in which the school system supplied enrollments and students bid on them. Because taxes supported schools, bids were free and all of equal value. System administrators regulated the market minimally. They halted bidding for a school when demand reached the supply of seats, though sometimes they responded to excess demand by increasing seats through part-time schooling. They reserved the right to reject any bid if they believed a request for a school was educationally unsound. The finitude of seats put students in competition for specific schools.

Normal market assumptions, however, poorly fit education. Unlike cars, for example, education is a service, not a good. It consists of—is created by—specific human relationships. The quality of education in a school depends on the teacher, the students, and their interactions—in addition to the adequacy of facilities, equipment, and materials. Automobiles are mass produced; all are presumably identical. Though drivers may use their vehicles differently, the nature of the car itself is not affected by the driver's identity or relations with other drivers. A market for automobiles puts buyers in competition for a limited number of finished products. In contrast, a market for schools puts families into a complicated game in which the "product" (the quality of education in a classroom) is determined only after families have made their choices, and the range of possible "products" is large. Parents who understand these contingencies try to manage them by influencing who teaches and who sits in class with their child. These parents want their child to have relationships with specific individuals or categories of persons. In other words, in trying to determine the educational "product" children receive, "consumers" are not bidding on objects that are separate from themselves, but are bidding on relations with one another, parts of other "consumers."

With schools, as with cars, "consumers" have various preferences. Three conditions are necessary for an enrollment market to work to broad satisfaction. First, most teachers must be "good" according to widely ranging standards and must teach in adequate facilities. Second, most children must have attributes valued by parents of many other children. Third, parents must make compatible choices: parents desiring a certain type of classmate for their child can get what they want only if parents of the classmates they desire make the same choice. If the first two conditions prevail, an enrollment market will work more efficiently when a central agency collects and distributes relevant information about teachers, students, and buildings. Otherwise, families will rely on prejudices, limited informal networks, and proxy indicators of school and student characteristics, such as where schools are located or teachers' or students' race.

In addition, to work efficiently, an enrollment market, as any market, must overcome the influences of "prior determinations." Past public policy and private actions, customs, and historical accident affect the nature and distribution of products available in a market, as well as the skills and assets consumers bring to exchanges. Markets that allocate products among actors as they are, that ratify the effects of prior determinations through indifference to them, cannot widely satisfy individual preferences. Efficiency in matching preferences with goods and services depends on actions by a central agency to reduce and remedy past inequalities so as to increase choices and individuals' ability to choose.[3]

Segregation was an overwhelming prior determination. The school system created colored schools that were physically undesirable by widely held standards. Segregation created two classes of black teachers: a minority who received scholarships to study out of state at good institutions and a majority who trained locally at a poorly staffed and equipped normal school. Many of the latter did not satisfy general expectations. Segregation isolated black children in schools where they often had fewer learning opportunities than whites. Particularly if they were poor, they were unlikely to have the attributes that middle-class parents wanted in children's classmates: cultivated intellectual skills, familiarity with "higher" culture, and connections to institutions of success.

These inequalities limited the efficiency of the enrollment market in providing families with choices that satisfied them. Beyond this, the market had a particular flaw as a means to desegregation, because families had conflicting preferences. Unlike a market for automobiles, which works when consumers have preferences for different products, a market for enrollment can desegregate schools only if "consumers" have similar preferences. While some black families wanted their children in schools with white classmates, most white families wanted their children in all-white classrooms. The chances that whites and blacks would choose compatibly so as to desegregate schools were small. Almost no whites used the market to choose historically or predominantly black schools. A small, growing number of blacks chose historically white schools, but as blacks moved in, whites moved out. After a decade of free choice, Baltimore schools were largely segregated and would become increasingly so.

Paradoxical Results of Free Choice

These flaws in free choice were not accidental. School officials valued a noncoercive policy on the assumption that voluntary desegregation would scare off the fewest whites. And yet, not only did open enrollment not significantly desegregate, but it also failed to deter white flight. White families left city schools even when their children had few black classmates. As late as 1972, when enrollment was 70 percent black, 81 percent of black students attended schools at least 90 percent black; two-thirds of white students attended schools at least 80 percent white, and half were in schools at least 90 percent white. Even when blacks and whites went to the same school, tracking often kept them apart.[4]

Whites left city schools for many reasons. The first moves, when the G.I. Bill let returning soldiers buy suburban homes, had nothing to do with race. Whites left Baltimore, where only 19 percent of 1940 residents were black and housing segregation limited whites' contact with them, to acquire American Dream homes. Federal Housing Administration discrimination ensured that suburbs would be white, and as blacks grew to 24 percent of the 1950 population and blockbusters stirred up anxiety, the suburban move gained racial meaning. Even so, white city public school enrollment increased until 1957.

The first declines in white enrollment were modest, less than 2 percent annually from 1957 to 1964, when the drop reached nearly 3 percent and began rising unevenly to 4 percent in 1967. However, the percentage decline diminished in 1968 and 1969 before rising to 4 and 5 percent in 1971 and 1972, respectively. Thus three years after school desegregation white enrollment started dropping, moderately. The rate of decline increased after the board's 1963 new desegregation policies but dropped the year of the riots. It rose again three years later. Undoubtedly white departure from city schools reflected unease about blacks. Time lags between desegregation actions and rises in white departures probably reflected some parents' decisions to let children finish neighborhood elementary schools before leaving. However, white departures increased at times when most white students attended class with few black students. For some white families any black classmates were unacceptable. Perhaps families whose children had more contact with black students were particularly likely to leave. Nevertheless, school desegregation was just one part of a larger calculation, in which neighborhood change, the civil rights movement, black power, and the riots also figured.[5]

Free choice contributed to white departure, however, not just by allowing black-white contact in schools, but also by adding to racial anxiety. A basic fact about the enrollment market was that no one was in charge: anyone could end up going to school with anyone. Thus a policy intended to affect race relations minimally unsettled race relations by transforming a situation of near certainty (Poly was the sole exception) into one of great uncertainty. White parents who might want or be willing to send their children to a nearby racially balanced school could not make a decision with any confidence about what the makeup would be when the school opened in the fall or how long those conditions would hold. They had little idea what other parents would choose and, in any case, no control over them. Free choice created a turbulent setting that left no place for rational individual action. In this context, a normal market strategy of choosing so as to maximize satisfaction made less sense than a strategy of trying to minimize (seemingly ubiquitous) risk. Parents might quickly shift from a desire to enroll their child in the neighborhood school to a plan to move to the suburbs. Thus a desegregation policy that avoided dealing with race increased racial anxiety and encouraged whites to leave.[6]

Baltimore school officials received national plaudits for adopting free choice right after *Brown* but two decades later became a target of federal civil rights enforcers. Three contexts make the course of events understandable. An examination of the national politics of school desegregation indicates why Baltimore started desegregation quickly, proceeded undisturbed with a modest policy for a long time, and then got into a confrontation with the Office for Civil Rights. A look at of the culture of Baltimore as a border city sheds light on why the Baltimore board took moderate steps when it started, why local officials resisted federal intervention, and why blacks did not sue. A review of liberalism shows how school officials' focus on individual choice limited their intervention and avoided overt consideration of race in policy while tacitly reinforcing racial discrimination.

The National Politics of School Desegregation

Geography, timing, and local culture mattered in school desegregation. Many districts in border states moved right after *Brown*. Because, like the South, they had legally segregated schools, the ruling required them to change enrollment practices. However, because they were geographically, economically, and culturally close to the North, they had significant numbers of liberal whites who wanted to end segregation. Wilmington, subject to the *Brown* decision, was already desegregating when the Supreme Court ruled. Although Washington was also one of the five school segregation cases, its move to desegregate in the fall of 1954 could be considered somewhat voluntary when contrasted with resistance in two of the other four districts, in Virginia and South Carolina. Baltimore, St. Louis, and Kansas City, three border cities, acted without a push.

Districts that desegregated in 1954 were trying something unprecedented, and no one could know what results specific strategies would bring. Washington, Wilmington, Kansas City, and St. Louis drew school zones, though Kansas City and Wilmington continued policies allowing students to transfer and St. Louis added transfers in 1963. Baltimore was the only early district adopting free choice alone as a desegregation strategy. Civil rights advocates, despite high hopes for desegregation, were uncertain what standards to use to measure the early efforts, and they gave generous benefits of doubts to those who acted first. Once a school board ended segregation policies, even if segregation continued, many local residents, particularly whites, thought of the schools as desegregated, and civil rights interests tended to give them a pass. Against the backdrop of entrenched segregation and determined defiance around the South, even modest changes seemed significant, and activists focused on districts engaged in massive or passive resistance.

The civil rights movement, the 1964 Civil Rights Act, the Office for Civil Rights, and the U.S. Civil Rights Commission changed expectations of desegregation in the 1960s. In 1961, the NAACP opened a campaign against segregation in Northern and Western districts. Gradually, the NAACP, OCR, and the Civil Rights Commission soured on free choice, and in 1968 *Green* rejected it unless it actually, and widely, integrated schools. In 1971, *Swann* required districts that had been legally segregated to prove that vestiges of segregation were gone and authorized busing and gerrymandered zones to integrate. Southern districts that had resisted desegregation and Northern districts that had avoided attention until the late 1960s or early 1970s confronted increasingly specific and stringent standards for implementing *Brown*. The NAACP forced court scrutiny of policies and practices that maintained segregation, and it sued Chicago, Philadelphia, Denver, Detroit, Boston, and other Northern districts, getting rulings requiring extensive desegregation.

Baltimore, as other districts that acted early, faced new challenges as the political and legal climate changed. In the late 1960s, OCR held administrative enforcement hearings to cut off federal education funds from Kansas City because schools were not desegregated very much. In response, the city ended transfers, reassigned teachers to create racial balance, and adopted a districtwide busing plan. By the late 1970s, the city concluded it could not desegregate schools two-thirds black without suburban involvement and initiated a suit that led to a metropolitan arrangement with voluntary black transfers to the suburbs and creation of magnets to attract whites into city schools. In St. Louis, parents sued the district in 1972 and were joined by the NAACP in broader litigation in 1977. The federal judge negotiated a settlement between the city and suburban districts that produced arrangements similar to those in Kansas City.

While federal laws, officials, and courts required districts to do more and more to desegregate, Baltimoreans remained committed to the open enrollment that received early national approval, despite growing segregation. Within that framework, the school board experimented with magnet schools, but no one took steps to develop metropolitan arrangements. The board refused to bus elementary school students to integrate, and it went along with union resistance to integrating teachers. Because no one ever sued school officials, no court held Baltimore to account against rising integration standards. The absence of such litigation led to the confrontation with OCR. However, without court involvement, as in Kansas City and St. Louis, OCR had limited negotiating leverage against Baltimore.

Baltimore Culture and Strategies for Racial Peace

Baltimore differed from other school districts in two respects. A liberal board that wanted desegregation adopted a free choice policy that did not produce it and adhered to the policy despite this inefficacy. Black leaders encouraged and endorsed open enrollment, continued to support it despite its failure to end racial separation, and never sued the board to integrate more actively. These peculiarities reflected both distinctive local circumstances and common American efforts to avoid conflict over race.[7]

Racial Laissez-faire

When national conflicts over slavery threatened to tear Baltimore apart in the mid-nineteenth century, Baltimoreans sought to maintain peace by adopting a laissez-faire policy on race. Private citizens were free to pursue their own positions for and against slavery, for and against segregation, but the government would not deliberately intervene in race relations. When the city government did adopt a policy that discriminated against blacks, it did so as an endorsement of private preferences or actions, not as an autonomous initiative. The 1911 racial zoning ordinance, for example, was framed as simply codifying private decisions, not enacting any new distinctions. School segregation was couched similarly as a formalization of community norms.

The 1954 school desegregation policy continued an historic open enrollment policy but also followed the tradition of racial laissez-faire. The Public Schools and the Housing Authority desegregated their facilities in the same month, and both gave their clients free choice about mixing. Whatever the historic precedents and philosophical justifications for open enrollment, it removed school officials from responsibility for determining or regulating school racial makeup. The policy put the onus for racial mixing on families, mainly black families.

Black leaders supported the enrollment policy for practical reasons. After nearly a century of government restriction of black education, free choice seemed the most emancipatory alternative. Rather than rely on mostly white school officials to set new rules controlling enrollment, black leaders believed self-reliance offered the greatest opportunities. Middle-class and elite black families had the confidence and resources to move their children into historically white schools. Laissez-faire, particularly if only a minority of blacks participated in it, seemed the approach least likely to arouse white resistance. And a policy that avoided a public position on the racial makeup of schools kept race out of public discussion, removing a spark to white opposition.

In general, Baltimore blacks' customary strategy of negotiating grievances with white officials used the laissez-faire political culture by establishing new private positions to which public officials might respond. That approach, coupled with the fact that most middle-class blacks liked free choice, kept civil rights activists away from the courts with regard to school desegregation. Thurgood Marshall, who would have been most likely to litigate, had left Baltimore for the New York NAACP offices in 1936 and from there took a national perspective on school desegregation. Although the Baltimore branch and the *Afro* talked about suing in 1975, by then the black constituency for integration was small.

Racial Ignorance and Silence

The quickness of the school board vote to desegregate on June 3, 1954, could be seen as a reflection of members' moral confidence in their action, but it can also be taken as a measure of their fear of talking about race. No one knew whether whites would react violently to ending segregation. In this context, the board's swift action followed the Baltimore habit of keeping peace by not letting race into public discussion. From that time on, officials suppressed talk about race in connection with desegregation in several ways.

First, on a number of occasions, the board and administrators simply ignored what many knew about racially unequal schools and anxious race relations. Superintendent John Fischer declared that transfers were unlikely because white and colored schools were equivalent. His facilities director said that the only challenge of desegregation was to accommodate growing enrollment; he saw no problems with school conditions. Probably most, if not all, of the white board members knew something about black school conditions, and all were aware of racial tensions. Perhaps they found these things too much to do anything about. Realistic action would have required campaigning for school bonds, taking on the teacher unions, and opening and managing public discussion. Apparent ignorance avoided even talking about these issues.

In addition, school officials directly and explicitly discouraged racial talk. When voting to desegregate, the board allowed no public discussion. In choosing a policy, the board endorsed Fischer's recommendation that "the race of the pupil shall not be a consideration" in enrollment decisions. This language rejected the strictures of segregation, but it also precluded taking students' race into account in devising remedies, thus eliminating racial talk in desegregation. Fischer warned that race-conscious integration efforts were dangerous "social engineering." School officials' view that desegregation meant simply removing restrictive laws avoided considering de facto segregation as a problem and made it unnecessary to examine race relations in schools. When the 28 Parents charged the system with de facto segregation, board member William Stone admonished his colleagues to stop talking about race and integration and keep to "educational" issues. When city solicitor George Russell Jr. stated that *Green* made the free choice policy unconstitutional, city council president William Donald Schaefer argued against reviewing the policy because doing so would require talking about race. When board president Mark Joseph retired in 1980 after the court battles with the federal government, he urged his colleagues to avoid controversy associated with race.

Stone's letter represented a third way of avoiding race: changing the subject to "education." This position asserted that racial issues such as desegregation had nothing to do with education, the only proper subject for school board deliberation. Stone said that racial talk just led to conflict that hindered school improvement. Even after the Coleman Report found that integration aided black children and after Baltimore test data showed that black students, most in segregated schools, performed lower than whites, those who raised the "education" flag still insisted on not talking about race. Rather than analyzing whether segregation contributed to racial educational differences, and whether integration would improve black children's education, school officials devised "compensatory education" for black students in predominantly black schools.

Liberalism and a Raceless Attack on Segregation

Baltimore officials also kept race from public debate simply by relying on liberalism in defining issues and making policy. Sociological individualism, an ethical emphasis on rights, and government minimalism focused diagnosis and prescription on whether raceless individuals were free to choose schools. This perspective served Baltimoreans who wanted to avoid conflict over race, but the liberal premises that obscured race and restrained government action also limited the scope and impact of desegregation policy. Moreover, people continued to think about race even if they did not talk about it, and liberal school officials who avoided overt racial discussion ended up unwittingly admitting invidious racial distinctions into their vocabulary and policy. Liberal-thinking officials failed to get a grasp on race as either an instrument of or obstacle to desegregation.

Liberal Resistance to Integration

Most Baltimore school officials' emphasis on the liberal concept of individual liberty—freedom from external constraint—led them to define segregation as the imposition of limits on students' enrollment and to define desegregation simply as the removal of restraints. They focused on legal policies that limited enrollment for several reasons. First, these policies were the most explicit and visible constraints on black children—more explicit than policies on districting overcrowded schools or locating new facilities and more visible than the historic racial identities or climates of schools. Second, recognizing and dealing with the latter constraints required looking at and talking about race, which liberals could barely see and did not consider important. Third, de facto segregation, because it resulted from limits on blacks as a group rather than black children as individuals, was a collective, rather than individual, condition, and liberals thought in terms of individual opportunities rather than group opportunities. Finally, de facto segregation referred to an outcome of enrollment decisions, rather than the process of enrolling students, and liberals were not directly concerned about outcomes. For all these reasons, liberal officials did not consider the deliberate mixing of black and white students that constituted integration as a goal of desegregation. Integration was a communal condition requiring individuals to have specific social relations, and recognizing a citywide interest in integration would require acknowledging children's race and limiting their choices according to their race.[8]

Liberalism as a Means of Resisting Desegregation

Not only did liberal board members focus narrowly on de jure desegregation, but when they rejected a public interest in racial integration and framed desegregation as a matter of individual rights, they gave whites language and authority for resisting desegregation. Thus some white Baltimoreans opposed desegregation by asserting a right of free association, a right to select their child's classmates. Soon after *Brown*, a *Sun* letter-writer defended segregation in these terms: "One of our highest rights in this country is that of every man to dislike and avoid whom he pleases." White parents protesting the appearance of black children at historically white elementary schools in 1954 carried signs proclaiming "We want our rights." Over the years, white families and neighborhood associations repeatedly invoked their "rights" in opposing desegregation. In 1974, when southeast parents resisted desegregation plans, they justified school sit-ins as protecting families' "rights" and said parents would take their children to "the school of their choice."[9]

The school board's language of rights had no explicit link to race. Thus desegregation opponents could invoke rights to segregated schooling without speaking of race or expressing racial animosity. The school board consistently gave in to southeast demands to reduce racial mixing. Part of the explanation was adept community organizing. Part may have been board members' sympathy for working-class whites, who bore the brunt of white participation in integration. However, in the end, the rights language of free choice left no alternative. Integration is a matter of degree, but rights are absolute. Moreover, they are undiscussable and nonnegotiable. If a right doesn't exist absolutely, it isn't a right. Hence the board, up against HEW demands to integrate and aware that yielding to desegregation opponents would hurt the city position, could not resist.[10]

How a Raceless Educational Strategy Reinforced Racial Discrimination

Free choice left many black children in predominantly black schools, and many of these students had academic problems. In the late 1950s, and increasingly in the 1960s, as poverty became a national concern, Baltimore school officials gave attention to poor black children with academic problems. Although *Brown* had identified segregation as an obstacle to black students' development, some Baltimore educators of both races adopted newly current terms that diagnosed problems in ways that had little to do with segregation or race and put blame on the students. These school officials labeled poor black children as "culturally disadvantaged" or "culturally deprived" and prescribed "compensatory education" in predominantly black schools as the remedy. The "cultural" language and "compensatory" strategy fit a liberal approach to educational policy in several ways.[11]

In general, the liberal perspective fit well with conventional images of education, which featured an encounter between two individuals, a teacher and a student. In this view, education depended simply on a teacher's skill and devotion and a child's motivation. A student's classmates, for example, didn't matter, and thus the racial makeup of a classroom was far less important than what a student brought into it. The new cultural language depicted poor black children as individuals whose families lived apart from mainstream society and failed to give their sons and daughters the culture and motivation to learn. If anything, coping with poverty led the poor to develop ways of thinking and habits that diverted them from success. In any case, it was poverty, and not race, that limited their ability to learn.

References to culture and poverty might lead to analysis of how social institutions constrained black children, but conventional usage of the new language connected most readily to a simplistic economic image of a world that held opportunities for all individuals who had the skills and motivation to struggle against circumstances. Hence Baltimore school officials simply aimed to alter black children through programs that "compensated" for their "disadvantages," without any consideration of how society or school system culture and practices limited black children's learning. With the untested assumption that economic opportunities were open to those who took them, "compensatory education" fit the liberal premise that unencumbered individuals rose or fell on their own. In addition, compensatory education could be used as a rationalization for not taking more forceful measures to desegregate schools. Although Houston Jackson took black children's "cultural deprivation" as an argument for integration, John Fischer and others saw the children's "culture" or "disadvantage" as an individual handicap that the system could hope to remedy without any institutional change: ending tracking, integrating teaching staffs, training teachers to work with racially mixed classes, and integrating student bodies were unnecessary.[12]

Corresponding to the "culturally deprived" label for black children was a related term often used for whites: "middle class." In a typical instance, when the Baltimore lawyer reassured Judge Hackerman that city officials wanted integrated schools, the attorney argued for moderate measures that would not drive out "middle class people." "White" was understood. The phrase both avoided race and indicated that any group differences were matters of economics. However, though the language of "class" might imply that society was structured in ways that offered different opportunities to different groups, typical usage gave a simple individualistic meaning to this term as well. "Middle class" referred to essentially autonomous individuals who had a culture and income that made them reasonably well off. Thus both "culture" and "class" bolstered the view of children as race-free individuals.

And yet the labels "middle class" and "culturally deprived" did more than just graft onto liberal individualism new ways of referring to racial groups without using racial language. Connotatively, the two phrases affirmed an old Manichaean distinction between good, industrious whites and bad, uncultured blacks. "Culturally deprived" echoed the Europeans who first encountered dark-skinned Africans and concluded that they were "heathens," not disciplined by religion or culture. American whites thought that blacks, lacking culture, following their animal instincts and emotions, had little chance for economic success because their passions got in the way of calculating their self-interests. In the mid-twentieth century, Edward Banfield drew together these assumptions about blacks while simultaneously denying that race mattered. Blacks' troubles, he argued, were merely the result of their poverty, and the reason many were poor was that they lacked a "culture" of "discipline" and "rationality." Without it, they succumbed to economically unrewarding "impulsive" "action."[13]

The language of "culture" and "class" worked against black children's interests in two ways. First, it tacitly endorsed moral distinctions between races that put blacks beneath whites. This racial dichotomy raised emotional doubts that blacks could learn or that they were suitable classmates for white children. In addition, the language affirmed the liberal norm of suppressing passions and governing action by reason. In this view, ignoring emotional impulses is essential for economic success, and the good individual does as much as possible to remain unaware of feelings. Because the idea of race, as Myrdal observed, emerged from "irrational," "impulsive" passions, the admonition to think only rationally encouraged ignorance of the origins and meanings of race and emotional and moral interests in it. Consistently, liberal Baltimore school board members (as their counterparts elsewhere) avoided examining the irrational thinking that led whites to resist contacts with blacks, the passions that posed the central obstacle to desegregation. Board presidents, certain they could not control emotional expressions, did all they could to suppress them. Instead, policymakers accepted assumptions about race as an ineffable given, which they would neither analyze nor try to change. The board took whites' unease about blacks as a parameter limiting action alternatives, within which officials considered incentives to influence families' behavior. In these ways, a language of "culture" and "class" both hindered overt recognition of race and reinforced black disadvantages.

Liberalism and the American Dilemma

In 1903, W. E. B. DuBois predicted that "the problem of the color line" would be "the problem of the twentieth century." Forty years later, Gunnar Myrdal affirmed DuBois's forecast and interpreted the problem as an American Dilemma. He described the dilemma as a conflict in Americans' hearts and minds between liberalism, a progressive, egalitarian, reasoning tradition with which he identified, and another tradition that he abhorred: many whites' assumption that they were morally superior to blacks and free, or even obliged, to degrade them. Myrdal was of two minds about remedies. On the one hand, he had faith in the power of education gradually to subjugate ignorance and prejudice and create a more equal society. On the other hand, he recognized that many whites had deep emotional interests in seeing blacks as inferior and that these wishes resisted gaining the realistic knowledge on which social reform depended.[14]

Thus Myrdal, an Enlightenment liberal, saw the Dilemma as a contest between reason and passion. And yet, in noting Americans' belief in ignoring statutes, such as antidiscrimination legislation, that violated their notions of higher, natural law, he recognized that liberalism had two strands. One emphasized the equal worth of all individuals; the other emphasized individuals' equal liberty. The latter allowed individuals wide freedom to act on their desires and anxieties before authorizing government restraint. Northern liberals, with their minds fixed on equality, put extraordinary faith in the power of reason eventually to discipline individual freedom. Southern liberals, in contrast, lived in explicit racial inequality and understood how untrammeled individuals indulged their desires in whatever ways society allowed.[15]

In other words, though Myrdal formulated the American Dilemma as a struggle of liberalism against ignorance and emotion, the dilemma was inherent to liberalism itself. Finding a way out required coming to terms with the ways that the castelike relations of race encumbered individuals and understanding the desires and anxieties that defined individual relations racially. Liberalism developed the emancipatory modern concept of the individual, but liberal premises are clearer on why individuals should have freedom from others than why and how persons should accept responsibility for and make common cause with one another. Liberalism is a philosophy of moderation, respectful of differences, concerned with balance, but establishing the American Creed in schooling demanded simultaneously respecting black and white concerns and articulating how all had interests in giving priority to black interests in equality over white interests in liberty. There were no clear paths.

Those who made policy on school desegregation needed answers to the original liberals' questions: how to understand human nature, how to demarcate individual liberty, how to resolve conflicts justly, and how to design social arrangements that elicit and serve what is most constructive in human beings. However, twentieth-century liberals lacked the moral language and conscious understanding of passions that informed their predecessors. They imagined ways of balancing the interests of individuals who happened to be white or black, while avoiding knowledge of the emotions that made them white or black. They held onto abstract liberal principles, but these, split off from the knowledge of human beings that gave rise to them, availed little.[16]

School desegregation involved more than a battle of ideas. The course of events was shaped by whites' wish to see themselves as good by seeing blacks as bad, the rationalization and institutionalization of this desire in slavery and segregation, and all ensuing anger and guilt. Liberalism provided the argument for black emancipation, but it also offered a way of thinking that hindered knowing about race. For policymakers who feared political conflict and for individuals who feared their own moral and emotional conflicts, thinking liberally was a culturally normal, commonsense way of avoiding talking or even knowing about race. Gunnar Myrdal put his hopes for enactment of the American Creed in reason. And yet, while he held out faith that conscience could remake social institutions, he concluded his study cautiously: "What we usually call 'social trends' have their main significance for the Negro's status because of what is in white people's minds." Extending black freedom and increasing equality required realistically confronting race, human desires, and anxieties, and the liberal dilemma to devise imperfect but good enough steps forward.[17]

Appendix

Table 1. Baltimore city public schools enrollment

YEAR	WHITE		BLACK		TOTAL
	NUMBER	PERCENT	NUMBER	PERCENT	
1923	82,222	83%	16,807	17%	99,029
1933	92,138	77	26,759	23	118,897
1943	77,286	71	31,287	29	108,573
1953	86,206	62	51,827	38	138,033
1954	75,624	60	57,064	40	143,688
1955	87,913	59	61,870	41	149,783
1956	88,083	57	66,913	43	154,966
1957	87,312	55	72,415	45	159,727
1958	85,988	53	77,611	47	163,542
1959	84,194	51	82,525	49	166,719
1960	82,588	49	87,634	51	170,222
1961	81,772	47	93,492	53	175,234
1962	80,822	45	99,216	55	180,032
1963	79,216	43	105,650	57	184,866
1964	76,903	41	111,584	59	188,487
1965	74,010	39	117,076	61	191,086
1966	71,534	37	120,882	63	192,416
1967	68,616	36	124,150	64	192,766
1968	66,826	35	126,224	65	193,050
1969	64,970	34	128,180	66	193,150
1970	63,035	33	129,852	67	192,887
1971	60,363	32	130,464	68	190,827
1972	57,295	31	129,711	69	187,006
1973	54,167	30	128,744	70	182,911

Sources: Baltimore City Public Schools, *Informational Materials for Desegregation Task Force* (Baltimore: BCPS, 1974); Board of School Commissioners, Baltimore City Public Schools, *Annual Report* (Baltimore: BCPS, 1945); Julia Roberta O'Wesney, "Historical Study of the Progress of Racial Desegregation in the Public Schools of Baltimore, Maryland" (Ph.D. diss., University of Maryland, College Park, 1970).

Table 2. Percentages of schools with different racial compositions

YEAR	100% WHITE	>90% WHITE	50–90% BLACK	>90% BLACK	100% BLACK
1953	60%				40%
1954	33				37
1955	26				39
1956	20	44%		39%	32
1957	20				33
1958	19				30
1959	20				31
1960					
1961		30		44	
1962		30		46	
1963		23		46	
1964		22		48	
1965		21		50	
1966		20		53	
1967	6	20		54	23
1968		19		54	
1969		18		54	
1970		18		56	
1971		18		57	
1972		16		55	
1973		17	.	57	

Sources: Baltimore City Public Schools, *Informational Materials for Desegregation Task Force* (Baltimore: BCPS, 1974); Joel Acus Carrington, "The Struggle for Desegregation of Baltimore City Public Schools 1952–1966" (Ph.D. diss., University of Maryland, College Park, 1970); Julia Roberta O'Wesney, "Historical Study of the Progress of Racial Desegregation in the Public Schools of Baltimore, Maryland" (Ph.D. diss., University of Maryland, College Park, 1970); Parents Committee, *Seven Years of Desegregation* (Baltimore: Parents Committee, 1963).

Table 3. Percentages of students attending schools with different racial compositions

YEAR	100% WHITE	>90% WHITE	>50% WHITE	>50% BLACK	>90% BLACK	100% BLACK
1954		96% of W students		97% of B students	97% of B students	
1955		84% of W 86% of W elem. stds.; 100% W sec. stds.		97% of B	91% of B	
1956		81% of W elem. stds.; 77% of W sec. stds.			87% of B	
1957		81% of W elem. stds.; 71% of W sec. stds.			85% of B	
1958		78% of W elem. stds.; 64% of W sec. stds.			82% of B	
1959	34% of W	70% of W elem. stds.; 65% of W sec. stds.			80% of B	55% of B
1960		74% of W elem. stds.; 61% of W sec. stds.			82% of B	
1961	26% of W	65% of W	97% of W	87% of B	80% of B	45% of B
1962	27% of W	64% of W	93% of W	90% of B	80% of B	41% of B
1963	19% of W					39% of B
1965		57% of W elem. stds.		92% of B elem. stds.	84% of B elem. stds.	
1972		49% of W			81% of B	

Sources: Baltimore City Public Schools, *Informational Materials for Desegregation Task Force* (Baltimore: BCPS, 1974); Julia Roberta O'Wesney, "Historical Study of the Progress of Racial Desegregation in the Public Schools of Baltimore, Maryland" (Ph.D. diss., University of Maryland, College Park, 1970); Parents Committee, *Seven Years of Desegregation* (Baltimore: Parents Committee, 1963); U.S. Commission on Civil Rights, *Racial Isolation in the Public Schools,* vol. 1 (Washington, DC: USCCR, 1967).

Notes

The following short titles are used to identify sources in the notes:

Afro: *Baltimore Afro-American*
Evening Sun: *Baltimore Evening Sun*
Marshall Levin Papers: documents shared with the author by Marshall
                        Levin
Office for Civil Rights Office for Civil Rights documents received by the
    documents: author under a Freedom of Information Act request
Sun: *Baltimore Sun*
SSN: *Southern School News*

PREFACE

1. Jomills Henry Braddock II and James M. McPartland, "Social-psychological Processes that Perpetuate Racial Segregation: The Relationship between School and Employment Desegregation," *Journal of Black Studies* 19 (1980): 267–289; James S. Coleman, Ernest Q. Campbell, Carol J. Hobson, James McPartland, Alexander M. Mood, Frederic D. Weinfeld, and Robert L. York, *Equality of Educational Opportunity* (Washington, DC: U.S. Government Printing Office, 1966); Robert L. Crain and Rita E. Mahard, "Minority Achievement: Policy Implications of Research," in Willis D. Hawley, ed., *Effective School Desegregation* (Beverly Hills: Sage, 1981), 55–84; Susan E. Eaton, *The Other Boston Busing Story* (New Haven: Yale University Press, 2001); James M. McPartland and Jomills Henry Braddock II, "Going to College and Getting a Good Job: The Impact of Desegregation," in Hawley, *Effective School Desegregation*, 141–154; Leonard S. Rubinowitz and James E. Rosenbaum, *Crossing the Class and Color Lines* (Chicago: University of Chicago Press, 2000); Janet W. Schofield, "Review of Research on School Desegregation's Impact on Elementary and Secondary School Students," in James A. Banks and Cherry A. M. Banks, eds., *Handbook of Research on Multicultural Education* (New York: Macmillan, 1995), 597–616.

INTRODUCTION

1. On *Baltimore Afro* reporting on the war and the Double V campaign, see Haywood Farrar, *The Baltimore Afro-American, 1892–1950* (Westport, CT: Greenwood Press, 1998), chap. 8.

2. On the postwar mood, see Alan Brinkley, *Liberalism and Its Discontents* (Cambridge: Harvard University Press, 1998); Henry Steele Commager, *The American Mind: An Interpretation of American Thought and Character Since the 1880s* (New Haven: Yale University Press, 1950); Eric F. Goldman, *The Crucial Decade—and After: America, 1945–1960* (New York: Vintage, 1960); David Halberstam, *The Fifties* (New York: Fawcett Columbine, 1993); William Manchester, *The Glory and the Dream: A Narrative History of America 1932–1972* (Toronto: Bantam Books, 1975); Margaret Mead, *And Keep Your*

Powder Dry: An Anthropologist Looks at America, exp. ed. (New York: William Morrow, 1965); and Richard H. Pells, *The Liberal Mind in a Conservative Age: American Intellectuals in the 1940s and 1950s* (New York: Harper and Row, 1985).

3. On the equation of free markets with the free world, see Yehoshua Arieli, *Individualism and Nationalism in American Ideology* (Baltimore: Penguin Books, 1964).

4. On the nonstructural view of society, see Seymour Martin Lipset, *The First New Nation: The United States in Historical and Comparative Perspective* (New York: W. W. Norton, 1979). On the suppression of passion, see Lewis Mumford, "The Corruption of Liberalism," *The New Republic* (April 29, 1940), 568–573.

5. On individualistic American thinking about poverty, see Alice O'Connor, *Poverty Knowledge: Social Science, Social Policy, and the Poor in Twentieth-Century U.S. History* (Princeton: Princeton University Press, 2001). For a sample of Lippmann's writing, see *The Method of Freedom* (New York: Macmillan, 1934); *The Good Society* (Boston: Little, Brown, 1943); and *Essays in the Public Philosophy* (Boston: Little, Brown, 1955). For an account of midcentury liberal thinking that notes little talk of race, see Pells, *The Liberal Mind in a Conservative Age*.

6. The discussion in this section draws on Gunnar Myrdal, *An American Dilemma: The Negro Problem and Modern Democracy* (1944; New Brunswick, NJ: Transaction, 2000).

7. Myrdal, *An American Dilemma*, 85. On the history of white Americans' thinking about blacks, see Winthrop Jordan, *White over Black: American Attitudes toward the Negro 1550–1812* (Baltimore: Penguin, 1969); and George M. Fredrickson, *The Black Image in the White Mind: The Debate on Afro-American Character and Destiny, 1817–1914* (Hanover, NH: Wesleyan University Press, 1987).

8. Myrdal, *An American Dilemma*, 100, author's italics. On the psychology of white thinking about blacks, see Jordan, *White over Black;* Elizabeth Young-Bruehl, *The Anatomy of Prejudices* (Cambridge: Harvard University Press, 1996); Isaac D. Balbus, "The Psychodynamics of Racial Reparations," *Psychoanalysis, Culture, and Society* 9 (2004): 159–185; James Baldwin, *Collected Essays* (New York: The Library of America, 1998); Wendell Berry, *The Hidden Wound* (Boston: Houghton Mifflin, 1970); George A. De Vos and Marcelo Suárez-Orozco, *Status Inequality: The Self in Culture* (Newbury Park, CA: Sage, 1990); Ralph Ellison, *The Collected Essays of Ralph Ellison*, rev. ed., John F. Callahan, ed. (New York: Modern Library, 2003); Frederickson, *The Black Image in the White Mind;* Joel Kovel, *White Racism: A Psychohistory* (New York, Columbia University Press, 1984); Toni Morrison, *Playing in the Dark: Whiteness and the Literary Imagination* (Cambridge: Harvard University Press, 1992); Lillian Smith, *Killers of the Dream*, rev. ed. (New York: W. W. Norton, 1961).

9. Myrdal, *An American Dilemma*, 100–101.

10. Ibid., 41, 48.

11. On lynchings, see James Allen, Hilton Als, John Lewis, and Leon F. Litwack, *Without Sanctuary: Lynching Photography in America* (Santa Fe: Twin Palms, 2000); Philip Dray, *At the Hands of Persons Unknown: The Lynching of Black America* (New York: Random House, 2002); Sherrilyn A. Ifill, *On the Courthouse Lawn: Confronting the Legacy of Lynching in the Twenty-first Century* (Boston: Beacon Press, 2007); and James H. Madison, *A Lynching in the Heartland: Race and Memory in America* (New York: Palgrave, 2001).

12. Smith, *Killers of the Dream*, 27, 83–84, 88, 90; C. Vann Woodward, *The Strange Career of Jim Crow* (New York: Oxford University Press, 1957).

13. Morton Sosna, *In Search of the Silent South: Southern Liberals and the Race Issue* (New York: Columbia University Press, 1977), 4, 162; David L. Chappell, *Inside Agitators: White Southerners in the Civil Rights Movement* (Baltimore: Johns Hopkins University Press, 1994), 20. Elizabeth Jacoway describes fear of miscegenation as the foundation for

school segregation in Little Rock in *Turn Away Thy Son: Little Rock, the Crisis that Shocked the Nation* (New York: Free Press, 2007).

14. Data for the states come from Patrick McCauley and Edward D. Ball, eds., *Southern Schools* (Nashville: Southern Education Reporting Service, 1959), tables 1, 2, 6, 8; data on Washington, DC, come from Jeffrey R. Henig, "Patterns of School-Level Racial Change in D.C. in the Wake of *Brown:* Perceptual Legacies of Desegregation," *PS: Political Science and Politics* 30, 3 (September 1997): 449. The early Southern Education Reporting Service data were sometimes imprecise, but they accurately represented orders of magnitude and racial differences.

15. Expenditure data, from McCauley and Ball, *Southern Schools,* draw on reports from six to ten states, depending on the measure; no border state is included; sources are tables 60, 26, 27, 32, 33, 70, 72.

16. Teacher data, from McCauley and Ball, *Southern Schools,* draw on reports from 12 to 16 Southern and border states, depending on the measure; sources are tables 43, 45, 47, 49, 50, 38, 40, 41, 52, 54.

17. The busing data, from McCauley and Ball, *Southern Schools,* draw on reports from 8 to 17 states, depending on the measure; sources are tables 61–64, 66–68.

18. On the cultural normality of liberalism in mid-twentieth-century America, see Robert N. Bellah, Richard Madsen, William M. Sullivan, Ann Swidler, and Steven M. Tipton, *Habits of the Heart: Individualism and Commitment in American Life* (New York: Harper and Row, 1985); Louis Hartz, *The Liberal Tradition in America* (San Diego: Harcourt, Brace, 1991); and Michael J. Sandel, *Democracy's Discontent: America in Search of a Public Philosophy* (Cambridge: Belknap Press of Harvard University Press, 1996). For analysis of the constraints of rights talk, see Mary Ann Glendon, *Rights Talk: The Impoverishment of Political Discourse* (New York: Free Press, 1991).

19. For examples of contract theories of society, see Thomas Hobbes, *Leviathan,* ed. by Richard E. Flathman and David Johnston (1651; New York: W. W. Norton, 1997); John Locke, *Two Treatises of Government* (1690; New York: Hafner, 1947). On early liberals' psychological views, see Stephen Holmes, *Passions and Constraint: On the Theory of Liberal Democracy* (Chicago: University of Chicago Press, 1995); Sheldon S. Wolin, *Politics and Vision: Continuity and Innovation in Western Political Thought,* expanded ed. (Princeton: Princeton University Press, 2004). On modern theories of narcissism, see Otto Kernberg, *Borderline Conditions and Pathological Narcissism* (New York: Jason Aronson, 1975); Heinz Kohut, *The Analysis of the Self,* The Psychoanalytic Study of the Child Monographs, No. 4 (New York: International Universities Press, 1971); Christopher Lasch, *The Culture of Narcissism: American Life in an Age of Diminishing Expectations* (New York: W. W. Norton, 1978).

20. Holmes, *Passions and Constraint;* Charles E. Lindblom, *Politics and Markets: The World's Political-Economic Systems* (New York: Basic, 1977); Wolin, *Politics and Vision.* Alan Wolfe observes that "distrust" of emotions is central to the "liberal disposition" (*The Future of Liberalism* [New York: Alfred A. Knopf, 2009]).

21. Alexander Hamilton, James Madison, and John Jay, *The Federalist Papers,* No. 51 (1788; New York: New American Library, 1961), 322; C. Fred Alford, *Psychology and the Natural Law of Reparation* (Cambridge: Cambridge University Press, 2006); Arieli, *Individualism and Nationalism in American Ideology;* Lipset, *The First New Nation;* Myrdal, *An American Dilemma,* 13–19; Sandel, *Democracy's Discontent;* Rogers M. Smith, *Civic Ideals* (New Haven: Yale University Press, 1997).

22. Walter Lippmann, *The Essential Lippmann: A Political Philosophy for Liberal Democracy,* Clinton Rossiter and James Lare, eds. (New York: Random House, 1963), 132, 138, 163, 147–148, 163, 137, 23.

23. Ibid., 323.

24. Reinhold Niebuhr, in *Moral Man and Immoral Society: A Study in Ethics and Politics* (New York: Charles Scribner's Sons, 1936), and Arthur M. Schlesinger Jr., in *The Vital Center: The Politics of Freedom* (Boston: Houghton Mifflin, 1949), were exceptional in writing about civil rights before *Brown*. Pells's account of liberal thinking in the 1940s and 1950s (*The Liberal Mind in a Conservative Age*) reports little talk of race. David Carroll Cochran (*The Color of Freedom: Race and Contemporary American Liberalism* [Albany: SUNY Press, 1999]) and Richard Schmitt ("Liberalism and Racism," in Curtis Stokes and Theresa Meléndez, eds., *Racial Liberalism and the Politics of Urban America* [East Lansing: Michigan State University Press, 2003], 15–24) note the silence of liberalism on race. Liberal theorists who have said little or nothing about race, even though writing after the civil rights movement, include Bruce A. Ackerman, *Social Justice in the Liberal State* (New Haven: Yale University Press, 1980); Ronald Dworkin, *Taking Rights Seriously* (Cambridge, MA: Harvard University Press, 1977); Richard E. Flathman, *Willful Liberalism: Voluntarism and Individuality in Political Theory and Practice* (Ithaca: Cornell University Press, 1992); William A. Galston, *Liberal Pluralism: The Implications of Value Pluralism for Political Theory and Practice* (New York: Cambridge University Press, 2002); Mary Ann Glendon and David Blankenhorn, eds., *Seedbeds of Virtue: Sources of Competence, Character, and Citizenship in American Society* (Lanham, MD: Madison Books, 1995); Holmes, *Passions and Constraint;* John Rawls, *A Theory of Justice* (Cambridge: The Belknap Press of Harvard University Press, 1971); John Rawls, *Political Liberalism* (New York: Columbia University Press, 1993); Nancy L. Rosenblum, ed., *Liberalism and the Moral Life* (Cambridge: Harvard University Press, 1989); and Paul Starr, *Freedom's Power: The True Force of Liberalism* (New York: Basic Books, 2007). Critics of liberalism Michael Sandel (*Democracy's Discontent; Liberalism and the Limits of Justice,* 2nd ed., Cambridge: Cambridge University Press, 1998) and Robert Paul Wolff (*The Poverty of Liberalism,* Boston: Beacon Press, 1968; *Understanding Rawls: A Reconstruction and Critique of* A Theory of Justice, Princeton: Princeton University Press, 1977), similarly, say little about race. Writers who have looked at the implications of liberalism for race are Jennifer L. Hochschild, *The New American Dilemma: Liberal Democracy and School Desegregation* (New Haven: Yale University Press, 1984); Carol. A. Horton, *Race and the Making of American Liberalism* (New York: Oxford University Press, 2005); and Smith, *Civic Ideals*.

25. On the transformation of individual freedom from means to end, see John Dewey, *The Public and Its Problems* (Denver: Alan Swallow, 1927). On contrasts between negative and positive concepts of liberty, see Isaiah Berlin, "Two Concepts of Liberty," in *Four Essays on Liberty* (Oxford: Oxford University Press, 1969).

26. These assumptions are widespread among liberal theorists cited in note 24, above. Writers who call particular attention to them, either as exponents or critics, include Benjamin Barber, *Strong Democracy: Participatory Politics for a New Age* (Berkeley: University of California Press, 1984); Seymour J. Mandelbaum, *Open Moral Communities* (Cambridge: MIT Press, 2000); Rawls, *A Theory of Justice;* Sandel, *Liberalism and the Limits of Justice;* Galston, *Liberal Pluralism;* and Michael Walzer, "On Involuntary Associations" in Amy Gutmann, ed., *Freedom of Association* (Princeton: Princeton University Press, 1998), 64–74.

27. These assumptions are held by many liberals identified in note 24. Writers who address them explicitly include Barber, *Strong Democracy;* Charles E. Lindblom, *The Market System: What It Is, How It Works, and What to Make of It* (New Haven: Yale University Press, 2001); Lindblom, *Politics and Markets;* Rawls, *Liberal Democracy;* Sandel, *Democracy's Discontent;* and Sandel, *Liberalism and the Limits of Justice*.

28. These assumptions are held by many liberals cited in note 24. On egalitarian and libertarian liberals, see Sandel, *Democracy's Discontent*. For additional specific discussion, see Barber, *Strong Democracy;* Holmes, *Passions and Constraint;* Theodore J. Lowi, *The*

End of Liberalism: Ideology, Policy, and the Crisis of Public Authority (New York: W. W. Norton, 1969); Lindblom, *The Market System;* Lindblom, *Politics and Markets;* John Stuart Mill, *On Liberty* (1859; Millis, MA: Agora Publications, n.d.); Sandel, *Liberalism and the Limits of Justice.*

29. For a discussion of how liberal jurisprudence ignores group claims and concerns about substantive outcomes, see Ruth Colker, "Anti-subordination above All: Sex, Race, and Equal Protection," *New York University Law Review* 61, 6 (December 1986): 1003–1066; Owen M. Fiss, "The Fate of An Idea Whose Time Has Come: Antidiscrimination Law in the Second Decade after *Brown v. Board of Education,*" *University of Chicago Law Review* 41 (1974): 742–773; Owen M. Fiss, "Groups and the Equal Protection Clause," *Philosophy and Public Affairs* 5, 2 (winter 1976): 107–177; "The Origins and Fate of Antisubordination Theory: A Symposium on Owen Fiss's 'Groups and the Equal Protection Clause,'" *Issues in Legal Scholarship,* Berkeley Electronic Press, 2002–2004; Cass R. Sunstein, "The Anticaste Principle," *Michigan Law Review* 92 (1994): 2410–2455; Laurence H. Tribe, *American Constitutional Law,* 2nd ed. (Mineola, NY: Foundation Press, 1988), chap. 16.

30. On appeal to contract theory in disobeying laws, see Myrdal, *An American Dilemma,* chap. 1.

31. On this tension, see Arieli, *Individualism and Nationalism;* Sandel, *Democracy's Discontent;* Schlesinger, *The Vital Center;* and Smith, *Civic Ideals.*

CHAPTER 1. AN AMERICAN BORDER CITY

1. Sherry H. Olson, *Baltimore: The Building of an American City,* rev. and exp. ed. (Baltimore: Johns Hopkins University Press, 1997), 1–2.

2. On Baltimore's mid-nineteenth-century economic growth and stagnation, see Olson, *Baltimore,* 102–111.

3. On Baltimore Catholics and nativist politics, see Jean H. Baker, *The Politics of Continuity: Maryland Political Parties From 1858 to 1870* (Baltimore; Johns Hopkins University Press, 1973), chap. 1; Robert J. Brugger, *Maryland, A Middle Temperament: 1634–1980* (Baltimore: Johns Hopkins University Press, 1988), chap. 6; William J. Evitts, *A Matter of Allegiances: Maryland from 1850 to 1861* (Baltimore: Johns Hopkins University Press, 1974); and Thomas W. Spalding, *The Premier See: A History of the Archdiocese of Baltimore, 1789–1979* (Baltimore: Johns Hopkins University Press, 1989), chap. 4.

4. On the city's relationship with state government, see Brugger, *Maryland,* 556; James B. Crooks, *Politics and Progress: The Rise of Urban Progressivism in Baltimore 1895 to 1911* (Baton Rouge: Louisiana State University Press, 1968); and Olson, *Baltimore,* 135–154.

5. Brugger, *Maryland,* 264; Barbara Jeanne Fields, *Slavery and Freedom on the Middle Ground: Maryland during the Nineteenth Century* (New Haven: Yale University Press, 1985), 2, 4–6, 11, 12, 37; Leroy Graham, *Baltimore: The Nineteenth Century Black Capital* (Lanham, MD: University Press of America, 1982); Olson, *Baltimore,* 183–185.

6. Brugger, *Maryland,* 214–215; Joseph Garonzik, "The Racial and Ethnic Make-up of Baltimore Neighborhoods, 1850–1870," *Maryland Historical Magazine* 71, 3 (fall 1976): 392–402; David K. Sullivan, 1973, "William Lloyd Garrison in Baltimore, 1829–1830," *Maryland Historical Magazine* 68, 1 (1973): 64–79.

7. James Silk Buckingham, *America, Historical, Statistic, and Descriptive* (New York: Harper and Brothers, 1841), 1:289; Matthew A. Crenson, "Learning to Lobby and Litigate: Baltimore's Contributions to the Civil Rights Movement," paper presented at the Annual Meeting of the American Political Science Association, August 30–September 2, 2006, Philadelphia, 9–11; Matthew A. Crenson, "Roots: Baltimore's Long March to the Era of Civil Rights," in Richardson Dilworth, ed., *The City in American Political Development* (New York: Routledge, 2009), 200–224; Graham, *Baltimore,* chap. 3; Christopher Phillips,

Freedom's Port: The African American Community of Baltimore, 1790–1860 (Urbana: University of Illinois Press, 1997), chaps. 7, 8.

8. Baker, *Politics of Continuity,* 34, 127; Crenson, "Learning to Lobby and Litigate," 11–14; "Kennedy, Anthony (1810–1892)," Biographical Directory of the United States Congress, http://bioguide.congress.gov/scripts/biodisplay.pl?index=K000103, accessed October 13, 2006.

9. Brugger, *Maryland,* 269–293; David Herbert Donald, *Lincoln* (New York: Simon and Schuster, 1995), 277–279.

10. Eleanor S. Bruchey, "The Development of Baltimore Business, 1880–1914, Part I," *Maryland Historical Magazine* 64, 1 (spring 1969): 18–42; Crooks, *Politics and Progress,* 141–142; Joseph L. Arnold, "Baltimore: Southern Culture and a Northern Economy," in Richard M. Bernard, ed., *Snowbelt Cities: Metropolitan Politics in the Northeast and Midwest since World War II* (Bloomington: Indiana University Press, 1990), 25–39; Garonzik, "Racial and Ethnic Make-up."

11. Bruchey, "Development of Baltimore Business, 1880–1914, Part I"; Olson, *Baltimore,* 240, 243.

12. On nationalization and progressivism, see Robert H. Wiebe, *The Search for Order, 1877–1920* (New York: Hill and Wang, 1967); Lawrence A. Cremin, *The Transformation of the School: Progressivism in American Education, 1876–1957* (New York: Vintage Books, 1961). On Baltimore's neighborhood autonomy, see Garonzik, "Racial and Ethnic Make-up"; Matthew A. Crenson, *Neighborhood Politics* (Cambridge: Harvard University Press, 1983).

13. Phillips, *Freedom's Port,* 155; Olson, *Baltimore,* 277. In 1900, the second largest black population, in St. Louis, was only 35,000 (Colin Gordon, *Mapping Decline: St. Louis and the Fate of the American City* [Philadelphia: University of Pennsylvania Press, 2008], 25). In 1950, just before *Brown,* only 24 percent of black Baltimore households owned homes, in contrast with 58 percent of white, and Baltimore's black homeownership was 29th of 42 major American cities, even though Baltimore homeownership overall was 12th. See U.S. Bureau of the Census, *Census of Housing: 1950,* vol. 1, *General Characteristics, Part 1: United States Summary* (Washington, DC: U.S. Government Printing Office, 1953), table 27. There were 14 black-owned banks in the United States, but still none in Baltimore (E. Franklin Frazier, *Black Bourgeoisie: The Rise of a New Middle Class in the United States* [New York: Collier Books, 1962], 53).

14. On the development of Baltimore's black middle class, see Graham, *Baltimore,* 63–76; Harold A. McDougall, *Black Baltimore* (Philadelphia: Temple University Press, 1993); Olson, *Baltimore,* 183; Phillips, *Freedom's Port,* 131–144, 168, 175; also Frazier, *Black Bourgeoisie* (Frazier grew up in Baltimore).

15. On racial zoning and deed restrictions, see Garrett Power, "Apartheid Baltimore Style: The Residential Segregation Ordinances of 1910–1913," *Maryland Law Review* 43, 2 (1983): 289–328; Gretchen Boger, "The Meaning of Neighborhood in the Modern City: Baltimore's Residential Segregation Ordinances, 1910–1913," *Journal of Urban History* 35, 2 (January 2009): 236–258; Antero Pietila, *Not in My Neighborhood: How Bigotry Shaped a Great American City* (Chicago: Ivan R. Dee, 2010). On Baltimore segregation, see Joel Acus Carrington, "The Struggle for Desegregation of Baltimore City Public Schools 1952–1966" (Ph.D. diss., University of Maryland, 1970), 35–36; Charles S. Johnson, "Negroes at Work in Baltimore, Md.," *Opportunity: A Journal of Negro Life* 1, 6 (June 1923), 12–19; Juanita Jackson Mitchell, oral history interview, McKeldin-Jackson Oral History collection, Maryland Historical Society, OH 8095, July 25, 1975; Elizabeth M. Moss, oral history interview, McKeldin-Jackson Oral History collection, Maryland Historical Society, OH 8140, July 13, 1976; Clarence M. Mitchell Jr., oral history interview, McKeldin-Jackson Oral History collection, Maryland Historical Society, OH 8154, July 29, 1976, August 3,

1976, 22; J. E. T. Camper, oral history interview, McKeldin-Jackson Oral History Collection, Maryland Historical Society, OH 8134, July 2, 1976, 8; David Taft Terry, "Tramping for Justice: The Dismantling of Jim Crow in Baltimore, 1942–1954" (Ph.D. diss., Howard University, 2002); Sidney Hollander Foundation, *Toward Equality: Baltimore's Progress Report* (Baltimore: Sidney Hollander Foundation, 1960).

16. Johnson, "Negroes at Work in Baltimore, Md.," 12.

17. Julia Roberta O'Wesney, "Historical Study of the Progress of Racial Desegregation in the Public Schools of Baltimore, Maryland" (Ph.D. diss., University of Maryland, College Park, 1970), 23; Phillips, *Freedom's Port,* 163–164, 226–227; Brugger, *Maryland,* 250–251, 266; Bettye Gardner, "Ante-bellum Black Education in Baltimore," *Maryland Historical Magazine* 71, 3 (fall 1976): 360–366; Graham, *Baltimore,* 23, chaps. 3, 4; Olson, *Baltimore,* 129.

18. Brugger, *Maryland,* 249; Olson, *Baltimore,* 128–129, 191.

19. Brugger, *Maryland,* 308–309; Richard Paul Fuke, "The Baltimore Association for the Moral and Educational Improvement of the Colored People 1864–1870," *Maryland Historical Magazine* 66, 4 (winter 1971): 369–404; Gardner, "Ante-bellum Black Education in Baltimore," 363; Olson, *Baltimore,* 186.

20. Brugger, *Maryland,* 307–308; Fuke, "The Baltimore Association," 399–400; Crooks, *Politics and Progress,* 93–94; Graham, *Baltimore,* 207; Olson, *Baltimore,* 187; Bettye C. Thomas, "Public Education and Black Protest in Baltimore 1865–1900," *Maryland Historical Magazine* 71, 3 (fall 1976): 383.

21. Andrea R. Andrews, "The Baltimore School Building Program, 1870 to 1900: A Study of Urban Reform," *Maryland Historical Magazine* 70, 3 (fall 1975): 267, 271; Brugger, *Maryland,* 390–391, 419; Olson, *Baltimore,* 191, 235.

22. Graham, *Baltimore,* 207–209, 222; Thomas, "Public Education and Black Protest," 384–387.

23. Andrews, "The Baltimore School Building Program," 271–272; Crooks, *Politics and Progress,* 94; Thomas, "Public Education and Black Protest," 389; Olson, *Baltimore,* 277.

24. Brugger, *Maryland,* 391; Thomas, "Public Education and Black Protest," 386–387; Olson, *Maryland,* 277; George Drayton Strayer, ed., *Report of the Survey of the Public School System of Baltimore, Maryland* (Baltimore: Public Improvement Commission, 1921), 1:214.

25. Strayer, *Report,* 1:147, 152, 161, 182, 183, 184, 185; table 14, 57–61; table 26, 119–120; table 21, 104; table 20, 91; table 23, 111; table 7, 31–35.

26. Strayer, *Report,* 1:73–83; quotation on 74.

27. Strayer, *Report,* vol. 1, table 24, chart 20, 92–117; Strayer, *Report,* vol. 2, table 13, 88; table 22, 112; tables 15 and 16, 94–96.

28. Strayer, *Report,* 2:18; O'Wesney, "Historical Study," 26; J. Le Count Chestnut, "Prof. Russell Quits When Power in School Dwindles," *Chicago Defender,* September 26, 1924; "West Holds Up Resignation of Supt. Russell," *Afro,* September 5, 1924; "School Board Elects Supervisor of Public Schools," *Afro,* July 18, 1925; Farrar, *The Baltimore Afro-American, 1892–1950,* 35–37.

29. Francis M. Wood, *A Survey of the Colored Division of the Baltimore Public School System from August 1, 1925 to February 3, 1933* (Baltimore: Colored Division, Baltimore Public School System, 1933), 2, 4, 12.

30. W. L. Fairbanks, with W. S. Hamill, *A Statistical Analysis of the Population of Maryland* (Baltimore: Maryland Development Bureau of the Baltimore Association of Commerce, 1931), 111, 114, Table 44.

31. Fairbanks, *Statistical Analysis,* table 46; also Bart Landry, *The New Black Middle Class* (Berkeley: University of California Press, 1987).

32. Arnold, "Baltimore: Southern Culture and a Northern Economy," 27; John Talbot Smith, quoted in Spalding, *The Premier See,* 289.

33. On Baltimore's black middle class and elite, see McDougall, *Black Baltimore*. On local black political activism, see Sandy M. Shoemaker, "'We Shall Overcome, Someday': The Equal Rights Movement in Baltimore 1935–1942," *Maryland Historical Magazine* 89 (fall 1994): 261–274; Frazier, *Black Bourgeoisie;* Crenson, "Roots: Baltimore's Long March to the Era of Civil Rights"; Davison M. Douglas, *Jim Crow Moves North: The Battle over Northern School Desegregation, 1865–1954* (Cambridge: Cambridge University Press, 2005), chap. 5; Andor Skotnes, "'Buy Where You Can Work': Boycotting for Jobs in African-American Baltimore, 1933–1934," *Journal of Social History* 27, 4 (summer 1994): 735–761; Bruce A. Thompson, "The Civil Rights Vanguard: The NAACP and the Black Community in Baltimore, 1931–1942" (Ph.D. diss., University of Maryland, College Park, 1996), chap. 3; St. Clair Drake and Horace A. Cayton, *Black Metropolis: A Study of Negro Life in a Northern City*, rev. and enl. ed. (Chicago: University of Chicago Press, 1993).

34. On employment, see Fairbanks, *Statistical Analysis*, table 46; Johnson, "Negroes at Work in Baltimore," 13–15. On Baltimore black attitudes toward whites, see Terry, "Tramping for Justice," 134–135; Gloster Current to Walter White, Roy Wilkins, and Thurgood Marshall, August 28, 1947, Papers of the NAACP, pt. 26, series A, Group II, Box C-76, Manuscript Division, Library of Congress; Douglas, *Jim Crow Moves North*.

35. Arnold, "Baltimore: Southern Culture and a Northern Economy," 25–39; William H. Chafe, *Civilities and Civil Rights: Greensboro, North Carolina, and the Black Struggle for Freedom* (New York: Oxford University Press, 1980).

CHAPTER 2. A LONG BLACK CAMPAIGN FOR EQUALITY

1. On ties to Marshall and the national NAACP strategy, see Juan Williams, *Thurgood Marshall: American Revolutionary* (New York: Times Books, 1998); Mark V. Tushnet, *The NAACP's Legal Strategy against Segregated Education, 1925–1950* (Chapel Hill: University of North Carolina Press, 1987).

2. On the early history of the *Afro-American*, see Farrar, *The Baltimore* Afro-American *1892–1950*, chaps. 1–2.

3. Juanita Jackson Mitchell and Virginia Jackson Kiah, McKeldin-Jackson Oral History Collection, Maryland Historical Society, OH 8094, July 15, 1975; Denton L. Watson, *Lion in the Lobby: Clarence Mitchell Jr.'s Struggle for the Passage of Civil Rights Laws* (New York: William Morrow, 1990), 76–80.

4. Shoemaker, "'We Shall Overcome, Someday': The Equal Rights Movement in Baltimore 1935–1942," 261–274; Thompson, *The Civil Rights Vanguard*, chaps. 2–3; Watson, *Lion in the Lobby*, 89–90.

5. On the Williams lynching, see Ifill, *On the Courthouse Lawn*, chap. 2. On the revitalization of the Baltimore branch, see Thompson, *The Civil Rights Vanguard*, 62, ff., 224–227, 231–234, 241–242, 245; Mitchell and Kiah, OH 8094, J-16; Clarence M. Mitchell Jr., McKeldin-Jackson Oral History collection, Maryland Historical Society, OH 8154, August 3, 1976, 50; Elizabeth Murphy Moss, McKeldin-Jackson Oral History collection, Maryland Historical Society, OH 8140, July 23, 1976; Juanita Jackson Mitchell, McKeldin-Jackson Oral History collection, Maryland Historical Society, OH 8095, July 25, 1975.

6. On the litigation, see Thompson, *The Civil Rights Vanguard*, chap. 6; Tushnet, *The NAACP's Legal Strategy*, 65–67; Williams, *Thurgood Marshall*, 76–81.

7. Carl Murphy to Lillie May Jackson, February 1, 1938, Carl Murphy Collection, Moorland-Spingarn Research Center, Howard University.

8. "NAACP Group to Probe School Jam," *Afro*, February 5, 1938; "Mayor Renames White Members," *Afro*, March 12, 1938.

9. "School Board Appointments," *Afro*, March 2, 1940.

10. An *Afro* article catalogued problems with portable buildings: "2,883 Children Use 68 School Portables, Majority Need Repair," *Afro*, February 12, 1944. The comparisons

of black and white schools draw on data collected in different years. Though they don't describe any single moment, they consistently show that the school system spent less on black students than on white. The student-teacher ratios are for 1940 ("City's Schools Are 'Short' 61 Teachers," *Afro*, April 13, 1940). The school building value data are for 1945 (School Board, *Annual Report*, 1945, tables 12 and 62). The operating budget data are for 1946; the teacher degree data are for 1950 (Maryland Commission on Interracial Problems and Relations and Baltimore Commission on Human Relations, *An American City in Transition* [Baltimore: MCIPR, 1955], 109–111).

11. "Colored Schools Being Robbed, Board is Told," *Afro* June 22, 1940; Carl W. Murphy to Forrest Bramble, September 19, 1940, Carl Murphy Collection; "Schools—Those for White Pupils Have Elevator Service, The One at Douglass High Is for Freight Only," *Afro*, June 15, 1940.

12. Murphy to Bramble, September 19, 1940; "Mayor, Dr. Weglein and NAACP Discuss Schools," *Afro*, October 8, 1940; Carl Murphy to Mayor Howard Jackson, November 23, 1940, Carl Murphy Collection; "Assistant Superintendent Ruled Out by School Board," *Afro*, December 3, 1940.

13. Thurgood Marshall letter to W. A. C. Hughes, February 24, 1941, Carl Murphy Collection. On dropping the litigation, see Terry, *Tramping for Justice*, 84.

14. Committee on Current Educational Problems of Negroes, "Memoranda to the Board of Education," n.d., 1942, Carl Murphy Collection; "Ask Board End School Inequalities," *Afro*, February 7, 1942; "Coppin Teachers' College is Not an Accredited Institution," *Afro*, February 14, 1942; "Survey Shows Jr. High Pupils a Year Behind Like White Pupils," *Afro*, February 21, 1942.

15. "Mayor Says No to Board Member Cry," *Afro*, March 7, 1942.

16. On the Detroit and Harlem riots, see Dominic J. Capeci Jr., *Race Relations in Wartime Detroit: The Sojourner Truth Housing Controversy, 1937–1942* (Philadelphia, Temple University Press, 1984); Thomas Sugrue, *The Origins of the Urban Crisis: Race and Inequality in Postwar Detroit* (Princeton: Princeton University Press, 1996); Dominic J. Capeci Jr. and Martha Wilkerson, *Layered Violence: The Detroit Rioters of 1943* (Jackson, MS: University of Mississippi, 1991); Alfred McClung Lee and Norman D. Humphrey, *Race Riot, Detroit 1943* (New York: Octagon Books, 1968); Robert Shogan and Tom Craig, *The Detroit Race Riot: A Study in Violence* (New York: Da Capo Press, 1976); Nat Brandt, *Harlem at War: The Black Experience in WWII* (Syracuse: Syracuse University Press, 1996), passim; Dominic J. Capeci Jr., *The Harlem Riot of 1943* (Philadelphia; Temple University Press, 1977). The following account of the March on Annapolis draws on Terry, *Tramping for Justice*, chap. 2; and Thompson, *The Civil Rights Vanguard*, conclusion.

17. Watson, *Lion in the Lobby*, 113–119, 133–134.

18. "Citizens Call on Mayor," *Afro*, April 11, 1942, 2.

19. "What Spokesmen Demanded at the Epochal March on Annapolis," *Afro*, April 28, 1942, 3.

20. Douglas, *Jim Crow Moves North*, 237; "Justice Committee Says Governor Used 'Whitewash' Brush," *Afro*, August 15, 1942.

21. Juanita Jackson Mitchell, OH 8095, McKeldin-Jackson Oral History Collection, Maryland Historical Society, July 25, 1975, 32; Terry, *Tramping for Justice*, chap. 2; Thompson, *The Civil Rights Vanguard*, conclusion; George H. Callcott, *Maryland and America 1940 to 1980* (Baltimore: The Johns Hopkins University Press, 1985), 81; "63,365 Registered," *Afro*, October 7, 1944.

22. "Open Letter to Mayor Jackson," *Afro*, May 16, 1942, 1; Howard Jackson to Citizens Committee for Justice, May 28, 1942, Carl Murphy Collection; Howard Jackson to Forrest Bramble, May 28, 1942, Carl Murphy Collection; Howard Jackson to Forrest Bramble,

June 1, 1942, Carl Murphy Collection; Forrest Bramble to Howard Jackson, June 3, 1942, Carl Murphy Collection.

23. Committee on Current Educational Problems of Negroes, report, December 10, 1942, 1, Carl Murphy Collection; Committee on Current Educational Problems of Negroes, report, December 10, 1942; *Missouri ex rel. Gaines v. Canada*, 305 U.S. 337, 1938. On NAACP legal strategy, see Tushnet, *The NAACP's Legal Strategy*.

24. "The Report of the Governor's Commission Demands Immediate and Close Attention," *Afro*, March 27, 1943; "Governor O'Connor's Next Move," *Afro*, June 17, 1943; "Three Vacancies on the School Board This Year," *Afro*, January 8, 1944; "School Disgraces," *Afro*, January 29, 1944; "The Proposed School Board Member," *Afro*, February 19, 1944.

25. "Legality of Dual School System to Get Court Test," *Afro*, February 19, 1944; "Jim Crow Robs School Children," *Afro*, March 4, 1944.

26. "The Mayor's Appointment," *Afro*, March 25, 1944; Power, "Apartheid Baltimore Style: The Residential Segregation Ordinances of 1910–1913"; Boger, "The Meaning of Neighborhood in the Modern City."

27. U.S. Bureau of the Census, *Census of Population: 1950*, vol. 2, *Characteristics of the Population, Part 20 Maryland* (Washington, DC: U.S. Government Printing Office, 1953); "Why Teachers Resign," *Afro*, September 30, 1944.

28. "Negroes Request School Control," *Sun*, February 16, 1945.

29. "An Assistant Superintendent," *Afro*, January 27, 1945; "Thomsen Admits Schools Inferior," *Afro*, February 17, 1945, 2.

30. "Board May Name Colored Superintendent—Thomsen," *Afro*, May 5, 1945; "A Vocational High School," *Afro*, May 19, 1945.

31. "Name School Superintendent," *Afro*, November 3, 1945; "What the School Appointment Means," *Afro*, November 10, 1945; "The No. 1 School Problem," *Afro*, November 17, 1945.

32. "Negroes Will Attempt to Enroll in School," *Sun*, January 4, 1946; "Speedup School for Negroes Set," *Evening Sun*, January 16, 1946; "NAACP Objects to New Class," *Afro*, January 26, 1946.

33. "Air School Hazards," *Afro*, January 19, 1946, 2.

34. "NAACP Objects to New Class," *Afro*, January 26, 1946; A. B. Koger, "Local School Problems," *Afro*, January 28, 1945; Ida Coole, "Washington Jr. High School Is Filthy!" *Afro*, February 9, 1946; "Washington Junior High School," *Afro*, February 9, 1946; "This Is What Parents Seek to Correct," *Afro*, February 9, 1946; "Two Schools Will Be Renovated," *Afro*, February 9, 1946; "Mayor to View School Inequalities," *Afro*, March 9, 1946; "Mayor Inspects Junior High," *Afro*, March 16, 1956, 22.

35. Louise Hines, "A School Outlet," *Afro*, April 20, 1946; "Makeshift School Plans," April 20, 1946; Ida Coole, "Condemned 26 Years Ago, School No. 127 Still Used," *Afro*, May 4, 1946; Ida Coole, "64-Year-Old School Held too Crowded Dank, Dingy," *Afro*, May 11, 1946; Ida Coole, "School Called Fire Trap 21 Years Ago Still Used," *Afro*, May 18, 1946; Ida Coole, "School No. 154 Revealed as Unfit to House Pupils," *Afro*, May 25, 1946; Ida Coole, "280 Retarded Children Hampered at School 105," *Afro*, June 8, 1946; Ida Coole, "School Board Decorates Hulk for Pupils for Use," *Afro*, June 15, 1946; Ida Coole, "Facilities at School No. 136 Below Modern Standards," *Afro*, June 22, 1946; Ida Coole, "Stowe School's Building Seen as Unfit for Pupils," *Afro*, July 6, 1946; "Only Word for It," *Afro*, October 4, 1946; Strayer, *Report of the Survey of the Public School System of Baltimore, Maryland*, 1:153, 181, 184.

36. Ida Coole, "School 137, Typical Hand-Me-Down, Found Unfit for Junior High School Use," *Afro*, March 14, 1947, 6; Strayer, *Report*, 1:162–163; on Harvey Johnson, see http://www.msa.md.gov/msa/stagser/s1259/121/6050/html/12414000.html, accessed January 5, 2009.

37. Harry O. Levin, "Segregated Facilities are Legally Indefensible," *Afro*, August 30, 1947; September 6, 1947; September 13, 1947; September 20, 1947; September 27, 1947; October 4, 1947; October 11, 1947; October 18, 1947.

38. "Tests Show Pupils Lag in Baltimore," *Afro*, November 8, 1947.

39. "Both Races Can Live Together in Harmony," *Afro*, November 8, 1947, M-3; "Residents of Mixed Areas Like Situation," *Afro*, April 3, 1948, 1, 20. On Baltimore blockbusting, see W. Edward Orser, *Blockbusting in Baltimore: The Edmondson Village Story* (Lexington: University Press of Kentucky, 1994).

40. "Equal Educational Opportunities Asked," *Afro*, April 16, 1949; "Inequalities Retard Pupils," *Afro*, April 16, 1949; "Baltimore Public School Inequality at a Glance," *Afro*, April 16, 1949. On changing NAACP thinking, see Tushnet, *The NAACP's Legal Strategy;* and Risa L. Goluboff, *The Lost Promise of Civil Rights* (Cambridge: Harvard University Press, 2007).

41. "1500 Residents in Protest Against New Carver School," *Afro*, September 24, 1949; "Thomsen Insists on School There," *Afro*, March 18, 1950; "Bentalou Area Site Opposed," *Afro*, March 18, 1950; Baltimore Branch of the National Association for the Advancement of Colored People, Committee on Education to the Board of School Commissioners, March 16, 1950, Carl Murphy Collection; "NAACP's Strong Plea for Carver Site Published," *Afro-American*, March 25, 1950; "Carver Issue Forced Out," *Afro*, April 8, 1950; "Board Okeys Carver Site," *Afro*, April 15, 1950.

42. "Templeton Head of Urban League," *Afro*, September 30, 1950.

43. O'Wesney, "Historical Study of the Progress of Racial Desegregation," 14; School Board, *121st Report of the Baltimore School Commission*, 1954, 154, 156; School Board, *124th Report of the Baltimore School Commission*, 1960, 154.

44. "School Needs Justify More Money," *Afro*, January 25, 1950.

45. "School Overcrowding Should Go to Court," *Afro*, March 7, 1951; "Court Suit Seeks to End High School Segregation in Virginia," *Afro*, May 26, 1951.

46. "School Picture Brighter, But Some Phases Still Dark," *Afro*, September 8, 1951.

CHAPTER 3. OPENING THE RACIAL DOOR SLIGHTLY

1. Carrington, "The Struggle for Desegregation of Baltimore City Public Schools," 16; "NAACP Sets School Goals," *Sun*, May 25, 1952.

2. This account relies on Furman L. Templeton, "The Admission of Negro Boys to the Baltimore Polytechnic Institute 'A' Course," *Journal of Negro Education* 23 (1954): 22–29. Information about board memberships comes from Terry, *Tramping for Justice*, 309; Baltimore Urban League memorandum, July 7, 1951, Maryland Historical Society; "Boards and Officers of Baltimore ADA 1953–1954," Marshall Levin papers; Margaret Neustadt Randol interview, May 27, 2003.

3. Marshall Levin interview, May 29, 2003; Carl Clark interview, March 28, 2005; Milton Cornish interview, March 22, 2005; Terry, *Tramping for Justice*, 324; Carrington, "The Struggle for Desegregation of Baltimore City Public Schools," 16; Aaron M. Glazer, "Course Correction: Two Years Before Desegregation Became the Law of the Land, a Baltimore High School Opened Its Doors to 13 Black Students—Very Quietly," *Baltimore City Paper*, September 5, 2001.

4. McKeldin letter quoted in Templeton, "The Admission of Negro Boys," 25; "Let Negroes Enter Poly, McKeldin Asks," *Sun*, August 23, 1952; "Governor for Mixing Polytechnic Students," *Afro*, August 26, 1952; Copy of Resolution Passed at Special Meeting of Maryland Commission on Interracial Problems and Relations, August 20, 1952, Marshall Levin papers.

5. Biddison opinion described and quoted in Templeton, "The Admission of Negro Boys," 24–25; *Pearson v. Murray*, 169 Md. 478, 1936, 483; *Briggs v. Elliott*, 342 U.S. 350, 1952.

6. Glazer, "Course Correction," 18; Templeton, "The Admission of Negro Boys," 26; Walter Sondheim interview, April 15, 2003; Marshall Levin interview, May 29, 2003; Carl Murphy to Edward S. Lewis, October 9, 1952, Carl Murphy Collection; "N.A.A.C.P. Sets School Goals," *Sun*, May 25, 1952; Walter Sondheim, McKeldin-Jackson Oral History Collection, Maryland Historical Society, OH 8172, September 27, 1976, 20–21.

7. "City School Board Opens Polytechnic Institute to 12," *Afro*, September 6, 1952.

8. Minutes of the Board of School Commissioners (hereafter, School Board minutes), September 2, 1952, 198, 200, 201.

9. Ibid., 201–211.

10. "Board Rules Negroes Can Enter Poly," *Sun*, September 3, 1952; "City School Board Opens Polytechnic Institute To 12," *Afro*, September 6, 1952; "Poly to Admit Negro Pupils," *Sun*, September 3, 1952; Marshall Levin interview, May 29, 2003; Marshall Levin notes for school board presentation, Marshall Levin papers; Roszel C. Thomsen, "The Integration of Baltimore's Polytechnic Institute: A Reminiscence," *Maryland Historical Magazine* 79, 3 (fall 1984): 235–238.

11. School Board minutes, September 2, 1952, 211–212A; "Board Rules Negroes Can Enter Poly"; Terry, *Tramping for Justice*, 319; M. Dion Thompson, "13 Bright Teens Stood for Many," *Sun*, February 28, 2002; Walter Sondheim interview, April 15, 2003.

12. Thomsen, "The Integration of Baltimore's Polytechnic Institute," 238.

13. School Board minutes, September 2, 1952, 212A–212E,

14. "The Polytechnic Issue and the School Board," *Afro*, September 6, 1952.

15. Edward S. Lewis to Carl Murphy, October 2, 1952, Carl Murphy Collection; Carl Murphy to Edward S. Lewis, October 9, 1952, Carl Murphy Collection.

16. "Parents Make Effort to Enroll Pupils at Western," *Afro*, September 27, 1952; Martha B. Pulley to Carl Murphy, February 26, 1953, Carl Murphy Collection.

17. "NAACP Report Tabs Schools as Unequal," *Afro*, January 10, 1953.

18. "Printing School Rejects 4 Pupils," *Afro*, February 7, 1953.

19. School Board minutes, February 5, 1953, 45–48; "Dr. Lemmel, School Head, Dies at 56," *Sun*, January 30, 1953; "Dr. Wm. Lemmel Dies Suddenly," *Afro*, January 31, 1953.

20. School Board minutes, February 5, 1953, 48–49; School Board private session minutes, February 5, 1953; "Mergenthaler Bars Negroes," *Sun*, February 6, 1953; "Printing School Rejects 4 Pupils," *Afro*, February 7, 1953; "Pitched Battle Looms on Printing Training," *Afro*, March 7, 1953.

21. Martha B. Pulley to Carl Murphy, February 26, 1953, Carl Murphy Collection; "NAACP Action Plans Slated," *Afro*, March 7, 1953; Jack Greenberg to Juanita Jackson Mitchell, March 31, 1953, Carl Murphy Collection; I. Shapiro, "An Appraisal of Printing Instruction in Baltimore, MD.," n.d., Carl Murphy Collection.

22. School Board private session minutes, March 5, 1953; "Mergenthaler Color Barrier Faces Test," *Afro*, March 7, 1953.

23. Donald G. Murray to Chairman of Education Committee, Baltimore Branch NAACP, April 7, 1953, Carl Murphy Collection; Lillie May Jackson to Roszel Thomsen, April 22, 1953, Carl Murphy Collection; Juanita Jackson Mitchell and Donald G. Murray to Roszel Thomsen, April 22, 1953, Carl Murphy Collection; "Plan Mergenthaler, Western High Test," *Afro*, April 25, 1953; "Lawyers Retained For 6 Who Seek Entry to Mergenthaler," *Afro*, April 25, 1953.

24. School Board private session minutes, May 7, 1953; John H. Fischer to Juanita Jackson Mitchell, May 14, 1953, Carl Murphy Collection.

25. Furman Templeton to Members of the Western Committee, May 28, 1953, Carl Murphy Collection.

26. Juanita Jackson Mitchell and Donald G. Murray to Roszel Thomsen, May 30, 1953, Carl Murphy Collection; School Board minutes, June 4, 1953, 157–159; "Lawyers Retained for 6 Who Seek Entry to Mergenthaler," *Afro*, April 25, 1953; Elinor Pancoast, *The Report of a Study on Desegregation in the Baltimore City Schools* (Baltimore: The Maryland Commission on Interracial Problems and Relations and the Baltimore Commission on Human Relations, 1956).

27. "Mergenthaler Printing School Case In Court," *Afro*, June 6, 1953; docket sheet for Smith v. Mayor and City Council, Baltimore City Court, Maryland State Archives, 1953, Liber JOR 16, f. 279, Case No. 028463, MSA T 549–13.

28. Department of Education, Office of the Superintendent, news release, June 19, 1953, Carl Murphy Collection; John H. Fischer, "Special Report to the School Board on the Application of Negro Students for Admission to the Western High School," July 17, 1953, Carl Murphy Collection; "Negro Girls to Enter Western High," *Sun*, June 21, 1953.

29. "Western Fight to Court," *Afro*, June 27, 1953; School Board minutes, June 23, 1953, 173–178; "Negro Girls are Barred at Western," *Sun*, June 24, 1953.

30. School Board minutes, June 23, 1953, 179–180; "Negro Girls are Barred at Western"; "School Board Would Bar 24 Students," *Afro*, June 27, 1953; "They Said 'No,'" *Afro*, June 27, 1953; Marshall Levin presentation notes, Levin papers.

31. School Board private session minutes, June 23, 1953; School Board minutes, June 23, 1953, 181–182.

32. Marshall Levin interview, May 29, 2003; Walter Sondheim interviews, April 15, 2003, February 7, 2004; U.S. Bureau of the Census, *Census of Population: 1950*, vol. 2, *Characteristics of the Population, Part 20, Maryland* (Washington, DC: U.S. Government Printing Office, 1952), tables 66, 76; Margaret Randol interview, May 27, 2003.

33. Juanita Jackson Mitchell, McKeldin-Jackson Oral History collection, Maryland Historical Society, OH 8095, July 25, 1975, 58; "School Board's Mind Made Up Before Meeting," *Afro*, June 27, 1953; "School Board Would Bar 23 Students," *Afro*, June 27, 1953.

34. Complaint, *Veronica A. Shipley et al. v. Roszel C. Thomsen, et al*, U.S. District Court of Maryland, July 15, 1953, Civil Action Case 6739, RG 21, Records of the U.S. District Court of Maryland, Civil Action Case Files, 1938–1982, ARC 567889, National Archives and Records Administration (NARA) Mid Atlantic Region, Box 533.

35. Motion for Preliminary Injunction and for Show Cause Order in Support Thereof, and Show Cause Order, Civil Action No. 6739, July 15, 1953, NARA Archives, Philadelphia; Juanita Jackson Mitchell, Mitchell-Jackson Oral History collection, Maryland Historical Society, OH 8095, July 25, 1975, 56. A document describing "Outstanding Achievements of the Baltimore Branch NAACP" (n.d., NAACP Archives) reported that the judges in the two cases asked that trial be postponed pending a Supreme Court decision.

36. "Two admitted to Mergenthaler," *Afro*, October 10, 1953.

37. "Public Meeting Set to Study Integration in Public Schools," *Afro*, March 6, 1954.

CHAPTER 4. DESEGREGATION BY FREE CHOICE

1. *Brown v. Board of Education of Topeka*, 347 U.S. 483, 1954, 495, 494; *Brown II* was 349 U. S. 294, 1955; on the *Brown* decisions, see Richard Kluger, *Simple Justice: The History of* Brown v. Board of Education *and Black America's Struggle for Equality* (New York: Notable Trials Library, 1994).

2. "High Tribunal Bans Race Segregation In Schools," *Evening Sun*, May 17, 1954, 1; "The School Segregation Cases," *Evening Sun*, May 18, 1954, 22; "Supreme Court Bans Segregated Schools," *Sun*, May 19, 1954, 1; "The Court's Decision Seen from Abroad," *Sun*, May 19, 1954, 16. For a view that Cold War considerations influenced the Supreme Court, see Derrick Bell, *Silent Covenants:* Brown v. Board of Education *and the Unfulfilled Hopes for Racial Reform* (New York: Oxford, 2004).

3. "Mix Schools," *Afro,* May 18, 1954, 1; "Leaders Comment on Supreme Court School Decision," *Afro,* May 18, 1954, 5–7; Pancoast, *The Report of a Study on Desegregation in the Baltimore City Schools,* 25.

4. "Dr. Fischer is Appointed School Chief," Baltimore *Sun,* February 21, 1953.

5. Eleanor Johnson, "Fischer Bases School Policies on Early U.S. Principles," *Evening Sun,* March 5, 1953; "The Fischer Letter," *Afro,* June 19, 1954.

6. Walter Sondheim interview, April 15, 2003; Walter Sondheim, McKeldin-Jackson Oral History collection, Maryland Historical Society, OH 8172, September 27, 1976, 1, 5–6; Paul A. Kramer, "White Sales: The Racial Politics of Baltimore's Jewish-Owned Department Stores, 1935–1965," in Dean Krimmel, Paul A. Kramer, and Melissa J. Martens, eds., *Enterprising Emporiums: The Jewish Department Stores of Downtown Baltimore* (Baltimore: Jewish Museum of Maryland, 2001), 37–66; Baltimore "'Policy' for Colored Buyers," *Afro,* January 6, 1945.

7. "Interracial Contributions," n.d., Papers of the NAACP, pt. 26, series A, Group II, Box C-76, Manuscript Division, Library of Congress; Walter Sondheim interview, April 15, 2003; Walter Sondheim, McKeldin-Jackson Oral History collection, Maryland Historical Society, OH 8172, September 27, 1976, biographical summary, 4; Rhoda Dorsey, "Reflections on *Brown:* A Conversation with Walter Sondheim, Jr.," *Maryland Humanities* (winter 2004): 5.

8. Juanita Jackson Mitchell, McKeldin-Jackson Oral History collection, Maryland Historical Society, OH 8095, July 25, 1975, 57; Elizabeth M. Moss, McKeldin-Jackson Oral History collection, Maryland Historical Society, OH 8140, July 13, 1976, 24.

9. Mike Bowler and Laurie Cohen, "The Painful Second Step in School Integration." *Sun,* September 8, 1974, K1; School Board private session minutes, May 20, 1954.

10. John H. Fischer, "Preliminary Statement to the Board of School Commissioners by the Superintendent on The Elimination of Racial Segregation in the Baltimore Public Schools," May 20, 1954, School Board private session minutes, May 20, 1954.

11. Juanita Jackson Mitchell, McKeldin-Jackson Oral History collection, Maryland Historical Society, OH 8095, July 25, 1975, 56–57; "Outstanding Achievements of the Baltimore Branch," n.d. [1954?], Mitchell Family Papers, Manuscript Division, Library of Congress; Clarence Mitchell, "Separate But Equal Has No Place," *Sun,* May 18, 1974.

12. "Opinion of the City Solicitor of Baltimore City," in Baltimore Department of Education, *Eliminating Racial Segregation in the Baltimore Public Schools,* 3; Walter Sondheim interview, April 15, 2003; "U. S. Supreme Court Lets Stand Harford County Gradual Program," *SSN* 5, 1 (July 1958): 5; Dorsey, "Reflections on *Brown:* A Conversation with Walter Sondheim, Jr.," 6.

13. Dorsey, "Reflections on *Brown:* A Conversation with Walter Sondheim, Jr.," 5, 7; Walter Sondheim, McKeldin-Jackson Oral History collection, OH 8044, October 19, 1971, II:6.; School Board minutes, June 3, 1954, 109–110; "Board Votes Unanimously To End School Segregation," *Afro,* June 5, 1954.

14. "39 Graduate from Gilman," *Sun,* June 8, 1954; U.S. Bureau of the Census, *U.S. Censuses of Population and Housing: 1960, Census Tracts, Baltimore, Md.,* Final Report PHC(1)-13 (Washington: U.S. Government Printing Office, 1961), table P-1; U.S. Bureau of the Census, *1970 Census of Population and Housing, Census Tracts, Baltimore, Md.,* Final Report PHC(1)-19 (Washington: U.S. Government Printing Office, 1972), table P-2.

15. Docket sheet for *Carl E. Smith, et al. v. Mayor and City Council,* Baltimore City Court, Maryland State Archives, 1953, Liber JOR 16, f. 279, Case No. 028463, MSA T 549-13. Petition of respondents, consent, and order of court, District Court of the United States for the District of Maryland, Civil Action No. 6739, June 9, 1954, NARA, Mid Atlantic Region Archives Facility, Philadelphia; "Board Votes Unanimously To End School Segregation," *Afro,* June 5, 1954; Order of Attorneys, filed in the District Court of the

United States for the District of Maryland, Civil Action No. 6739, June 16, 1958, NARA, Mid Atlantic Region Archives Facility, Philadelphia.

16. School Board minutes, June 10, 1954, 114–117; "School Board Adopts Policy Erasing Racial Basis for Registration," *Sun,* June 11, 1954.

17. Pancoast, *Report of a Study on Desegregation in the Baltimore City Schools,* 39.

18. School officials' expressed views echoed Locke's *Two Treatises of Government* and Mill's *On Liberty.* See the Introduction for a general discussion of mid-twentieth-century liberalism.

19. John H. Fischer, "Report on Our Duty and Our Opportunity," in George B. Brain, ed., *Desegregation Policies and Procedures, 1954–1963* (Baltimore: Baltimore City Department of Education, 1963), 6, 4; "School districting in Baltimore and Washington," *Sun,* June 12, 1954, 10.

20. "Fischer reviews Baltimore desegregation course he directed." *SSN* 6, 1 (July 1959): 5.

21. U.S. Commission on Civil Rights, *Fourth Annual Education Conference on Problems of Segregation and Desegregation of Public Schools* (Washington, DC: U.S. Commission on Civil Rights, 1962), 19; Lipset (*The First New Nation*) observed that "free choice" was a dominant American theme proceeding from stories of the Revolution as an association of free individuals casting off British shackles.

22. The 1871 school board provided for student transfers among schools with permission (Baltimore Board of Commissioners of Public Schools, *Rules* [Baltimore: BBC, 1871], 84). The 1900 board approved rules essentially identical to the 1954 free choice policy:

> Parents upon first entering their children, either into a primary or grammar school, shall have the right to choose any school, provided the school selected has accommodations. If the school into which entrance is desired is outside of the district in which the pupil resides, principals must have evidences in writing, of the parent's choice. In the event of a school having more applicants for admission than it can accommodate, children living within the district of said school shall have the preference. (School Board minutes, September 18, 1900, 84)

On Baltimore public housing desegregation, see Rhonda Y. Williams, *The Politics of Public Housing: Black Women's Struggles against Urban Inequality* (New York: Oxford University Press, 2004), 107–113.

23. Fischer in Brain, *Desegregation Policies and Procedures,* 1954–1963, 5; Walter Sondheim interview, April 15, 2003.

24. "We Must Learn to Live with It," *Afro,* June 5, 1954, 4; "Residents of Both Races Happy about School Ruling," *Afro,* June 5, 1954, 1; "Outstanding Achievements of the Baltimore Branch NAACP," Mitchell Family Papers.

25. On the scholarship program, see Mike Bowler, "Black Students Sent Away," *Sun,* May 16, 2004; and R. Scott Baker, *Paradoxes of Desegregation: African American Struggles for Educational Equity in Charleston, South Carolina, 1926–1972* (Charleston: University of South Carolina Press, 2006), 31.

26. On the Baltimore black middle class and the black middle class generally, see McDougall, *Black Baltimore;* Frazier, *Black Bourgeoisie;* Bart Landry, *The New Black Middle Class.*

27. Lula Jones Garrett, "What the Baltimore Schools Offer Your Child: Integration Means More Opportunities," *Afro,* June 26, 1954, 8.

28. Betty Murphy Phillips, "What Integration Means to You, Me," *Afro,* June 5, 1954, 4. Phillips became Betty Murphy Moss after a second marriage.

29. Betty Murphy Phillips," This Won't Happen under Integration," *Afro*, June 26, 1954, 6. E. Franklin Frazier, who grew up in Baltimore, observed in *Black Bourgeoisie* that many middle-class blacks sought a nonracial identity based on class and demeanor.

30. On how whites elsewhere used free-choice language to resist desegregation, see Kevin M. Kruse, *White Flight: Atlanta and the Making of Modern Conservatism* (Princeton: Princeton University Press, 2005).

CHAPTER 5. MODEST CHANGE

1. "Public School Building Plan Is Unchanged," *Sun*, June 5, 1954, 40.

2. Maryland Commission on Interracial Problems and Relations and Baltimore Commission on Human Relations, *An American City in Transition* (Baltimore: MCIPR and CHR, 1955), 99–100; Board of School Commissioners of Baltimore City, *One Hundred Twenty-First Report* (Baltimore: BSCBC, 1954), tables 24–26; O'Wesney, "Historical Study of the Progress of Racial Desegregation," 38.

3. Junior Association of Commerce of Baltimore, *What Baltimoreans Think of Their Public Schools* (Baltimore: JACB, 1952), 4, 13.

4. On constraints on choice in historically segregated systems, see Paul Gewirtz, "Choice in the Transition: School Desegregation and the Corrective Ideal," *Columbia Law Review* 86, 4 (1986): 728–798. For examples of how other school districts conducted community discussion as part of desegregation, see Willis D. Hawley, et al., *Strategies for Effective Desegregation: Lessons from Research* (Lexington, MA: LexingtonBooks, 1983), chap. 5.

5. Garrett, "What the Baltimore Schools Offer Your Child"; Terry, *Tramping for Justice*, 371–380; Keiffer Mitchell Sr., interview, January 4, 2005.

6. Keiffer Mitchell Sr., interview, January 4, 2005; David Taft Terry, interview, July 1, 2004; Terry, *Tramping for Justice*, 373–375, 377–378, 389; Carolyn Cole interview, July 7, 2004.

7. "Many Mixed Classes As Schools Open," *Afro*, September 4, 1954; "Segregation Concluded as Schools Open," *Sun*, September 8, 1954, 34; "1,200 Classes in 47 Schools Mixed," *Afro*, September 11, 1954; "'School Days' Take on New Meaning," *Afro*, September 11, 1954, 15. October 31 numbers were extrapolated from "Schools List 140,957-Pupil Enrollment," *Sun*, September 17, 1954; "Mixed Classes in 52 Schools, Board Reports," *Afro*, September 18, 1954; and O'Wesney, "Historical Study of the Progress of Racial Desegregation," 32, 33, 38.

8. Pancoast, *The Report of a Study on Desegregation*, 55–56; "Pickets Use NAAWP Technique," *Afro*, October 2, 1954; School Board minutes, September 30, 1954, 180A; "School Board," *Afro*, October 2, 1954; "Policy Restated by School Board," *Sun*, October 1, 1954.

9. Walter Sondheim, interview, April 15, 2003; Pancoast, *The Report of a Study on Desegregation*, 59–62; "Integration at Southern Stirs Unrest: Six Arrested in Disorders over Desegregation at School," *Sun*, October 2, 1954.

10. "Will Ober Punish Glass This Time?" *Afro*, October 17, 1953, 4; "Grand Jury Says in Effect that Col. Ober Should Resign," *Afro*, September 15, 1951; "Is Commissioner Ober Protecting Officer Glass?" *Afro*, October 20, 1951; "How Does Commissioner Ober Measure an Officer's Guilt?" *Afro*, October 20, 1951; "History Repeats Itself and Ober Ought to Step Down," *Afro*, November 24, 1951; "Police Have Black Record Under Ober," *Afro*, December 1, 1952; "The Title of Dictator Applied to Colonel Ober," *Afro*, October 17, 1953; "Broken Glass," *Afro*, November 7, 1953.

11. Leon Sachs, McKeldin-Jackson Oral History collection, Maryland Historical Society, OH 8136, July 30, 1976, 55–58; Pancoast, *The Report of a Study on Desegregation*, 62–74; "Schools Back to Normal," *Afro*, October 9, 1954.

12. Pancoast, *The Report of a Study on Desegregation,* 44–48.

13. Jo Ann Robinson, *Education as My Agenda: Gertrude Williams, Race, and the Baltimore Public Schools* (New York: Palgrave McMillan, 2005), 66; Liz Wolfson, interview, September 20, 2004; Gertrude Williams interview, December 1, 2005.

14. Clarence Mitchell, "Foes of Integration in Baltimore and Washington," *The Crisis* (November 1954), 533–537; Watson, *Lion in the Lobby,* 270–271; Walter Sondheim, interview, April 15, 2003.

15. Keiffer Mitchell Sr., interview, January 4, 2005; Rachel Sams, "Political Pioneers," *Baltimore Business Journal,* September 10. 2004; Keiffer J. Mitchell, "Strong Foundation," *Sun,* September 21, 2004; Eric Siegel, "A Nonpolitical Mitchell, Who Is a Doctor and an Artist," *Sun,* February 5, 1984.

16. Orser, *Blockbusting in Baltimore,* 49, 110–113, 123–127.

17. Mike Bowler, "Voices of Brown," *Sun,* May 16, 2004; Carolyn Holland Cole, interview, July 7, 2004.

18. Liz Wolfson, interview, September 20, 2004; Terry, *Tramping for Justice,* 387.

19. Elinor Pancoast, *Desegregation in the Baltimore City Schools* (Baltimore: Maryland Commission on Interracial Problems and Relations and Baltimore Commission on Human Relations, 1995), 28; Pancoast, *The Report of a Study on Desegregation,* 105; Terry, *Tramping for Justice,* 387; "Maryland," *SSN* 1, 10 (June 8, 1955).

20. Emily Sachs, "Wants Segregation," *Evening Sun,* May 31, 1954, 26.

21. "Maryland," *SSN,* 1, 7 (March 3, 1955); "Maryland," *SSN,* 1, 6 (February 3, 1955): 8; "Maryland Asks Supreme Court to Say How Far Ruling Goes," *SSN,* 2, 2 (August 1955); Pancoast, *The Report of a Study on Desegregation,* 102.

22. Lillie M. Jackson to John Fischer, May 20, 1955, Mitchell Family Papers, Library of Congress; Gertrude Samuels, "School Desegregation: A Case History," *New York Times Magazine,* May 8, 1955, 70.

23. O'Wesney, "Historical Study of the Progress of Racial Desegregation," 33, 34, 38, 52; Baltimore City Public Schools, *Informational Materials for Desegregation Task Force* (Baltimore: BCPS, 1974, n.p.); "Maryland Board Rulings to be Appealed to Court," *SSN* 4, 10 (April 1958); "Desegregation Passes Half-way Point in Baltimore's Public School System," *SSN* 5, 9 (March 1959); "Negro Pupils Outnumber Whites For First Time in Baltimore," *SSN* 7, 9 (March 1961); "Majority of Baltimore Negro Pupils in Biracial Schools," *SSN* 8, 9 (March 1962); Parents Committee, *Eight Years of Desegregation in the Baltimore Public Schools; Fact and Law* (Baltimore: Parents Committee, 1963), tables 1, 3; Carrington, "The Struggle for Desegregation," 52; Dollie Walker, Arthur L. Stinchcombe, and Mary S. McDill, *School Desegregation in Baltimore* (Baltimore: Center for the Study of Social Organization in Schools, Johns Hopkins University, 1967), 5–7.

24. "Dr. Fischer Gets Hollander Prize," *Sun,* May 25, 1955; Sidney Hollander Foundation, *Toward Equality* (Baltimore: Hollander Foundation, 1960); "Dr. Fischer Wins Honor For Educational Role," *Evening Sun,* January 16, 1957; "John H. Fischer," *Afro,* May 16, 1959, 4.

25. "Fischer Reviews Baltimore Desegregation Course He Directed," *SSN* 6, 1 (July 1959): 5. For a cultural view of race and class, see Edward C. Banfield, *The Unheavenly City: The Nature and Future of our Urban Crisis* (Boston: Little, Brown, 1968). For an example of the use of cultural language in education, see Frank Riessman, *The Culturally Deprived Child* (New York: Harper, 1962). On the integration of cultural language into an individualistic liberal view of economic well-being, see O'Connor, *Poverty Knowledge.*

26. Stephen E. Nordlinger, "City Schools Head Named," *Sun,* July 3, 1959; "New School Head," *Sun,* July 3, 1959; "Dr. Brain Is Our New Superintendent," *Afro,* July 4, 1959; Neil H. Swanson, "Dr. Brain Talks Education Sense," *Baltimore American,* September 6, 1959;

"Dr. Brain To Become Head Of Schools On January 4," *Sun,* November 30, 1959; Stephen E. Nordlinger, "New School Head Arrives, Unpacks," *Sun,* January 3, 1960; Corinne Hammett, "Dr. Brain Takes Over School Job," Baltimore *News-Post,* January 4, 1960; Stephen E. Nordlinger, "From Teacher To Superintendent In 14 Years," *Sun,* January 10, 1960; "Educational Tools," *Sun,* January 20, 1960; Stephen E. Nordlinger, "Dr. Brain Gives Views on Classes," *Sun,* February 2, 1960; "Hard-Core Subjects," *Evening Sun,* February 2, 1960; "Schools and Causes," *Sun,* February 3, 1960; "Brain Aims To Cut Frills," Baltimore *News-Post,* February 3, 1960; Moses J. Newson, "Meet Dr. Brain…New School Head," *Afro,* July 18, 1959, 9.

CHAPTER 6. PARENTS' PROTEST AGAINST CONTINUING SEGREGATION

1. "Written Statement of Dr. George B. Brain, Superintendent of Schools, Baltimore, Md.," in U.S. Commission on Civil Rights, *Conference before the United States Commission on Civil Rights,* February 25, 1961, 37–39; "Statement of George B. Brain, Superintendent of Schools, Baltimore, Md.," in U.S. Commission on Civil Rights, *Conference Before the United States Commission on Civil Rights,* February 25, 1961, 30.

2. "Negro Educator Sees More Baltimore Segregation," *SSN* 8, 2 (August 1961): 10–11.

3. "On Whose Side Is Dr. Jackson," *Afro,* August 12, 1961.

4. The following account relies on Billie Bramhall interview, June 12, 2003; and Robert L. Crain, *The Politics of School Desegregation* (Chicago: Aldine, 1968), 72–80.

5. Edward Holmgren interview, June 18, 2003; Michael L. Mark, *But Not Next Door: Baltimore Neighborhoods, Inc.: The First Forty Years* (Baltimore: Baltimore Neighborhoods, 2002); Shirley Bramhall to George Brain, January 27, 1962, in author's possession.

6. Dorothy Sykes, "Summary of Conference with Superintendent, August 6, 1962, Mrs. Zenas M. Sykes, Jr.," in Brain, *Desegregation Policies and Procedures,* appendix, 1–13, quotation on 9; Crain, *Politics of School Desegregation,* 72–80.

7. Edward Holmgren interview, June 18, 2003; Billie Bramhall interview, June 12, 2003; Crain, *Politics of School Desegregation,* 72–80.

8. Melvin Sykes interview, May 30, 2003; Edith Furstenberg and Sidney Hollander interview, May 24, 2006; Private practice lawyer profile for Melvin J. Sykes, Martindale. com, http://www.martindale.com/xp/Martindale/Lawyer_Locator/Search_Lawyer_Locator/search_detail.xml?STS=&LNAME=sykes&CN=&PG=1&bc=65&CRY=&FN=&FNAME=melvin&STYPE=N&a=8DC3F5296297CD&l=A6DC0F427BB0E4&type=2&pos=2&cnt=2, accessed May 25, 2006.

9. Complaint, §§ 13(b)(1–5), 16–23, 11, 2(a)(I), 12, 3(c), 3(e).

10. Complaint, §§ 4(a-p), IV.

11. Parents Committee, *Seven Years of Desegregation in the Baltimore Public Schools: A Report* (Baltimore: Parents Committee, 1963); "Baltimore School Commissioners Ask Progress Report," *SSN* 9, 10 (April 1963).

12. G. H. Pouder, "People of the Town: Man for All Seasons," *Baltimore,* February 1963, 15, 69, 70; "Eli Frank, Noted Judge, Dies at 84," *Sun,* July 26, 1958; Edith Furstenberg and Sidney Hollander interview, May 24, 2006.

13. Parents Committee, *Seven Years,* 3, 4.

14. Ibid., 16–18, 20, appendix E.

15. Board of School Commissioners, *One Hundred Twenty-first Report to the Mayor and City Council, July 1, 1952 to June 30, 1954* (Baltimore: BSC, 1954), table 24, 154; O'Wesney, "Historical Study of the Progress of Racial Desegregation," 33, 50; Parents Committee, *Seven Years,* 27–28.

16. Parents Committee, *Seven Years,* 7–9; "Carrington, "The Struggle for Desegregation," 104–106.

17. Parents Committee, *Seven Years*, 4; U.S. Commission on Civil Rights, *Commission on Civil Rights Report, Book 2: Education* (Washington, DC: U.S. Commission on Civil Rights, 1961), 47.

18. Parents Committee, *Seven Years*, 30–33; School Board minutes, June 6, 1963, 106.

19. "NAACP to Push School Desegregation Drive," *Afro*, July 28, 1962.

20. Williams, *Thurgood Marshall*, 206–207; Jack Greenberg, *Crusaders in the Court* (New York: Basic Books, 1994), 158; June Shagaloff Alexander interview, June 9, 2006.

21. Kluger, *Simple Justice*, 615–616; June Shagaloff Alexander interview, June 9, 2006; Kenneth B. Clark, "Desegregation: An Appraisal of the Evidence," *Journal of Social Issues* 9, 4 (1953): 64, emphasis in original; Greenberg, *Crusaders in the Court*, 180–181.

22. June Shagaloff, "Public School Desegregation—North and West," *The Crisis* 70, 2 (February 1963): 92–95, 103; Jack Dougherty, *More than One Struggle: The Evolution of Black School Reform in Milwaukee* (Chapel Hill: University of North Carolina Press, 2004), 76; NAACP, *NAACP In Action: Report for 1961* (New York: NAACP, 1961), 49–51; "NAACP To Push School Desegregation Drive," *Afro*, 32; "Five More Counties Admit Negroes to White Schools, "*SSN* 9, 3 (September 1961): 13.

23. Brain, *Desegregation Policies and Procedures*, 30, 31, 34, 37–38, 10–11, 109, 60, 149–150.

24. "School Board Suspends Action on Appointments," *Afro*, June 8, 1963; Ralph Matthews Jr., "Citizens Condemn Segregation Here," *Afro*, June 8, 1963; Parents Committee, *Eight Years of Desegregation in the Baltimore Public Schools: Fact and Law* (Baltimore: Parents Committee, 1963).

25. Adam Clymer, "School Drive Planned Here By NAACP," *Sun*, June 7, 1963, 26; Parents Committee, *Eight Years*, 5, 6, 7.

26. *Eight Years*, 36, 37; Ralph Matthews, Jr., "Citizens Condemn Segregation Here," *Afro*, June 8, 1963.

27. School Board minutes, June 6, 1963, 105–113.

28. "Board Hears Three-Pronged Attack on Racial Policies," *SSN* 10, 1 (July 1963); School Board minutes, June 6, 1963, 120–121; "NAACP," *Afro*, June 8, 1963, 2; "New Board Policies Termed 'Unacceptable,'" *Afro*, June 8, 1963, 1.

29. School Board minutes, June 6, 1963, 121–122; Adam Clymer, "School Drive Planned Here by NAACP"; "NAACP," 1–2.

30. Clymer, "School Drive Planned Here by NAACP," 2.

31. Carl Murphy, "The School Board Shouts," *Afro*, June 22, 1963; "Not Schools Alone," *Sun*, June 8, 1963, 12.

32. Adam Clymer, "Fischer Says School Heads Should Push Integration," *Sun*, June 9, 1963, 48.

33. "Board Hears Three-Pronged Attack," *SSN* 10, 1 (July 1963): 18; Crain, *The Politics of School Desegregation*, 77, 79; Melvin Sykes interview, May 30, 2003; Adam Clymer, "School Race Talks Sought," *Sun*, June 13, 1963; Robert Lloyd interview, January 12, 2005; Adam Clymer, "Shift in Schools' Race Policy Seen," *Sun*, June 14, 1963; School Board minutes, June 19, 1963, 125; Ralph Matthews Jr., "'Tokenism' In Schools Assailed," *Afro*, June 22, 1963.

34. Stone letter published in School Board minutes, June 26, 1963, 149–150; 347 U.S. 493, 494, 495, 1954, bracketing in the Supreme Court decision.

35. Billie Bramhall interview, June 12, 2003; James S. Coleman, Ernest Q. Campbell, Carol J. Hobson, James McPartland, Alexander M. Mood, Frederic D. Weinfeld, and Robert L. York, *Equality of Educational Opportunity* (Washington, DC: U.S. Government Printing Office, 1966).

36. Ralph Matthews, Jr., "NAACP Studying New School Move," *Afro*, July 20, 1963; on Boston desegregation, see J. Anthony Lucas, *Common Ground* (New York: Vintage Books,

1986); "Superintendents to study integration," *Afro* July 20, 1963; George B. Brain, *School Superintendents Conference on the Practical Problems of Public School Desegregation* (Washington, DC: U.S. Department of Health, Education and Welfare, Office of Education, 1964).

37. School Board minutes, July 31, 1963, 179; June Shagaloff Alexander interview, June 9, 2006; Ralph Matthews, Jr., "More Picketing for Local Schools," *Afro*, August 3, 1963; Adam Clymer, "School Board Is Picketed by NAACP, *Sun*, August 1, 1963.

38. Adam Clymer, "Harm Seen in School Segregation," *Sun*, August 5, 1963.

39. Brain, *School Superintendents Conference*, 14.

40. Ibid., 21–23; "Slum Schools Should Be Best, School Aides Told," *Evening Sun*, August 6, 1963.

41. Brain, *School Superintendents Conference*, 18–21; Adam Clymer, "3 Groups Ask School Move," *Sun*, August 7, 1963; for the 1961 NAACP endorsement of open enrollment, see NAACP, *NAACP In Action: Report for 1961* (New York: NAACP, 1961), 50.

42. Brain, *School Superintendents Conference*, 26, 9, 7.

43. Ralph Matthews, Jr., "Dr. Brain Indicates More Speed in Local Desegregation," *Afro*, August 10, 1963; Adam Clymer, "Brain Plans for Schools," *Sun*, August 8, 1963, 37.

44. Kay Mills, "She Frets About Taxpayers' Money," *Evening Sun*, May 2, 1969.

45. Joseph Allen to Eli Frank Jr., August 29, 1963, 27, 29–30, 30, 32.

46. "600 Overcrowded Students Start School Year In Buses," *Sun*, September 5, 1963; "2,917 Pupils Affected by School Board Bus Plan," *Afro*, September 14, 1963; "District Enrolls First Negroes With Whites," *SSN* 10, 4 (October 1963): 19; George W. Collins, "Segregation, Overcrowding Target of New School Policy," *Afro*, September 7, 1963; George B. Brain, "Equality of Educational Opportunity: A Progress Report for the Baltimore City Public Schools," School Board minutes, March 19, 1964, A61–A68.

47. School Board minutes, September 5, 1963, 181–185, 192–193; Adam Clymer, "School Board Votes to Remedy Effects of Racial Imbalance," *Sun*, September 6, 1963; Collins, "Segregation, Overcrowding Target of New School Policy"; George W. Collins, "A School Board Talk Sized Up: You Were 'Loud, Clear, Wrong,'" *Afro*, September 21, 1963.

48. Charles V. Flowers, "Order Vowed by McKeldin," *Sun*, September 6, 1963; "Rally Seeks to Bar More Negro Pupils," *Sun*, September 8, 1963; "Negro Pupil Shifts Spur 2 Protests," *Sun*, September 10, 1963; "Transfer Opponents Attack School Board," *Afro*, September 28, 1963; School Board minutes, September 19, 1963, 205–206; School Board minutes, September 26, 1963, 217; "Not Racial," *Sun*, September 7, 1963, 12; Crain, *Politics of School Desegregation*, 76; George W. Collins, "Segregation, Overcrowding," *Afro*, September 7, 1963, 11; "Major Win for NAACP in Baltimore Schools," September 13, 1963, Papers of the NAACP, pt. 3, Series D, Group III, Box A-102, Manuscript Division, Library of Congress.

49. Brain, "Equality of Educational Opportunity," A46.

50. Ibid., A72–A73; Baltimore City Public Schools, *Informational Materials for Desegregation Task Force*, table B; "Superintendent Reports Progress in 'Racial Integration' Last Year," *SSN* 10, 10 (April 1964): 18; Walker, Stinchcombe, and McDill, *School Desegregation in Baltimore*, 5–7.

51. Brain, "Equality of Educational Opportunity," A62, A64, A68.

52. Ibid., A71, A62.

53. Ibid., A82, A74–A80, A92.

54. Ibid, A81, A84.

55. Ibid., A86.

56. Baltimore City Public Schools, *Informational Materials for Desegregation Task Force*, table B; "Superintendent Reports Progress in 'Racial Integration' Last Year," *SSN* 10, 10 (April 1964); Carrington, "The Struggle for Desegregation," 99–100. On tracking, see Jeannie Oakes, *Keeping Track: How Schools Structure Inequality* (New Haven: Yale University Press, 1985).

**CHAPTER 7. GROWING INTEGRATIONISM AND
THE MURDER OF MARTIN LUTHER KING JR.**

1. Civil Rights Act of 1964, P. L. 88–352, July 2, 1964, Sections 401, 602.

2. Stephen K. Bailey and Edith K. Mosher, *ESEA: The Office of Education Adminis-ters a Law* (Syracuse: Syracuse University Press, 1968); Beryl A. Radin, *Implementation, Change, and the Federal Bureaucracy; School Desegregation Policy in HEW, 1964–1968* (New York: Teachers College Press, 1977); Gary Orfield, *The Reconstruction of Southern Education: The Schools and the 1964 Civil Rights Act* (New York: Wiley-Interscience, 1969); Leon E. Panetta and Peter Gall, *Bring Us Together: The Nixon Team and the Civil Rights Retreat* (Philadelphia: J. B. Lippincott, 1971).

3. Robert A. Dahl, *Who Governs? Democracy and Power in an American City* (New Haven: Yale University Press, 1961); *School Desegregation in the Southern and Border States*, Compiled by Southern Education Reporting Service (hereafter, *School Desegrega-tion*), July 1965, Maryland-3; Barbara Mills, *"Got My Mind Set on Freedom": Maryland's Story of Black and White Activism 1663–2000* (Bowie, MD: Heritage Books, 2002), 400; Ralph Matthews Jr., "Who Revealed School Board Choice to Replace Brain?" *Afro*, August 1, 1964; John Eddinger, "School Superintendent Expected To Be Named," *Evening Sun*, August 27, 1964; Joann Rodgers, "Dr. Paquin Appointed School Superintendent," *News-American*, August 28, 1964; "Dr. Paquin Is New School Head," *Afro*, August 29, 1964; Gerald Clarke, "New School Head Has Dealt With Slum School Problems," *Sun*, August 30, 1964; Ralph Matthews Jr., "New School Chief Will Do Right By Pupils," *Afro*, September 5, 1964; "Superintendent of Schools Talks about Changing Times," *Afro*, April 3, 1965; "LGP—New School Head," *Afro*, s24 July 10, 1965; "New Superintendent Turns Deaf Ear on School Rumors," *Afro*, July 10, 1965.

4. "CORE Members—1961," Sidney Hollander Sr., collection, Maryland Historical Society; James Griffin to Advisory Board Members, June 6, 1966, Sidney Hollander Sr., collection, Maryland Historical Society; James Griffin interview, June 30, 2003; August Meier and Elliott Rudwick, *CORE: A Study in the Civil Rights Movement, 1942–1968* (New York: Oxford University Press, 1973), 304–305, 359, 383–384.

5. School Board minutes, December 16, 1965, 243–245; Gene Oishi, "Teachers Seek Pay Increases," *Sun*, December 17, 1965; "CORE, Teachers Hit School Segregation, Poor Quality," *Afro*, December 18, 1976; *School Desegregation*, December 1965, Maryland-3.

6. Laurence G. Paquin, *The Senior High Schools in the Years Ahead 1966–1971* (Balti-more: Baltimore City Public Schools, 1966); James B. Conant, *The American High School Today: A First Report to Interested Citizens* (New York: McGraw Hill, 1959).

7. Melvin J. Sykes et al., *City Forever? A Tradition at the Crossroads* (Baltimore: Sykes et al., 1965); Gene Oishi, "City College Stirs Debate," *Sun*, January 21, 1966; "Both Sides Argue 'City Forever?'" *Afro*, January 22, 1968; *School Desegregation*, January 1966, Mary-land-2–8; *School Desegregation*, February 1966, Maryland-6–8; *School Desegregation*, March 1966, Maryland-5–6; Mills, *"Got My Mind Set on Freedom,"* 395–399.

8. Paquin, *Senior High Schools*, A4, A11; "School 'Position' Paper," *Afro*, February 5, 1966; Roger J. Nissly, "De Facto Bias, Course Labels Target of Plan," *Afro*, February 5, 1966; "NAACP Hails Paquin Plan," *Afro*, February 5, 1966; "Paquin Raps 'Selfish Interests' of Some Critics of School Plan," *Afro*, February 27, 1966; "Elite Alumni," *Afro*, March 5, 1966; "Paquin's 'Volunteers' Plan Wins Backing of Teachers," *Afro*, May 21, 1966; School Board minutes, June 9, 1966, 131–145; "Paquin Plan Approved with Several Changes," *Afro*, June 11, 1966; Roger J. Nissly, "Paquin Plan Changing High Schools," *Afro*, June 18, 1966; *School Desegregation*, February 1966, Maryland-6–8; *School Desegregation*, March 1966, Maryland-4–6; *School Desegregation*, May 1966, Maryland-3–4, 6–7; Mills, *"Got My Mind Set on Freedom,"* 395–399.

9. George Rodgers, "Segregation Rate Drops in Schools," *Evening Sun,* August 11, 1966; Baltimore City Public Schools, *Informational Materials for Desegregation Task Force,* table B.

10. Louis C. Goldberg, "CORE in Trouble: A Social History of the Organizational Dilemmas of the Congress of Racial Equality Target City Project in Baltimore (1965–1967)" (Ph.D. diss., Johns Hopkins University, 1970), chap. 1; James Griffin interview, June 30, 2003; Meier and Rudwick, *CORE,* chap. 12, 409–410.

11. Richard E. Levine, "CORE Chief Here to Heal Rights Rift," *Sun,* June 18, 1966, B18; Mills, *"Got My Mind Set on Freedom,"* 560–562; "Interracial Drive Backed," *Sun,* July 8, 1966.

12. *Report of the National Advisory Commission on Civil Disorders,* chap. 1, charts; Phillip Potter, "Mayor Tells of Means to Prevent Riot," *Sun,* October 6, 1967, C24.

13. Goldberg, "CORE In Trouble," 139; Mills, *"Got My Mind Set on Freedom,"* 564–568; "Mayor Says Target City Could Be Summer's Safest," *Afro,* July 5, 1966; "SNCC Firebrand Raps Non-Violence," *Evening Sun,* July 2, 1966; Peter Marudas interview, December 11, 2003.

14. Mills, *"Got My Mind Set on Freedom,"* 609–610; Goldberg, "CORE In Trouble"; Meier and Rudwick, *CORE,* 420; Levine, "CORE Chief Here to Heal Rights Rift," *Sun,* June 18, 1966; Howell S. Baum, *The Organization of Hope: Communities Planning Themselves* (Albany: SUNY Press, 1997); Kenneth D. Durr, *Behind the Backlash: White Working-Class Politics in Baltimore, 1940–1980* (Chapel Hill: University of North Carolina Press, 2003); Howard F. Stein and Robert F. Hill, *The Ethnic Imperative: Examining the New White Ethnic Movement* (University Park: Pennsylvania State University Press, 1977).

15. U.S. Commission on Civil Rights, *Southern School Desegregation, 1966–67* (Washington, DC: U.S. Government Printing Office, 1967), 23–25; School Board minutes, September 22, 1966, 229–232; Gene Oishi, "Task Force Urges Speed-Up in Integrating School Staffs," *Sun,* September 23, 1966.

16. *School Desegregation,* October 1966, Maryland-4–5.

17. School Board minutes, June 1, 1967, 227–229, 242–247, quote on 228; *School Desegregation,* May 1967, Maryland-5–7; "Dr. Paquin to Push School Staff Mixing," *Afro,* June 10, 1967, 1,

18. U.S. Commission on Civil Rights, *Racial Isolation in the Public Schools* (Washington, DC: U.S. Government Printing Office, 1967), 4, 67–69; Mayor's Task Force for Equal Rights, "Series of Recommendations on Integration and Quality Education in the Inner City," June 26, 1967; School Board minutes, September 20, 1967, 404–409; *School Desegregation,* July 1967, Maryland-3–4.

19. Martin D. Jenkins and Hans Froelicher Jr., to Theodore R. McKeldin, July 26, 1967; *School Desegregation,* October 1967, Maryland-3–4.

20. Walker, Stinchcombe, and McDill, *School Desegregation in Baltimore.*

21. *School Desegregation,* August 1967, Maryland-4.

22. *School Desegregation,* August 1967, Maryland-2–5; *School Desegregation,* October 1967, Maryland-7–8.

23. *School Desegregation,* February 1967, Maryland-3–4; "Major Cities Face School-Race Problems," *SSN* 10, 5 (November 1963).

24. "Nondiscrimination in Federally Assisted Programs of the Department of Health, Education, and Welfare—Effectuation of Title VI of the Civil Rights Act of 1964," 45 C.F.R. 80, 1964; "General Statement of Policies Under Title VI of the Civil Rights Act of 1964 Respecting Desegregation of Elementary and Secondary Schools," Washington, DC: U.S. Government Printing Office, 1965; Orfield, *Reconstruction of Southern Education,* 1969, 92–101; Radin, *Implementation,* 1977, chap. 6; "School Desegregation," *The Crisis,* 72, 8 (October 1965): 524; U.S. Commission on Civil Rights, *Survey of School Desegregation in the Southern and Border States, 1965–66* (Washington, DC: U.S. Government Printing Office, 1966); *Kier v. County School Board of Augusta County,* 249 F. Supp. 239, 1966

25. "Revised Statement of Policies for School Desegregation Plans under Title VI of the Civil Rights Act of 1964," 45 C.F.R. Part 181; Orfield, *Reconstruction of Southern Education,* 1969, 135–147; Radin, *Implementation,* 1977, 110–114; U.S. Commission on Civil Rights, *Southern School Desegregation 1966–67,* 12–19; Roy Wilkins to John W. Gardner, March 18, 1966, excerpted in "School Desegregation Guidelines," *The Crisis* 73, 4 (April 1966): 217–219; U.S. Commission on Civil Rights, *Southern School Desegregation 1966–67,* 95–97.

26. Greenberg, *Crusaders in the Courts,* 383–384.

27. "Pimlico School PTA Asks End Of Congestion," *Sun,* September 29, 1967; "Pimlico's Real Problem," *Afro,* October 7, 1967; "Suspicions Remain," *Afro,* October 21, 1967; "Pimlico Explained," *Afro,* October 28, 1967; "Gene Burns—Libertarian," http://www.theadvocates.org/celebrities/gene-burns.html, accessed June 29, 2006; "Talkers Magazine—Gene Burns," http://www.talkers.com/greatest/24rBurns.htm, accessed June 29, 2006; Baltimore City Public Schools, *Informational Materials for Desegregation Task Force* (Baltimore: BCPS, 1974); School Board minutes, November 18, 1967, 542.

28. School Board minutes, November 4, 1967, 490; "Pimlico's Real Problem," 8.

29. School Board minutes, November 16, 1967, 520–522, 525–527, 537–552; Roger J. Nissly, "No Use of Drugs Found at Pimlico," *Afro,* November 4, 1967; Stephen A. Bennett, "Size Blamed at Pimlico," *Sun,* November 17, 1967; Roger J. Nissly, "School Board Report Shows Pimlico Charges Exaggerated," *Afro,* November 18, 1967.

30. "Urban Office Set by D'Alesandro," *Sun,* November 18, 1967; Jane L. Keidel, "Study Says Negro Firstborn In City Are 61% Illegitimate," *Sun,* November 18, 1967.

31. Thomas J. D'Alesandro III, McKeldin-Jackson Oral History collection, Maryland Historical Society, OH 8119, June 17, 1976; Thomas D'Alesandro III, interview, November 4, 2003; Peter Marudas interview, December 11, 2003; Peter Bachrach and Morton S. Baratz, *Power and Poverty: Theory and Practice* (New York: Oxford University Press, 1970).

32. Dorothy Pula Strohecker, "Tommys Two: The D'Alesandros," in Lenora Heilig Nast, Laurence N. Krause, and R. C. Monk, eds., *Baltimore: A Living Renaissance* (Baltimore: Historic Baltimore Society, 1982), 232; Mike Bowler, *The Lessons of Change: Baltimore Schools in the Modern Era* (Baltimore: Fund for Educational Excellence, 1991), 12; National Education Association, *Baltimore, Maryland: Change and Contrast—The Children and the Public Schools,* Report of an Investigation (Washington, DC: NEA, 1967).

33. George Rodgers, "Murnaghan Is Eyed to Succeed Frank," *Evening Sun,* November 16, 1967; John E. Woodruff, "Mayor, Murnaghan Tour Schools," *Sun,* December 12, 1967; "To Head the Schools," *Sun,* December 12, 1967; "School Board Head," *Afro,* December 16, 1967; Roger J. Nissly, "'I Do Not Buy that Children Are Not Educable,'—Murnaghan," *Afro,* December 16, 1967; Thomas J. D'Alesandro III, interview, November 4, 2003; James Griffin interview, June 20, 2003; Kay Mills, "Griffin, Former Demonstrator On Outside, Fights For Change Within School Board," *Evening Sun,* October 15, 1968.

34. Kay Mills, "City's New School Chief Maps Poverty Area Push," *Evening Sun,* March 26, 1968, C24; Richard D. O'Mara, "Dr. Sheldon: A First Impression," *Evening Sun,* March 27, 1968; Stephen A. Bennett, "New Yorker Named City School Head," *Evening Sun;* Kay Mills, "New School Chief Maps Poverty Area Push," *Evening Sun;* "Welcome, Dr. Sheldon," *Evening Sun,* July 1, 1968; Tom Callahan, "New City School Head Got Start As Teacher-Coach," *Evening Sun,* July 24, 1968; "Dr. Sheldon Takes Over," *Afro,* August 3, 1968; Bowler, *Lessons of Change,* 1991, 11; "Sheldon's Pay Tops In U.S.," newspaper clipping, Enoch Pratt Thomas Donald Sheldon Vertical File; Edgar L. Jones, "$50,000 a Year," *Evening Sun,* March 7, 1969; Kay Mills, "Hempstead Praises Work of Dr. Sheldon, Especially In Community Relations Area," *Evening Sun,* April 5, 1968.

35. This and the following account of actions just after King's death and rioting is based on Stephen J. Lynton, "Mayor Pays King Tribute," *Sun,* April 5, 1968; Phillip Potter,

"Troops," *Sun,* April 6, 1968; Oswald Johnston, "Appeal," *Sun,* April 5, 1968; "Unrest Rises in Wake of King's Death," *Sun,* April 6, 1968; David L. Maulsby, "Many On Street Unwilling to Discuss King Tragedy," *Sun,* April 6, 1968; Robert A. Erlandson, "City To Mark Monday As Day Of Mourning For Dr. King; Schools, Offices Will Close," *Sun,* April 6, 1968; Stephen J. Lynton, "Baltimore Sad But Peaceful As Negro And White Mourn," *Sun,* April 6, 1968; "Guard Called Out In Baltimore Riot; Three Killed; U.S. Troops Sent To Chicago, Bolstered In D.C.," *Sun,* April 7, 1968; "1,900 U.S. Troops Patrolling City; Officials Plan Curfew Again Today; 4 Dead, 300 Hurt, 1,350 Arrested," *Sun,* April 8, 1968; "Mayor Tours A Scarred City, Seeking To Avert A Second Night," *Sun,* April 8, 1968; Edward G. Pickett, "Efficient, Weary Guardsmen Unable To Prevent Looting," *Sun,* April 8, 1968; "1,900 More GI's Join Riot Forces As Snipers Peril Police, Firemen; Arrests In 3 Days Rise To 3,450," *Sun,* April 9, 1968; "Baltimore's Weary Firefighters Get Help From Two Counties," *Sun,* April 9, 1968; Richard Basoco, "West Baltimore Is An Ugly No-Man's Land," *Sun,* April 9, 1968, "55,000 Troops, Apparently Most In U.S. History, Are Deployed," *Sun,* April 9, 1968; "Today Must End It," *Sun,* April 9, 1968; "Backbone Of Riot Reported Broken; Return To Normal Could Be Near," *Sun,* April 10, 1968; Edward G. Pickett, "Negro Peace Meeting Dispersed By Troops," *Sun,* April 10, 1968; John E. O'Donnell Jr., "600 Treated, 19 Admitted With Wounds From Rioting," *Sun,* April 10, 1968; "City Begins Clean-Up After Riots; Sightseers Tour Ravaged Areas," *Sun,* April 10, 1968; George W. Collins, "City In Turmoil As Rioters Roam," *Afro,* April 9, 1968; Jewell Chambers and Al Rutledge, "Riot Brings Misery, Suffering to Innocent," *Afro,* April 9, 1968; Callcott, *Maryland and America,* 165–166; Olson, *Baltimore,* 382–384; University of Baltimore, "Timeline," http://www.ubalt.edu/template.cfm?page=1639, accessed July 1, 2008.

36. Gene Oishi, "Negroes Quit Conference with Agnew," *Sun,* April 12, 1968; Robert A. Erlandson, "Mayor, Reacting To Agnew's Remarks, Asks For Restraint," *Sun,* April 13, 1968; "Text Of Governor Agnew's Statement To Civil Rights Leaders," *Sun,* April 13, 1968; "Angry Leaders Walk Out on Agnew," *Afro,* April 20, 1968; Mills, *"Got My Mind Set On Freedom,"* 625–627; Thomas J. D'Alesandro III, McKeldin-Jackson Oral History collection, Maryland Historical Society, OH 8119, June 17, 1976, I-2:19; Callcott, *Maryland and America,* 215; Brugger, *Maryland,* 626–628.

37. Callcott, *Maryland and America,* 5–8.

38. Thomas J. D'Alesandro, III, McKeldin-Jackson Oral History collection, Maryland Historical Society, OH 8119, June 17, 1976, I-2:17; Thomas D'Alesandro III, interview, November 4, 2003.

39. Gene Oishi, "Telegrams," *Baltimore Sun,* April 13, 1968.

40. Olson, *Baltimore,* 383; "What's the Answer," *Baltimore Jewish Times,* 98, 9 (April 12, 1968), 8.

41. U.S. Bureau of the Census, *Population,* Second Series, *Characteristics of the Population, Maryland* (Washington, DC: U.S. Government Printing Office, 1942), table 41; U.S. Bureau of the Census, *Census of Population: 1950,* vol. 2, *Characteristics of the Population, Part 20, Maryland* (Washington, DC: U.S. Government Printing Office, 195), table 44; U.S. Bureau of the Census, *U.S. Censuses of Population and Housing: 1960,* Final Report PHC (1)-13 (Washington, DC: U.S. Government Printing Office, 1961), table P-4; U.S. Bureau of the Census, *1970 Census of Population,* vol. 1, *Characteristics of the Population, Part 22, Maryland* (Washington, DC: U. S. Government Printing Office, 1973), table 92; U.S. Bureau of the Census, *1980 Census of Population and Housing,* Census Tracts, Baltimore, Md., PHC80-2-82 (Washington, DC: U.S. Government Printing Office, 1983), table P-14.

42. Erlandson, "Mayor, Reacting To Agnew's Remarks, Asks for Restraint"; Weldon Wallace, "Priests," *Sun* April 13, 1968; "Racism Is Good Friday Theme," *Sun,* April 13, 1968.

43. 391 U.S. 430, 1968, 435, 439, 442.

44. George W. Collins, "Glenn Sees 'Lot To Be Done,'" *Afro,* May 26, 1962; Baltimore Community Relations Commission, *Survey of The Baltimore City Public Schools—1965* (Baltimore: BCRC, 1965); John E. Woodruff, "School Board Criticized on Racial Stand," *Sun,* September 15, 1967.

45. George L. Russell Jr., Ambrose T. Hartman, and Blanche G. Wahl memorandum to David L. Glenn regarding "Integration in the Baltimore City Schools: Impact of *Green v. County School Board,"* Department of Law File No. 118889, November 29, 1968, quotations, 4, 6, 7, 8, 9; John B. O'Donnell Jr., "City School Integration Held Lagging," *Sun,* December 1, 1968, 24, 12; George Russell interviews, March 26 and March 29, 2004; Southern Education Reporting Service, *School Desegregation,* May, 1968, Maryland-6.

46. George Russell interview, March 26, 2004; Alvin P. Sanoff, "Change Denied on Open Schools," *Sun,* November 19, 1968; "Open Enrollment In Schools Is Wasteful, Pressman Says," *Sun,* November 30, 1968; "Murnaghan Poses Two Integration Problems," *Sun,* December 2, 1968; Roger J. Nissly, "Baltimore Schools Have No Master Plan For Desegregation," *Afro,* December 14, 1968; Sanoff, "Change Denied On Open Schools," C6.

47. Melvin Sykes interviews, May 30, 2003 and July 13, 2005.

48. Bowler, *Lessons of Change,* 1991, 11–12; "Dr. Sheldon's First Year," *Afro,* August 30, 1969.

49. George Collins, "Sam Daniels—Seeker of Challenges," *Afro* August 4, 1963; Jane Jasper, "TJD: New School Board 'Makes Me Very Happy,'" *Afro,* January 28, 1969; Mills, *"Got My Mind Set On Freedom,"* 404, 508, 513, 626; Larry Gibson interview, August 4, 2003,

50. "Racial Tension Blamed For Disruption At Girls' School," *Afro,* February 14, 1970; "Protests Force School Shut-down," *Afro,* February 17, 1970; School Board minutes, February 12, 1970, 64–67; Joshua Watson, "Murnaghan Threatens to Quit School Post," *Afro,* February 14, 1970; Allen Feld, "Murnaghan Talks of Future Plans," *Afro,* February 28, 1970; "The Murnaghan Era," *Afro,* February 28, 1970.

51. "TJD Choice Hit For Role In Police Beating Probe," *Afro,* February 24, 1970; "New School Prexy," *Afro,* February 28, 1970; Alfonso A. Narvaez, "Henry Green Parks Jr. Dies at 72; Led Way for Black Entrepreneurs," *New York Times,* April 26, 1989; Mike Bowler, "Karwacki's 21 Months on Board Helped Avert Disaster, He Believes," *Sun,* November 9, 1971.

52. Paul Evans, "TJD's School Board Threat Meets with Fire from Black Community," *Afro,* January 16, 1971; Bowler, *The Lessons of Change,* 12; Antero Pietila, "City School Segregation Rises," *Sun,* November 18, 1970; Antero Pietila, "Race Issue Foils City's School Plan," *Sun,* November 6, 1970; School Board minutes, November 5, 1970.

53. Paul Evans, "Macht Leaves Board, Banks Gets Raise," *Afro,* December 5, 1970; Kay Mills, "Hempstead Praises Work Of Dr. Sheldon, Especially In Community Relations Area," *Evening Sun,* April 5, 1968; Sue Miller, "School Board Head Assails D'Alesandro," *Evening Sun,* January 23, 1971, 2; Paul Evans, "To Consult Sheldon on Leaving," *Afro,* January 9, 1971; School Board minutes, January 6, 1971; Sue Miller, "Baltimore School Discord Isn't Unique," *Evening Sun,* January 19, 1971.

54. Paul Evans, "Leaders Ask TJD to Name 2 Blacks to School Board," *Afro,* November 24, 1970; "TJD Picks His Aide for School Board," *Afro,* January 9, 1971; Paul F. Evans, "Hettleman Replaces Macht on School Board," *Afro,* January 9, 1971; Kalman Hettleman interview, June 13, 2003; Sue Miller, "Board, Once Placid, Clashes All The Time," *Evening Sun,* January 22, 1971; Gerald Parshall, "Mayor Puts Aide In Board Vacancy," *Evening Sun,* January 7, 1971; "The Peacemaker," *Evening Sun,* January 8, 1971; Paul Evans, "TJD's School Board Threat Meets With Fire From Black Community," *Afro,* January 16, 1971; Gerald Parshall, "Entire Board Target Of Scolding: Mayor," *Evening Sun,* January 21, 1971; Gerald Parshall, "D'Alesandro On Verge Last Week Of Asking School Board's Ouster," *Evening Sun,* January 16, 1971; Sue Miller, "Mayor Demands Board Show Cooperation," *Evening Sun,* January 15, 1971.

55. Paul Willis, "'Circus' Atmosphere Is Blamed For 2 School Board Resignations," *News-American,* January 23, 1971; Paul Evans, "Three New Members on School Board," *Afro,* January 26, 1971; Paul Evans, "Dr. Sheldon Leaves Post Monday," *Afro,* January 30, 1971; "City to Get First Black School Head?" *Afro,* February 6, 1971; Paul Evans, "Interim School Head Hassle Called 'Trick,'" *Afro,* February 9, 1971; Paul Evans, "Keyes, 36, First Black School Head," *Afro,* February 13, 1971; Paul Evans, "All 4 black Councilmen Oppose Thieblot's Vote," *Afro,* February 20, 1971.

56. 402. U. S. 1, 1971, 15, 17, 23A, 24; Davison M. Douglas, *Reading, Writing, and Race: The Desegregation of the Charlotte Schools* (Chapel Hill: University of North Carolina Press, 1995); Stephen Samuel Smith, *Boom for Whom? Education, Desegregation, and Development in Charlotte* (Albany: SUNY Press, 2004).

57. "Explore Magnet School Plan Alternate to Open Enrollment," *Afro,* April 3, 1971; School Board minutes, April 22, 1971, 141–189, quote on 142–143; School Board minutes, March 18, 1971, 103–105.

58. School Board minutes, May 13, 1971, 229–238; "School Board," *Afro,* May 15, 1971; "City's Magnet School Plan—What It's All About," *Afro,* May 22, 1971, 4.

59. Paul Evans, "Griffin, Gibson Expose Move to Make Keyes Superintendent," *Afro,* June 26, 1971; "Karwacki Departure," *Afro,* November 13, 1971; Paul Evans, "Citizens Rally for Patterson," *Afro,* November 23, 1971; Paul Evans, "TJD Calls for Support of Patterson," *Afro,* December 7, 1971; G. Jefferson Price 3d, "School Board Chief Resigns," *Sun,* November 9, 1971.; C. Fraser Smith, *William Donald Schaefer: A Political Biography* (Baltimore: Johns Hopkins University Press, 1999), 61–93, 135–136; Kalman Hettleman interview, June 13, 2003; Larry Gibson interview, August 4, 2003; James Griffin interview, June 30, 2003; Robert Thieblot interview, June 16, 2003; Robert Schaefer interview, June 17, 2003.

60. S. D. Gordon, "Mr. McNierney: His Interest Is in School Curriculum," *Afro,* January 20, 1971; W. C. Rhoden, "School Board Member Quits," *Afro,* October 20, 1973; Sue Miller, "2 Resignations Leave School Board in State of Flux," *Evening Sun,* October 25, 1973; Sue Miller, "Hettleman Is Third Member to Quit City School Board," *Evening Sun,* October 19, 1973; Mike Bowler, "McNierney Resigns from School Unit, Giving Job Pressure as His Reason," *Sun,* August 3, 1973; "Stephen W. McNierney," *Evening Sun,* February 19, 1971; Sue Miller, "School System Urgency Stressed," *Evening Sun,* October 3, 1973.

61. O'Wesney, "Historical Study," 54; Baltimore City Public Schools, *Informational Materials for Desegregation Task Force,* tables B, C.

62. McDougall, *Black Baltimore.*

CHAPTER 8. FEDERAL INTERVENTION

1. 356 F. Supp. 92, 1973, 95, 97, 101; Frederic B. Hill, "Court Tells HEW to Force Schools to Desegregate," *Sun,* February 17, 1973.

2. Thomas B. Edsall, "HEW Enforcer Deems Full Integration Impossible," *Sun,* September 11, 1974; Peter Holmes interview, April 6, 2005.

3. Panetta and Gall, *Bring Us Together,* 176; Edsall, "HEW Enforcer Deems Full Integration Impossible."

4. Edsall, "HEW Enforcer Deems Full Integration Impossible"; Peter Holmes interview, April 6, 2005; Panetta and Gall, *Bring Us Together;* Deposition of Peter E. Holmes before the United States District Court for the District of Maryland, in *Baltimore v. Mathews,* N-76–23, January 20, 1976, 3–5.

5. Roland N. Patterson to Peter E. Holmes, June 4, 1973, in Baltimore City Public Schools, *Informational Materials for Desegregation Task Force.*

6. Harold Davis testimony before the United States District Court for the District of Maryland, in *Mandel v. Mathews* and *Baltimore v. Mathews,* N-76–1 and N-76–23, January 30, 1976, 107–108.

7. Peter E. Holmes to Roland N. Patterson, April 17, 1973, OCR documents obtained under FOIA request; Patterson to Holmes, June 4, 1973; 156 U.S. App. D.C. 267, 1973; Mike Bowler, "Federal Court Upholds Enforcing Desegregation," *Sun,* June 13, 1973.

8. Peter E. Holmes to Roland N. Patterson, February 5, 1974, OCR documents.

9. Mike Bowler, "71% of Students Absent; Hearing Set on Injunction," *Sun,* February 6, 1974; Mike Bowler, "School Attendance 16%; Talks Break Off Again," *Sun,* February 7, 1974; Bill Rhoden, "New Teachers' Contract Costs City $6 million," *Afro,* March 9, 1974.

10. School Board minutes, February 21, 1974; Roland N. Patterson to Peter E. Holmes, February 14, 1974, in Baltimore City Public Schools, *Informational Materials for Desegregation Task Force;* "City Schools Get Extension to Submit Integration Plan," *Sun,* February 23, 1974; School Board minutes, March 14, 1974; Martin H. Gerry to Roland Patterson, February 27, 1974, in Baltimore City Public Schools, *Informational Materials for Desegregation Task Force.*

11. School Board minutes, March 14, 1974; Glen Fallin, "School Deseg Task Force to Meet," *News American,* March 18, 1974; "Patterson Asks Coexistence of HEW Rule, Open Enrollment," *Sun,* March 16, 1974.

12. Herbert Goldman interview, June 24, 2003.

13. Betty Deacon interview, August 25, 2003; "Betty Deacon Named to School Board Task Force," *East Baltimore Guide,* March 21, 1974.

14. "School Integration Panel Off to a Stumbling Start," *Sun,* March 19, 1974; Sue Miller, "Neighborhood School Defender," *Evening Sun,* March 22, 1974; DeWayne Wickham, "Massive Busing Ruled Out By HEW Unit," *Evening Sun,* March 23, 1974; "Nixon Pushes School Aid, Busing Plans," *Evening Sun,* March 23, 1974; Michael P. Weisskopf, "Busing Not Needed in City, HEW Says," *Sun,* March 24, 1974; Glen Fallin, "'Massive' School Busing Proposal Held Unlikely," *News American,* March 24, 1974; "Rose Granger Elected To School Deseg Task Force," *East Baltimore Guide,* March 28, 1974; Theodore W. Hendricks, "City Task Force Works on School Integration Report," *Sun,* April 16, 1974; Betty Deacon Interview, August 25, 2003.

15. Glen Fallin, "Merger of City, County School Units Urged," *News American,* March 27, 1974.

16. Tom Linthicum, "Pairing of 94 Elementary Schools Suggested to End Segregation in City," *Sun,* April 5, 1974; Glen Fallin, "Plan to Pair Schools Opposed," *News American,* April 6, 1974; Sue Miller, "Pairing-Clustering Desegregation Plan Given To Panel," *Evening Sun,* April 5, 1974.

17. On SECO, see Matthew Crenson, *Neighborhood Politics* (Cambridge: Harvard University Press, 1983), chap. 6; Lee Truelove, *SECO History* (Baltimore: South East Community Organization, 1977).

18. Glen Fallin, "Plan to Pair Schools Opposed," *News American,* April 6, 1974; Sue Miller, "Pairing-Clustering Desegregation Plan Given To Panel," *Evening Sun,* April 5, 1974; "Councilman Schaefer Takes Firm Stand against Busing," *East Baltimore Guide,* April 11, 1974, 3; "School System Member Suggests Mass Busing to Desegregate," *East Baltimore Guide,* April 11, 1974.

19. Betty Deacon interview, August 25, 2003; Sue Miller, "Betty Deacon Learns To Speak Out," *Evening Sun,* June 10, 1974; Durr, *Behind the Backlash,* 166, ff.

20. Theodore W. Hendricks, "200 Attend Stormy Session on School Desegregation," *Sun,* April 12, 1974; Theodore W. Hendricks, "City Task Force Works on School Integration Report," *Sun,* April 16, 1974; Theodore W. Hendricks, "Task Force Votes 25 to 20 to Send 5 Desegregation Plans to School Unit," *Sun,* April 17, 1974; Glen Fallin, "Six Deseg Plans Offered," *News American,* April 17, 1974; Edgar L. Jones, "Racial Isolation in Baltimore Schools," *Evening Sun,* April 22, 1974; Antero Pietila, "Hearing Set on Plans to Desegregate," *Sun,* April 25, 1974.

21. "Five Plans, No Desegregation Policy," *Sun,* April 18, 1974, A16.

22. Betty Deacon interview, August 25, 2003; Irona Pope interview, July 1, 2003.

23. "Parents Say 'We're Staying,'" *East Baltimore Guide,* April 25, 1974; "Letters to the Editor," *East Baltimore Guide,* May 2, 1974, 2.

24. "Busing Inescapable," *Afro,* April 27, 1974, A-4.

25. "Desegregation Sentiments," *Sun,* April 26, 1974; Antero Pietila, "Placards and Prayer Meld at Desegregation Hearing," *Sun,* April 26, 1974; Glen Fallin, "Parents Flay Deseg Plans," *News American,* April 26, 1974; Deposition of Peter E. Holmes before the United States District Court for the District of Maryland, in *Baltimore v. Mathews,* N-76-23, January 20, 1976, 15; Glen Fallin, "Schools Seek HEW Extension," *News American,* April 30, 1974; Sue Miller, "Desegregation Delay Sought," *Evening Sun,* April 30, 1974; Sue Miller, "City Gets Extension On Desegregation," *Evening Sun,* May 1, 1974; Glen Fallin, "City Has Extra Month to Submit School Deseg Plan," *News American,* May 1, 1974; "School Board Faces Desegregation," *Sun,* May 4, 1974.

26. SECO Congress—May 4, 1974, agenda; Special Collections, Langsdale Library, University of Baltimore, Series II, folder 1; "SECO Bars Busing, Curfew," *Sun,* May 6, 1974.

27. Marion Banfield, "Only Together," *Evening Sun,* May 1, 1974, A18; Marc Shelby Silver, "Glen Area—Interracial Stability?" Baltimore *Jewish Times,* May 3, 1974; "The Glen Avenue Area," Baltimore *Jewish Times,* May 3, 1974, 12.

28. School Board minutes, May 28, 1974; Antero Pietila, "School staff told to devise desegregation plan," *Sun,* May 10, 1974; Glen Fallin, "Grade School Busing Ruled Out," *News American,* May 10, 1974; Antero Pietila, "Students Protest New Plan," *Sun,* May 30, 1974.

29. "Twenty Years after *Brown,*" *Sun,* May 17, 1974; Corinne F. Hammett, "After 20 Years, It's Not That Simple," *News-American,* May 19, 1974, 3A; "After 20 Long Years," *Afro,* May 4, 1974, A-4; "Cut Out the Rhetoric," *Afro,* May 11, 1974; "Stop Pussyfooting," *Afro,* May 25, 1974.

30. Baltimore City Public Schools, *Desegregation Plan for Baltimore City Public Schools* (Baltimore: BCPS, 1974).

31. Nicole Fuller and Kelly Brewington, "'Matriarch of NAACP' dies at 102," *Sun,* October 25, 2006; Adam Bernstein, "Enolia McMillan, First Woman to Lead NAACP," *Washington Post,* October 26, 2006.

32. "William L. Marbury Dead at 86; Lawyer and a Fellow of Harvard," *New York Times,* March 7, 1988; Pietila, *Not in My Neighborhood,* chap. 3; Stephen Derby interview, July 23, 2003.

33. Mike Bowler, "School Plan Is Mild Medicine," *Sun,* May 30, 1974, C1, C3; "School Desegregation," *News American,* May 30, 1974; "An Imaginative Plan for the Schools," *Evening Sun,* May 29, 1974.

34. "Zoning Urged for Patterson," *East Baltimore Guide,* May 30, 1974; "Preregistration Slated For Eastside Schools," *East Baltimore Guide,* May 30, 1974; John Jennings and Glen Fallin, "Students Protest Board's Plans," *News American,* May 29, 1974; Sue Miller and Larry Carson, "6 Schools' Students Refuse To Attend Classes in Protest," *Evening Sun,* May 30, 1974; Antero Pietila, "Students Protest New Plan," *Sun,* May 30, 1974; Edward Colimore, "Mayor Pelted by Busing Protesters," *News American,* May 30, 1974, C1; Sue Miller and Larry Carson, "6 Schools' Students Refuse To Attend Classes In Protest," *Evening Sun,* May 30, 1974; Theodore W. Hendricks, "Students Cut Class to March," *Sun,* May 31, 1974; Kelly Gilbert and Sue Miller, "Students Protest School Plan," *Evening Sun,* June 3, 1974; "Desegregation Protest Grows As Pupils of 9 Schools March," *News American,* June 3, 1974.

35. School Board minutes, June 4, 1974.

36. "Federal Court Suit Looms in School Desegregation," *Afro,* June 8, 1974; Antero Pietila, "School Court Fight Due; City, NAACP Each Vow Suit on Race Plan," *Sun,* June 6,

1974; Glen Fallin, "NAACP Asking U.S. Court To Stop City School Funds," *News American,* June 6, 1974; Sue Miller, "'Attitude' Is School Problem: NAACP," *Evening Sun,* June 6, 1974, C5; Antero Pietila, "Changes Delay Integration Plan," *Sun,* June 8, 1974; "We Told You So!" *Afro,* June 8, 1974.

37. Edgar L. Jones, "Where Were Our Top People, While Students Howled?" *Evening Sun,* June 14, 1974, A10.

CHAPTER 9. FEDERAL OFFICIALS, THE SCHOOL BOARD, AND PARENTS NEGOTIATE

1. Peter E. Holmes to Roland N. Patterson, July 29, 1974, OCR documents; "Integration in Baltimore," *Sun,* July 26, 1974; Bill Rhoden, "Aug. 15 Deadline Now for New Deseg Plan," *Afro,* July 27, 1974; Antero Pietila, "HEW Threatens City School Aid Cut," *Sun* July 31, 1974.

2. 418 U.S. 717, 1974; "The Desegregation Dilemma," *Sun,* August 1, 1974.

3. Richard Ben Cramer and Antero Pietila, "Board's Whites Try to Fire Patterson," *Sun,* August 9, 1974; Bill Rhoden, "Board for Patterson Scalp," *Afro,* August 10, 1974; James Griffin interview, June 30, 2003; Robert Schaefer interview, June 17, 2003; Richard Ben Cramer, "Patterson's Status Unsure Following Vote," *Sun,* August 10, 1974; Antero Pietila, "Patterson Ouster Seems to Founder," *Sun,* August 13, 1974.

4. School Board minutes, August 13, 1974; "City School Board Approves Parts of Fall Integration Plan," *Sun,* August 14, 1974.

5. Betty Deacon interview, August 25, 2003; "Mass Meeting Scheduled for Tonight," *East Baltimore Guide,* August 29, 1974; Tracie Rozhon, "Liberal Dedication to City Schools Dwindles under HEW Pressures," *Sun,* August 19, 1974; Jeanne Saddler, "Desegregation Pushing Pupils to Catholics," *Sun,* August 20, 1974; *The Official Catholic Directory* (New York: P. J. Kenedy and Sons, 1950–1980).

6. Antero Pietila, "City School Assignments Held Back," *Sun,* August 21, 1974; Antero Pietila, "Teachers Face Posting by Race," *Sun,* August 23, 1974; Antero Pietila, "Borders Pleads for School Plan," *Sun,* August 30, 1974; Mike Bowler, "MTA Is in State of 'Mass Confusion' over Schools' Busing Requirements," *Sun,* August 31, 1974; Antero Pietila, "School Security Boosted," *Sun,* September 5, 1974.

7. Peter E. Holmes to John Walton, August 23, 1974, OCR documents.

8. Richard Ben Cramer, "City Maps School Plan Resistance," *Sun,* August 30, 1974; Pietila, "Borders Pleads for School Plan"; Antero Pietila, "Speak Out on School Plan, Urban Coalition Appeals," *Sun,* September 2, 1974; Richard Ben Cramer, "Mayor Bars Changes in School Plan," *Sun,* September 3, 1974; Antero Pietila, "School Security Boosted."

9. Pietila, "School Security Boosted"; Jeanne E. Saddler, "Schools Ask Parents, Teachers: Let's Work Together," *Sun,* September 5, 1974; "Pickets, Absenteeism Mark Schools' Opening," *Sun,* September 6, 1974; Antero Pietila, "1 in 5 Pupils in City Skips Opening Day," *Sun,* September 6, 1974; Mike Bowler, "Student Boycotts Continue; Attendance under Par at Paired Schools," *Sun,* September 7, 1974; Mike Bowler, "4 Out of 5 Whites Skip Black Jr. High Classes," *Sun,* September 10, 1974.

10. "Students Obey Law of the Land," *Afro,* September 7, 1974; Widgeon, Schatzman, and Badham, "Harlem Park, Houston, Booker T. Have Calm and Stormy Openings," *Afro,* September 7, 1974; "Integration Is Working Well at Clifton Park Junior High," *Afro,* September 14, 1974; "Black Students Suffer Harassment at Poole J.H.," *Afro,* September 28, 1974.

11. "Pickets, Absenteeism Mark Schools' Opening," *Sun,* September 6, 1974, A12; Betty Deacon interview, August 25, 2003; Durr, *Behind the Backlash,* 166ff; Jeanne E. Saddler, "At the Eye of Picketing, Sit-in Storm, One Calm Canton Teacher Carries On," *Sun,* September 7, 1974; Mike Bowler, "Modify Integration, School Board Asked," *Sun,* September 12, 1974.

12. Deposition of Peter E. Holmes before the United States District Court for the District of Maryland, in *Baltimore v. Mathews*, N-76–23, January 20, 1976, 48ff.

13. Notice of Opportunity for Hearing, Docket No. S-82, September 9, 1974.

14. School Board minutes, September 19, 1974; Mike Bowler, "Transfers Allowed at 6 Junior Highs," *Sun*, September 20, 1974.

15. Mike Bowler, "Southeastern Sit-in Ended by Board's Junior High School Retreat," *Sun*, September 21, 1974; Mike Bowler, "500 Parents Apply for Transfers for Children at 6 Assigned Schools," *Sun*, September 24, 1974; Mike Bowler, "Boycott Empties One City School," *Sun*, September 26, 1974; "Integration Plan Is Weakened," *Sun*, September 27, 1974; Mike Bowler, "School Rally, Boycott Fizzles," *Sun*, October 1, 1974.

16. "Desegregation without Direction," *Sun*, September 21, 1974, A16; "Intolerable School Situation," *Sun*, October 1, 1974; "Time for the NAACP to Act," *Afro*, September 28, 1974.

17. Deposition of Peter E. Holmes before the United States District Court for the District of Maryland, in *Baltimore v. Mathews*, N-76–23, January 20, 1976, 51; "U.S. Troops Asked in Boston," *Sun*, October 16, 1974; "Beaten Junior High Student Refuses to Go Back to Desegregated School," *Sun*, October 16, 1974; Nick Thimmesch, "Working Class Boston Wants Upper Class Whites Bused, Too," *Sun*, October 14, 1974.

18. School Board minutes, October 24, 1974.

19. "NAACP Lawyers Study a Desegregation Suit," *Afro*, October 26, 1974, B13.

20. Peter E. Holmes to Norman P. Ramsey, November 5, 1975, Exhibit 18, Deposition of Peter E. Holmes before the United States District Court for the District of Maryland, in *Baltimore v. Mathews*, N-76–23, January 20, 1976; School Board minutes, October 31, 1974; Mike Bowler, "City Requests Delay on Integration Plan," *Sun*, November 1, 1974; Testimony of Harold Davis, Hearing in the United States District Court for the District of Maryland, Civil Action N-76–23, January 30, 1976, 141–144.

21. John E. Woodruff, "4 on School Board Facing Mayor's Ax," *Sun*, December 19, 1974; John E. Woodruff, "Ramsey Made President of 5–4 Black School Board," *Sun*, January 4, 1975; "Ramsey, Busy Trial Lawyer, Takes on Another 'Tough Case'—The Schools," *Sun*, January 4, 1975; "3 Board Members New to City Posts," *Sun*, January 4, 1975; "Fresh Start for the School Board," *Sun*, January 4, 1975, A14.

22. Peter E. Holmes to Roland N. Patterson, January 8, 1975, Exhibit F, *Baltimore v. Mathews*, Civil Action N-76–23, United States District Court for the District of Maryland; School Board minutes, October 31, 1974; Mike Bowler, "City Requests Delay on Integration Plan," *Sun*, November 1, 1974; Testimony of Harold Davis, Hearing in the United States District Court for the District of Maryland, Civil Action N-76–23, January 30, 1976, 141–144.

23. "HEW's Latest School Orders," Baltimore *Sun*, January 15, 1975, A12.

24. Roland N. Patterson to Peter E. Holmes, January 20, 1975, Exhibit G, *Baltimore v. Mathews*, Civil Action N-76–23, United States District Court for the District of Maryland.

25. Baltimore City Public Schools, *Senior High School Desegregation Plan for Baltimore City Public Schools*, 1975; School Board minutes, January 30, 1975; Mike Bowler, "School Plan Ends Open Enrollment," *Sun*, January 22, 1975; "Zone Plan for City High Schools," *Sun*, January 22, 1975; Mike Bowler, "It's Back to Zones for the City's High Schools," *Sun*, February 2, 1975; "School Board Strives for Feb. 3 Deadline on Deseg Plan," *Afro*, January 25, 1975; "Desegregation Plan Approved by Unanimous School Board Vote," *Afro*, February 1, 1975.

26. Mike Bowler, "Parent Councils Calm," *Sun*, January 23, 1975; Jeanne E. Saddler, "Blacks Said to Oppose Integration Plan," *Sun*, January 30, 1975; Bowler, "It's Back to Zones for the City's High Schools," K3.

27. Peter E. Holmes to Roland N. Patterson, February 24, 1975, Exhibit I, *Baltimore v. Mathews*, Civil Action N-76–23; United States District Court for the District of Maryland.

28. Jeanne E. Saddler, "Plan to Shift 14,000–16,000 in Junior Highs," *Sun*, February 20, 1975; Jeanne E. Saddler, "Southeast Baltimore Residents Threaten Boycott of Canton Junior High over Desegregation Plan," *Sun*, February 22, 1975; Jeanne E. Saddler, "Southeast Group Tiredly Tries Again," *Sun*, February 26, 1975; "Junior High Neighborhoods under Anti-bias Plan Listed," *Sun*, February 26, 1975; "Gerrymandered Zones for City Schools," *Sun*, March 1, 1975; "Southeast, Northeast Parents Relay Ire to School Board," *Sun*, March 5, 1975; "Another School Boycott," *Sun*, March 6,. 1975; Jeanne E. Saddler, "More Staff, Parent Help Urged at Lombard Junior High," *Sun*, March 12, 1975; Mike Bowler and Jeanne E. Saddler, "Angry Parents Protest Beating of Girl," *Sun*, March 13, 1975; Mike Bowler and Jeanne E. Saddler, "School Plan Passed after Pupil Shift," *Sun*, March 14, 1975; "SE Deseg Coalition Presents New Junior High Zoning Plan," *East Baltimore Guide*, February 6, 1975; "Neighborhoods United Endorse Deseg Plan," *East Baltimore Guide*, February 20, 1975; "Parents Call For Junior High Boycott Friday," *East Baltimore Guide*, February 27, 1975; "Officials Back Parents Against Lombard High," *East Baltimore Guide*, February 27, 1975; "Junior High Boycott a Huge Success," *East Baltimore Guide*, March 6, 1975; "Coalition Claims Victory—No Lombard!" *East Baltimore Guide*, March 13, 1975; "Deseg Plan Improves Jr. Hi Racial Balance," *Afro*, February 22, 1975, 1; "Canton Parents Warned of Arrest," *Afro* March 1, 1975; Portia E. Badham, "New Deseg Plan Moves 700 Lombard Pupils to Canton and Hampstead," *Afro*, March 15, 1975; Baltimore City Public Schools, *Junior High School Desegregation Plan for Baltimore City Public Schools*, 1975; School Board minutes, March 13, 1975.

29. *Adams v. Weinberger*, 391 F. Supp. 269, 1975, 271, 272.

30. Mike Bowler, "School Board to Evaluate Patterson Tenure," *Sun*, April 18, 1975; Jeanne E. Saddler, "Patterson Hires Gibson as Lawyer," *Sun*, May 2, 1975.

31. Peter E. Holmes to Roland N. Patterson, May 2, 1975, Exhibit L, *Baltimore v. Mathews*, Civil Action N-76–23, United States District Court for the District of Maryland; Mike Bowler, "City's School Desegregation Plan Rejected," *Sun*, May 3, 1975;

32. "HEW Cloud over City Schools," *Sun*, May 6, 1975; Norman P. Ramsey to Peter E. Holmes, May 8, 1975, Exhibit M, *Baltimore v. Mathews*, Civil Action N-76–23, United States District Court for the District of Maryland; Portia E. Badham, "Board Points Out HEW Errors, Asks Conference," *Afro*, May 10, 1975.

33. Mike Bowler, "School Integration Defended," *Sun*, May 23, 1975.

34. Jeanne E. Saddler, "Some on School Board Defiant on HEW Rejection," *Sun*, May 13, 1975; Mike Bowler, "Board Spends 7 Hours on Patterson," *Sun*, May 13, 1975; Jeanne E. Saddler and Mike Bowler, "Board Votes 7 to 2 to Oust Patterson; Griffin Arrested in Protest at Meeting," *Sun*, June 10, 1975; Jeanne E. Saddler, "School Board Appeals Judge Howard's Order Enjoining it from Dismissing Superintendent," *Sun*, June 21, 1975; "School Case Injunction Fight Begun," *Sun*, June 24, 1975; Joseph J. Challmes and Robert P. Wade, "Gibson Asks Court to Reopen Patterson Case," *Sun*, June 30, 1975; Mike Bowler and Jeanne E. Saddler, "School Hearing Set Today," *Sun*, July 2, 1975; Jeanne E. Saddler, "School Hearing Opens," *Sun*, July 3, 1975; Mike Bowler, "Board Denied Data," *Sun*, July 9, 1975; Mike Bowler and Robert A. Erlandson, "School Chief Is Fired," *Sun*, July 18, 1975; Mike Bowler, "Crew Is Named to School Post," *Sun*, July 19, 1975; Portia E. Badham, "Patterson 'Lynched,'" *Afro*, July 19, 1975; Mike Bowler, "Possible Federal Cut-off of School Aid Averted," *Sun*, June 24, 1975; "HEW Hearings May Be Delayed," *Afro*, June 21, 1975.

35. John Crew interview, August 2, 2003; "Interim Chief Chosen for Yet Another Crisis," *Sun*, July 19, 1975; Bowler, *The Lessons of Change*, 15–16.

36. "In the Nation: Boston Girds for School Violence," *Sun*, July 31, 1975; Dean Mills, "Busing: Some Civil Rights Advocates Want Off," *Sun*, August 14, 1975; "Judge Bars Busing

in Detroit's Schools," *Sun,* August 17, 1975; "Louisville Starts City-Suburb Busing," Baltimore *Sun,* September 5, 1975; Mike Bowler, "Massive Security Keeps Boston's Schools Quiet," *Sun,* September 9, 1975; "Louisville Quiet; Buses Carry Guards," *Sun,* September 9, 1975; Mike Bowler, "Harder Times Ahead for Boston Schools," *Sun,* September 14, 1975; "City-County Busing in Louisville," *Sun,* September 14, 1975.

37. Transcript of Proceedings, Prehearing Conference in the Matter of Baltimore City School District, Baltimore, Maryland, and Maryland State Department of Education, Docket No. S-82, August 4, 1975, 6.

38. Eric Carriker interview, August 5, 2003.

39. Transcript of Proceedings, Prehearing Conference, 19, 20.

40. Ibid, 22; the ruling was *U.S. v. Texas Education Agency,* 467 F. 2d 848, 1972.

41. Transcript of Proceedings, Prehearing Conference, 24–28.

42. "Aug. Is Open House Month for Desegregated Schools," *Afro,* July 26, 1975; "Deseg Confabs Set," *Afro,* August 16, 1975; "400 Set to Attend 3-day Deseg Confab," *Afro,* August 23, 1975; "Group to Meet Mayor to Ask Support for Integration Plan," *Sun,* August 15, 1975; "We Can Make It If We Try," *Sun,* August 17, 1975; Jeanne E. Saddler, "School Crisis Teams Tutored on Biases," *Sun,* August 26, 1975; "Getting Ready for the Test," *Sun,* August 30, 1975; "After Flirt with Chaos, Schools Have Integration Ready to Roll," *Sun,* September 1, 1975; "9 'Rumor' Lines Set Up," *Sun,* September 1, 1975; "Officials Reassure Public on Security," *Sun,* September 3, 1975.

43. Portia E. Badham, "Schools Open Peacefully but 2,000 Parents Seek Transfers," *Afro,* September 6, 1975; Mike Bowler, "Schools Remain Peaceful," *Sun,* September 6, 1975; "Schools Still Segregated," *Afro,* October 4, 1975.

44. "Schools Still Segregated," *Afro,* October 4, 1975.

45. Jeanne E. Saddler, "School-transfer Bids Pour in as Headquarters Lifts Freeze," *Sun,* September 17, 1975; Portia E. Badham, "Schools Open Peacefully but 2,000 Parents Seek Transfers," *Afro,* September 6, 1975; "School Transfer Policy May Witness Changes," *Afro,* November 1, 1975; Mike Bowler, "Lake Clifton Head Asks Transfer Ban, Hints School Plan Is Being Subverted," *Sun,* October 27, 1975; Beverly Ellinwood interview, February 9, 2005.

46. Albert Sehlstedt Jr., "Coleman, Former Busing Advocate, Testifies It Is Counterproductive," *Sun,* October 22, 1975; Christine H. Rossell, "Integration and White Flight," *Sun,* October 5, 1975, K2.

47. "School Figures Indicate Black Flight," *Sun,* November 3, 1975, A1, A5; "Student Rolls Here Dip Again," *Sun,* November 1, 1975.

48. Peter E. Holmes to Norman P. Ramsey, November 5, 1975, Exhibit 18, Deposition of Peter E. Holmes; Mike Bowler, "HEW Sends Back Lower School Plan," *Sun,* November 13, 1975; School Board minutes, November 13, 1975, 4.

49. Mike Bowler, "Schaefer Silent on Ramsey Exit," *Sun,* September 24, 1975; "Ramsey Got the Board on Course," *Sun,* September 25, 1975; "Ramsey Spurns Resignation Queries," *Sun,* September 27, 1975.

50. Peter Holmes interview, April 6, 2005; Transcript of Proceedings, Department of Health, Education, and Welfare, In the Matter of Title VI of the Civil Rights Act of 1964 Involving the Baltimore City School District, Baltimore Maryland, Docket No. S-82, November 17, 1975, 32, 102–103; Mike Bowler, "February Desegregation Hearings Set," *Sun,* November 18, 1975.

51. Mike Bowler, "Joseph Well Versed in Urban Affairs," *Sun,* December 4, 1975, C1; "Schaefer Turns to School Post," *Sun,* November 6, 1975.

52. Request for Admissions of Fact and Genuineness of Documents, Administrative Proceeding, Docket No. S-82, December 16, 1975; Response to Respondent School District's Request for Admissions of Fact and Genuineness of Documents, Administrative Proceeding, Docket No. S-82, December 23, 1975, 5.

CHAPTER 10. THE CITY'S COURT VICTORY

1. Jeanne E. Saddler, "Some on School Board Defiant on HEW Rejection," *Sun,* May 13, 1975, C4.

2. "Beleaguered City Seeks Justice," *Sun,* January 9, 1976; "Metropolitan Desegregation," *Sun,* November 20, 1975.

3. Reports describing "two cities" are Melvin R. Levin, *A Viable City: Baltimore in the 1980s* (Baltimore: School of Social Work and Community Planning, University of Maryland at Baltimore, 1979); and Peter Szanton, *Baltimore 2000: A Choice of Futures* (Baltimore: Morris Goldseker Foundation, 1986). On William Murphy's "two Baltimores" campaign against Schaefer for mayor in 1983, see Smith, *William Donald Schaefer,* 221–226.

4. On the individualistic bias of American civil rights law, see Owen M. Fiss, "The Fate of An Idea Whose Time Has Come: Antidiscrimination Law in the Second Decade after *Brown v. Board of Education,*" *University of Chicago Law Review* 41 (1974): 742–773; "The Origins and Fate of Antisubordination Theory: A Symposium on Owen Fiss's 'Groups and the Equal Protection Clause,'" *Issues in Legal Scholarship,* Berkeley Electronic Press, 2002–2004; Cass R. Sunstein, "The Anticaste Principle," *Michigan Law Review* 92 (1994): 2410–2455; Tribe, *American Constitutional Law,* 1493–1521.

5. On Title IX responsibilities, Peter Holmes interview, April 6, 2005.

6. Herbert Goldman interview, June 24, 2003; Jeanne E. Saddler, "City Sues HEW Over School Aid," *Sun,* January 9, 1976; Response to Respondent School District's Request for Admissions of Fact and Genuineness of Documents, Administrative Proceeding, Docket No. S-82, December 23, 1975, 3.

7. Equal Educational Opportunity Act, 20 USC §§ 1701, et seq.

8. Office for Civil Rights Policies on Elementary and Secondary School Compliance with Title VI of the Civil Rights Act of 1964, 1968, 12; Civil Rights Act of 1964, Section 602, 42 USC § 2000d-1.

9. Memorandum of Law in Support of Plaintiffs' Application for Temporary Restraining order, with Notice, and its Motion for Preliminary Injunction, in the United States District Court for the District of Maryland, in *Baltimore v. Mathews,* Civil Action N-76–23, January 9, 1976, 2–3.

10. Frank Krueger interview, July 25, 2003.

11. Memorandum of defendants in opposition to plaintiffs' application for preliminary injunction, in the United States District Court for the District of Maryland, in *Baltimore v. Mathews,* Civil Action N-76–23, January 23, 1976, 152–153.

12. Ibid., 169.

13. Jeanne E. Saddler, "City Sues HEW over School Aid," *Sun,* January 9, 1976; "Beleaguered City Seeks Justice," *Sun,* January 9, 1976; "Court Asked to Block HEW Cut-off," *Afro,* January 10, 1976; "Gamble with HEW," *Afro,* January 17, 1976.

14. Adam Bernstein, "Edward S. Northrop, Md. Senator And Chief Federal Judge, Dies at 92," *Washington Post,* August 15, 2003; Johnathan E. Briggs, "Edward S. Northrop, 92, Chief Judge of U.S. District Court," *Sun,* August 14, 2003; David Leeman interview, July 24, 2003; Alexander Ross interview, April 8, 2004; *United States v. Philip Berrigan, David Eberhardt, Thomas Lewis, and James Mengel,* 283 F. Supp. 336, 1968.

15. Deposition of Peter E. Holmes before the United States District Court for the District of Maryland, in *Baltimore v. Mathews,* N-76–23, January 20, 1976, quote on 84.

16. Transcript of Proceedings, in the United States District Court for the District of Maryland, in *Mandel v. HEW,* Civil Action N-76–1, *Baltimore v. HEW,* Civil Action N-76–23, January 30, 1976, 47, 49–50, 52.

17. Alexander Ross interview, April 8, 2004.

18. Transcript of Proceedings, in the United States District Court for the District of Maryland, in *Mandel v. HEW,* Civil Action N-76–1, *Baltimore v. HEW,* Civil Action N-76–23, January 30, 1976, 54, 61.

19. Alexander Ross interview, April 8, 2004; Transcript of Proceedings, in the United States District Court for the District of Maryland, in *Mandel v. HEW,* Civil Action N-76–1, *Baltimore v. HEW,* Civil Action N-76–23, January 30, 1976, 80, 81.

20. Transcript of Proceedings, in the United States District Court for the District of Maryland, in *Mandel v. HEW,* Civil Action N-76–1, *Baltimore v. HEW,* Civil Action N-76–23, January 30, 1976, 95.

21. Ibid., 102.

22. Ibid, 104–156.

23. Defendants' Post-Hearing Memorandum, in the United States Court for the District of Maryland, in *Baltimore v. Mathews,* Civil Action N-76–23, February 9, 1976.

24. Transcript of Proceedings in the United States District Court for the District of Maryland, in *Mandel v. HEW,* Civil Action N-76–1, *Baltimore v. HEW,* Civil Action N-76–23, February 20, 1976, 3–30, quote on 20.

25. Ibid., 38–58, quotes on 56.

26. Ibid., 59; *Leedom v. Kyne,* 359 U.S. 184, 1958; Transcript of Proceedings in the United States District Court for the District of Maryland, in *Mandel v. HEW,* Civil Action N-76–1, *Baltimore v. HEW,* Civil Action N-76–23, February 20, 1976, 58–68, quote on 68.

27. Eric Carriker interview, August 5, 2003; Frank Krueger interview, July 25, 2003.

28. Transcript of Proceedings in the United States District Court for the District of Maryland, in *Mandel v. HEW,* Civil Action N-76–1, *Baltimore v. HEW,* Civil Action N-76–23, February 20, 1976, 75.

29. *Baltimore v. Mathews* (411 F. Supp. 542), 1976, 14.

30. Ibid., 44, 41, 36, 51, 41, 59, 43, 65, 66.

31. Order, in the United States District Court for the District of Maryland, in *Baltimore v. Mathews,* Civil Action N-76–23, March 12, 1976; Frank Krueger interview, July 25, 2003.

32. Notice of Appeal, *Baltimore v. Mathews,* Civil Action N-76–23, for the District of Maryland, March 22, 1976; "U. S. Files Appeal on Funds," *Sun,* July 1, 1976.

33. Brief Amicus Curiae of the NAACP Legal Defense and Educational Fund, Inc., in the United States Court of Appeals for the Fourth Circuit, in *Baltimore v. HEW, Mandel v. HEW,* No. 76–1493, June 30, 1976 (filed July 2).

34. Brian Landsberg interview, February 10, 2004.

35. Ibid.; Cynthia Attwood interview, March 18, 2004; Appellees' Suggestion for Hearing in Banc, in the United States Court of Appeals for the Fourth Circuit, in *Mandel v. HEW,* No. 76–1494; Appellees' Suggestion for Hearing in Banc, in the United States Court of Appeals for the Fourth Circuit, in *Mathews v. Baltimore,* No. 1493, April 23, 1976, filed April 26, 1976; Appellants' Memorandum in Response to Appellees' Suggestion for Hearing en Banc, in the United States Court of Appeals for the Fourth Circuit, No. 76–1494, April 27, 1976, filed April 28, 1976; Order, United States Court of Appeals for the Fourth Circuit, in *Baltimore v. Mathews,* No. 76–1493, *Mandel v. HEW,* No. 76–1494, December 10, 1976.; Edward Coltman, "HEW Asks U.S. Appeals Court to Lift Bar to Segregation Sanctions on City, State," *Sun,* February 15, 1977; Lee Baylin, "Lawyers Argue When HEW Review Will Be," *Evening Sun,* February 15, 1977.

36. "Remembering the Fourth Circuit Judges: A History from 1941 to 1998," *Washington and Lee Law Review* 55 (spring 1998): 524; Albert Sehlstedt Jr. and Dennis O'Brien, "Eminent Federal Jurist Harrison L. Winter Dies," *Sun,* April 11, 1990; "Harrison L. Winter," *Sun,* April 11, 1990, 14A; Frederick Rasmussen, "Beautiful Architecture Amid Nature's Bounty," *Sun,* December 23, 2001; David Feldman interview, August 21, 2006; Frank Henry, "Dean Howell—He Built Up A Law School," *Sun,* June 3, 1982.

37. *Baltimore v. Mathews,* 562 F. 2d 914, 1977, 919, 923.

38. "Battle Lost, Peace Won," *Sun,* August 14, 1977, K4.

39. *Baltimore v. Mathews,* 562 F. 2d 915, 1977, 1.

40. Stephen Derby interview, July 23, 2003; *United States v. American-Foreign Steam-ship Corp.,* 363 U. W. 685, 1969; 80 S. Ct. 1336, 1960; Motion of Baltimore City Plaintiffs-Appellees to Vacate Judgment Affirming the Order of the District Court, and, in the Alternative, Petition for Rehearing, in the United States Court of Appeals for the Fourth Circuit, in *Baltimore v. Mathews,* No. 76–1493, August 23, 1977, 3–4; Response to Petitions for Rehearing, in the United States Court of Appeals for the Fourth Circuit, in *Baltimore v. Mathews,* No. 76–1493, September 20, 1977.

41. *Baltimore v. Mathews,* 571 F 2d 1237, 1978.

42. Michael J. Himowitz, "Order To Bar HEW From Cutting Funds From Md. Schools Upheld By Court," *Evening Sun,* February 17, 1978; Timothy M. Phelps, "Reversing Itself, Appeals Court Bars $88 Million State-aid Cut-off," *Sun,* February 18, 1978, A1.

43. Albert T. Hamlin to Lawrence G. Wallace, Deputy Solicitor General, Department of Justice, April 1978, OCR documents; Harry M. Singleton to William Bradford Reynolds, September 20, 1982, OCR documents; Brian Landsberg interview, February 10, 2004

44. Lloyd R. Henderson to David S. Tatel, November 16, 1978, OCR documents; Roma J. Stewart to Secretary Patricia Roberts Harris, January 29, 1980, OCR documents.

45. Brian Landsberg interview, February 10, 2004.

46. David Tatel interview, May 26, 2005; United States Court of Appeals for the District of Columbia Circuit, Biographical Sketches of the Judges, http://www.cadc.uscourts.gov/internet/home.nsf/content/VL+-+Judges+-+DST, accessed July 23, 2008; Alexander Ross interview, April 8, 2004.

47. Lloyd Henderson interview, July 31, 2003.

48. Lloyd R. Henderson to David S. Tatel, November 16, 1978, OCR documents.

49. Stephen Derby interview, July 23, 2003; Roma J. Stewart to Patricia Roberts Harris, January 29, 1980, OCR documents; David Feldman interview, August 21, 2006.

50. Roma Stewart interview, May 27, 2005.

51. Roma J. Stewart to Patricia Roberts Harris, January 29, 1980; Nicholas Carroll interview, July 25, 2003; David Leeman interview, July 24, 2003.

52. Antonio Califa to Harry Singleton, August 18, 1984, OCR documents; David Feldman interview, August 21, 2006; Stephen Derby letter to Sandra Lynn Beber, December 8, 1982, OCR documents; Daniel Oliver memorandum to Margaret Heckler, January 14, 1983, OCR documents; Stipulation and Order, in the United States District Court for the District of Maryland, in *Baltimore v. Mathews,* Civil Action N-76–23, January 21, 1983.

53. School Board minutes, June 26, 1980.

54. Ibid., September 2, 1982.

55. Ibid.

56. Ibid.

57. Antonio J. Califa to Harry M. Singleton, [March, 1983?], OCR documents; Antonio J. Califa to Harry Singleton, June 27, 1983, OCR documents; Antonio J. Califa to Harry Singleton, October 18, 1983 [?], OCR documents; Antonio J. Califa to Harry Singleton, October 25, 1983, OCR documents; Harry Singleton to William Donald Schaefer, September 8, 1983, OCR documents; Antonio J. Califa to Harry Singleton, October 18, 1984, OCR documents.

58. Philip Kiko to Alicia Coro, March 6, 1987, OCR documents.

59. Alicia Coro to Alice Pinderhughes, May 12, 1987, OCR documents.

CONCLUSION

1. Test data for 1993–94 show typical racial differences at this time. Black boys in Baltimore placed around the 31st percentile and black girls around the 40th percentile

in the nationally normed Comprehensive Test of Basic Skills. Baltimore's white boys and girls placed around the 52nd and 54th percentiles, respectively (Baltimore City Public Schools, *Maryland School Performance Program Report, 1994: School System and Schools— Baltimore City* [Baltimore: BCPS, 1994], 17). Racial makeup data for 2004 come from Joseph Harkness, e-mail to author, April 28, 2009. On Baltimore racial isolation, see Erica Frankenberg and Chungmei Lee, *Race in American Public Schools: Rapidly Resegregating School Districts* (Cambridge: The Civil Rights Project, Harvard University, 2002), table 14.

2. As a means for coordinating individual actions, markets may allocate either publicly or privately produced goods or services; see Lindblom, *The Market System.*

3. On prior determinations, see ibid., 169–177.

4. United States Commission on Civil Rights, *Statement on Metropolitan School Desegregation* (Washington: USCCR, 1977), 9; Baltimore City Public Schools, *Informational Materials for Desegregation Task Force.*

5. Baltimore City Public Schools, *Informational Materials for Desegregation Task Force.*

6. On turbulent environments see Fred E. Emery and Eric L. Trist, "The Causal Texture of Organizational Environments," *Human Relations* 18 (1965): 21–32.

7. One other place where blacks strongly advocated open enrollment was in Greensboro, North Carolina, where in 1971 a group of blacks opposed a court-ordered integration plan including massive busing as imposing high costs with few gains and demanded free choice instead (Chafe, *Civility and Civil Rights,* 325).

8. On the distinction between desegregation as an individual condition and integration as a communal condition, see john a. powell, "Living and Learning: Linking Housing and Education," in john a. powell, Gavin Kearney, and Vina Kay, eds., *The Pursuit of a Dream Deferred: Linking Housing and Education Policy* (New York: Peter Lang, 2001), 31–32.

9. Gene Sullivan, "Segregation," *Sun,* September 28, 1954, 12; Pancoast, *Report of a Study on Desegregation,* 56, 59; "Deacon Attacks HEW Rejection Of SE Desegregation Proposal," *East Baltimore Guide,* May 8, 1975, 2; "Residents Say: 'We're Staying,'" *East Baltimore Guide,* May 16, 1974, 18. For a liberal assertion of a right of association against *Brown,* see Herbert Wechsler, "Toward Neutral Principles of Constitutional Law," *Harvard Law Review* 73, 1 (November 1959): 1–35.

10. On the use of rights language to express racial prejudice, see Kruse, *White Flight.* On the divisiveness of a rights framework, see Mary Ann Glendon, *Rights Talk; The Impoverishment of Political Discourse* (New York: Free Press, 1991).

11. For an example of "cultural" labeling, see Riessman, *The Culturally Deprived Child.* On blaming students for school failures, see William Ryan, *Blaming the Victim,* rev. ed. (New York: Vintage, 1976), chap. 2.

12. On how liberalism downplays structural explanations for poverty in favor of individual and associated cultural explanations, see O'Connor, *Poverty Knowledge.*

13. Banfield, *The Unheavenly City,* chap. 3.

14. W. E. Burghardt Du Bois, *The Souls of Black Folk* (1903; Greenwich, CT: Fawcett, 1961), 23.

15. On Southern thinking and Southern liberalism, see Wilbur J. Cash, *The Mind of the South* (New York: Vintage, 1941); James C. Cobb, *Away Down South: A History of Southern Identity* (New York: Oxford University Press, 2005); John Hope Franklin, *The Militant South, 1800–1861* (Cambridge: Belknap Press of Harvard University Press, 1956); George B. Tindall, "The Central Theme Revisited," in Charles Grier Sellers Jr., ed., *The Southerner as American* (Chapel Hill: University of North Carolina Press, 1960), 104–129; George Brown Tindall, *A History of the South,* vol. 10, *The Emergence of the New South, 1913–1945* (Baton Rouge: Louisiana State University Press, 1967).

16. On the loss of moral language in twentieth-century America, see Reinhold Niebuhr, *The Nature and Destiny of Man,* vol. 1, *Human Nature* (New York: Charles Scribner's Sons, 1964); Andrew Delbanco, *The Death of Satan: How Americans Have Lost the Sense of Evil* (New York: Farrar, Straus and Giroux, 1995).

17. Myrdal, *An American Dilemma,* 998.

Index

Page numbers in bold refer to figures or tables